The Hanging Gardens of Vedic Philosophy

Also by Ashish Dalela:

Semantic Atomism
Semantic Reasoning
The Journey of Perfection
Material and Spiritual Natures
Conceiving the Inconceivable
The Science of God
Time and Consciousness
Conceiving the Inconceivable
The Balanced Organization
The Yellow Pill
Cosmic Theogony
Emotion
Mystic Universe
Moral Materialism
Signs of Life
Uncommon Wisdom
Gödel's Mistake
Quantum Meaning
Sāṅkhya and Science
Is the Apple Really Red?
Six Causes

The Hanging Gardens of Vedic Philosophy

SHABDAVERSE
VOLUME 7

Ashish Dalela

The Hanging Gardens of Vedic Philosophy —SHABDAVERSE
Volume 7
by Ashish Dalela

Published by Shabda Press
press.shabda.co
ISBN 978-93-85384-58-5

SHABDA
PRESS

Contents

Series Preface

SHABDAVERSE is a series of article collections, organized by topics. The articles in these collections were originally published online on the SHABDA website over many years. A series of articles written from 2014 to 2019 were earlier published in chronological order under the series title *Western Questions Eastern Answers*. The SHABDAVERSE series organizes articles from 2019 to 2025 by categories, rather than dates. This is for multiple reasons—(a) there are enough articles in each category to produce collections organized by categories, (b) readers wanting to read topic-focused collections might find this approach more convenient and cohesive than the chronological one, and (c) the topic-focused approach allows us to make unique covers for each book, after all, in the ultimate analysis, a book is judged by its cover!

All these articles follow an interdisciplinary approach to every topic—everyday experience, empirical evidence, problems with different ideas advanced in the past and present, how ideas may have evolved historically, how certain issues were seen and understood differently across cultures, and with a solution to any and all related open and unsolved problems, which can be validated through ordinary experience, empirical evidence, and rational arguments. I often cite statements and ideas from Vedic texts, not to substantiate my claims, but to establish that my ideas are not new, and that I as the author of these articles don't claim authorship of the ideas. I only aim to present ancient ideas in a modern language, so that present audiences may understand and appreciate them based on what they already trust.

Pursuant to the science-religion divide created during European Enlightenment, we see two opposite approaches to the study of ancient texts—(a) the religious approach takes an ancient text as a divine revelation to be trusted on faith at best, and (b) the scientific approach, which rejects these texts as the personal opinion of dogmatic scribes, unprovable through or contradictory to the available evidence, and focuses on collecting evidence, followed by speculation to find an explanation that fits that evidence.

The Vedic tradition differs from both of these. Ancient texts have been preserved in a written form for thousands of years, but in every successive era, those texts were explained through commentaries. The texts and the commentaries were never merged. That trend continues today, and those who like to read ancient texts with explanations can do so. However, these explanations do not contrast their ideas with those in present-day sciences and religions, because the Vedic tradition was historically inward-looking, not outward-looking. By continuing the same trend, commentaries on Vedic texts appear to most people as different ideas, not better or true ideas, when contrasted to the ideas found in other worldviews. In fact, those ingrained in other worldviews consider Vedic texts primitive because the Vedic ideas don't match the ideas they have received through their culture and education. Therefore, the inward-looking historical trend of the Vedic texts is not adequate for the present time. For the present time, the Vedic tradition must become outward-looking, and contrast itself to the ideas of the other worldviews.

Therefore, in these articles, we—(a) sometimes we begin with unsolved problems created by prevalent ideas and theories and try to solve them using reasoning and evidence, and then connect the solution to the ideas in ancient texts, and (b) sometimes we begin with ideas and theories in ancient texts and show how they are relevant to the present time by showing how they solve unsolved or open problems.

I have seen with consternation a tendency among many authors to take ancient ideas, reformulate them in convenient ways, disconnect them from the sources from where these ideas were taken, and present these ideas as an author's original work. I think that this approach constitutes a theft, disrespectful to the teachers and texts from where ideas were taken. But more importantly, it filters the tradition of texts and teachers through the opinionated lens of the author who takes ideas without attribution, and closes the door for readers to go back to the tradition for more exploration in the future. Authors with such attitudes present themselves as prophets of original ideas, while masking the actual prophets.

I aim to show people of the present time a path to the Vedic tradition, not pretend to be a prophet of original ideas. Personally, I'm convinced that everything I have written about is a miniscule fraction of all that can be written, understood, or derived from the Vedic texts, and hopefully, future generations will do more of what I have tried to do. My primary goal is to dispel the myth that the Vedic texts are like the texts of other religions which have to be accepted on faith, rather than reason and observation. I call the dispelling of this myth, the *scientific study of Vedic texts*, pursuant to the common definition of science as truth based on reasoning and evidence, in contrast to a religion based on blind faith or belief.

Ashish Dalela

The Supreme Personality of Godhead

Most religions speak about the Supreme Person simply as "God". In Vedic texts, He is described as *Īśvara*. But in the Gaudīya Vaishnava literature, since the time of Śrīla Bhaktisiddhānta Sarasvati Thakur, the term "Supreme Personality of Godhead" is often employed to describe what is otherwise simply referred to by the word "God". Why use this complex term when a simpler "God" suffices? This post discusses the meaning of the term "Supreme Personality of Godhead" and why it is different from the conventional notions of "God". Many nuances of Vaishnavism are illustrated by this usage.

The Concept of Leadership

Every nation, society, institution, or organization has a leader. The leader is a part of the whole, and yet he or she represents the whole. A country, for instance, has a national leader who is a citizen of the country and yet represents the entire country. A business organization has a CEO who is an employee of the business and yet represents the entire business. The country or the business are the whole, and citizens of the country and employees of the business are its parts. However, *one* citizen of the country or employee of the business becomes a symbolic representation of the whole. The leader is a part of the country or the business, and yet he or she is a representative of the whole.

In one sense, the country or organization are "bigger" than the leader who represents them. After all, the leader is a citizen of the country or a member of the organization, and there are many other citizens and members besides the leader. And yet, in another sense, the entire country or organization is represented by the leader. The leader is a part of the whole, and a symbol of the whole.

Godhead is the Whole Truth

To understand the term "Supreme Personality of Godhead", we need to distinguish between the country and the leader of the country. Godhead means the entire created world, of which God is one citizen. The other citizens are the individual spiritual souls. Just as a country has many citizens, similarly, Godhead is the country that has many citizens. God is one of the citizens of Godhead.

The term "Supreme Personality of Godhead" represents the *leader* of the creation. Like a nation has a president or an organization has a CEO, similarly, Godhead has a leader—the Supreme Person *of* Godhead. However, we must remember that this Supreme Person is also a *citizen* of Godhead.

Thus, in one sense, the Supreme Person is *part* of Godhead—like the president is a citizen of the country. In another sense, the Supreme Person is a *representative* of Godhead—like the president represents the entire country. As a citizen, the Supreme Person is one part of the whole truth. As a representative of the whole, the Supreme Person is representing the whole truth. Thus, "Supreme Personality of Godhead" is both a *part* of the whole and a *representative* of the whole.

Who Created the Whole Truth?

And yet, this description of Supreme Person is only a partial understanding of Godhead. The bigger question is: How did Godhead come into existence? For example, a president of the country doesn't create the citizens of the country. The leadership of the country is different from creating the country itself. In the same way, leadership of Godhead is different from the creation of Godhead.

This is where a more nuanced understanding of Godhead is described: Godhead expanded out of the Supreme Person. Like a spider expands a web out of itself, and then becomes a part of the web, in the same way, the Supreme Person expands Godhead, and then becomes its Supreme Personality. The leadership of the president of a country can be challenged because the president did not create the country. But the leadership of the Supreme Person cannot be challenged because He expanded the world out of Himself. The world is *non-different* from Him. Notably, the world is not *identical* to the Supreme Person because it is expanded from His person. And it is not *different* from the Supreme Person because it previously existed in God's person. While other religions say that God "created" the world, in the Vaishnava system of philosophy, God "expanded" the world from His person.

The Role of the Supreme Person's Śakti

This 'expansion' of the world from the Supreme Person is much like an artist externalizing his personality on a canvas, or a reflection of a person into a mirror. The 'canvas' or 'mirror' are the Supreme Person's Śakti or energy. Thus, Godhead or the created world is not the Supreme Person *per se* but His Śakti.

In one sense, this Śakti is *within* the Supreme Person, and in another sense the Śakti is not identical to the Supreme Person. When the Śakti is considered to exist within the Supreme Person, it is described as the Supreme Person's power to know and express Himself. The Śakti is nothing other than the Supreme Person's 'consciousness' by which the Supreme Person becomes aware of His own existence. When the Śakti is described as different from the Supreme Person, the difference is simply that the power can lie dormant and hence unused. The Supreme Person is simply the *possibility* of bliss and knowledge. The possibility *exists,* so the Supreme Person exists. And yet, to convert this possibility into the experience of knowledge and bliss, Śakti is required. The Śakti is the Supreme Person's power. And yet, just like the power can lie unused and therefore dormant, similarly, the Śakti can remain inactive.

Thus, the Supreme Person is by Himself the dormant state of possibility in which Godhead doesn't exist. When the Supreme Person activates His Śakti, then Godhead is manifest from the Supreme Person, through the act of converting the possibility into reality in knowing and expressing His personality.

In a simple sense we can say that the Supreme Person exists, but when the Śakti is inactive, then He doesn't know and express Himself. When Śakti is activated then He knows Himself by expressing Himself. Godhead is the manifest world, which is expanded from the Supreme Person in His endeavor to know and express Himself. And this expansion is mediated by the Supreme Person's Śakti.

Dormant and Reactivated Persons

There is hence a Supreme Person before He expands into a Godhead or the world. Then, when the Supreme Person has expanded into Godhead, He is the "Supreme Personality of Godhead".

The "Supreme Personality of Godhead" is the self-aware stage of the Supreme Person in which His Śakti is active. But because the Śakti can be inactive, there is a Supreme Person who is not "Supreme Personality of Godhead". He exists although in a non-self-aware state. This state in which the Śakti is inactive is called the "deep-sleep" state of the Supreme Person. When He goes to "sleep", He loses consciousness of His own existence, and the world expanded from His person merges back into His person. When He "wakes up", and becomes self-aware, the word expands from His person.

Certain forms of Supreme Person are never in "deep sleep", and the Godhead created from their person is never merged back into His body. The spiritual world is such a Godhead in which the Śakti never becomes inactive and God never loses awareness of His own nature. But there is also the Godhead of the material world in which God sometimes goes into "deep sleep" and loses consciousness of His person. In this state, His Śakti becomes dormant, and the material creation disappears. When the Supreme Person wakes up again, the Śakti is reactivated, and the world appears. Notably, the material world must also be considered Godhead because it is expanded from the Supreme Person. Thus, the leader of the material world is also referred to as the "Supreme Personality of Godhead".

But since the Godhead may not always be expanded, therefore, the "Supreme Personality of Godhead" is technically different from the eternal "Supreme Person". The former is simply the self-aware state of the Supreme Person, while the latter is the non-self-aware of state of the Supreme Person. In the self-aware state, the Supreme Person has reactivated His Śakti to create His experience. But in the non-self-aware state, the Śakti exists in the Supreme Person but remains dormant and inactive.

God and Mathematics

The following is a somewhat extended version of a reply to some questions that I sent today to an interested reader. I thought this description would be relevant and useful even to others, and hence I decided to post it.

The current doctrine of numbers is *physical* and by physical, I mean that if you add 1 to 1, then you get 2. There is, however, another way to think of numbers as *concepts*.

For example, suppose you know Newton's three laws of motion, and then I tell you again about the 3rd law. This doesn't add to your knowledge, because you already knew of the three laws. Thus, in this case 3 + 1 = 3. The nature of conceptual addition is that it increases upon addition *if only if* the meaning wasn't previously present. If you already know of Newton's three laws, and I again tell you about these three laws, then the result of that addition will be 3 + 3 = 3, because knowledge has not increased. Again, concepts don't increase if we add the same concept.

So, there are two ways of thinking about numbers. In the present conception of numbers, we think about them as physical things, and when you add two physical things you always get a greater number of things. But in the conceptual addition, you can sometimes get two things (e.g., if you add new knowledge), exactly the same thing (e.g., if you add the same knowledge), and even nothing (e.g., if the new concept negates the previous concept). Thus, the simple operation of 'addition' becomes unpredictable if we consider numbers as concepts. From this problem, however, we can open the doors to a new kind of understanding that predicts how knowledge *grows*.

For example, knowledge doesn't always grow linearly, even if you add new ideas. Rather, knowledge has a *structure*, and ideas get added, reformulated, some ideas are removed, and some are moved (or given a new kind of place in the system of ideas), and then these ideas are expressed without a reduction. This complicated dynamic of the nature of ideas, namely, addition, removal, reformulation, movement, and expression, constitutes a new science.

These five processes of the dynamic of knowledge are called the five *prāna*, or "life force". By their presence, every system of knowledge becomes a 'living organism'. Thus, we are living organisms, because we add, remove, reformulate, reorganize, and express ideas. The addition is called *prāna*, the removal *apāna*, reformulation *samāna*, reorganization *vyāna*, and expression *udāna*. This is the dynamic of knowledge that occurs in every knowledge system—our individual bodies, the society of knowing beings, and further stages of complexity.

Now, to relate this problem to the nature of God, let us look at the 1st verse from Iśopaniśad:

"That is complete, this is complete. From the complete comes the complete. And after the complete is removed from the complete, the balance is complete".

It is impossible to understand this verse if we think physically. But it is possible to understand it if we treat the complete conceptually. In this case, God must be understood as 'knowledge'. From this 'knowledge', many varieties of knowledge, which are parts of knowledge, expand. But after all this knowledge has expanded, God hasn't become ignorant! Thus, even if you remove the complete from the complete, the balance is still complete. Why? Because the complete that you removed was knowledge, and the source that created that knowledge was knowledge.

Thus, we can describe the paradoxical relation between science and religion by the simple operation of number addition: $1 - 1 = 0$ in science, and $1 - 1 = 1$ in (Vedic) religion. But the solution to this paradox, by treating reality conceptually, opens the door to their reconciliation.

To understand this resolution, let us see how conceptual addition exists in set theory in a primitive form as Union of sets, where a Union of two sets equals the same set if these two sets are identical. Even if they are not identical, the union of sets only produces a set that combines the unique elements, not the duplication of elements that already existed.

For example, let's consider two sets A and B, such that A := {P, Q, R} and B := {Q, R, S}. Then the union of A and B is denoted as A U B := {P, Q, R, S}. This is how knowledge addition works; we add new knowledge only when the knowledge was previously missing. If the knowledge was previously existing, we don't say that anything new has been acquired.

However, the conceptual addition is not extended to conceptual subtraction in set theory. The set theory subtraction is called 'Difference', and it removes elements. Thus, for example, if A := {P, Q, R}, and B := {Q, R}, then the difference A – B := {P}. This is like saying that if I taught you some scientific theory, then I must have become ignorant of the theory that I previously taught you. As ridiculous as that sounds, that is precisely what set theory Difference leads us to.

Now, lots of problems arise due to the mistaken idea about 'Difference' in set theory, because then we stop treating the sets as conceptual entities. We rather treat them as physical entities. The correct set theory would be where 'Difference' is also just like Union — you remove some elements from a set, and they are still there, just like by giving knowledge, knowledge is not lost.

Now, while number theory is based on set theory, the concept of number addition is not like set Union, because 1 + 1 is not 1. It is rather 2. Therefore, the idea of number addition is different than the idea of set Union. However, the idea of number subtraction is exactly like the idea of set Difference. For example, 1 – 1 = 0, and if you subtract a set from itself, you get a null set.

So, even though set theory starts by using a novel idea of Union, because it is incompatible with the idea of Difference, the definition of sets has to be modified to be simply a collection of physical things. In this new conception of sets, if you add two sets of 3 and 5 cars, you must get a set of 8 cars. You cannot say that the set of 8 cars is simply one thing – i.e., cars. Because if you said that, then you would be led to a paradox: Are there 8 different things, or just 1 thing?

Of course, the fact is that both kinds of statements are true, although in different ways. You must say that there are 8 individual cars. And you must say that there is just one *type* of thing—i.e., car. But we cannot do this in sets because it requires the notion of *modalities* (these are called the 'modes of nature' in Vedic philosophy). In the individual modality, you must say that there are 8 cars, and in the universal modality you must say that there is only one type of thing—i.e., car.

The mode in which we see that one type of thing is called *sattva-guna*, and the mode in which we see eight different things is called *tamo-guna*. Then there is also a mode called *rajo-guna* in which we create contrasts between things by comparison – e.g., cars are defined by their distinction to trucks, so by a car, we also mean something that it is not a truck (but the distinction to a horse can be contextually applied or removed, depending on the context). This third mode creates contextuality in the study of concepts, where something is *not* other things, but what it is *not* only depends on the context (a car can also be towed by a horse, in which case, it now becomes a 'carriage', not a 'car').

So, there is just one reality, but, based on different modes we must be able to say that there is only one thing and that there are eight things, and then some unspecified number of things based on the context. These modes are like "perspectives" on the same reality. In one perspective, you see eight individual things, and in another perspective, you just see one thing. Then by relating to another group of things, you assign it additional attributes. So, by changing the perspective, the same thing is just a single entity, or it is many individual entities or few different types of entities. These are statements about the exact same reality, and therefore, they are simultaneously true. However, without modes, they lead to a contradiction: How can we say that the same thing is just one thing, and then say that it is eight different things, and then say something else purely based on the context in which the truth is presented?

So, the modes of nature, or modalities, constitute a radically different way of viewing reality in which reality is known completely through many perspectives. Vedic philosophy identifies three fundamental perspectives – universal, individual, and contextual – and these combine in innumerable ways to create infinite perspectives. Due to these infinite perspectives, the reality is just One, and yet it is simultaneously known in infinite ways through infinite perspectives.

We cannot reconcile these perspectives because they are indeed contradictory. However, each of these perspectives is *true*. This leads to the paradox that truth must be self-contradictory. This principle of contradiction is called Achintya-Bheda-Abheda Tattva, where two things are simultaneously different from each other, and yet they are the descriptions of the same thing, and because we cannot logically reconcile them, therefore, the reality is said to be 'inconceivable'.

There is, however, a solution to this inconceivability, and that is the notion of reality and its *perspectives*. And that means that we must reconceive reality in terms of many modes. This modal conception of reality constitutes a step forward from the Achintya doctrine and can be called the *Chintya* doctrine. This is the essence of the Vedānta Sutra commentary entitled "Conceiving the Inconceivable" that was published recently. This commentary demonstrates how reality is described in contradictory ways from different perspectives—called *modes*.

As noted above, in addition to this perspective approach, we also require a conceptual approach, so that we can say that by removing the complete from the complete, the balance is still complete. And these two ideas can be reconciled if we say that the original 'complete' is the 'Reality' and the removed complete is the infinite 'Perspectives' on that reality. The original 'Reality' – the supremely beautiful Lord Kṛṣṇa – manifests infinite perspectives, but by manifesting this knowledge, He doesn't become ignorant. So, even when the complete is removed from the complete, the balance is still complete, and that is because the complete is knowledge. If this was some physical entity being removed from another physical entity, the removal would reduce the thing it is removed from, and that will lead to *reductionism.*

The key point is this: The basis on which we understand God is also the basis on which we can understand concepts, and the basis on which we understand concepts is also the basis on which we can solve the paradoxes of mathematics. The first is religion, the second is philosophy, and the third is science. These are not fundamentally different subjects if properly understood.

If this provokes your interest, then you can read "Gödel's Mistake" and "Conceiving the Inconceivable". The former is the description of the problem and its solution in mathematics, and the latter is the discussion of the same problem and its solution in Vedānta philosophy.

Philosophizing in Six Perspectives

Introduction and Overview

In my first book—Six Causes—I described a theory of creation that comprises six causes, namely, Material Cause, Efficient Cause, Personal Cause, Formal Cause, Instrumental Cause, and Systemic Cause. This was in a way a contrast to the Greek use of four causes (Final, Efficient, Material, and Formal). Now, as I work on the Six Systems of Vedic Philosophy, there is another set of sixes—Vedānta, Sāñkhya, Yoga, Vaiśeṣika, Nyāya, and Mīmāṃsā. Is the use of six categories serendipity? This article argues that it is not. Reality must be described from six perspectives, which are necessary to complete the understanding.

Six Causal Questions

Without undue complexities, we can state the doctrine of six perspectives by noting the six questions necessary to completely describe causality—What, When, Where, Why, Who, and How. If any of these questions remain unanswered, causality is incomplete.

Then we must note that the answer to one of these questions *underdetermines* the answer to others. What happens—i.e., the events that occur in the universe—can happen in different places, and times, caused by different people, in different ways, and for different reasons.

For instance, let's consider the event of a war. What happened? A war. When did it happen? Such and such a year. Where did it happen? So and so place. Why did it happen? It was perhaps ideological conflict, economic competition, political control, etc. Who fought? We can name the individuals who participated, and the rulers who triggered it. How did it happen? A certain number of soldiers, tanks, ships, and airplanes were mobilized from one place to another. These six questions are neither mutually *independent* nor mutually *determined*.

For example, since tanks did not exist at a certain time, hence, they could not be mobilized for war at that time. But even if tanks exist at certain times, the war could be fought with drones instead of tanks. The answer to "how" (drones vs. tanks) is neither independent of "when" (since tanks did not exist at one time) nor completely determined by "when" (even when tanks exist, a war could be fought using drones).

Similarly, the answers to "why" (e.g., religious vs. economic objectives) neither determine the answer to "how" (since both drones and tanks could be used for winning wars based on religious or economic objectives) nor are the answers to "how" independent of the answers to "why" (nuclear weapons will not be used if the purpose of the war is to get control over resources and people for economic growth).

Likewise, the answer to "why" (e.g., a religion) neither completely determines the answer to "where" (e.g, one or another country, because two religions may not fight everywhere) nor is the answer to "why" (e.g., a religion) completely independent of "where" (because the religions that might fight each other may not exist everywhere). The answer to "why" (e.g., a religion) neither completely determines the answer to "when" (e.g., one century vs. another, because the religions that could have fought may not necessarily fight at some time) nor is the answer to "why" (e.g., a religion) is completely independent of the answer to "when" (because that religion may not have existed then).

We could go on listing how the answers to each of the six questions underdetermine the answers to the other five questions, but it would greatly elongate this post. Therefore, we can summarize: Even as the six questions are different, they are not independent. Arbitrary combinations of answers will not work, but many combinations will. We cannot reduce the six questions to one, and we cannot provide answers to each question *independently*. There has to be a relation between answers, but many variations are possible.

Classical Deterministic Causality

At the dawn of modern science, these six questions were combined into two—predictions and explanations.

What is a prediction? It is the combination of three questions—What happened, where it happened, and when it happened. The where, when, and what was collectively called "prediction". What is an explanation? It is the combination of three answers—How it happened, why it happened, and who participated in the events. The answer to "why" was a "force". The answer to "who" was a "particle". And the answer to "how" was a "trajectory". Thus, there were two tiers of reality—an observational tier of events, places, and times, and an explanatory tier of particles, forces, and trajectories. The observational tier required empiricism and the explanatory tier required rationalism.

There was however a problem of philosophical indeterminism: The same observation could be explained in many ways, and we could never establish the necessity of one explanation over another. Many explanations could be called *sufficient* but neither was *necessary*.

However, this problem could be overlooked or disregarded by dissolving the difference between the observer and reality. This dissolution required us to equate the observer as one of the particles, situated in space and time, evolving according to a trajectory, pushed by forces exerted by other particles, with their experiences being described as the collision of particles. This merged the observational tier of events, places, and times into the explanatory tier of particles, forces, and trajectories. Space, time, events, particles, forces, and trajectories were all merged into a single description. This methodology also collapsed the distinction between the above-mentioned six questions.

Now, "what" happened fully determined "how" it happened because the events were merely points on a trajectory. Similarly, "why" it happened—i.e., why the force was exerted—fully determined the answer to "where" because force varied with locations in space. Since force varied with motion, therefore, "when" something happened fully determined the answers to "what" happened. In this way, a model of scientific description was constructed in which the answer to one question fully determined the answers to the other five questions.

The Collapse of Classical Causality

But, slowly, cracks begin to appear in this model. For example, if reality is a possibility, then space is a domain of possibilities, which is different from the space of observations or events. Now you cannot reduce reality to observation, or an observer to a space-time entity, because the observer experiences events while reality is just possibilities. All possibilities are not always observed as events.

Similarly, time is measured in classical physics by motion, and this time cannot be measured if events are discrete because then the idea of continuous motion collapses. What is happening, when events are not occurring? The classical view would say that time isn't passing because there is no motion. But we cannot say that; we must insist that time passes even when nothing is happening. The result is that time has to be disconnected from the idea of events. It is now a cause that produces the event. Now, an event (what) is the manifestation of a possibility (that exists in a space of possibilities–where), caused by something called time (when). The simple idea that matter exists as a possibility thus separates what, where, and when. The question of predictions is no longer a single question; it is three separate questions.

Likewise, indeterminism reappears in science if the same event in the same place and time could be caused by a different particle, by the intersection of different trajectories, or due to different forces. This is just like saying that if I did not do something, then someone else could, in a different way, for alternative reasons. Even if what, when, and where are fixed by observation, the who, why, and how are not.

Indeterminism in science is simply the fact that there are six distinct questions, and fixing the answer to one doesn't fix the answer to others. Determinism in science collapsed the six questions into one, whereas indeterminism in science separates these six questions.

The Problem of Contradictions

Some scientists still dream of a time when indeterminism did not exist, and they try to find a single theory in which all these six questions can be combined again as they were in classical physics. But this has proven to be impossible for rather unprecedented reasons.

If we try to combine six answers in a single theory, we get logical contradictions, rendering the theory self-contradictory. And if we separate these questions, then each theory is self-consistent, but it is also incomplete—it only answers *one* of the six questions. Atomic theory, for instance, can say what will happen, but don't expect it to answer where, when, why, who, and how. Its predictions are just like saying "food will be cooked" but don't ask who will cook it, where and when it will be cooked, how it will be cooked, and why it will be cooked.

We have two possible approaches to this problem. One, where we can say that we will one day find a complete description of reality in which six questions will be reduced to one and then answered completely without a contradiction. Two, where we can say that these six questions cannot be reconciled in any theory, and science will forever remain incomplete. Different people prefer different kinds of answers.

The View of Complementarity

There is also a third view in which there are six questions, and even as they cannot be reduced to a single question, they can co-exist as six complementary perspectives on reality. So, if you want an answer to one of the six questions, you shift into a certain type of perspective and get the answer to that specific question. But the answers you get from that perspective will not fully determine the answers to the other five questions. You will also not get the answers to all the six questions within a single perspective. To know something completely, you have to look at the same thing from six perspectives, each time obtaining an answer to one of the six questions. The six together are the full truth.

Complementarity doesn't mean independence. While there are many how, when, where, who, and why of what happens, any random how, why, where, who, and why doesn't answer what happens. So, there is some connection between the six questions. This connection appears as the probabilities of atomic theory. While we cannot accurately predict where, when, how, why, and who, we can say that certain things are more and less likely. The more or less likelihood of something happening becomes the probability of atomic theory predictions.

This problem can never be overcome in the classical deterministic sense because we cannot find a single description or perspective that will answer all the six questions. We have to rather find a description in which we need six different perspectives, to be used alternately.

The Fungibility of Six Perspectives

The six questions of what, where, when, how, who, and why is just an example of the six questions we can ask. If we take the complementarity view, then these are not necessarily the only possible perspectives. We can, in fact, construct any arbitrary six perspectives to describe reality.

For instance, in the book Six Causes, I presented these six perspectives as Personal, Material, Efficient, Instrumental, Systemic, and Formal causes. These six causes are a different set of six perspectives than those noted above. The first chapter in Six Causes provides the following illustration of this idea.

While these causes are distinct and perform different roles in the universe, they are not independent. They act concertedly with each other and this can be understood through a simple example. Consider a potter who shapes pots out of clay, by turning clay on the potter's wheel. What are the causes responsible for creating the pot? First, there must be a potter. The presence of the potter is the personal cause of the pot; the pot comes about because there is a potter. A potter is an individual person and the existence of this person is the first cause of the pot. Second, the existence of the potter is not sufficient to create pots. The potter must act like a potter. That is why the actions for the creation of a pot are called efficient causes. Third, the potter needs instruments to create pots. The potter's wheel on which the clay is turned is an instrumental cause of the pot because it plays a supporting role in the creation of the pot. Fourth, the potter must have the shape of the pot in mind to create the right kind of pot and so the formal cause determines the shape or form of the pot. Fifth, having instruments and acting with a purpose is insufficient without the matter on which these actions happen. The potter needs clay from which to create the pot, and clay is, therefore, the material cause of the pot. Sixth, the potter creates pots because he is rewarded and remunerated within an ecosystem of pot consumers, so the economic environment of purchasing pots is a systemic cause of the pot. A potter is both intrinsically motivated as well as forced by external and systemic circumstances to act towards pot creation.

This system of Six Causes elucidates the need for multiple perspectives in describing causality. But as this system of Six Causes is different from the foregoing example of who, where, what, when, why, and how, we must also note that there are multiple ways to conceive the six perspectives.

Once we realize that there are many such six perspectives on reality, then a revolution in philosophy occurs, which is that (a) there are numerous ways to describe reality, and (b) in order to be complete, they must describe it from six perspectives. The first conclusion leads us to the idea that there can be many different descriptions of reality, and the second conclusion obviates the apparent relativism arising from different perspectives—if you fix one perspective, then the alternatives in the other five are reduced too.

Six Systems of Philosophy

With that general background in mind, we can now understand the Six Systems of Vedic philosophy as yet another way of describing reality from six perspectives. Any curious onlooker naturally asks: Why should there be six systems? Why not just one? Or why not a hundred? The number six is not arbitrary. But it is one way to construct a complete philosophy of nature.

The Six Systems of Philosophy divide the reality into the following components—Object (Vedānta), Qualities (Sāñkhya), Activities (Yoga), Atomism (Vaiśeṣika), Logic (Nyāya) and Semantics (Mīmāṃsā). In fact, by putting these singular words against each system of philosophy, I am most likely committing the error of oversimplification because these philosophies certainly discuss other topics. However, this is necessary for two reasons. First, since no answer is ever complete unless it accounts for the other five perspectives, therefore, each system delving into other topics is inevitable—to create some completeness. Second, each aspect can itself be further divided into multiple other aspects.

Nevertheless, in these Six Systems, we can see a different way of describing reality than the examples I employed previously. The choice of dividing the whole truth into the above six perspectives is a choice that the Vedic tradition made collectively. It is not some random people who came up with some random ideas, formed some random groups, and produced a random tradition to say some random things. There is a precise system of six perspectives, although those were chosen collectively. The goal of my Six Systems of Vedic Philosophy project is to show how these perspectives form a coherent system. But a side effect of that project is the ability to see why six perspectives are necessary for completeness.

Jīvā Goswami's Six Treatises

Jīvā Goswami, one of the six prominent disciples of Sri Chaitanya, who were tasked to create the philosophical texts pursuant to Gaudiya Vaishnavism, wrote six treatises known as the Six Sandarbha. These are Bhagavat Sandarbha (Transcendent Person), Paramātma Sandarbha (Immanent Person), Krishna Sandarbha (the Whole Truth), Tattva Sandarbha (the Whole-Part relationship), Bhakti Sandarbha (the process of attainment), and Prīti (the goal of the process). This is another set of six perspectives.

In my previous writing, I have presented a description in which reality is said to exist in three aspects called Brahman, Paramātma, and Bhagavan. Bhagavan is transcendent, Paramātma is immanent, and Brahman is the collection of everything. Brahman is everything; Bhagavan is One Thing. Paramātma is each thing.

We can think of this in terms of ordinary ideas such as a "mammal". The idea mammal is transcendent; the idea mammal is immanent in each cow, dog, horse, etc. And the idea mammal is the collection of all the cows, dogs, horses, etc. Thus, Bhagavan is Supreme Being, Paramātma is the same Supreme Being inside everything. And Brahman is that Supreme Being expanded into everything such that everything is inside the Supreme Being as His part. Through the course of the evolution of Vedānta philosophy, there has been a shift in the presentation of what Brahman truly means. In Advaita philosophy, Brahman is an impersonal existence. In subsequent Vaishnava interpretations, Brahman is Lord Vishnu. And in Jīvā Goswami's presentation, Brahman is Krishna. Brahman is everything. And Krishna is everything.

Then, if you are familiar with the three aspects of the soul, which are described as Sambandha, Abhidheya, and Prayojana, Tattva Sandarbha is about the relation or Sambandha, Bhakti Sandarbha is the Abhidheya or the cognition and conation, and Prīti Sandarbha is the emotional goal of life. These three are described as the three aspects of the soul—*sat*, *chit*, and *ānanda*—and I have presented them as three aspects of reality in many different forms (you can find more on these aspects here).

Thus, Jīvā Goswami's philosophy presents the three aspects of the soul, and then three aspects combined into three types of souls—the Transcendent Truth, the Immanent Truth, and the Whole Truth. His presentation of the six aspects of reality is a different view on how to create six perspectives.

As a follower of Gaudiya Vaishnavism, I consider Jīvā Goswami's presentation of these six aspects—i.e., three types of souls and three aspects of the soul—as the preeminent philosophy to employ in presenting Vedic philosophy in modern time. For example, all science and philosophy fall into the category of Tattva and their goal is to establish Sambandha—the relationship to God. They are not directly Abhidheya or Prayojana, or Bhakti and Prīti, but steps leading toward these two stages.

Veda Vyās's Six Divisions of Vedas

Veda Vyās is credited to have classified and divided the Vedic knowledge into six aspects (the term Vyās means dividing and organizing). These six aspects are Samhita (Worship), Upaniśad (Philosophy), Purāṇa (Stories), Tantra (Worship), Itihāsa (Stories), and Darśana (Philosophy). There are two sets of texts devoted to three aspects—Philosophy, Worship, and Stories—one set that is mostly God-given and the other that is mostly created by advanced souls based on the God-given set. For example, Samhita is mostly worship prescribed by God, while Tantra is mostly worship presented by advanced souls. Upaniśads are God-given philosophies, and Darśanas are philosophies created by advanced souls. Purāṇa is mostly God-related pastimes whereas Itihāsas are mostly stories about advanced souls. (While Rāmāyana is considered an Itihāsa, it is not Veda Vyās's composition, but of Vālmīkī; hence it presents the story of Lord Rāmachandra, but it is quite different from Mahabhārata composed by Veda Vyās which predominates in stories of the advanced souls, and the pastimes of Lord Krishna occur occasionally in that broader narration. Vālmīkī thus combined things in Rāmāyana that Veda Vyās separated in the Vedas).

Similarly, there is a parallel system of Six Vedāñga, called Vyākaraṇa (grammar), Nirukta (etymology), Chandha (prosody), Śhikśā (pronunciation), Kalpa (rituals), and Jyotiśa (time and place). Together, these six systems create a view of language in which there are atoms of meaning (Nirukta), combined into sentences by grammar (Vyākaraṇa), composed in a poetic form for memorization (Chandha), to be pronounced in a specific manner (Śhikśā) so that language can be employed for performing rituals and sacrifices (Kalpa) at appointed places and times (Jyotiśa). These six systems of Vedāñga comprise the aspects or perspectives on what Vedas mean by "language".

An important side effect of this understanding is that Vedic cosmology or what we call Jyotiśa cannot be separated from the other five aspects dealing with etymology, prosody, pronunciation, grammar, and ritual. If we make that separation, then we don't understand what Jyotisha is. Most people may find it strange that cosmology has a connection to language, but the Vedic tradition has studied Jyotiśa as a part of linguistic performances. Mystic Universe, therefore, upholds this principle and includes a chapter on "The Theory of Language". This connection has to be upheld from the beginning in understanding that all places in the universe are different representations of meaning. The space of the universe is a domain of varied linguistic propositions because reality is itself text.

Many Possible Six-Way Constructions

The above are samples of how the six-way philosophizing system works. There are numerous such systems of philosophy that present reality through six perspectives and they are not the only possible systems. For instance, we can divide modern technical education into six areas—Logical Sciences, Physical Sciences, Life Sciences, Mind Sciences, Social Sciences, and Philosophy—because most people today are comfortable with this way of looking at things.

The problem in this division of knowledge into six perspectives is that people tend to separate these six areas from each other. For example, physical science cannot be about the study of meanings because meaning only exists in mind sciences. Matter cannot make choices because choices are only studied in life sciences. Society cannot be a living organism because social sciences are not life sciences. Logic and mathematics cannot be applied to the study of the mind because that is the domain of meaning and not of mathematics. And philosophy has nothing to say about anything other than some transcendent questions which are by definition outside the scope of every science.

The philosophy of six perspectives tells us there are indeed six different perspectives, but they are not *independent*. We cannot construct a theory of atoms unless we treat atoms as symbols of meaning. We cannot have a perfect understanding of logic and mathematics unless numbers can represent meanings. We cannot have a theory of material causality unless we take into account conscious choices. We cannot construct a social theory unless we understand the interconnected nature of a living organism. And we cannot formulate any theory without realizing its purpose and moral implications, because these philosophical questions underpin why we want to know anything.

Thus, when we look at the modern world through six perspectives, the problem is not the perspectives but their supposed *independence*. We can teach perfect knowledge through a system of six perspectives—Logical Sciences, Physical Sciences, Life Sciences, Mind Sciences, Social Sciences, and Philosophy—in a new way by breaking that independence. And that description of reality through six perspectives can be quite different from the types of six perspectives traditionally employed in Vedic philosophy. (This, by the way, is how I think of Shabda Academy, as the means to bring Vedic knowledge through modern fields of knowledge by acknowledging their usefulness, but breaking their supposed independence.) We did not create this system of six perspectives, but we can adapt to this perspective system.

That adaptation would constitute yet another method of presenting the Vedic system of philosophy, although in a way that people today can understand. Those who understand Vedic philosophy deeply can also transform the philosophy into yet another system of six complementary perspectives. This would also constitute a "scientific presentation of the Vedas", although through a modern scheme.

Absolute Truth and Perspectives

There is an overarching philosophy that underlies this way of thinking, which is that there is an Absolute Truth but it can be described through infinite systems of six perspectives. Each individual can have a different way of understanding, describing, presenting, and explicating that Absolute Truth. All these descriptions are various "branches" of the Absolute Truth in which the same reality is presented using different words and schemes, but these are not contradictory to the other perspectives.

There is hence radical freedom in knowing the truth, although the truth itself is fixed. God is a person in the sense that there is a certain way that He views Himself. But that is just one of the infinite views! Similarly, each soul can be perfect in the sense that it can view God through one of the many established perspectives—the "branches" established by Achāryas—or, even create a new perspective. The only criterion is that there must be six complementary perspectives that describe the Whole Truth. This "relativism" in the understanding of the Absolute Truth constitutes free will. It doesn't mean arbitrary conceptions. But it means multiple perfect understandings of reality.

This radical philosophy of Absolute Truth and infinite perspectives constitutes the Vedic system. In one sense, there is only one system. In another sense, there are many different presentations of the same truth through six perspectives. These include the system of Veda Vyās (Samhita, Upaniśad, Purāna, Tantra, Itihāsa, and Darśana), the Six Darśana (Vedānta, Sāñkhya, Yoga, Nyāya, Vaiśeṣika, and Mīmāṃsā), Jīvā Goswami's Six Sandarbha (Bhāgavat, Paramātma, Krishna, Tattva, Bhakti, and Prīti), and the study of reality as language in six aspects (Vyākaraṇa, Nirukta, Chandha, Shikśā, Kalpa, and Jyotiśa). Even God is presented as a composite of six aspects called Knowledge, Beauty, Renunciation, Wealth, Power, and Heroism. Hence, it would not be unfair to say that what we call the "Vedic system" is actually many *systems of six perspectives*.

The same system of six perspectives can also be presented differently as six questions (What, Who, Why, Where, When, and How), a collection of Six Causes (e.g., Personal, Material, Efficient, Instrumental, Systemic, and Formal), or a description in terms of six sciences—Logical Science, Physical Science, Life Science, Mind Science, Social Science, and Philosophy.

The soul lives eternally. What are we going to do for eternity? If truth is fixed, static, or eternal, then life would be infinitely boring and painful. But it is not. That's because there are infinite ways to know the Absolute Truth. The Absolute Truth interacts with the different parts because each part brings a new perspective. That is a way for the Absolute Truth to discover something new. By looking at things from a new perspective, He sees things that always existed but were never highlighted. Eternal life is thus not scary because there is a continuous novelty. And temporary life need not mean something false—it can also mean the same eternal Absolute Truth.

Material vs. Spiritual Realism

Introduction and Overview

Vedic vs. Western Notions of Realism

There is a sense in which Vedic philosophy is realist—a soul moves in a space of meaning-states called childhood, youth, and old age (higher) and hungry, thirsty, lusty (lower). All these states are fixed and eternal, but the soul's connection to these states is temporary.

This sense of realism is different than Western material realism which upholds that object move in a material space and time, and if the soul exists, then it is carried in the body. Descartes for instance believed that the soul is somewhere in the brain. Thereby, the body moves according to material realism and the soul (if it exists) moves along.

Confusions in the Vedic Notion of Realism

The issue of realism is considerably complicated by the use of seemingly material realist analogies in Vedic texts such as (a) the soul is a passenger on the chariot of the body, (b) the soul rides on a material machine, and (c) the soul is situated in the heart. All these analogies seem to talk about moving with the body, rather than moving from one body to another.

Owing to such analogies, many people think that any rejection of material realism is (a) contrary to commonsense, (b) contrary to Vedic texts, and (c) identical to impersonalism and voidism, which are antirealist in some sense. Of course, if we accept material realism, then we cannot solve the soul-body interaction problem. The materialist would say: Whatever is in the brain or heart, is a part of the brain or heart, so it must also be material. Thus, accepting material realism leads to the annulment of soul-body distinction and of the soul.

I will discuss the resolution of this problem in two parts. The first part discusses the failures of material realism in Western science and philosophy, and how they have led to antirealist positions. The second part discusses how spiritual realism is established in Vedic philosophy, but the rejection of material realism is not impersonalism or voidism. We need to become convinced that material realism is false before we try to understand spiritual realism.

Two Notions of Inside and Outside

To make a long story short, we need to redefine the meaning of "inside" and "outside". The soul is "inside" the body in the sense that the body can control the soul. And the soul is "outside" the body in the sense that the soul can control the body. So, when the body controls the soul, then the material realist analogies like a passenger on the chariot, riding on the material machine, or being situated in the heart are true. However, because the soul can control the body, therefore, when the soul is able to control the body, then it is outside the body and always moves from one body to another. There is hence no contradiction between the two.

This definition of "inside" and "outside" is consistent with the rest of Vedic philosophy. For instance, the soul is a part of God in the sense that God controls the soul. Everything, including the soul, is "inside" God due to this control. Similarly, as we will see, something is "outside" us if we cannot control those things. Material realism is based on the inability to control.

The body controls the soul by *throwing* the soul from one body to another. Since the body throws the soul, therefore, the body controls the soul, and the soul is inside the body. However, because the soul moves from one body to another and its identity is not changed by this throwing, hence, it is none of the bodies and not in any of the bodies. Accordingly, the body can be called *prakṣepātmikā* or the "throwing potency" because it throws the soul from one state to another. The body can also be called *āvaraṇātmikā* or the "covering potency" because it is a covering of the soul and the soul is temporarily inside the covering of some body.

Illustration Through An Example

We can imagine toothpaste inside a tube. The tube is squeezed, and the toothpaste is pushed out, but then it enters another tube, which then squeezes the paste into yet another tube. The tube is separate from the paste, but the paste is also inside some tube temporarily, squeezed by the tube, and pushed forward from one tube to another by the squeezing of the tube.

The person squeezing the tube is God, in the form of Time. The tube is material energy or Prakṛti. And the soul is the paste in the tube. Thereby, the tubes are not moving, however, the paste is moving from one tube to another. If the successive tubes are similar to each other, then we call that the movement of the body as it looks like incremental change. But if the new tube is quite different from the previous one, then it is called rebirth. However, in both cases, the mechanism of the movement of the paste from tube to tube is the same. Material life is getting squeezed like paste inside some tube. And spiritual life is finding that tube that doesn't squeeze the paste because there is no need to push the paste to another tube.

Part I – The Failures of Material Realism

Antirealism in Greek Philosophy

The problem of realism in Greek philosophy goes back to Socratic times. Socrates presented an allegory of cavemen who see shadows projected on cave walls cast by things or people behind them. Since they cannot see those things behind them, they cannot know the nature of reality. They can only try to infer the nature of reality from the shadows, but all those inferences are most likely false. A modern upgrade to that Socratic allegory would be the projection of a movie on a screen by a projector behind us. Whatever you see on the screen is not real, although there is something that creates shadows.

This kind of antirealism does not assert the *absence* of reality. It just says that what we think is real is actually not real. For example, in the case of a movie projector, there is a reality—the projector—but the dialogues we hear, or the people we see in the movie, are not real. They are illusions created by the projector. Therefore, this anti-realism is opposed to material realism but not to realism per se.

Antirealism in Empiricist Philosophy

Similar opposition to material realism appeared at the dawn of science, and it drew a distinction between primary properties (length, mass, energy, momentum, etc.) and secondary properties (color, taste, smell, touch, sound, etc.). This distinction stated that *everyone is hallucinating* because all sense perceptions are unreal. The reality behind those perceptions is completely unlike perceptions.

Many early philosophers, including David Hume and George Berkeley, argued against this antirealism. Berkeley for instance said that we can never assert the realism of primary properties, because even when you conduct a measurement—e.g., of weight—you are not observing weight; you are simply observing the movement of a pointer on a scale. David Hume then said that even if you assert the realism of primary properties, you cannot establish causal necessity between two events. Without that necessity, you can never say that any of the primary properties are the causes of appearances.

Thus, we can distinguish between two kinds of antirealism in the modern era: (a) the claim that everything we see is an illusion because all secondary properties are false, and (b) the claim that the assertion of primary properties is also false because we never perceive them, nor can we assert causal necessity even if we postulate their existence. Those postulates will forever remain unconfirmable.

Antirealism in Modern Physics

Then there were four big waves of anti-realism in science that followed one after another.

Antirealism in Classical Mechanics

The first wave arose in Newton's mechanics where mass, energy, momentum, and angular momentum are conserved, however, the total number of *particles* is not conserved. This meant that only properties are real, and objects are not real. Whatever is not conserved (i.e., eternal) cannot be called real. Therefore, if you think that the world is particles with properties like mass, then you are making a false claim, because particles are not real. Instead, some properties temporarily coagulate for reasons that we don't understand. That coagulation of properties is euphemistically called a particle, but because particles are not conserved, therefore, we cannot call them real. The coagulation of properties is simply a fact, which has no explanation in current science. But let's not dwell too much on that problem.

Antirealism in Classical Thermodynamics

The second wave arose in thermodynamics in trying to explain the irreversibility in the conversion between heat and work. Thermodynamics says that, over time, heat becomes less convertible to work. But how do we know that energy is not disappearing? You might say: Well, because it gets converted to heat and we can measure that using a thermometer. But a thermometer is also doing work—expanding the mercury—so detecting the presence of heat also requires converting heat to work. If we say that we cannot convert heat to work, then we also cannot detect it using a thermometer. Now, there is no evidence for the existence of energy. The honest answer to this problem would be to say that energy, momentum, angular momentum, etc. are not conserved, but that would destroy physics.

Therefore, Boltzmann used a trick to say that the energy gets *dispersed*. Recall from classical mechanics where physical properties can coagulate or disperse. If we say that energy disperses over time, then we can solve two problems—(a) we don't get any work, and (b) we don't detect an increase in temperature. But this claim is empirically indistinguishable from energy not being conserved. The fact is that the reality of all physical properties ended with thermodynamics, but the situation was salvaged by Boltzmann using an unverifiable premise that energy disperses and becomes undetectable.

Antirealism in Relativity Theory

The third wave arose in relativity theory which demonstrated how classical conceptions like distance and duration were not objective realities; they were tied to an observer, and hence each observer could measure a different length and time. This destroyed the idea that space and time were objectively real. Now, we were only left with one property—energy—assuming you buy into Boltzmann's solution to the problem of energy not being measurable. This energy could split and combine in many ways creating fictions called trajectories. As those trajectories intersected, then the fiction called a location in space and a moment in time was created. Those fictions were collectively called space and time.

Antirealism in Quantum Mechanics

The fourth wave arose in quantum mechanics which demonstrated that even as we claim the reality of physical properties, their existence does not simultaneously produce an effect, and hence cannot be detected. All this energy exists as a *potential*, and it manifests into different events one after another. In thermodynamics, some energy disperses gradually and becomes permanently undetectable. In quantum mechanics, even when it has not permanently disappeared, its presence is often not detectable.

Summary of Antirealisms in Physics

In short, classical mechanics destroyed the idea of particles. Relativity destroyed the idea of space and time. And quantum mechanics and thermodynamics destroyed the idea of physical properties in different ways. You still have observations—but all the methods used to explain them are unreal. You either find a different way of explaining them, or you accept that there is no physical reality.

Antirealism in Modern Philosophy

While all this antirealism was going on in physics, philosophers were creating their own antirealism. For instance, they said there is no meaning to properties like pressure and temperature other than the instrument that is used to measure them, and that instrument is arbitrarily chosen by us. This was called Operationalism. Then, looking at the fact that any data can be interpreted in many ways, philosophers stated that we can never be sure about the truth of any theory. A theory can only be falsified, but never verified. Finally, tired of all these problems of realism in science, philosophers advanced the idea that a scientific theory is not about reality or truth; it is just a model for predictions, which can be revised at any time and can stake no claim to knowing the nature of truth or reality despite its success.

Antirealism of Geometrical Entities

Meanwhile, mathematicians were struggling with their own problems of realism in the case of numbers and geometry. We cannot define a point denoted by a number unless we can *completely define* the number. Since we can never completely define an irrational number (it has infinite digits), therefore, we cannot define any point in space represented by irrational numbers. These irrational numbers are exponentially more numerous than rational numbers, so we cannot simply ignore them. Since all irrational numbers were traditionally created via geometrical constructions, hence, a point in space has no existence. Rather, that point arises by the intersection of straight lines—the simplest construction.

But what gives us the authority to say that lines are fundamentally real? It could also be said that lines are created by the intersection of surfaces. Then, what gives us the right to say that surfaces are real? We could also say that three-dimensional shapes are real. We might go back to the idea of Platonic solids, acknowledging basic shapes in nature. We could say that by the intersection of shapes, we get surfaces. By the intersection of surfaces, we get lines. By the intersection of those lines, we get points. So, a point, line, and surface are not real. However, the problem is that we have no basis to assert that space is three-dimensional. So, the three-dimensional shapes could be defined by the intersection of higher-dimensional shapes. Once you say that points are not real, then the smallest thing is not real. When you start postulating bigger things, there is no limit to how complex or big that thing has to be. The net result is that even though you can *talk* about anything, you cannot say that anything is *real*.

Antirealism in Number Theory

Then, Gödel dealt an even more severe blow to the capacity to talk about the world. Geometry had assumed that if we can construct something, then it *exists* in some sense, and a statement that says that such a thing exists is true. All that is true is not necessarily real, because points can exist, but they are not real. However, at least we can say that such and such point exists in our observation or experience, and the sentence that makes that claim is true. Gödel's Incompleteness took away that ability when he showed that a sentence that exists—and can be logically proven—may be asserting a false claim.

The root cause of that problem is that words have multiple meanings. For example, consider the three statements: (a) I am nobody, (b) nobody is great, and (c) therefore, I am great. You can prove the third statement based on the first two statements, but the third statement contradicts the second statement. Therefore, even when you have proven things logically and mathematically, they might not be true.

To eliminate this problem, you have to fix the meaning of each word. And to do that, you must forbid one of the following two statements: "I am nobody" or "nobody is great" as something meaningful. By forbidding statements, you lose the ability to say and know everything that can be said and known. That is called the *incompleteness* of mathematics. It is the only way to avoid logical contradictions.

Gödel's incompleteness means that we cannot know the complete truth about numbers, and hence about anything else. Since everything uses numbers, therefore, every theory of science is incomplete. You could still *believe* in claims that cannot be proven, and Gödel was a *believer*—he believed that there is a Platonic world of forms that have to be grasped intuitively rather than through proof. However, if we use the mathematical standards of proof, then infinite claims are unprovable and hence unreal.

Antirealism in Computing Theory

Once you start forbidding statements, then you realize that there are infinite questions that can never be answered. One such question is the capacity to predict what a program will do. It might draw a circle, or triangle, or a sphere, but we cannot know what it will do—unless we execute the program. We need the ability to predict the outcomes *before* we use something. But if we forbid that question itself, then we have forbidden the inquiry into whether a program is good or malicious. Then, we have forbidden the inquiry into whether creating such a program is morally right or wrong. The net result is that you tell everyone to stop asking all these questions because they will lead you to logical contradictions.

There are further antirealist theories, such as the idea that the world we see is a computer simulation. Even though you think that something is heavy or big, it is not actually heavy or big; it is the result of a number produced by a simulation. Then you can ask: Who created the computer and wrote the simulation software? And the answer is: Whatever question you ask, and whatever answer you get, is produced by the simulation. It appears in your mind because your mind is a simulation. So, if such questions are appearing in your mind, followed by some answers, it doesn't mean that they are true. Whether you ask the question, whether you get an answer, whether you debate the question and answer, and whether you judge some question or answer to be true, right, or good, is all simulation. Even the idea that we are simulated by a computer is an idea planted by the computer simulation. Hence, think and do whatever comes to your mind, because you cannot do anything otherwise.

Summary of Antirealist Ideas

Let us summarize the various kinds of antirealist theories and what they say:

1. There is some reality, but it cannot be known by reason and observation
2. While everything we see is a hallucination, we might know reality by speculation
3. Whatever we know by speculation can never be rationally or empirically guaranteed
4. Yes, we understand, but let's speculate anyway, and we'll see what we get
5. Speculation: The world is space and time, particles and waves, and their properties
6. Observations show that particles and waves are not real things as they are not conserved
7. Irreversibility takes out the reality of energy, momentum, and angular momentum
8. Observations show that space and time are not objectively real things
9. Observations show that there is no "hard" reality because everything is a potential
10. There is no meaning to any property other than arbitrarily chosen instruments
11. There is no truth or reality in any theory other than the current pragmatic usefulness
12. Numbers and points are not real things, because they depend on lines
13. We don't know what is real because we can't define the highest dimensional space
14. We cannot ask all the questions because they will lead us to logical contradictions
15. There are infinite unanswered questions due to the problem of contradictions
16. Let's not worry about that problem because it is a simulation anyway

Realism appeared briefly in Platonism when he said that there is another world of ideal forms, of which the present world is a poor reflection, but Plato could never define any ideal form. Then Aristotle threw away Platonism and introduced a new realism in which four substances—earth, water, fire, and air—and geometrical forms are real. Then, physicists threw out the reality of earth, water, fire, and air, and mathematicians threw out the reality of geometry because they could not find any solid foundation.

There is no scientific or philosophical theory that justifies realism. That doesn't mean the absence of reality. But it means that it is not to be found in these philosophies and sciences.

Part II – The Basis of Spiritual Realism

The Perceptual Problems of Realism

Even if we set aside all these problems, and take a classical realist stance, there are still serious issues in establishing realism based on our perception. Let's suppose a person is seeing an apple—i.e., properties like red and round. These are pictures in his mind. So, how can we say that they are real—i.e., outside the mind? Most people respond by saying that another person can see the same thing, and because we are mutually exclusive, therefore, their ability to see what we see means that it is outside both persons.

Note the irony. We are establishing the reality of an apple by *presupposing* the reality of persons. If the second person is real, then the apple is real. If that second person is simply an image in my mind, then the apple is also an image in my mind. The fact is that we cannot establish realism like this.

Solipsism in Western philosophy and certain forms of impersonalism in the Vedic tradition take this view. They say: The idea that there is another person, or a world of things, is a metaphysical claim. For those who might not know, metaphysics is often used as a bad word in philosophy, quite like the unspeakable four-letter words. To call something metaphysical is a philosopher's use of four-letter words.

Realism Based on Free Will

We establish realism by *suffering*. If we were always satisfied, then we could say that everything is in my consciousness, and there is no external reality because everything conforms to my will and I'm creating my experience willingly just to remain satisfied. However, if things work against our will, then we are compelled to say that there must be an external reality that is forcing me to suffer, against my will.

Therefore, if we enter a world where there is no suffering, then we could say: Everything is happening exactly how I want, which is giving me satisfaction, therefore, everything is being created due to my will, and in accordance to my will, hence everything is *within me*. Now, there is no need for realism.

Realism appears in the material world because we are suffering, which is against our will, so we cannot claim that I'm creating this suffering. Rather, we must say that it is forced upon me externally. To explain suffering, we must assume a real world, and we use that assumption to explain enjoyment too.

Another type of realism appears when an image appears in my consciousness, which I have not willed, and says: "Do this". If I do it, then I *automatically* become happy. The command "Do this" is not caused by my will, and yet it causes my happiness. So, I cannot say that things are happening according to my will, but they are giving me happiness. Therefore, they must originate outside my consciousness, and hence there is a reality. Now, external reality is justified not by suffering but by happiness.

In both cases of suffering and happiness, what establishes realism is that things happen without my will. They may be against my will and cause suffering, or they may be compatible with my will and cause happiness. Therefore, realism depends on *unwilled* happiness and suffering. If instead everything happens according to my will, then there is no need for realism. In Vedic philosophy, there is such a realm called the Brahman, in which the soul is self-absorbed and there is no external world.

Many Levels of Reality

Once we define external reality by the fact that we cannot control it, or that it operates against our will, or without our will, then we get a new way to construct many levels of realism. For example, we have greater control of will over some body as compared to other bodies, therefore, the body that we can control more by our will is *our body*, and the bodies that we cannot control by our will are *other bodies*. Our identification with some body as "my body" is based on this ability to control that body. We are also attached to a body to the extent that we think we can control it. If we become convinced that we cannot control the body, then we will stop identifying with the body. Sickness is a good example of this.

Similarly, we have more control over our thoughts than the process of digestion or circulation. Hence, circulation and digestion are more external than our thoughts. If you are an introspective person, and you have tried to control or change your emotions, thoughts, judgments, intentions, values, etc. then you can identify many layers of reality that are successively more external to the soul because we have lesser control over them. They are all lumped into something called the "mind" in Western philosophy because philosophers have not used the appropriate criteria for externality—namely, something is less external if I can control it more by my will, and more external if I can control it less by my will.

If we follow this introspective method of trying to gain control, which is what some yoga processes teach, then we can come to the same conclusion as Sāñkhya philosophy, which describes the layers of material realities that are successively "outer" to the previous reality. The inner reality is also called the "higher" reality, and the outer reality is also called the "lower" reality. Thus, the body is lower than the senses, the senses are lower than the mind, the mind lower than the intellect, and so on. This is not merely a theory or philosophy. It is amenable to empirical confirmation if we are introspective.

The Genesis of Material Realism

But remember, this conclusion depends on how much we are able to control our body and mind by our will. If we have no control, then we will not be able to distinguish between *more* and *less* control, and thereby not be able to distinguish between multiple layers of reality. By the loss of control, we will think that there is no soul, and by the absence of different extents of control, we will think there are no layers.

Materialism is effectively the total loss of control over emotions, thoughts, judgments, values, sensations, and actions. The materialist flattens this hierarchy from the soul to the gross body into the gross body. Why? Because he is unable to control any of the levels. His thoughts are as much out of his control as his digestion. Therefore, there is no reason to believe that thinking is different than digestion.

Once a person has lost all this control, it is very difficult to recover it. The Vedic system prescribes yoga processes to deal with this problem, and the general rule is that they begin from the outermost layer of the body, then into the senses, then into the mind, and so on, progressively deeper toward the soul. This is just like peeling an onion; you regulate the outer layer, and by regulation, you get some control over it. When you get control, then you can distinguish it from yourself. Then, you regulate the next inner layer, and by that, you get some control over it and distinguish it from yourself. Over time, as you get control over all these layers, then you can see the full hierarchy, and see yourself separate from the hierarchy.

But this process generally takes a long time. Most people, while performing this process, are not in control over their body, thoughts, emotions, etc. Their thinking is as much out of control as digestion. Therefore, if anyone says that the mind is "outside" the body, nobody will accept it. Why? Because the body is digestion and the mind is thinking, and they are equally out of the person's control.

Such a person may also not understand Sāñkhya philosophy, or how there are many layers of existence that can be progressively more in control of the soul. How the mind is "higher" than the "body" or how the "ego" is higher than the "mind" is never experienced. Then, it is very hard to understand how the ego controls the thoughts, which then control the senses, which then control the body because they are not in control of the ego. Finally, how the mind is outside the body and how the ego is outside the mind—in the specific sense that the mind can control the body, and the ego can control the mind—is not understood. Then it should not surprise us if someone says: The soul is not outside the body; it is in the heart or in the brain, and like money is carried in the pocket, similarly, the brain or the heart carry the soul along.

Since a person has lost control over their ego, mind, senses, and body, therefore, he correlates the motion of external bodies as the *cause* of changes into his or her body, senses, mind, judgments, values, etc. This is the genesis of Locke's *tabula rasa* thesis in which everything we do is based on what the world has taught us. Therefore, if we have some values, then they are society's values. If we have some ideas, they are because society has taught us to think in that way. This is also the genesis of Newton's physics in which a particle moves autonomously until another particle exerts a force on the particle. Now, there is no "internal" existence, because everything is "external". Newton in fact collapsed a planet into a point particle! Why? Because there is no "inside". If the planet can be collapsed into a point particle, then surely the human body can be collapsed similarly. Now, we are all point particles moving around in space, pushed by external forces acting on the particle. This externality of causation is called material realism—or that bodies are moving in space and time through push and pull.

In short, material realism arises due to the loss of free will, or the willing control over the ego, mind, senses, and the body. If such control is gained through yoga practice, then that realism can be rejected. But because regaining this control is hard, therefore, many yoga practitioners can also believe in material realism. This is where philosophy becomes important: It teaches us why that realism is false.

The Process of the Soul's Movement

The Vedic texts describe how the soul is moving from one body to another using two processes called *prakṣepātmikā* or the "throwing potency" and *āvaraṇātmikā* or the "covering potency". I have, in earlier articles, described this process as the tightening or loosening of the "ropes" that bind the soul. The material *guna* are also called "ropes", the soul is described as an animal tied by the rope, and the Lord is the person tugging on the rope. You can imagine a dog tied by a leash. The master pulls on the leash, and the dog moves. When the master stops pulling, then the dog stops moving. Therefore, the soul is called an animal or *paśu*, and the master of the animal is called *Paśupatī*.

This analogy, however, doesn't fully explain the process of movement, although it is not incorrect. The more complete understanding is that the material covering *squeezes* the soul and then shows an *alternative* state. That squeezing is *prakṣepātmikā* and showing the alternative is *āvaraṇātmikā*. That alternative is simply a possibility but because the soul is squeezed in the present state, therefore, it is desperate to get out of the situation, and it quickly accepts the alternative, thinking that it will be better. We can also say that the squeezing is like a tight leash and the alternative is like a loose leash. To get out of the tight leash state, the soul willingly accepts the movement to the loose leash state. But it is not will that is voluntarily coming out of the soul. It is rather the coercion of nature, accepted by the soul.

Therefore, we can say that the material energy is controlling the soul. And we can say that it is the soul that ultimately acquiesces to this pressure, so the soul is moving based on its will or acceptance.

Hence, Lord Krishna states that everything is being done by Prakṛti and the soul falsely thinks of itself as the doer. This is because the Prakṛti has forced the alternative. And yet, if the soul was not willing, then it could not be assigned any responsibility for its actions. Therefore, the complete understanding is that the soul is not the *doer* but it is the *approver.*

The statements that (a) the soul is moving on the chariot, (b) the soul is riding the machine of material nature, and (c) the soul is in the heart, arise because the soul approves what is forced upon it. The material nature compels the soul, and the soul acquiesces. By coming under the control of material nature, the soul comes "inside" that nature. However, because the soul can disapprove, and the Prakṛti will not be able to force the soul, therefore, the soul can control the movement of the chariot through a hierarchy of charioteer, reins, whip, etc.

As noted earlier, we can compare this process to the toothpaste, the tube, and the squeezing of the tube. Time is the person squeezing the tube, material energy is the tube that contains the toothpaste, and the result of that squeezing is that the soul is pushed into another tube by its acquiescence. However, if the soul does not acquiesce, then the soul can remain in a fixed tube for a very long time.

How the Material Energy Moves the Soul

With this background, we can go even deeper into how material energy squeezes the soul. As you can probably tell, it is not a physical squeezing. The process of squeezing is called *māyā* or "that which is not". This is the deepest covering of the soul and is identical to *prakṣepātmikā*. The Tantra scriptures identify these as five kinds of limitations called *kañchuka*. These limitations are those of place, time, ability, knowledge, and liking. The limitation of the place says: I'm stuck to this place, society, country, or institution, and I'm not able to get out of it. The limitation of time says: I'm stuck to this era, and forced by things happening at this time, and have no control over things. The limitation of ability says: I have so few abilities that I'm not competent or capable of what is expected of me. The limitation of knowledge says: I am ignorant and not capable of understanding many things. Finally, the limitation of liking says: Even if I tried to acquire ability, knowledge, or tried to get out of this place and time, I may not like the new place and time, or it will be so hard to get new abilities and knowledge that I will not be able to bear the pain, difficulty, hardship, and the humiliating process of change.

Basically, the function of *māyā* is to make the soul feel emasculated, and then gain control over the soul. Thereby, the soul feels worthless, insignificant, and powerless, and is forced to accept whatever *māyā* tells it. This results in endless suffering and the illusion of the soul. The illusion is that there is no other way than to go on suffering in this way. And this illusion arises because the soul is emasculated to an extent that it feels it cannot do anything about it. Therefore, *māyā* is described as abnegation, illusion, and suffering. They are the same thing. Even the most powerful, rich, famous people always feel insecure internally because *māyā* constantly emasculates them from within.

When this pressure of *māyā* reaches its limit, then the soul becomes *angry*. He says: I am not useless, worthless, or insignificant. I will prove that I am great, worthy, and invincible. Then, *āvaraṇātmikā* says: Here are the options that you could use to prove your greatness. Due to its anger, the soul forgets that such proposals have been entertained in the past and they have not worked permanently. The anger, frustration, and pressure from *māyā* compel the soul to accept those proposals. And by that acceptance, the soul moves into another body, which is another entrapping tube for the toothpaste, which means that it will squeeze the soul again, and then force it into the next situation.

How Yoga Stops the Soul's Movement

The essence of all yoga systems is to stop the squeezing. By that, the throwing is also stopped. For example, if you can relax the body and mind, then you will stop feeling squeezed in any situation. Then, you will also not feel compelled to move to a new situation.

In the mantra chanting process, the soul takes shelter of the Lord and feels protected by Him. By the remembrance of the Lord, he stops feeling the squeeze of the mind, body, and circumstances. Even if there is a squeeze, there is no acquiescence. Thus Lord Krishna says that the yogi tolerates hot and cold as mere sensations produced by the interaction of the senses with the world. These sensations cannot do anything to the soul because the soul is eternal. However, by creating the impression that the soul is being hurt, the material energy forces the soul to change its current state. Therefore, if you are feeling hot, and you get up to switch on a fan, this is because material energy is pushing you. In the perfectional state, when the soul is perfectly devoted to the Lord, it stops feeling the squeezing of material nature. The consciousness is fixed on the Lord, and anything else happening in the world doesn't matter. Such a soul becomes inactive in the sense that it is not pushed by the material squeezing. However, if the Lord says: "Do this", then the soul is immediately active. Basically, one goes from tight rope to lose rope to no rope to being voluntarily bound by the rope of love. This is the path of perfection in the yoga system.

If the soul is surrendered to the Lord, then in response to the instigations of *māyā*, it says: I'm actually ignorant, incapable, bound by time, place, and circumstance, suffering in so many ways, but I beg the Lord to place me as one of the dust particles on His lotus feet. There is no anger or sense of inferiority and then the desire to prove one's superiority. There is instead *humility*. This humility is not just prostrating the body. It is the prostration of the soul. If *māyā* cannot instigate anger in the soul, then it cannot force the soul to move.

Therefore, Vaishnava Acharyas teach that one must simply conquer pride, anger, aggression, frustration, feeling of superiority, greatness, worthiness, and invincibility, and surrender to the Lord. If we surrender to the Lord, then *māyā* cannot touch us.

Material Realism in Christian Thinking

Even as Christianity asserted the reality of the world as God's creation, there is no understanding of how the material energy controls the soul, how it forces to move the soul from one body to another, and how the soul can be liberated from this condition. The philosophers who have no control over their emotions, thoughts, judgments, sensations, and the body, then stated that the soul is carried in the body like money in one's pocket. And anyone who is in the same situation as these philosophers believes that this is just commonsense.

However, this commonsense idea has been going on for over two millennia and nobody is able to explain how the soul exists in the body. The Cartesian mind-body dualism itself is going on for many centuries, and nobody is able to solve the problem. So, there is no use in calling it commonsense if we cannot overcome the flaws of that commonsense, which then lead to the rejection of the commonsense.

Spiritual Realism in Vedic Philosophy

We have to find that understanding in which these flaws can be overcome, and accept it as the most rational solution. This transcendence can be established by direct observation through the practice of yoga. And this understanding is also presented in the Vedic texts.

Hence, by rational argument, we can show that science has never been able to establish material realism. Then, we can show that there is an alternative spiritual realism in which the soul moves from one body to another. Then, we can show how this spiritual realism leads to false material realism when the soul loses control. Then we can show how both being in control and not in control are presented in Vedic texts. Finally, we can experience the in-control situation by practicing yoga. So, there is a rational and empirical rejection of material realism and rational, empirical, and scriptural confirmation of spiritual realism. If anyone is seriously inclined to understand, there is ample knowledge.

Under this spiritual realism, whatever we experience as hard, hot, rough, sweet, bitter, smooth, etc. is *real* because it is *outside* our control. However, it is *inside* another consciousness called Prakṛti because She is in control. For example, when we cannot control our digestion, it is not happening randomly. It is occurring under the control of Prakṛti. And because that situation is forced upon us, therefore, we are under the control of Prakṛti, and *inside* Prakṛti. If we become free of the control of Prakṛti and are not forced, then we are *outside* Prakṛti.

Spiritual realism means changing the meaning of the words "inside" and "outside". What is inside me? That which I control. What is outside me? That which I don't control. When am I inside matter? When matter controls me. When am I outside matter? When matter doesn't control me. Thereby, even if we see the Lord in front of us, we are "inside" the Lord, because "inside" means that the Lord controls us by His will.

In material realist ideas of "inside" and "outside", there is force only upon things that are "outside" a thing and no force on things that are "inside", either because there is no "inside" or because if we try to describe that "inside", we run into infinities (this is a separate topic, but to note it in passing, the self-force of a particle becomes infinite). In spiritual realist ideas, there is a force on things only if they are "inside", and no force if they are "outside". Hence, Prakṛti controls us if we are "inside" Prakṛti but doesn't control us if we are "outside" Prakṛti.

If we can accept this alternative idea of control, causation, inside, and outside, then there is a spiritual science that applies to matter as well as the soul. However, if we are conditioned by the material realist ideas of "inside" and "outside" then we cannot understand spiritual realism. However, then, we also cannot establish any other kind of realism, including modern scientific material realism.

Rejection of Material Ontologies

What is "outside" my consciousness is not "stuff", "substance", "object", etc. It is also a conscious state of a superior personality who has the power to control us. Those conscious states are produced by the will of a superior personality, and they are inside that consciousness.

The material realist says that what is outside *my* consciousness is outside consciousness *per se*. It is objective in the sense that it exists independent of *all* observers. The world then has to be observed from a *third-person* perspective. But the spiritual realist says that what is outside my consciousness is inside another consciousness. I cannot control your mind, so it is outside my control, but it may be inside your conscious control. Then there are things that neither of us control, but they are under the control of a superior personality, so they are inside their consciousness. Therefore, the world has to always be understood from a *first-person* perspective. It may not be *my* perspective, but it is the perspective of another person or a superior personality who controls everything by their will. By converting all third-person thinking into first-person thinking, we don't become solipsists, impersonalists, or idealists (i.e., the world is an idea only in *my* mind) because we accept that it is always an experience, idea, or meaning in the mind of a superior personality, and it is almost always outside my control.

Material realism is tantamount to saying that nobody controls the world. The world is working on its own due to mathematical laws. This idea is also called Deism in which God made the world and then left it to operate on its own. Thereby, the world is *outside* God's control, and that gives each scientist the freedom to start speculating on the mathematical laws of nature, formulate constants of nature, and if you are a theist, then call those laws "God's intelligent design". This so-called "design" is rejected in Vedic philosophy because we reject Deism.

The world is *not* operating independently of the Lord. It is directly under His control and supervision. However, because the Lord is not irrational, whimsical, capricious, or illogical, therefore, His will is also rational, scientific, and moral. We can use our logic and reason to understand the order in nature, and by that, we are studying Lord's will. The irony is that even Deists and Christian design theorists will say the same thing: We are studying God's will. And that is why the next important distinction has to be made: The world is *inside* the Lord.

Lord Krishna showed mother Yashoda the universe inside His mouth. So, mother Yashoda is inside the universe which is inside the Lord, and that mother is also holding the Lord forcibly by her arms, showing Him a stick, and scolding Him. Similarly, the Dāmōdarāṣṭakaṁ states that the entire universe is inside the belly of the Lord. And a rope, which is a part of that universe, has now bound the Lord's belly. So, the Lord is controlling the rope, and the rope is controlling the Lord. The rope is inside the Lord, and the Lord is inside the rope. This is because of love. The rope is a devotee of the Lord, and He has agreed to be bound by the rope. But if we are not devotees, then the Lord controls us. In both cases, everything is under the Lord's control. But if there is love, then the Lord also comes under the control of that which He controls. Hence, the preliminary step is to understand how the universe is inside the Lord. It may be within His mouth or within His belly; those are different understandings and require a deeper discussion. But the high-level description is that the universe is inside the Lord.

Therefore, instead of rejecting hard, hot, rough, sweet, bitter, smooth, etc., as illusions of our experience (as modern science does), we have to accept them as real—outside and not in our control. However, they are not "stuff", "substance", "object", etc. They are conscious states produced by the will of a superior personality, and they are inside the consciousness of that personality. Likewise, instead of saying that the world is particles, with properties like energy and momentum, moving in an empty space according to some mathematical laws, we have to reject that idea because science can never prove the reality of these things, and every step leads to more antirealism.

When we are studying hard, hot, rough, sweet, bitter, smooth, etc., then we are studying our mother. We are not studying "stuff", "substance" or "object". If you cannot get over the impersonalist ideas of modern science, then due to the mind-body problem, you will reject the soul and then reject God. After all these rejections, you will find that even the body is not real. Thereby, you end up in nihilism.

The rejection of material realism is not impersonalism. Rather, reducing the mother to a collection of particles is impersonalism.

And when that reduction fails, then we get nihilism and voidism. Therefore, if one begins in material realism then the progressive conclusion is impersonalism and voidism. But if we begin by rejecting material realism then we get to personalism, and thereby to spiritual realism.

Matter is also consciousness, which controls us. Then the soul is consciousness which is controlled by matter. And matter controls the soul under the direction of God, which is also consciousness. So, everything is consciousness, but due to differences in the qualities of consciousness, they are different. In one sense, Vedic philosophy is monism—because there is only consciousness. Then, it is dualism—because there is matter and soul. Then, it is trialism—because there is matter, soul, and God. And finally, matter and soul are parts of God, therefore, there is just God. Being part of God, or being "inside" God, means that God controls them. He is the Supreme Person.

QUANTITY AND QUALITY NOTIONS OF TRUTH

Distinction Between Truth and Existence

What is truth? Some people say that truth means *existence*. If a tree exists, then it is true. But it also means that if you think that the tree doesn't exist, that thought is also true, because your thought exists. To allow for the distinction between truth and existence, we have to invoke *meanings*. The thought that the tree doesn't exist exists, but it is not true, because truth pertains to the meaning of the thought rather than the existence of the thought.

Once truths are tied to meanings, and not to existence, then we can consider the fact that the bigger meanings are truer than the smaller ones because they are found in more thoughts. For instance, animal is a bigger meaning that dog because animal is more pervasive than dog. Now, consistency with the bigger meaning is a greater criterion for truth than the consistency with the smaller meanings. Thereby, we can say that if the tree's existence is inconsistent with the bigger truth, then even if the tree exists, thoughts about the tree are not true.

This criterion can now be extended into religion. For instance, if God is the bigger truth, and the world is inconsistent with God's nature, then we must say that the world exists, but is *false*—like a dream or false thought. Then, there is no contradiction between the claims—(a) the world exists, and (b) the world is false. The world's existence is like that of a false sentence. This is one of the many examples of non-binary truths, and this post discusses their nature.

The Problem of Fundamental Truth

One of the central problems with binary truths is that all truths are equally true, and all falsities are equally false. For example, if God is true, and a table is true, then God and table are equally true. The nature of equal truths is that you can derive one truth from another. Thus, if God and table are equally true, then, we can derive the table from God, and God from the table.

The ability to derive one truth from the other means that no truth is *fundamental*. God may be an axiom for one person, and the table may be an axiom for another person. Since both are equally true, therefore, simply by changing the axioms, we can alter what we consider fundamental. Thereby, someone can say that tables are fundamental truths, and God is a derived truth.

In Vedic philosophy, we can derive God from the table, and the table from God. And yet, God is the fundamental truth. This is because God is pervasively true, while a table is contextually true. The pervasive truth is also *immanent* in the contextual truth; hence, it is possible to derive God from the table. But since God is *transcendent* to all other truths, hence, it is possible to derive everything from God. Thus, we arrive at a nuanced position in which there is a *fundamental* truth, which can also be derived from the non-fundamental truths, and yet, the ability to derive the fundamental truth from the non-fundamental truth doesn't mean all truths are equal.

The fundamental and non-fundamental truths are reconciled by a *hierarchy* of truths, which are organized like the root, trunks, branches, twigs, and leaves in an inverted tree. The properties of the root, trunk, branch, and twig are immanent in the leaf. Hence, by knowing the leaf *fully*, we can know everything. If the soul is the leaf, then by fully knowing itself, it can know everything else. Likewise, by fully knowing the table everything else can be known perfectly. And yet, that doesn't make the soul or the table fundamental truths, because they are not pervasively true.

Qualities Break Classical Logic

This system of hierarchically organized truths depends on *qualities*. The deeper quality—e.g., color—is embedded in the shallower quality—e.g., red. And yet, because color is more pervasive than red, hence, it is a more fundamental truth. Likewise, sight is more pervasive than color (because of colorless shapes), hence it is even more fundamental than color. The system in which all truths are equally true, and no truth is fundamental (as a result of which, we can arbitrarily switch the axioms, changing the definition of the fundamental truth), depends on quantities.

The system of qualities, however, leads to serious issues in binary notions of truth. For example, if red is color, but color is not red, then the principle of identity (one thing is itself) in logic is broken. Since both red and blue are colors, but color is *neither* red nor blue, therefore, the principle of mutual-exclusion (either red or blue) is broken. Likewise, since color includes both red and blue, therefore, the principle of non-contradiction (not both red and blue) is broken.

When all the principles of binary logic are broken, then the doctrine of *oneness-and-difference* is employed, because binary logic means *oneness-or-difference*. This is called Bhedābheda.

Equivalent Ways of Describing Qualities

We can see an intimate connection between (a) hierarchy, (b) non-binary logic, (c) qualities, (d) immanence and transcendence, (e) oneness and difference, and (f) more or less true.

If we emphasize that two things are separate, we would be *partially correct* because even if we emphasized that two things are identical, we would be partially correct. This partial correctness is the result of things being *more* or *less* true. Other than the Absolute Truth or God, everything is less true, because it is less pervasively true. But that doesn't mean it is *false*. When certain truths are widely true, but not pervasively true, we can call them *contextual truths*. But when certain truths are true only for an individual, then they are *individual truths*. In contrast, the Absolute Truth or God is *universally true*. Hence, the above principles are also equivalent to the distinction between universal, contextual, and individual truths as grades of more or less true.

As we divide the qualities into smaller parts, we arrive at something that is initially contextually true and then individually true.

For example, 'man' and 'woman' have several contextual definitions in different societies, and then, each person carries a unique idea of what it means to be a 'man' or 'woman', which will not be identical to the views of other men and women.

However, there is still an *ideal* man and woman, partially represented in each contextual and individual definition, which constitute the universal truth. Thereby, we can connect all the above ideas to *degrees of ideality*. The universal truth is most ideal, but contextual and individual truths are less ideal. And yet, those may be the most ideal things needed in a given context.

The most ideal truth is also the most *complete*, and the less ideal truth is less complete. For example, the most ideal man is the most complete man, and the less ideal man is a less complete man. Therefore, we can connect ideality to most true to the completeness of the truth. The path to that completeness goes through non-binary logic involving qualities through a hierarchy of steps that are progressively more ideal and complete, and end in the most complete and ideal.

The most ideal and complete is *self-justified*, hence it becomes the *fundamental truth* because it doesn't need anything else for its justification. A table is not self-justified. But God is self-justified because He is the ideal and complete truth. Every other non-ideal and incomplete truth is a partial truth, less true relative to the complete truth, and a part of the complete truth.

Since the understanding of this complete truth passes through qualities, hierarchy, non-binary logic, immanence and transcendence, oneness and difference, recognizing less and more true truths, that are successively more ideal, therefore, whenever we try to describe the complete truth using a system of linearity (all truths are equally true), binary logic (identity, mutual exclusion, and non-contradiction), quantities (that are either one or different), and objects (that are either inside or outside, never immanent and transcendent), then we get many *contradictions*.

The Cause of Gödel's Incompleteness

These contradictions are noted in Gödel's Incompleteness as "no system of arithmetic can be both consistent and complete".

The simple reason is that complete truth can only be obtained in a system of non-binary logic, using hierarchies, less and more true truths, that are successively more ideal and complete, with oneness and difference, immanence and transcendence.

Modern thinking is flawed not in the narrow sense that some of the formulae do not fully account for the data, or there are too many formulae, or some formulae contradict other formulae. It is flawed in a much more serious sense that it employs binary logic, quantities, treats all truths as being equally true, and objects which can never be inside and outside another object. Objects, quantities, and formulae also lack the notions of ideality, and hence self-justification.

Thereby, even if there were a complete formula that described all reality, we would still ask: Why this formula and not another one? Of course, contradictions in the path to that formula entail that such a formula would never be attained. There can, of course, be millions of formulae that are selectively useful in different contexts, but those cannot be called *universal truths*. At best, we can call them *contextual truths*, and as the contexts become more complex (requiring more additions to the formula) each formula would simply become an *individual truth*—i.e., it seems true to one person, in one situation, for one kind of problem, at one place and time.

Implications of Quantity Thinking

When quantity thinking is extended to all reality, then God must be quantitatively bigger. Then, He cannot be a person with a form, because all these forms are quantitatively finite. How can God appear within the universe as an incarnation if He is bigger than all universes? How can anyone ever see God, if they are not able to see all the universes at once? How can God fit within the arms of a mother, when the mother is just like us? The conclusion is always that God cannot be known, except as an infinity. That infinity is imperceptible because we are finite. The only way to know the infinite is to become infinite ourselves. Therefore, either the word 'infinity' is meaningless (the word 'infinity' is not like the word 'table' because we can point to something finite called a table, but the word 'infinity' doesn't refer to anything finite) or it is meaningful only if we become infinite. The former is materialism and the latter impersonalism.

Once you designate 'infinity' as a meaningless word, then you can start eliminating all other words that cannot be reduced to something finite and measurable in terms of something you can point to as a thing. For instance, either 'love' is a certain number of particles or it is meaningless. Similarly, either 'beauty' is a certain number of particles, or it must be meaningless. Now, a 'bigger person' is simply one who is taller and bulkier. The definition of 'big' is simply a larger quantity, and what cannot be measured in terms of a smaller quantity is meaningless. Due to the equality of all truths, you can define each thing in terms of interchangeable axioms. For example, you can say that something is either 1 kilogram or 0.001 tons. Thereby, neither kilogram nor ton is fundamental truth; they are equally arbitrary because either of these can be used to measure, hence, whatever we call fundamental truth is an arbitrary choice of a measuring standard.

Now, the 'soul' must be either all the particles in the body, or it is a meaningless word. Thereby, if you urinate or defecate, then the 'soul' must be reduced in proportion. When you eat, then the soul must expand. And when the body disintegrates, then the soul has ceased to exist.

Theism Necessitates Non-Binary Logic

When quantities, binary logic, inside vs. outside, and all truths are equally true, take hold of our worldview, then atheism is inescapable. That atheism can come in the form of materialism or the sense that there is no soul or God. Or, it can come in the form of impersonalism, namely, that there is an infinite truth, but it can never be known by the finite unless the finite dissolves into the infinite. Therefore, anyone who thinks that they can reconcile theism with modern science hasn't actually worked out the nature of the problem before they seek the solution.

The solution is non-binary thinking based on qualities, that involves a hierarchy of more and less true truths, some of the things that exist are not true, the truth is immanent even in falsities, which make the falsity simultaneously one and different from the truth. Yes, the world is false, the world exists, God is immanent in the world, so it is neither true nor non-existent. By knowing the false, we can know the truth, because the truth is within the falsity. This solution is incredibly difficult and seemingly inconceivable, but it is the only possible solution. When all that is impossible has been eliminated, then whatever remains, however difficult, must be accepted.

Why Metaphysics Is Pointless

Physics vs. Metaphysics Definition

Western philosophy has a famed distinction between appearance and reality. This distinction began with the idea that appearances are outward projection, while reality is the thing in itself. For example, consider a cheater, who talks suavely and pretends to have your best interests at heart, but in fact, he is trying to deceive you. Here, the bodily appearances (things that we can see) are called *physics* and the cheater's thoughts (that we cannot see) are called *metaphysics*.

The assumption inherent in the appearance vs. reality distinction is that we can never know the reality—e.g., the mind of the cheater. Or that we can only observe the cheater's behaviors. Thereby, the idea that the cheater has a mind also becomes metaphysics. Now, if someone says that the cheater's mind can be deduced from his behaviors—e.g., that he sometimes avoids eye contact, or says contradictory things at different times—this would be called the *reduction* of metaphysics to physics, whereby the mind is an unnecessary hypothesis.

In this article, I will discuss why metaphysics rests on limiting our perception to senses. If the perceptual capacities are broadened to include other faculties that exist in everyone although might be dimmed, then there is nothing *behind* the appearances; all those things that we thought were behind appearances—and called metaphysics—are seen in the appearances.

The Sixth Sense in Vedic Philosophy

In Bhagavad-Gita 15.7, Lord Kṛṣṇa calls the mind the *sixth sense*, in addition to the five senses of smell, taste, sight, touch, and sound. This sixth sense is sometimes called *intuition* in Western thinking, but it has been systematically ignored by almost all philosophers and scientists. The mind, like all other senses, however, has the same four capacities of emotion, cognition, conation, and relation. By emotion, the mind can have desires or revulsions, just the way the senses have them. By cognition, the mind perceives meanings, just like the five senses perceive sensations. By conation, the mind creates meanings, just like the five senses create sensations during dreams. And by relation, the mind can approach or withdraw from things other than itself (including approaching and withdrawing from the five senses).

Let's begin with the cognitive aspect of the mind. The mind assigns concepts to percepts. For example, if you see something red, round, and sweet, then the mind can attach the concept apple to it. In general, percepts and concepts underdetermine each other. For example, the combination of red, round, and sweet could also be a nectarine. Likewise, an apple could also be green.

Due to underdetermination, the senses and the mind are *complementary* senses, which perceive complementary realities. The general principle of underdetermination is that concepts define what the percepts cannot be (e.g., that apples cannot be purple) and percepts define what the concept cannot be (e.g., that something red, round, and sweet is not a tree). As we gather more and more sensations, we progressively eliminate more and more conceptual possibilities. Thereby, we narrow the conceptual assignment to percepts to a very small subset; we have defined what the thing is *not*. That is not the same as saying what the thing *is*. This is why the mind becomes necessary. Even otherwise, a mind may be pressed early into service to preempt gathering more and more sensations; if you can tell early on what a thing *is*, then you can use sensations to confirm things that it is *not*.

The conative aspect of the mind is responsible for creativity, speculation, interpretation, imagination, invention, and so on. Lord Kṛṣṇa doesn't emphasize this in the above verse, but they are present in everyone. Like the five senses create sensations during dreaming, the person whose mind is involved in creativity, speculation, interpretation, imagination, or invention is also sometimes said to be *dreaming*. The mind can alternate between dreaming and perceiving states. For example, when the mind creates some ideas, it is in the conative state; then it alternates to the cognitive state and perceives its own creation. Therefore, when we are dreaming while being awake—e.g., speculating on the nature of reality—we are alternating between conative and cognitive states. Even during dreaming, we are alternating between cognitive and conative states. However, during the waking state, we are only in the cognitive state. Thereby, in one sense, the waking state is an *inferior* state—it is mostly cognition and little conation. In another sense, the waking state is *superior* to dreaming, because we are not speculating.

The Western Approach to the Mind

In the West, the cognitive powers of the mind—i.e., the capacity to intuit meanings—are almost completely disregarded. Conversely, the conative power of the mind—i.e., to speculate—is greatly emphasized. We can say that Western intellectuals emphasize daydreaming.

Since the cognitive powers of the mind are almost completely neglected, therefore, a problem of metaphysics is created—the senses can cognize but the mind cannot cognize. What the mind could cognize is, however, reality while what the senses can cognize are mere appearances. Since the mind cannot cognize in Western thinking, therefore, it must *speculate* on the nature of reality. Those speculations are arbitrary and beyond physics—i.e., what we can perceive by the senses. Nevertheless, society must encourage this speculation to allow everyone to create their own metaphysics.

Thereby, a hypocritical stance on mental conation is created—speculation is encouraged as everyone's birthright and yet its results are generally derided as metaphysics. It depends on what seems convenient to whom at which place and time. If you like someone's speculation, you laud them as creative people. If you dislike their ideas, you call their ideological products metaphysics.

Modern science is a good example of this hypocrisy. Scientific concepts such as energy, momentum, mass, charge, gravitational force, electromagnetic field, etc. are speculative ideas, and therefore *metaphysics*. However, scientists will laud this kind of speculative metaphysics. Conversely, someone else's metaphysics—e.g., mind, soul, angels, demons, and God—would be derided as being speculation, imagination, invention, storytelling, and guesswork, that has no basis in observation or reality. The fact is, as far as the Western stance on conceptual realities is concerned, both are equally metaphysical.

Immanuel Kant tried to solve this problem by saying that some metaphysical ideas are *innate in us*; he called them *synthetic a priori*. They are *synthetic* because they are not vacuous. And they are *a priori* because they are innate in us. He proclaimed that ideas like space, time, particle, causality, force, and law are innate in us. Carl Jung then extended his stance to say that the Warrior Hero, Loving Mother, Dutiful Father, Enlightened Teacher, etc. are also innate *archetypes*, and religion was based on such archetypes. Thereby, both science and religion are equally metaphysics, but they are still entertained as valid subjects because they only seek to uncover the deep-seated or hard-wired notions in our psyche. Neither science nor religion are about a truth separate from us; they are rather *our self-discovery*. By creating science, or practicing religion, we are simply uncovering the ideas hidden in our psyche.

The Pointlessness of Metaphysics

After Kant and Jung, who rationalized the respective metaphysics of science and religion, the word became pointless, because the question was always: It is metaphysics as opposed to what? Metaphysics was no longer a bad word—an accusation to deride someone you disagree with—because (a) both science and religion use concepts not given by sense perception, and (b) both these concepts are called hard-wired truths in our psyche. This, however, meant that everyone had to agree on some universal science and religion.

With the dawn of liberalism, which permitted everyone to create their own version of the truth, right, and good, a problem arose. Since everyone has the freedom to practice their own religion, which differs in theological doctrines, therefore, you can no longer claim the ubiquity of the same theology. You can no longer say that some religious ideas are innate to the human mind. Likewise, since scientists are free to create their own theories, therefore, you cannot insist on some scientific ideas being ubiquitous hard-wired structures of the mind that everyone had to think in terms of. Basically, freedom to speculate, invent, create, and guess undermined Kantian and Jungian ideas.

The only way you could justify a particular scientific theory or religious ideology is by asserting the *superiority* of some minds over others. You could, for example, say that European minds are superior to other minds. Therefore, they have pure and perfect innate ideas, which when translated into their science and religion produce the ideal science and religion. This was a great impetus for racism, cultural superiority, and ethnic differentiation. Thereby, all minds are free to speculate, but some minds are culturally superior to others.

What we call modernism today, and is contrasted to post-modernism, was rooted in the purported and assumed superiority of European culture. It led to colonialism, racism, slavery, and exploitation of others because this is the only solution to the problem of metaphysics in Western thinking.

To overcome this problem, there is post-modernism, which counters the claim of superiority and advocates *liberalism*. Under this liberal idea, everyone is *equally free* to speculate, and European science and religion are not superior to any other science or religion. Post-modernists emphasize the primacy of the subject in interpreting the object because that is how Kant and Jung rationalized metaphysical ideas of religion and science. The difference simply is that post-modernism rejects the superiority of some minds, considering them equally speculative as any other mind. Ultimately, there is no truth, right, or good. You are free to choose whatever you like and you should not deny others the freedom to choose what they want to. Thereby, liberalism is tied to post-modernism and the politics of racism in the West.

You cannot solve this problem unless you go back to saying that the mind has both cognitive and conative aspects, the conative aspect is not the way to know reality, and reality is to be known by mental cognition. Thereby, truth is decided by better perception, and not by racial superiority. Of course, since people reject intuition as a method to know, this is not an easy path. But that means that society will be lost in the debate of racial superiority, rather than the superiority of mental perception. It will assert mental superiority through bodily factors of skin color, body shape, and history, rather than mental acuity. Since the body underdetermines the mind, and vice versa, therefore, this debate will never be resolved. This is also the pointlessness of metaphysics.

Metaphysics in Vedic Philosophy

Vedic philosophy also uses a metaphysics of three qualities called *guna*—sattva, rajas, and tamas. According to this metaphysics, the experience of taste is an appearance, and reality is one combination of sattva, rajas, and tamas. Likewise, the experience of smell is an appearance, and the reality is another combination of sattva, rajas, and tamas. Then, your thoughts, judgments, intentions, morals, conations, emotions, and relations, are all different combinations of the three modes of nature. They *appear* to be different kinds of things in our experience, but under the hood, the reality is simply a combination of qualities. Hence, there is a distinction between appearance and reality, but appearance includes all experiences—senses, mind, intellect, ego, moral sense. And the reality is the three qualities comprising them.

To understand this metaphysics, we have to understand the three qualities of nature. This means: We have to analyze all of our experiences in terms of sattva, rajas, and tamas. Thereby, sweet taste is sattva, sour and spicy taste is rajas, while bitter taste is tamas. The color yellow is sattva, the color red is rajas, and the color blue is tamas. Your food, clothing, housing, emotions, relationships, work, ideas, beliefs, habits, abilities, and everything else that you can imagine, are all comprised of sattva, rajas, and tamas. Therefore, if you learn to see the metaphysical reality in the appearances of smell, taste, sight, touch, and sound, then you can use the same metaphysics to understand the mind, intellect, ego, moral sense, emotions, relations, conations, food, clothing, housing, and everything else that you can imagine.

A good example of this metaphysical perception appears in Ayurveda, in which a physician analyses a person's pulse by putting three fingers at a suitable place on your right-hand wrist. The Vāta pulse is felt under the index finger. The Pitta pulse is felt under the middle finger. And the Kapha pulse is felt under the ring finger. Then, there is a system of qualities such as slow and fast, rough and smooth, sharp and dull, hard and soft, hot and cold—all qualities that you can perceive by touch—which will help you determine the current state of Kapha, Vāta, and Pitta. The Ayurveda physician simply knows how to transform this *appearance* into a *metaphysics* of three qualities of sattva, rajas, and tamas. By assessing the domination of different qualities in the pulse, he can tell you everything about your body, senses, mind, intellect, ego, moral sense, emotions, relations, conations, and many other things.

Of course, the pulse is not the only way to gauge this metaphysics. A good physician will also observe traits about your body, speech, the way you sit, the tone of your voice, etc. They will use that information to refine the metaphysics of sattva, rajas, and tamas, and prescribe a medicine. They will tell you which foods to avoid, what to eat, and other things to change.

Thereby, a person's mind is not *hidden* from a physician just because he is perceiving the body. The mind is therefore not metaphysics, while the body is physics. Rather, both mind and body are appearances of another metaphysics of three qualities. This metaphysics covers your body, senses, mind, thoughts, emotions, relations, works, and so on. It is *in physics*, not *behind physics*. In simple words, the reality is in the appearances rather than behind the appearances. The appearances are not the facades that hide or obscure reality. The appearances instead reveal the same reality in many ways, if only we know how to analyze the appearance to understand the reality.

The Capacity to Know the Reality

There is, however, a serious problem in understanding this reality, namely, that if the body, senses, mind, intellect, ego, and moral sense are all themselves constructed out of sattva, rajas, and tamas, then how can they perceive the qualities different from their own qualitative nature? For example, how will a person addicted to lying understand that someone else may be telling the truth? How will a person habituated to speculation understand that someone else is not speculating, but perceiving the truth?

The fact that our apparatus for cognition, conation, emotion, and relation is itself comprised of the three modes of nature is called *material conditioning*. It obscures, limits, and hides numerous things from our cognition; it biases us toward certain kinds of actions; it forces us to feel certain likes and dislikes, and it pushes us toward certain kinds of relationships and away from other kinds of relationships. Material conditioning hinders our knowledge.

Therefore, reality, or what we can call metaphysics of three qualities, is not easily perceived by everyone correctly. People misinterpret one quality as another, are drawn toward some qualities over others, act under the influence of quality conditioning, and feel differently toward qualities.

Therefore, in Bhagavad-Gita, Lord Kṛṣṇa speaks about *transcending* the qualities. This transcendence is presented in many different ways: (a) a description of qualities and how to identify them, (b) regulating our life by duties such that we resist untoward attraction or revulsion toward qualities, (c) drawing the consciousness inward and away from the qualities, and (d) acquiring a nature that transcends these qualities by the practice of devotion. Everyone can identify the three qualities to greater or lesser extents, and that is the starting point. Then, they can regulate their lives by associating with better qualities than the worse ones. Then, they can detach themselves from the world of qualities to reduce the influence of qualities on the apparatus of cognition, conation, emotion, and relation. Finally, they can sustain all these things only if the self is situated in a state beyond the three qualities.

This freedom from material conditioning is called the *purification of consciousness*. Once the consciousness is purified, the body, senses, mind, intellect, ego, and moral sense are all purified. Then, cognition is pure, conation is pure, emotion is pure, and relation is pure. Since we are primarily discussing the cognition of reality here, the pure consciousness perceives reality *as it is*. This simply means that the metaphysics of three qualities is perceived clearly in every kind of sensual and mental appearance.

We could rephrase this: You can know the reality by detaching yourself from that reality and standing apart from it. Only if you are not conditioned by the three qualities, will you perceive the qualities clearly. Therefore, metaphysics doesn't require *speculation* about what lies *behind* appearances. Rather, metaphysics requires us to clearly see what is *in the appearances*, which is possible if the observer is not itself influenced, biased, conditioned, or prejudiced toward certain limited aspects of the appearances.

The Knower-Knowing-Known Distinction

The three qualities are said to have many manifestations, one of which is the knower, knowing, and known distinction. The knower is predominant in sattva, the knowing is predominant in rajas, and the known is predominant in tamas. For example, the property of taste has three manifestations: (a) the property of taste conditioned by sattva becomes the knower and is called the *sense* of taste, (b) the property of taste conditioned by tamas becomes the known and is called the *object* of taste, and (c) the property of taste conditioned by rajas becomes the knowing and is called the *activity* of tasting.

The first consequence of this description is that the activities of tasting, seeing, touching, smelling, or hearing, are not simply the *interactions* of a knower and known; rather they are different *kinds of interactions*, which is why we cannot reduce these interactions to one type. These are loosely responsible for what modern science calls "forces" of nature; there are many *kinds* of forces. We cannot perceive these forces by a physical measurement; we can only perceive their effects. To understand their differences, one has to note the experiential difference between seeing and tasting.

The second consequence of this description is that taste is not simply in the observer; it is also in reality. Therefore, the world has to be described as taste, smell, sound, touch, and sight, not as quantitative or primary properties like mass, charge, energy, momentum, etc. The observer is qualities or secondary properties, and the observed is also qualities or secondary properties. The difference is simply that the observer's senses are dominant in sattva, while the observed reality is dominant in tamas. Every observer thus comprises senses (the knower), body (the known), and prāṇa (the power of knowing). Thereby, a person's "body" comprises three distinct components called senses, the thing to be known, and the power of knowing.

In aśtānga-yoga, first, the thing to be known is regulated, then the power of knowing is regulated, and then the senses are regulated—gradually progressing from tamas to rajas to sattva. These three steps are called āsana (known), prāṇāyāma (knowing), and pratyāhāra (knower) in Yoga Sūtras. Similarly, the power of knowing is manifest from the knower, and the known is manifest from the power of knowing. Thereby, if one is able to master their senses, then they can change their body to a different one. This change of body includes the capacity to control urges like hunger and sleep. It also includes the capacity to heal your illnesses. In a more radical sense, by controlling the senses, it is possible to completely change the species.

The third consequence of this description is that the mind is another kind of sense that perceives meaning. Its capacity to perceive is due to sattva. Its capacity for creativity is due to rajas. And its capacity to store meaning as memories is due to tamas. Thus, a person influenced by tamas has a fantastic memory, some limited creativity, and almost non-existent mental intuition. Thereby, in modern society, people who can memorize subjects pass the exams, but they have very little creativity; they can apply their knowledge to repeated problems, but they cannot solve new problems. Those who have some creativity tend to fail in exams, but they can do better in life afterward, as they can solve new problems. Finally, rare people have the mental intuition to solve a problem in a way that doesn't create new problems.

The result of qualities is that there is no reason for the mind-body divide. The mind is one combination of three qualities, and the body is another combination of three qualities. These two combinations can interact because they are simply three qualities. And yet, the combination is such that the body underdetermines the mind, and the mind underdetermines the body. Underdetermination is neither full determination nor complete independence. Hence, bodily changes have mental effects, and mental changes have bodily effects, and yet, the mind is not the body, nor is the body the mind. The mental effect doesn't fully determine the bodily effect, and the bodily effect doesn't fully determine the mental effect. But since there is an effect, therefore, we cannot say that mind and body are independent.

Tattva vs. Ontology and Metaphysics

Western philosophy doesn't have a word for what Vedic philosophy calls *tattva* which equals *reality*. It employs two words—metaphysics and ontology—both of which are misleading. Metaphysics means that which lies behind appearances, and ontology means appearance. Thereby, there is nothing that is *in experience*, and yet, not experienced by everyone. This *in experience* and yet *not experienced* thing is called *tattva* or reality in Vedic philosophy. Sometimes, *tattva* is translated as "essence", but even that translation is misleading because it is imbued with Platonic notion of essences under which the concepts of chair and table are essences.

Basically, there is no equivalent word for *tattva* in Western terminology, so whenever we use the terms metaphysics or ontology as translations of *tattva*, we are misleading people in different ways—by the former reality is behind appearances and the by the latter the reality is equated to appearances. Since we are compelled to use misleading words, it is very hard to explain what we mean by reality in Vedic philosophy. For most people, it is impossible to understand what we mean by knowledge of reality, called Tattva-Jñāna.

The Nature of Tattva-Jñāna

Śrīmad Bhagavatam 1.2.11 states: *vadanti tat tattva-vidas tattvaṁ yaj jñānam advayam brahmeti paramātmeti bhagavān iti śabdyate.* Here, *tattva-vidas* means "those who know the tattva". The word *tattvaṁ* means "reality" which is neither ontology nor metaphysics. Then what is it? It is described as *jñānam advayam* or "nondual knowledge". This is a radical leap in philosophy, where *reality is knowledge*. Thereby, if we know something perfectly, then our knowledge comprising percepts and concepts *is reality.* Reality and appearance are just two copies of the same percept and concept. If, however, we don't have the knowledge, then our version of percepts and concepts is an illusion. That doesn't mean that reality is *not* percepts and concepts. It just means our version of percepts and concepts is not what reality is.

This knowledge is further described in three ways: (a) a source, (b) a clone of the source, and (c) the source within the clone. We can think of knowledge. Suppose a person speaks about himself; his self-knowledge is the source, the speech is the clone of that knowledge, and the speaker is present in the speech as describing himself. If a person says "I am tall", the sentence doesn't become tall, because "I" doesn't refer to the sentence; it refers to the speaker. This reference to the source is the immanent form of the source. Thus, Bhagavān is the source, Brahman is His speech, and Paramātma is His innate presence in the speech. For example, Bhagavān is "I", Brahman is the sentence "I am tall", and Paramātma is the "I" in "I am tall" referring to Bhagavān.

Thereby, everything is an expansion of Bhagavān, and it is sentences like "I am tall", "I am strong", "I am beautiful", etc. In these sentences, there is an "I", represented by Paramātma. Thereby, Paramātma is *tattva*, and words like "tall", "strong", "beautiful" are His *pratyaya* or attributes. When we see these attributes, we think of *objects*, but they are not objects; they are sentences, spoken by Bhagavān, which describe Bhagavān. Therefore, when we see a table or chair, we are seeing a description of Bhagavān, spoken by Bhagavān. However, we disconnect that sentence from the source and see the table or chair. If we develop Tattva-Jñāna, then we will not see the table; instead, we will see a *description* of Bhagavān. This is also like five blind men observing an elephant; instead of saying that they are seeing the leg and stomach of the elephant, they call it cylinder and sphere. What we call table and chair is just like cylinder and sphere. It is the result of our blindness. However, if we become *tattva-vidas*, or knowers of *tattva*, then we will call it God's parts.

The soul is Brahman, which is the speech of Bhagavān. That sentence may be "I am tall", "I am beautiful", "I am male", etc. This "I" in the sentence, however, doesn't refer to the sentence itself; it refers to the *speaker* of the sentence. The foolishness is to think that "I am tall" refers to the sentence's properties, rather than to the speaker's properties. If that foolishness is destroyed, then the soul realizes that I am a property of God. Realizing the Paramātma simply means separating the attributes from the object of those attributes.

The other revolutionary idea in calling reality non-dual knowledge is that everything in appearance and reality has to be described as meaning. It is not substance, stuff, physics, or other such things. Even the material world is non-dual knowledge, which appears in the problem of underdetermination—mind and body are distinct but not separate; percepts and concepts are distinct but not separate. This is *non-duality*; it is neither *ekatva* (oneness) nor is it *dvaya* (duality). It is non-duality, which means distinct but not separate. All this becomes trivially easy when we think of reality as meaning; cow is neither identical to mammal nor is it separate from the concept of mammal.

The Process of Tattva-Jñāna

The process of Tattva-Jñāna is going *deeper*. For example, we might see someone's body right now, which is an appearance. Then we go a little deeper and we get prāṇa. Then we go a little deeper and we get senses. Then we go a little deeper and we get mind. As go deeper and deeper, we get the three qualities of sattva, rajas, and tamas. Then we go even deeper and we get a soul. Then we go even deeper and we get the immanent form of God, present in everything. This *deepest* truth is also the *broadest* truth because everything is produced from that truth. Hence, there is no conflict between the process of going *deeper* and going *broader*. Depth and breadth give identical results.

Thereby, sattva, rajas, and tamas are not the deepest level of reality, although they are far deeper than the observed phenomena of body, prāṇa, senses, mind, intellect, ego, moral sense, and so on. Our ability to see something *in appearance* gives us a *complementary* description of the appearance. For example, at the grossest level, we describe the world as objects. Then, we describe it as activities. Then we describe it as perceptions. Then we describe it as meaning. Then we describe it as judgments. Then we describe it as experiences. Then we describe it as omniscience. This is seeing reality *in the appearance*; it is a different description of the same appearance. It is not other than the appearance, but it is also not the appearance.

Tattva is a difficult concept if we are accustomed to Western terms because it is neither ontology nor metaphysics. If we can grasp it, then we can use the word *tattva* to speak about reality and forego ontology and metaphysics. Since most people are not going to be able to do that, it is imperative that we know what we mean by *reality*, because it is not metaphysics and not ontology.

What Is a Machine?

Article Introduction and Overview

In the last article, I discussed the nature of Personhood as six traits—self-awareness, intention, emotion, cognition, conation, and relation. Modern science depersonalizes persons as machines governed by laws. Therefore, in this article, I will discuss what I mean by a *machine* in contrast to a *person*. I will then discuss how the progressive influence of matter converts a person into a machine and its multifarious implications. Then I will discuss why a process of demechanization and dematerialization is prescribed to regain the lost personhood.

Six Traits of Personhood Revisited

The six traits of personhood entail very specific things in life. A person is self-aware, self-searching, self-satisfying, self-analyzing, self-organizing, and self-correcting. By the six-fold processes of the self, the self becomes *self-perfecting*. The self-awareness is "I", the self-searching is "Who am I?", self-satisfying is "How can I be happy with myself?". To answer these questions, there is self-analysis, followed by self-correction. If faults are corrected leading to self-satisfaction, whatever satisfies us more is designated as our *primary nature*. Conversely, the things we are dissatisfied with, are designated as our *secondary nature*. Due to this primary-secondary difference, people may not see their faults easily; they remain satisfied with whatever they are. Others, however, may see numerous faults in their persona. This contrast is presented by psychologists as between "How I see myself" vs. "How others see me".

Due to our need to become self-satisfied, there is considerable arbitrariness to self-satisfaction. For example, I could be riddled with faults and say: "I'm happy with myself". This arbitrariness arrests the process of self-perfection. The person who is more self-dissatisfied remains restless but keeps perfecting himself. Conversely, the person who is more self-satisfied remains content with imperfection. Thus, for example, there is a sense in which even the beasts, birds, fishes, and trees are self-satisfied.

However, self-satisfaction is not, ultimately, arbitrary because there is a *standard* for self-satisfaction in God. This standard of self-satisfied nature is called *complete* self-satisfaction, which means that we have a choice for arbitrary self-satisfaction, but that choice is not contrary to the standard of self-satisfaction.

Bhakti vs. Mukti Processes

If we remain unaware of God, then we can be satisfied with anything. But if we become aware of God, then we will try to perfect ourselves in comparison to God. This perfection takes two forms.

- First, we see the perfection in God, find ourselves lacking, and try to perfect ourselves. When the self gets more perfect and satisfied by it, then God becomes even more perfect and satisfied, because the self is a part of God. This is an *indirect* satisfaction of God called *mukti* in the sense that the self is satisfied first, and God is more satisfied as a consequence.
- Second, after we see the perfection in God, the attention never returns to the self. We forget about self-perfection and simply admire and love God. This process is *bhakti*. By it, the self is also satisfied because God is in each self as the innermost core. This is the *direct* satisfaction of God, in the sense that God is satisfied and the self is satisfied as a consequence.

These two ways of perfection and satisfaction can be understood through the relation between a parent and a child. When a child gets educated, self-reliant, independent, and successful, the parent gets very satisfied—I produced a child who is now independently successful, self-reliant, and prosperous. However, the parent gets even more satisfied if the child returns to the parent and cares for them. Now, the parent becomes the child of their former children and depends on their care and love. The process of liberation or *mukti* is the parent getting satisfied by the children's self-perfection. And the process of devotion or *bhakti* is the child getting satisfied by the parent getting satisfied due to the child's love.

Two Kinds of Spiritual Personalism

Thereby, there are two kinds of Personalism in Vedic philosophy. In the first—called liberation—a person is defined as something that is *self-perfecting*. As mentioned, to perfect oneself, there is self-awareness, self-searching, self-diagnosis, self-correction, and self-organization. As a person perfects themselves, there is more self-satisfaction. However, because God becomes even more satisfied by seeing His children's perfection and satisfaction, therefore, the standard of satisfaction and perfection *expands* or increases. Thereby, the process of self-satisfaction and self-perfection is unlimited, because the standard is God, and God gets more satisfied as the children become more perfect and satisfied by that perfection.

In the second kind of Personalism—called devotion—a person is defined as something that loves and serves God, which increases God's satisfaction, and because God is the deepest level reality in the self, therefore, each person becomes more satisfied by loving God. This is also never-ending because God's satisfaction increases the soul's satisfaction, which inspires and motivates the soul to love God more, which then increases God's satisfaction. Therefore, even the world of devotion is ever-expanding. They are different simply as greater perfection leading to greater satisfaction vs. greater satisfaction leading to greater perfection. The emphasis on perfection is *mukti* and that on satisfaction is *bhakti*.

The Genesis of Impersonalism

Once we understand these two kinds of personalisms, we can contrast them to spiritual impersonalism. Impersonalism is produced from a simple problem—the process of perfection and satisfaction is *never-ending* because there is no limit to perfection and satisfaction. We can imagine a carrot tied to a donkey using a stick; the donkey sees the carrot and tries to move toward it, but the carrot moves further. This example is imperfect because in it the donkey never eats the carrot; the carrot keeps moving forward. The spiritual world is not like that; it is a process in which you eat a carrot, and the carrot gets *bigger*. However, even this process can be quite dissatisfying—Why can't I eat the full carrot *at once*?

I'm reminded of the farmer who kills the goose that lays the golden eggs—one per day—to get all the eggs at once. Life means never-ending, ever-increasing perfection and satisfaction. But there is a death wish in the soul to attain a *static state of perfection*. It is like the farmer killing the golden goose to get all the eggs at once. By that process, however, the farmer just gets one golden egg. That attainment is not *personalism* but *impersonalism*, because personalism is defined as never-ending progress.

The personhood that ends in a static state is called Brahman. In this state, the soul has the self-awareness, self-searching, self-satisfying, self-diagnosing, self-correcting, and self-organizing abilities. However, the *verbs*—i.e., awareness, searching, satisfying, diagnosing, correcting, and organizing—become *nouns* by putting an end to the process, to attain a static state. Great Acharyas, therefore, have considered impersonalism a *spiritual suicide* arising out of the death wish of *finality* in the soul.

Many people come to spiritual life with a sense of *finality*—nothing more after this. No more progress, no improvement, and what is already perfect can never become *more perfect*. In fact, they might argue that more perfect and most perfect are contradictions in terms because perfection cannot be improved upon. The idea that you attain perfection and there is nothing to improve upon is *impersonalism*.

There are many variations of impersonalism—(a) eternal heaven, (b) Brahman, and (c) dissolution of the self. Personalism is the idea that you keep progressing eternally because there is no limit; the spiritual world keeps growing in perfection, although it was not imperfect, to begin with. Impersonalism is the converse idea that you work hard right now, and you attain a state of *final* perfection thereafter. Impersonalism is born out of the desire for finality. Under this idea, eternity becomes *static.*

The Genesis of Materialism

In Bhagavad-Gita 2.40, Lord Kṛṣṇa describes eternity as *nehābhikrama-nāśo 'sti pratyavāyo na vidyate*, which means there is no loss or diminution in this process. There are two key words here—*abhikrama* which means progress, process, sequence, and *na-iha nāśah* which means no destruction in this. It is not *static* and *final*, because there is progress. And yet, it is eternal because there is no reduction.

Impersonalism creates a stark contrast between *eternity* and *progress*—what is progressing cannot be eternal. Personalism provides a different definition of eternity—what is eternal is *non-reducing.*

The material world is produced due to a contradiction between eternity and progress because it is a *partial truth* compared to Personalism where there is eternity and progress. Since Impersonalism is incomplete—finality without progress—the material world compensates it: *progress without finality.* Just as the soul has a death wish for finality, similarly, it also has a life wish to see progress. Therefore, when the soul gets dissatisfied by the death wish of finality, it falls into matter to see progress.

In Śrīmad Bhagavatam 10.2.32, this is called patanty adhah (which literally means "falling down, falling under, or falling below"): **O lotus-eyed Lord, although non-devotees who accept severe austerities and penances to achieve the highest position may think themselves liberated, their intelligence is impure. They fall down from their position of imagined superiority because they have no regard for Your lotus feet.**

The material world becomes problematic because both endless progress (Spiritual Personalism) and endless finality (Spiritual Impersonalism) are rejected. The world remains endless, but it is neither progress nor finality. The negation of both progress and finality produces a *cycle* of change. That cycle would end if it were endless finality. And it would be a straight line if it were endless progress. When the soul rejects both endless progress and endless finality, then it gets an endless cycle of change.

The Genesis of Mechanization

The material world is deterministic due to the effect of time—it operates in cycles of changes. Due to the effect of time, there is the rise and fall of societies, cultures, ideologies, and economies. The same types of things happen over and over again. However, the soul is not required to be a part of the same society, culture, ideology, or economy. The universe is *what* deterministic but not *who* deterministic, because time controls the material energy, but the soul still has free will due to its personalism of never-ending progress. Mechanization is the denial of the existence of this personhood of the soul and reducing the soul to the predictable, repeatable, and controllable process in matter controlled by time.

This happens if the soul turns from God-awareness and self-awareness to matter-awareness. When self-awareness becomes matter-awareness, then self-seeking becomes matter-seeking (seeking material things), self-satisfied becomes matter-satisfied (fulfilled by possessing material things), self-analyzing becomes matter-analyzing (trying to understand the world), self-organizing becomes matter-organizing (trying to create an ordered world), and self-correcting becomes matter-correcting (trying to fix the problems in the world). All the six aspects of the self are thereby materialized. Furthermore, since matter is working deterministically due to the effect of time, the soul becomes deterministic.

Materialization of the self is due to the identification of the *consciousness* with the *content*. The content is *in* the consciousness, and *outside* it. For example, when we see an apple, there is a picture of the apple in our consciousness, but there is also an apple outside our consciousness. If we remember both, then we say: We are seeing an apple—i.e., the image in our consciousness is *non-different* from the apple. Not different means it is not an orange or a banana, and different means that by knowing the apple we don't become the apple. Together, different and not different are called *non-difference*. However, if non-difference is equated to *identity*, a person becomes a material mechanism.

The process is simple: Substitute the apple you are seeing with a reflection of you in a mirror. You are unlikely to identify with an apple, and hence by seeing an apple, you don't think you become an apple. But when you see a reflection of yourself in a mirror, you say—I am actually the thing that I am seeing. This reflection in the mirror is called the *ahaṃkāra* or the ego. It is the reflection of the soul in matter. It is just like an apple, and yet, we don't identify with an apple, although we identify with the ego. The question is: Why? And the answer is: We *want* to be a certain kind of thing. It is that which we wish to be, aspire to be, analyze ourselves to be, organize ourselves to be, and are satisfied by being so.

The Genesis of Delusion

The material energy works on the soul just like flattery works on almost everyone. The flatterer says: My dear lord, you are beautiful, powerful, knowledgeable, famous, and rich. And the soul approves because he wants to believe all that. Flattery works if we want it to be true and if someone flatters us, we think that it is indeed the truth. Thereby, the soul identifies itself with flattery and becomes what it is not. Unlike the progressive and final versions of self-satisfaction, flattery gives us temporary satisfaction. When the soul wants to be praised like God, but without perfection, it accepts a life of flattery.

The *ahaṃkāra* or the ego is false flattery. It is not the true nature of the soul, but the soul wants it to be true and accepts it as its true nature. Thus, the self, which is separate from matter, identifies as what it is not. Flattery would not work if we knew our true nature and realized that the flatterer is deceiving us. But due to the absence of self-awareness and God-awareness, and the desire for the self to become great, the soul accepts flattery as the truth. The rest of the material creation proceeds from this false flattery called *ahaṃkāra* or the ego, as described in Sāñkhya philosophy, and it is all false. This falsity doesn't mean the world is unreal. It means that it is flattery and not the soul's true nature.

In Bhagavad-Gita 18.61, Lord Kṛṣṇa says *bhrāmayan sarva-bhūtāni yantrārūḍhāni māyayā*, which means: All the living entities are wandering seated on the machine of delusion. The world is māyā or delusion because it is produced from the flattery of ego. It is real because it is separate from the soul, and yet, the soul identifies itself with the flattery, like its own reflection in a mirror. Then, it is a machine because it is operating deterministically and predictably under the control of time. The soul is seated on this machine because the soul goes wherever the delusion of the ego takes it. Lord Kṛṣṇa's greatness is that He can summarize the complete situation of the material world into a single perfect sentence.

Basically, the reflection in the mirror moves due to the effect of time, the soul identifies with it and says: I am moving; the reflection is moving because of my movement. In Bhagavad-Gita 3.27, Lord Kṛṣṇa says: *All activities are carried out by the three modes of material nature. But deluded by the false ego (ahaṃkāra), the soul considers itself the doer.* We can also understand this description through the lively proverb—"the tail wagging the dog"—where the soul is the dog, and the tail is its flattering ego.

The soul's free will would be seen if it stopped enjoying the flattery and actually tried to become perfect. This happens when the flattery turns into criticism. By suffering, we wake up to our real situation. Thereby, the spiritual journey begins due to suffering and is hampered by material success after we have begun, if we start enjoying the flattery. The advanced soul is not disturbed by flattery. He says: Whatever I have attained is due to the grace of my spiritual master and the Lord wanting to glorify His devotees.

The Meaning of Mechanization

Once the soul identifies with the flattering ego, then it becomes completely mechanized, because the ego is moving according to natural laws. Now, its self-awareness is ego-awareness; its intention is whatever the ego intends; its emotion is whatever emotions the ego produces; its cognition is whatever the ego cognizes; its relations are whatever the ego considers itself related to; and its conations are whatever the ego does under the control of time. There is absolutely no free will. The soul loses its capacities for self-diagnosing, self-correcting, self-organizing, self-cognizing, self-seeking, and self-awareness. Everything is delegated to the material energy, which moves deterministically.

By the presence of intention, the soul has the capacity for free will; it cannot be controlled by force. By the presence of emotion, the soul feels self-satisfied and has the capacity for love, and doesn't need to be selfish. By the presence of cognition, knowledge springs automatically within the soul, and ideas need not be fed into the soul from outside. By the presence of conation, the soul has enormous power to do things under the control of its will and doesn't need to be given any power from outside. And by the presence of relation, the soul has complete freedom to associate or dissociate from the world.

But when the soul identifies with the ego, it progressively loses everything. Of course, the ego is not uniform in everyone, because the ego has literally infinite flavors depending on its composition by the effect of three qualities called sattva, rajas, and tamas. Thereby, some ego is better than others.

The ego of sattva has the capacities for self-analysis, self-diagnosis, self-correction, self-seeking, self-organization, and self-awareness, where the "self" pertains to the inner reality such as the senses, mind, intellect, ego, and morals. The ego of rajas has the capacity to analyze, diagnose, correct, seek, organize, and know the world. Finally, the ego of tamas is confined to analyzing, diagnosing, correcting, seeking, organizing, and knowing one's body. Thus, under sattva, a person can understand mental reality very easily. Under rajas, a person can grasp the problems of the world and solve them easily. And under tamas, a person can only take care of his or her body.

When the consciousness is focused on the body, then a person cannot see how he is connected to the world at large, and how there is a deeper reality unperceived by the senses. The world is then modeled as distinct bodies, separated from each other, giving rise to the idea of modern science which studies the world as separated objects, quantities, mathematical laws, destroying all notions of personhood.

Worsening of Mechanization

Once the self and world understanding are lost, then the sense of meaning and purpose in life is completely destroyed. There is no morality. The tamas ego is moved by fear and greed—sticks and carrots—and not by any rational or ethical principle. There is no capacity even for mundane love or the ability to see the pains and joys of other people. The ideas of truth and right are lost; only the good remains, which is nothing more than sensual pleasure. There is no desire to serve anyone, help anyone, or assist anyone because these are not sensually pleasing. All relationships are based on demands of pleasures with minimal supply.

Once this worst form of material control is attained under the influence of the tamas ego, a person is almost completely mechanized. Thus, materialization exists even under sattva and rajas. But mechanization arises due to tamas. All the traits of personhood are progressively destroyed as the ego descends from sattva to rajas to tamas. Under tamas, spiritual personhood is completely destroyed.

Trait of Personhood	Personalism	Mechanization
Self-Awareness	Self-diagnosis Self-analysis Self-correction	Diagnosed by Others Analyzed by Others Corrected by Others
Intention	Free Will Goal Selection Motivated	Forced by Situations Purposeless Depressed
Emotion	Love Empathy Self-sacrifice	Selfishness Cold and Insensitive Survivalist
Cognition	Meaning Truth, Right, Good Spontaneous Knowledge	Things Agnostic Externally Input Data
Conation	Volunteerism Serving Others Creativity	Employment Dominating Others Repetition
Relation	Structure Self-control Interactive	Chaos Controlled by Others Unilateral

Every single definition of a machine—e.g., that it is repetitive, has no free will, can be controlled by force, lacks creativity and cognition, makes no judgment, has no love, emotion, or empathy, does what it is programmed to do, and lacks self-correction ability—is a contrast to the definition of a person. And all these effects are caused by the soul identifying itself with a deterministically operating tamas ego.

The Effects of Mechanization

The modern world is excessively dominated by tamas, which means there is literally no capacity for introspection. Vedic philosophy rests on understanding the nature of personhood, which is also partially reflected in the working of the senses, mind, intellect, and ego. All these things require introspection. However, a tamas ego cannot introspect and hence cannot grasp the philosophy of personality. By the inability to understand the self and see it differently from mechanical instruments, personhood is completely destroyed. People can only understand the working of machines, and model everything as a machine, which are objects working under the control of mathematical laws. Thus, due to the near-complete absence of introspection, the capacity to understand Vedic philosophy is almost completely destroyed.

Similarly, any spiritual practice requires self-control, which manifests into sense-control, mind-control, action-control, and ego-control. When there is no self-control, then there can be no spiritual practice.

Likewise, spiritual progress requires self-diagnosis and self-correction. But people cannot see their faults because the ego prevents acknowledging faults. People keep shifting the blame to others: The system is bad, we were not taught properly, the teachers are not good, and the books are incomprehensible. They simply cannot see that the fault lies within them, and they have to make a greater effort.

Finally, spiritual progress requires a sacrifice of pleasures and acceptance of difficulties. However, the tamas ego is extremely sensual. Under its influence, people cannot renounce any pleasures, or undertake hardships. Everything has to be very easy and palatable, like popping a pill into the mouth. Anything that involves endeavor, effort, sacrifices, or hardships, is rejected as being too painful. Instead, whatever seems easy, is understood to some extent, becomes popular, and is elevated to the level of truth.

The net effect of tamas is that (a) people cannot grasp philosophy, (b) they cannot practice self-control, (c) they cannot renounce pleasures or accept hardships, and (d) they cannot see any faults in themselves to make improvements. If we cannot grasp philosophy, then jñāna-yoga is out of the question. If we cannot practice self-control, then aśtānga-yoga is out of the question. If we cannot renounce pleasures and accept hardships, then karma-yoga is out of the question. And if we cannot see any fault in ourselves, then we cannot accept that the rational, mystical, and practical explanation is not grasped due to our faults.

Extreme Reliance on Faith

Once life is mechanized, then the only difference between humans and machines is *emotions*. Machines don't need to be motivated, but people do. You don't tell a machine: You are doing a fantastic job. But you do that for people. Machines don't feel pain and pleasure, but humans still do. Machines are not sad or happy, but people are. In every other way, humans have become almost completely identical to machines. Emotions are the only way that we can still distinguish humans from machines.

Hence, spiritual progress also totally depends on emotions. Chant and dance, eat sanctified food, love each other, avoid all kinds of aggression or violence (e.g., stop meat-eating), and even those things that can potentially lead to aggression or violence (such as intoxication, gambling, or illicit sex).

Of course, people will say: You are emotional people, not rational and practical people; you rely on blind faith in scriptures, and you don't have the capacity to prove anything by reason or observation.

But there is nothing we can do because by reason they mean the mathematical modeling of objects rather than the rational understanding of personhood, and by observation they mean meter readings on instruments rather than an introspective method to know the self through the self. People have lost the capacity to understand personhood which is gained via introspection and self-analysis. They can only understand impersonalized, mechanized, materialized, and lawful study of objects, which are external to their minds and senses. Even as problems arise in studying this world, those are marginalized, postponed, rationalized, and ultimately accepted as "the best we can do".

Now, those who come to religion—dissatisfied by the mechanical life devoid of purpose, meaning, morals, and love—accept things on faith: (a) soul and God, (b) soul vs. matter, and (c) a simple and repeatable process—e.g., the chanting of the Hare Krishna mantra—to purify themselves. All faith-based religions however seem equally irrational.

The minor difference is that some religions teach humility, love, and tolerance, rather than aggression, violence, and exclusivism. This distinction is the sole obvious external discriminator between religions presently because the philosophical, introspective, meditative, mystical, and inward approach to religion is either deemphasized or marginalized in favor of the external or outward differences. The noticeable attractions are confined almost exclusively to dresses, rituals, and places of worship.

Why Mechanization is Not Better

We claim that humans are different from machines because they have the capacity to self-diagnose, self-correct, self-organize, self-cognize, self-seek, and be self-aware, which machines do not. But we also know that all the traits of humans that distinguish them from machines—with the exception of emotions—are disappearing rapidly. Meanwhile, the machine capacities are getting better. As the gap between declining humans and advancing machines narrows, there will come a time when it is cheaper, easier, and better to have machines do all the work, and leave the humans to starve and die.

That is when we will realize why the philosophy of personhood is still much better than mechanization because there is at least one thing (emotions) that machines don't have but persons do. Religions based on faith and love will therefore remain, and more people will turn to them over time. However, they will be driven by emotional needs. They will accept the religion of love and devotion just to be happy.

Why Atheism is Simply Ignorance

The skeptics can say that religion is irrational faith, although it is not. It is a perfect science. However, to understand that science, one has to have the capacity to self-diagnose, self-correct, self-organize, self-cognize, self-seek, and be self-aware. We cannot teach philosophy to a machine. We cannot ask a machine to meditate. We cannot demand a machine to act morally. And we cannot expect a machine to self-correct. When people become just like machines, all scientific aspects of religion also disappear.

For religion to become rational again, people have to recover their personhood. If they can rise to rajas, then we can teach them perfect philosophy through the analysis of worldly scientific subjects. If they can rise to sattva, then we can teach them perfect philosophy through the principles of personhood gained by introspection. If they can realize that their current personhood is flawed, and they can fix these flaws, then we can teach them the perfect science of God by comparing it to a perfect self. But what can we do, if people cannot analyze the world, analyze the self, and correct flaws in the self?

If one takes to the chanting of the Hare Krishna mantra, then all declining or lost capacities in humans can be revitalized. By the revival of the capacities to self-diagnose, self-correct, self-organize, self-cognize, self-seek, and be self-aware, people will begin to understand how they are different from machines, why are they persons, why they cannot be reduced to impersonal objects and their laws. When humans are superior to machines, then they become indispensable to society—even if machines exist.

If humans advance in their personhood, then they can understand why mechanization has far bigger costs than benefits. We can carry bombs in our pockets to protect ourselves from an attack. However, it is likely that the bomb will explode in the pocket before the attack. When the bomb makes the situation far more dangerous, then the cost-benefit analysis says that we don't carry bombs in our pockets. However, even to do this cost-benefit analysis, one has to be much better than a machine.

The Modal Conception of Reality

Human Modes of Understanding

Even as Western epistemology is defined as the theory knowledge, owing to numerous dualisms in Western philosophy, such as the separation of the observer and the observed, it has never been clear if epistemology can meet its goals. In this article, I will discuss the problems of epistemology, and what they tell us about the observer and the observed.

The first problem of knowledge is that the world must conform to *our modes of understanding*. These include sensations like smell, taste, sight, touch, and sound, concepts such as table and chair, and judgments like truth, right, and good. Without a correspondence between our modes of understanding and the world, everything we perceive, think, and judge would be false.

If reality was not smellable, tasteable, seeable, touchable, or hearable, then properties of the world corresponding to the senses of smell, taste, sight, touch, and sound would not register anything in our senses. For instance, a speedometer cannot measure temperature. If our senses were like a speedometer, while the world was temperature, then they would not register anything. If our senses were only like a thermometer while the world was both speed and temperature, then sense-perception would only produce a *partial* understanding of the world.

Likewise, we conceptualize the world through ideas such as tables and chairs. Western philosophy has, for a very long time, considered these unreal; they are called our ideas about a world that is completely different. However, Western philosophy has also held that the world is *conceivable*. Scientific concepts include ideas like particles and waves, space and time, interrelationships and causality, logic and mathematics. But there is no clarity on the double standard with regard to concepts—Why are some concepts real and other concepts unreal? Similarly, how can we establish that certain concepts like beauty and justice are unreal when they are more pervasive, successful, and practical than the concepts of science?

Let's assume that our minds are like thermometers whereas the world is like speed speed. Just like a thermometer cannot register speed, similarly, everything our minds conceive would be unlike reality. That dissimilarity between the observer and the observed would preclude any knowledge. Then, if reality was a superset of properties only a subset of which were conceivable by the mind, reality would be known *partially*. Finally, if our minds were capable of a superset of concepts, only a subset of which apply to reality, we would have to justify why a certain subset of the mind applies to the world and restrict all attempts at knowing the world to that subset.

We can summarize these problems as follows. If our modes of knowing are a subset of the modes of reality, then we cannot know reality completely. If our modes of knowing are a superset of the modes of reality, then we cannot justify our knowledge. In the former case, there is no *method* to knowledge; in the latter, there is no *justification* for knowledge. Knowledge is possible *if and only if* our modes of understanding precisely coincide with reality.

The Contradiction in Knowing

The second problem with knowing is that knowledge must be *rational*, but knowledge gained through the senses and the mind violates ordinary principles of binary logic. For example, when you see an apple and use concepts such as red, round, sweet, and apple to cognize it, all these concepts are both in the mind and the world. If the concepts were only in the mind and not in the world, then our cognition would be *false*. If the concepts were only in the world, and not in the senses and the mind, then the world would not be known. The simultaneous presence of the same concepts creates problems.

The main problem is that since the apple exists outside of our senses and the mind, therefore, the apple is different from us. The apple doesn't cease to exist if we don't know about it. And yet, at the point of knowing, all those concepts also exist in the senses and the mind, therefore, the state of the senses and the mind is not different from that of the apple. In brief, the observer and the observed are neither totally different nor totally identical. More precisely, the observer and the observed are distinct individuals and yet they are conceptually identical at the point of truthful observation.

Universals and individuals are two modalities of knowing. If we remove the modalities, then the fact that the observer and observed are neither identical nor different creates a logical paradox. The resolution of the paradox necessitates the use of modalities. Hence, knowledge is inconceivable in non-modal logic, and conceivable in modal logic. Modality implies that two entities can be different in one sense and identical in another sense. For example, the apple in our senses and the mind is identical to the apple outside our senses and the mind conceptually, but the two are different individuals.

Likewise, the identity between the observer and the observed only exists in some contexts—e.g., when we are observing the apple. It is not a universal conceptual identity. For instance, we don't become an apple by observing an apple. Likewise, a context will reveal different things for different individuals.

Since knowledge is possible only when our modes of understanding are identical to that of the world, therefore, the presence of modalities in our knowing requires that reality must also be modal. Just as knowing requires the use of universality, individuality, and contextuality, similarly, reality must also comprise modes. If modes are restricted to our knowledge, then reality will be contradictory. If modes are restricted to reality, then our knowledge would be contradictory. In the former case, our knowledge claims will not pertain to reality; in the latter, even these claims will contradict each other.

The Modal Conception of Reality

Based on the above problems, we can conclude that the mere

possibility of knowledge requires a modal conception of the observer and the observed. By the first problem, the observer itself is modal—there are multiple modes of knowing—sensation, conception, and judgment—to which the world must conform. By the second problem, each mode must be subdivided into universality, contextuality, and individuality. For example, the idea of yellow is universal; there are many individual instances of yellow; and the same thing can be called yellow or not yellow in different contexts, without a contradiction.

The mere possibility of knowledge thus tells us many things: (A) that the observer and the observed must be modal, (B) they must be modal in the same way to avoid ignorance and contradictions, (C) the existence of modalities like sensation, conception, and judgment in the observer entails that these exist in the observed as well, and (D) the existence of modalities like universality, individuality, and contextuality in the observed entails that these exist in the observer too. Now, we can dissolve all the dichotomies in philosophy, such as the idea that the observer and the observed are fundamentally different. This is because they are both constructed out of a certain set of common and shared modalities.

Thereby, the observer can be observed, and the observed can be an observer. The relation between observer and observed—what we call observing—defines a connection between the two. In simple words, the mind and the senses can also be known but knowing these is not the same as being them because when we know them, they are the observed, but when they know, they are observers. Knowing that someone is in pain is not the same as being in that pain. This is again due to modalities.

The Linguistic Form of Modalities

Once we understand that reality and its knowledge are modalities, then we need yet another modality to linguistically express that knowledge. The problem is that linguistic communications can be fictional; they exist but they are not knowledge. Conversely, they can be used to convey knowledge and reality. Hence, linguistic communication is neither totally identical nor totally different from reality.

If only reality and its knowledge were possible, then we could know, but we could not *impart* that knowledge to others through the use of language. The fact that we can communicate knowledge, but the linguistic representation is not identical to knowing, and yet not different from that knowledge, requires us to formulate reality, knowledge, and language as modes. Hence, what we call a table is also a linguistic-symbolic representation. Likewise, when we think of a table, that too is a linguistic-symbolic representation. If and only if these two representations are identical can we claim to know the reality.

The practice of science requires a linguistic communication of reality. It cannot be different from reality. And it cannot be different from how we perceive and conceive reality by our senses and the mind. This doesn't mean that reality, its sensation, and the linguistic-symbolic representation are identical. It just means that they cannot be different. Language is a mode of knowledge and reality, that allows us to communicate reality and knowledge, but reality and knowledge can exist without communication. When communicated, the linguistic-symbolic representation cannot be called *not* knowledge or reality. And it cannot be equated to reality and knowledge. This conclusion necessitates the use of modalities.

The Reduction of Modalities

We have discussed several modalities—(A) observer, observed, observing, (B) sensing, conceiving, and judging, (C) universal, individual, and contextual, and (D) reality, knowledge, and language. All these modalities, we have noted, must exist in us and the external reality for the reality to be knowable, for knowledge to be consistent, and for the consistent knowledge to be communicable to others who know reality via language. But are these the only modalities? If not, how many such modalities can exist?

The answer is infinite because, in a modal conception of reality, everything becomes a mode. For example, the color, shape, and size are different modes of a table; the object, its properties, and the attachment of some property to some objects are also modalities. Therefore, there are as many modes as there can be words. The fact that we can express all knowledge and reality in words gives us the mechanism to say that all of science can be reduced simply to the study of words in a natural language.

Now, just as we can reduce language to fewer elementary sounds, similarly, we can reduce the modalities to some *elementary modes* from which more complex modes can be constructed. The possibility of reducing infinite diversity to a parsimonious list of elementary modes creates the *science of modes* under which everything can be reduced to and constructed from an elementary mode-set.

Why Vedic Philosophy Seems Strange

All the above conclusions don't require anything from Vedic philosophy. These could be derived from purely technical, observational, and rational analyses of our everyday world. This analysis, however, has never been done in Western philosophy. Instead, Western philosophy went down the path of creating numerous dichotomies such as a physical conception of reality different from the conception of the observer, the use of binary logical inferences, the use of objectivity instead of contextuality and individuality along with universality, the separation of language from reality, and so forth.

Vedic philosophy seems so strange to the modern mind because it rejects dualisms and dichotomies. For example, to overcome the observer-observed dichotomy, the observed must be described in terms of our modes of understanding. Most people are just not able to accept this idea; they prefer describing the world in terms of instrument measurements. Similarly, to overcome the mind-body dichotomy, the body must be described in terms of the categories of the mind. Again, most people are not able to accept this idea. They believe that making the body an idea would make it imaginary. They just cannot conceive that ideas are real things, because of Western dualisms. Likewise, to overcome the language-reality dualism, the reality must be described as text, which can expand to elaborate and contract to summarize without losing its essence. Again, most people cannot accept this idea. They think that matter must be conserved because only the mind can expand or contract. They think that material change requires push-and-pull forces because they cannot imagine that matter can be altered simply by our speech–quite like we can ask another person to do something just by speech.

Vedic philosophy seems strange and inconceivable because people are accustomed to dualistic dichotomies despite all their problems. A workman can have bad tools, and yet, refuse to let go of them because he doesn't want to learn new tools and seeks comfort in the familiar. Even as his tools are irrelevant to new problems, the workman says: My old tools have worked in the past, so they should work in the future. Rather than focusing on solving the problem, he mocks and questions the problem. The workman doesn't realize that the work will find the workmen with better tools, and he will become worthless.

Modal Nature of Vedic Philosophy

Vedic philosophy begins from the idea that reality is modal. Nature is said to comprise three modes called *sattva, rajas,* and *tamas*. The soul is said to comprise three modes called *sat, chit,* and *ānanda*. Similarly, reality is described both as meaning and language, because that reality is knowable, and the knowledge is expressible for communication and transmission to other knowers.

Language is no longer a human creation; it must be natural because there is no other way for knowledge to exist. Likewise, the world must be described in terms of our modes of understanding because there is no other way to ensure that knowledge is possible. This knowledge must employ a neither-identity-nor-difference method of thinking because there is no other way to ensure that knowledge is possible. Thus, the mere *possibility of knowing* asserts numerous conditions on the nature of reality.

When someone hears the description of reality, their cognitive apparatus shifts from the mode of language to the mode of meaning and then to the mode of reality, because the cognitive apparatus is also modal. Thereby, the problems of Western philosophy—those of epistemology, ontology, linguistics, observation, rationality, sensation, conception, and judgment—never arise in Vedic philosophy. This gives Vedic philosophy a distinct flavor from Western philosophy because modality is assumed.

All the discussion then is about why there are three modes, how these three modes are complete accounts for all reality, how these modes combine and separate, and how innumerable modes are created by their combination. Everything seems strange in Vedic philosophy if we don't know the reason why this modal conception is employed. That modal conception is assumed in Vedic philosophy, without an explanation. We can surmise that it wasn't explained because it seemed natural to everyone.

Understanding Vedic Philosophy

This grasp of the modal nature of reality has disappeared at present. Instead, everything is influenced by dichotomies and contradictions. People have even given up asking fundamental questions: Is knowledge possible? If so, how? What will be the nature of reality that is also knowable and communicable?

Unless we return to these fundamental questions and lay out the problems of arbitrarily assuming knowledge and its communication without explaining how reality can be known and communicated, Vedic philosophy will remain strange. This, however, creates a new role for philosophy in the modern world, which is quite like Western philosophy in the sense that it explores the same dichotomies and contradictions, although this time to show why and how they are resolved by modal conceptions.

This kind of philosophy wasn't actually practiced in the Vedic system, nor is it practiced in the West today. It is, however, a *bridge* between Western and Vedic systems of philosophy. That bridge must be built and crossed for everyone who understands Western philosophy but not Vedic philosophy yet.

Why the Material World Is Called an Illusion

The Illusion of Perceptual Location

Imagine that you are sitting inside a room. You will likely say that there is a space, inside which there is a planet, in which there is a country, inside which there is a city, inside which there is a house, inside which there is a room, inside which the body is currently situated. If you believe in the existence of a soul, you would likely say that the soul is inside the body, and hence it is limited in what it perceives by the fact that the body is inside space, planet, country, city, house, and room. Modern science will agree.

This idea of being inside the space, planet, country, city, house, room, and body is an illusion in Vedic philosophy. The reality is as follows: There is a conscious person—or a soul—which is outside of space, planet, country, city, house, room, and body. However, the soul's *perspective* is limited to a certain body, whose perspective is limited to a succession of perspectives called the material space, a planet, a city, a house, and a room. By limiting the perspectives successively, the *illusion* of being inside space, a planet, a country, a city, a house, a room, and a body is created. Factually, the soul is outside all this.

Thereby, the world is *real* in the sense that the perspectives exist even if our vision is not limited to those perspectives. But the idea that I'm inside something because it is precluding my vision of other things, is an illusion. I'm not inside the body, room, house, city, country, planet, or space.

Houdini's Escape Tricks

You might have heard about Harry Houdini who was well-known for his escape tricks. The standard trick involved being locked into a room or a trunk followed by an escape from those enclosures. This is considered a magic trick because we assume that the person is locked *inside* the trunk or the room.

Now imagine the converse in which the person is not inside the room, although his perspective is limited to seeing the walls of a room to the exclusion of all else. You can imagine that you are seeing the inside of a room through a camera installed in the room, while you are outside the room, looking at the pictures generated by the camera. If the camera moves, then you see something different.

Now take this a step further. Even the camera is not inside the room; the camera is merely *interacting* with the room such that at the moment it seems to be close to *all* the walls of the room, and hence seemingly *inside* the room. An appearance of proximity is created by a strong interaction between the camera and the room, quite like you can have a video call with a friend and he or she appears close on the screen, although they are far away. In modern science, the strength of interaction increases by reducing the distance; we can flip that idea to say: The distance reduces by increasing the strength of interaction. Things far apart seem close and those that are close seem far. But that seeming proximity and distance are not real. Only the things that you see are real. *Things are real, proximity is an illusion.*

If we adopt this alternative idea of what puts us inside a room or a trunk, then there would be no mystery if a person disappeared from the room. That disappearance is simply disconnecting their consciousness to the camera, connecting it to another camera, or connecting the camera to another room, and thereby seeing something else. They were never inside the room or the trunk; those were simply perspectives, which created the illusion of being inside something else. By changing their perspective, they could enter into something else.

The difference between these two views is as follows: If we think Houdini's escape tricks involve magic, then the *body moves* from one place to another. If instead, we think that moving from one room to another is a change in perspective, then *consciousness moves* from one perspective to another. What we call a *place* in ordinary thinking (and modern science) is a *perspective* in the alternative view. It is impossible for a body locked in a room to escape. But it is possible for consciousness to move, and thereby change the "camera" through which it sees things, or by connecting the camera to something else by changing its focus and interaction.

The Soul and Houdini's Escape Tricks

We begin to understand Vedic philosophy when we grasp these basic ideas about reality and illusion. The world is real in the sense that some cameras and the pictures they can show exist. However, the world is unreal in the sense that while seeing those things, we are not "inside" space, planet, country, city, house, room, and body. These are also not material things. They are just the images to be seen. If the soul is locked into some camera and image, then it is said to be locked into a perspective. The sense of being "locked" into some perspective, camera, or image is an illusion because the soul is not locked.

This idea is described by saying that you are not this body, sensation, ideas, judgments, morals, desires, etc. That doesn't mean those things are unreal or don't exist. It is also described by saying that the soul is "covered" by the material energy through successive layers of matter. Those coverings give the impression of being *locked* inside *if* we think of the covering as a trunk locking in Houdini. But the covering is not a trunk. It is an image attached to the soul's consciousness and it can be removed.

When we were children, we used to play with kaleidoscopes. You turn the kaleidoscope and it shows you a different image. Now imagine that the whole world is simply a kaleidoscope and we are looking into it. The body we consider as "I", followed by the room, house, city, country, planet, and space that we consider "mine" are just perspectives created by a kaleidoscope. The kaleidoscope, and the visions it produces, are real but the idea that I am these things, or that they are mine, is completely false.

Similarly, the soul moves from one perspective to another. At each step, it performs Houdini's escape tricks, which means it exits one perspective and enters another one. At the time of death, the soul changes perspective one more time and enters a new body, house, country, planet, or even a universe. Each of these is a version of Houdini's escape tricks. Even during this lifetime, when we walk from one room to another, the process is a succession of entries and exits. At the time of death, it is yet another entry and exit. The changes can *seem* small or big, but they are both *appearances*. The reality is that they are different perspectives, but because the perspective excludes the other perspectives, therefore, we think we are locked *inside* a body, room, house, city, country, planet, and ultimately the material space.

How Illusion Creates Binary Logic

That mutual exclusion of inside and outside a room creates binary logic, and then the rest of modern science. We think: Either I'm inside or I'm outside. I cannot be both inside and outside, or neither inside nor outside. But the soul is outside the room and yet inside the room as the illusion of proximity, so it is inside and outside simultaneously. Likewise, the room is outside the soul, and yet inside the consciousness simultaneously. Therefore, binary logic or the idea of mutual exclusion, non-contradiction, and identity is an illusion.

This illusory experience of binary logical separation is called *duality* in Vedic philosophy. The truth is *non-dual*, which means duality is an illusion. The term māyā is hence used in many ways simultaneously: (a) that which exists, (b) but as an illusion, (c) the illusion is duality, and (d) the duality is unreal. Since everyone gets confused by these things, hence, we can summarize it differently: The reality is non-dual but seems dual. If you *describe* reality by binary logic, your description is an illusion. If you *describe* it non-dualistically, it is reality.

Non-duality isn't just about the "other world". Even this world is non-dualistic. This is why in quantum mechanics, people are puzzled about how a quantum particle can be here and there simultaneously. How can something be in more than one place at once? The classical description is dualistic, and the quantum reality is non-dualistic. Classical descriptions cannot capture this non-duality, hence all the trouble in physics. It arises because scientists try to describe non-dualistic reality using a dualistic idea of space, distance, and proximity.

But just for a moment, think of ideas: The same idea can exist in two heads at once, so it is here and there at once. Likewise, if you acquire a new idea, it doesn't mean others who had the same idea before have now become ignorant. The idea hasn't *moved* like a classical particle. Rather it has *spread* to other places. Hence, the idea is localized as a particle and it spreads like a wave, so it is both particle and wave. There is no problem, except that we have to give up dualistic thinking arising out of object contemplation. If we just elevated ourselves to idea contemplation, we will understand this non-dualism, and that sets us on the road to understanding many kinds of non-dualism.

Two Ideas of Change, Law, and Reality

The dualistic and non-dualistic conceptions of reality result in two distinct ideas about change. Under the illusory conception, the body is moving from one room to another and evolving from one age to another. Under the reality conception, the soul is moving from one perspective (body, room, country, life) to another (body, room, country, life).

Likewise, these two distinct ideas about change alter our conception of space. Space under the illusory conception is a container and it contains things like planets, countries, cities, houses, rooms, and bodies. Space under the reality is conception is a set of perspectives produced by a kaleidoscope. You look at one perspective and you create a new conception of I and mine, but it is not you and not yours.

Accordingly, there are two different conceptions of natural laws. Under the illusory conception, the laws pertain to the motion of objects, planets, galaxies, etc. Under the reality conception, the laws pertain to the succession of perspectives—i.e., which perspective follows another perspective, based on our choices, a history of consequences, and abilities produced based on previous choices.

Finally, there are two different conceptions about matter. Under the illusory conception, the material world comprises things or objects with properties and their evolution. But under the reality conception, the material world comprises information about color, shape, size, taste, smell, hardness, roughness, heat, tone, pitch, etc. When you feel you are inside a room with hard walls, neither are you inside the room nor are those walls hard. The sense of being inside a room is an illusion created by a perspective, and the sense of the wall being hard is another impression on awareness by some information.

Qualitative Conception of Reality

We can understand this by analogically thinking of digital files. If we see color on a computer screen, the computer doesn't store color. It stores information bits. Those bits are converted into color by a display. In the same way, whatever we call 'matter' is information, but our senses generate a color by interacting with those bits. So, color is an illusion, because the reality prior to perception is bits of information. But color is not an illusion because there are indeed bits of information that produce color in our experience.

Similarly, reality is some combination of the three modes of nature (*sattva*, *rajas*, and *tamas*). But what we perceive is not these modes; instead, we perceive taste, color, smell, shape, size, hardness, etc. This is because the soul chooses some combination of modes as its definition of the self. By this choice, it picks its material personality and identity. Once the personality is chosen, everything downstream from that self-definition is automatically defined.

This is just like you choose an arbitrary origin of a coordinate system in space, and every location in space is thereafter designated by different numbers. The values we assign to the points in space using a coordinate system are not real. But they become real after the choice of an origin. Likewise, the modes of nature are not truly sensation, thought, judgment, or pleasure. But they are designated as such after we choose a definition of the self—the origin of space.

Hence, in Vedic philosophy, the first thing to define after the soul's entry into the material space is a self-adopted conception of a self, called the "ego". The ego is the origin of space that renumbers all locations in space to create personal qualitative reality. In short, it designates one combination of three modes as sensation, another one as thought, another one as judgment, another one as pleasure, etc. This is the construction of a *relative space* in which an objective reality of mode combinations is redesignated as personal experience. Without the choice of the ego, reality is simply some combination of three qualities but not sensation, thought, judgment, pleasure, etc.

Therefore, if we change our self-conception, then we will change our idea of pleasure. Once that idea of pleasure is changed, then what we consider true, right, and good will also change. Once those changes have occurred, then our thoughts will change. After those changes, our actions will change. And by those changes, our sensations will be altered. When everything beginning from the ego to the sensation is completely redefined, the consciousness starts interacting with others who have the same self-conception and stops interacting with those with different self-conceptions. With this change in interaction, the person disappears from one world and appears in another.

Why Modern Science is an Illusion

The simple difference between modern science and Vedic philosophy is that science describes the bits as three quantities (three coordinate directions) while Vedic philosophy describes them as three qualities. Just like you can specify an object by describing the X, Y, and Z coordinates of its particles in modern science, likewise, in Vedic philosophy, we can specify all the properties of matter by three qualities. Matter in science is a collection of {X, Y, Z} tuples, and matter in Vedic philosophy is a collection of {S, R, T} tuples. The primary difference is that {X, Y, Z} are quantities and {S, R, T} are qualities.

1. The order between {X, Y, Z} doesn't matter; you can change the order without altering the reality. The order between {S, R, T} is, however, immensely important. Changing the

order in {S, R, T} changes the reality itself. Thus, qualities are hierarchical because {S, R, T} have a dominant-subordinate structure, which results in a strict order between them, while {X, Y, Z} are independent and non-hierarchical variables so the order among them is not strict.

2. Due to the hierarchical structure of qualities, the space of qualities is like an inverted tree, rather than like a box for a space of quantities. The box-like space is relative because you can flip the order of {X, Y, Z}. The inverted-tree space is absolute because you cannot flip the order between {S, R, T} without changing reality.
3. The dominant-subordinate structure within {S, R, T} changes cyclically allowing each mode to dominate alternately. Therefore, time is cyclical; that cyclical change is described as a vibration, pulsation, or sound. It can also be *interpreted* as probabilities since different orders appear at different times. Thus, vibration, probability, and cyclical time are intertwined, as a result of alternating mode domination. Every location in space is sound because it is some {S, R, T} tuple and it is flipping in order. Meanwhile, {X, Y, Z} extend linearly and hence time is linear.
4. {X, Y, Z} describe things-in-themselves, while {S, R, T} describe conscious experiences. {X, Y, Z} is independent of any observer, but {S, R, T} are always dependent on some observer (because it is redesignated as sensation, thought, judgment, and pleasure). Hence, matter is personalized instead of impersonalized. It is always the conscious experience of some person, caused or produced by some person, and controlled by that person.
5. Even as {S, R, T} tuples exist objectively, the observer has a choice to accept or reject one or more of the qualities (the tuples can attach partially or completely to the observer). Thus, it is possible to know the same thing in different ways. Due to the dominant-subordinate change, the same thing is also revealed and hidden with time. Therefore, even if something exists, it may not be known to everyone in the same way at all places, times, and situations. Hence, matter is seen as a potentiality rather than a universal fact.

6. Since choices are involved in observation and action, therefore, the laws of experience pertain to the succession of quality attachments to consciousness, which means that they are the laws of choice and consequence, rather than the motion of matter. Matter is evolving too, but why we perceive some evolution and state in an objective reality, rather than others, becomes the primary law.
7. The temporal objective evolution of matter is designated as *time* selecting and deselecting aspects of matter, as the secondary law. Thereby there is objective evolution of matter, and a subjective evolution of the soul through that objectively changing reality. The objective evolution is the evolution of space, while the subjective evolution is the trajectory through this space. Due to the effect of time, the world evolves objectively even if we don't exist. But due to our choices, we experience parts of this evolution.
8. Qualities are governed by a non-binary logic unlike quantities governed by binary logic. For example, under non-binary logic, a person is inside a room and yet outside. Likewise, the room is inside the person and yet outside. Binary logic necessitates the mutual exclusion of inside and outside. Non-binary logic allows inside and outside simultaneously, although in different *modalities*.
    - Consciousness, content, and pleasure are three modalities of a person; the person is outside the room in the consciousness modality, inside the room in the content modality, and neither inside nor outside (or both inside and outside) in the pleasure modality.
    - The pleasure or pain while within a room are not necessarily due to the room (others in the same room may not feel the same pain or pleasure) nor is the room sufficient to cause it (pain and pleasure are partly self-created based on our desires).
    - When a person is neither happy nor sad in a room, then he is neither inside nor outside. If a person is partly happy and partly sad as a consequence of a mixture of his own state and the surrounding

triggers, then he is both inside and outside.

- We use different ideas of inside and outside to explain different kinds of effects. For one effect, we must say that the person is inside; for another, we must say that he is outside. This results in the problem that the person is simultaneously inside and outside.

9. Quantity addition is associative, distributive, and commutative, but quality combinations are not. For example, if I give you bad news after good news, the result is not the same as giving you good news after bad news. The result of criticism after appreciation is different from the result of appreciation after criticism. This is due to the non-commutative, non-associative, and non-distributive properties of quality additions. Quantitative arithmetic depends on associative, distributive, and commutative properties. Since nature is qualitative, and qualities break the rules of quantitative arithmetic, therefore, we cannot model nature using quantities.

Thereby, every single idea in modern science regarding logic, number, space, time, causality, matter, property, change, and law is rejected. These rejections are consequences of quality vs. quantity. The change is very subtle in one sense—quality vs. quantity. But it has huge ramifications for everything.

Whatever modern science calls reality, law, and change, is false in Vedic philosophy. That characterization, however, doesn't mean we are hallucinating, that the world is self-created, or nothing exists objectively. These are Western philosophical contrasts to realism, and entail idealism or solipsism, which are egocentric descriptions of experience. They stumble upon a simple question: Nobody wants to suffer, but we are suffering. So, are we creating our suffering for ourselves despite not wanting it? We are not talking about such egocentric ideas. We are talking about reality and science that is qualitative rather than quantitative. They are so radically different as to change every other idea.

The Illusion of Inside and Outside

The most precarious of these illusions is the idea that I'm inside a body, room, house, city, country, planet, and space. We are not. These are just limitations on what we are seeing right now. One who perfectly realizes this can perform Houdini's magic tricks without magic—he can escape any prison, room, or trunk, by changing his perspective to something else—because he was never inside.

Two things are involved in appearances and disappearances: (a) the soul remains attached to the same bodily perspective, and (b) the soul changes the association of the body with the prison, room, or trunk to associate with something else. By changing the association to other things, the person appears and disappears. If someone has the capacity to make these changes, then they can escape a locked room.

Such appearances and disappearances are called *avatār* in Vedic philosophy (the word doesn't mean a different image or form as commonly used in internet parlance, but an appearance into this world). God appears in this world, without leaving His world. He simply associates with the material world, and He appears in this world. And when He dissociates from the material world, then He disappears from this world. In the same way, an advanced yogi disappears from one place and immediately appears in another place.

Hence it is said that even when God appears in this world, He is beyond this world. This is not unique to God. Rather, everyone is beyond a room even when they think they are locked in a room. They just don't know how and why. The sense of being locked inside a room with hard walls is an illusion.

Applications of Consciousness Movement

Through the same process, one can have easy journeys to other planets—change the perspective from one planet to another. Through the same process, one can understand how the soul migrates from one body to another—the soul is changing the perspective from one body to another. Through the same process, one can understand why the soul is not burned when the body is burned—the feeling of being burned is one perspective and the feeling of relief is another perspective. Through the same process, one can transcend this world—we can change the perspective to the spiritual world. Finally, by the same process, one can also understand that the soul is never "fallen" into the material world. Rather the perspective of the soul is fallen. Hence, the soul cannot be "lifted" out of the world. The soul's perspective can be lifted by education.

Thus, all of Vedic science is about the movement of consciousness, the laws of this movement based on choice and consequence, and how we can zoom into the perspective to see deeper and deeper, or zoom out from the perspective to see broader and broader. The entire universe can be seen even when the present body is situated inside a room, because that body is only a perspective, while the entire universe is another perspective.

While dreaming, the consciousness leaves the body's perspective and goes to another perspective. When we wake up, the consciousness leaves the other perspectives and returns to the body perspective. If we leave the body perspective during the waking stage, then we are said to be *daydreaming*. This is because both dreaming and waking are simply different inside and outside movements of consciousness.

How Dreams Can Change Science

During the waking experience, if you lift a ball, you feel some heaviness. Science explains this by the gravitational law: We are not aware, but the Earth is pulling objects downward to create the impression of heaviness. However, when we lift a ball during a dream, we feel the same heaviness, although there is nothing being lifted from the perspective of modern physics. You could say: The mind recreates the external reality. But why do the dreaming people remember nothing about calculating the gravitational force, with prior knowledge of the mass of earth and the object they are lifting? Even those who know nothing about gravitational force, masses of objects, and computation of forces experience the same heaviness as those who know. The mind recreating heaviness in a dream thus has nothing to do with gravity computation.

Likewise, we feel hot due to the presence of the sun while dreaming during the night, although there is no sun because it is night, and there is no electromagnetic field, let alone the capacity to compute partial differential equations during the dream. Even those who know nothing about the mathematics involved in the computation of electromagnetic fields feel the heat, so it cannot be called a purely mental creation of reality.

The question is: If we can feel heaviness without a gravitational force during a dream, then why not explain the waking experience of heaviness without the gravitational force? If we can feel the heat without an electromagnetic wave during a dream, then why not explain the waking experience of heat without electromagnetic waves? Unless we can explain both experience in the same way, we cannot assume that the explanation is correct. Otherwise, we have two sensations of heat, and one involves an electromagnetic wave and the other doesn't. We have two sensations of heaviness, and one involves a gravitational field and the other doesn't. Why have double standards for waking and dreaming?

The answer to all these problems is that there is no electromagnetic or gravitational field. Rather, the consciousness moves from one quality to another, and it can escape the body during the dream to see and do things that it would otherwise do during the waking. The result is the same in both cases. We can also associate and dissociate with these qualities to feel the heat without heaviness or the heaviness without heat. This is why dreams are beyond science because they violate physical laws frequently.

The Futile Desire for Miracles

People at present are attracted to miracles. They consider something "science" only if it performs new miracles that were impossible by the previous science. Under that view, to "prove" Vedic knowledge, there must be people who can perform Houdini's escapes. It is also true that such things are possible. But acquiring such powers requires considerable practice. This is why we don't emphasize them.

We rather focus on things that everyone can see most of the time. For example, everyone knows that we must appreciate before criticizing, or giving good news before bad news. Have we sought a scientific explanation of this fact? Everyone perceives qualities at every moment of our living experience. Have we sought an explanation of that? Everyone breaks many laws of physics during dreams, and when such laws seem to be followed, there is no computational apparatus behind its existence. Have we sought an explanation of both how laws seem to be preserved in dreams and often broken during dreams?

These things need a little curiosity, and a lot of patience, determination, and effort. By those things, we don't need to perform Houdini's escape tricks. We can rather seek to understand what is around us. This means that we must bring new ordinary experiences to the table and seek an explanation, which will also show the possibility of mystical powers, and explain the appearance and disappearance of God in this world. We may not see mystics, and we may not see God in this world, but the *theory* that explains numerous ordinary waking and dreaming experiences will naturally necessitate these truths too.

Therefore, people demanding miracles, expecting to see mystics, or asking for proof of God are a waste of time. The focus can also be on ordinary experiences. That kind of "science" is this-worldly rather than other-worldly. It is available to everyone, not just some advanced souls. Why don't we focus on those things? Why should religion be obsessed with mysticism, miracles, and proofs of God, when the existence of those things is also necessitated by the explanation of ordinary experiences?

The Inversion of Reality and Illusion

The main reason for the decline in religion is that everyone has been indoctrinated with a false idea of reality and illusion. Anything you can measure and quantify is reality, and all qualitative experiences are illusions. The reality is numerical objectivity and illusion is qualitative subjectivity. Basically, everything you experience by your senses is an illusion, and anything you measure using an instrument is real.

Therefore, even if you see God with your eyes, it is still an illusion because all experience is an illusion. God must be measured by a weighing scale, speedometer, thermometer, gyroscope, and pressure gauges to prove that *something* exists. But even then, you will still not be able to prove that He is the cause and controller of the universe: God would be yet another object, governed by the same laws as those that cause ordinary measurements. Hence, there is no way to prove that God exists. And God must subject Himself to futile tests to prove His existence, which will always be denied. This nonsensical caricature of religion and God is the output of intellectually impoverished individuals. They cannot imagine that something can be here simply by its choice to associate and not here by its choice to dissociate.

When God wishes to interact, He appears in everyone's vision. He happily seeks interaction with His devotees due to their love. Without an interaction, God cannot be perceived. Through a weak interaction, a crude image of God is perceived. And through a strong interaction, the same person is seen accurately and intimately. Hence, the "distance" to God has to be bridged by a bidirectional strengthening of desire: We have to want to see God, and God has to want to see us. Under that bidirectional strengthening of desire, a strong interaction between soul and God creates the appearance of proximity. Hence, God can be near everyone who loves Him, and far from everyone who doesn't care about Him. Since God is near someone, therefore, they can see Him. But since He is far from others, therefore, they cannot see Him.

These principles of proximity and distance being produced by a strong or weak interaction are scientific because they apply to every other interaction, proximity, and distance. Hence, the process by which we see God is the same process by which we see other things. The process of seeing God is therefore not religion, while the process of observing the world is science. They are identical processes.

To go to a new place, one has to leave the current place. The place is not coming to us. Every new experience is a different place. To get there, we have to leave the current place. People with deep attachments to the present claim that free will doesn't exist. But it is not the absence of free will. It is the unwillingness to cut the rope that binds a boat to the shore that makes rowing futile.

Reality is Seen Only After Detachment

Truth is understood when we start detaching ourselves from this body, room, house, city, country, planet, and material life. If we can detach, then we can understand that what we see is merely due to a temporary attachment. Then we can ask: What *else* could I attach to? Therefore, the people who are attached to this body, room, house, city, country, planet, or material life are not considered knowledgeable. They are treated as dumb, ignorant, unintelligent, noobs. Although they have no clue about reality, they cannot stop talking and pontificating.

In Vedic philosophy, all experiences are real, but the identification of the self with those experiences is false. So, yes, you experience being inside a room. But if you believe that you are inside the room, it is an illusion. Treat that experience of being inside the room just like you treat images in a movie. This detachment from what you are seeing, putting a distance between yourself and the world, is a precondition to understanding the truth. If we can detach, then we understand what *free will* is: We can attach and detach to different things. If we cannot detach, then free will doesn't exist, because the material machine is moving, and we are being dragged by that machine. We have to get off this train onto another train to realize that even as the train could be moving deterministically, we are not bound to a train.

Likewise, all qualities are real, but if we quantify them by measurements, it is an illusion. When the pointer moves on a dial of an instrument, that is an effect on an instrument. But since the instrument is dumbed down, it cannot capture the reality accurately. We cannot measure a tiger to know the tiger. Even if we observe the tiger with human senses, we still don't know the tiger accurately. We have to become the tiger to know the tiger. Likewise, we cannot measure a tree to know what the tree is. Even if we observe a tree with human senses, we don't know it fully. We have to become the tree to know what it is.

In simple words, the third-person instrument measurement is an illusion. The second-person observation of something is a partial truth. And the first-person experience is real. That reality of first-person experience doesn't mean that we have become our experience; the experience is real but identification with it is false; likewise, the quantification of experience is an illusion, and the qualities of experience (especially when they include the deeper recesses of our conscious experience) are real.

Modern science has inverted the reality-illusion distinction employed in Vedic philosophy, whereby, everything considered an illusion in Vedic philosophy is called reality in modern science, and vice versa. Thereby, the first-person experience is completely illusory. The second-person experience (e.g., of color, shape, size) is partially based on reality, but it is not completely real. And the third-person instrument measurement is the only reality. This is worse than theological dogmas because you deny the reality of what everyone can see.

Escaping the Illusion into Reality

The way out of this false inversion is to reexamine ordinary experiences and demand a causal explanation of the illusion. Don't just accept the verdict that it is an illusion because science says it is so. Demand an explanation, of how scientific reality creates an illusion. How does a molecule become an emotion? How do neural connections create judgments of truth, right, and good? How do moving particles create thought? How do electromagnetic waves become taste and smell? How do we feel pain and pleasure as a result of molecules?

If they cannot do that, then ask them: How can one particle be in many places simultaneously? How can something be both particle and wave? How can two things separated by a large distance be entangled? Why do you say that gravity causes heaviness when I can feel heaviness during my dream without gravity? Why do you insist that heat is caused by an electromagnetic wave, when I feel the heat during a dream without such a wave? Modern science cannot even explain basic experiences. But they like to call them illusions.

So, how do you prove that something is an illusion? You test it more and more to check if it stands up to rigorous and intensive scrutiny. Illusions fall apart on scrutiny and the truth is strengthened upon scrutiny. The same is true of the reality-illusion divide.

Scrutinize the scientific reality and you will know that it is an illusion. Then scrutinize the scientific illusions, and you will know that they are real.

Summarizing the Illusion

We can summarize this article into two words: *quantification* and *identification*. If we quantify the experience, the result is dualistic separation, binary logic, and mathematical equations that cannot explain the simplest of our experiences. This is the first type of illusion. If we identify with the experience, then we have the illusion of being inside the body, room, house, city, country, planet, and space, and then we cannot explain why we ended up here or how we could enter another life, planet, or experience. This is the second type of illusion.

Both illusions are dispelled not by the volume of our voice or the extent of our popularity. They are dispelled by seeking answers to different questions. The illusion of quantification is dispelled by questioning the failure of scientific theories in explaining numerous first-person experiences, second-person observations, and third-person measurements. The illusion of identification is dispelled by questioning how I came to this space, planet, country, city, house, and body, and how I could be in another place, body, or life, of my choosing.

It is easy to remember two words—quantification and identification—and it is not hard to see how the former is modern science and the latter is atheism. Scientists say: Nature is numbers. Atheists say: You are these numbers. The Vedic response to this illusion is: Nature is not numbers; Nature is qualities. Likewise, the soul is not material qualities, but it is qualities nevertheless. The soul-matter interaction is between two kinds of qualities, not between quality and quantity (as in Cartesian mind-body dualism). How hard can it be to remember two words, and completely dispel the illusion? It is only as hard as we want it to be.

Laws of Increasing and Decreasing Returns

Article Overview and Summary

Laws are supposed to predict and explain. Predict means to describe the future relative to the present. Explain means to justify that prediction based upon ideas about reality.

The Law of Diminishing Returns is a law that predicts that returns on investment must diminish over time but does not explain it. Without the explanation, we don't know when, where, to whom, or what, the law must be applied.

In this article, I will provide that explanation—discuss when the law must be applied, and when it should not be. Then I will discuss an alternative Law of Increasing Returns, and the conditions that make it possible. We will finish this post with comparisons between the two.

Examples of Diminishing Returns

We are familiar with the concept of division of labor: Add more people to a task and you can get it done faster. As we divide the work and distribute it among many people, initially we see an almost linear growth in productivity. But slowly, the incremental productivity attained by adding more people begins to decline. Ultimately, we find that adding more people to the task reduces productivity.

Likewise, when children go to primary school, in the initial phase they learn a lot. Over a slightly longer period, they start questioning the value of that education as it doesn't seem very relevant. Ultimately, they realize that education ossified their minds and killed their critical thinking, intuitive, and creative capacities, which are more important over time than the information they got from education.

In the initial phase of a romantic relationship, small investments create much excitement. Then the couple gets married and finds that the additional investments in the relationship are not producing proportional excitement—the kind that they saw during the initial phase of the relationship. Over a longer period of time, they find that additional investments reduce their excitement rather than increase it.

In the initial phase of technological development, we feel a dramatic improvement in the quality of life. Over time, gadgets do not produce proportional returns for the investment—we work harder to get the same returns. In the long run, we realize that technology got us addicted and dependent, and we spent our life building and acquiring gadgets while destroying health, relationships, and happiness.

Initially, some criticism or penalty produces dramatic improvements. Over time, penalties and criticisms produce declining benefits as they are ignored. Sustained criticisms and penalties reduce productivity by demoralizing those who are critiqued. The same is the case with rewards and praises—initially great progress, then declining progress, and then rewards and praises cause regress due to laziness.

Three Successive Phases

The Law of Diminishing Returns divides the succession of events into three phases—useful, useless, and harmful. In the useful phase, you get good returns for a small investment—the investment is profitable because the returns are good, even for a small investment. Then in the useless phase, your returns match the investment and you start searching for alternative avenues of investment to get higher returns. Finally, in the harmful phase, all the investments are lost and the situation gets worse due to continued investment.

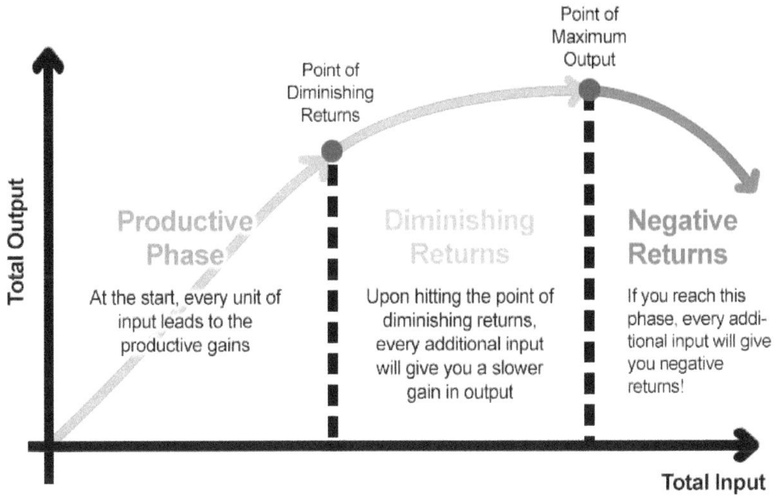

When returns begin diminishing, most people are unable to wean themselves away from the status quo and start anew. They think—It worked in the past, so it must work in the future. The diminishing returns are seen as a temporary glitch or headwind in the path. By doubling down on the efforts, people hope to conquer the glitches or headwinds and return to progress. They invest more, and for a while, they do see higher returns, although not similar to the gains that small investments produced in the initial phase. So long as investments produce some gains, greater and greater investments are made on the same path. This process continues until the return on investment becomes negative: Initially, the returns are lesser than the investment, and eventually, the situation gets worse with investment.

The change that follows is disruptive and discontinuous: We have to throw away the older approach and restart with a new approach. For example, if criticisms and penalties are not working, then we try praises and rewards. If one technology is no longer solving the problem, then we move to new technology. If one type of diet and exercise is not working, we try another type of diet and exercise. If we are bored and frustrated with one philosophy, then we try another. If some people are proving incapable of solving a problem, they are fired, and new ones with different skills are hired. If we are not getting happiness via romance, then we seek happiness through work and friendships.

Cosmetic vs. Novel vs. Drastic

In all such cases, if the new thing is only cosmetically different from the previous thing, then one keeps progressing on the same path from useful to useless to harmful. If the new thing is significantly novel than the previous one, then one enters a new cycle of the same three phases—useful, useless, and harmful—and much excitement is generated in the initial phase of usefulness, although the new cycle also eventually enters the useless and harmful phases. To get into a continuously progressive path, drastic changes have to be made.

The definition of *cosmetic* is that it keeps us in the current cycle of rise and fall. The definition of *novel* is that it puts us into a new cycle of rise and fall. And the definition of *drastic* is that it puts us on a non-reducing path—the progress on this path may be slow, but there is no loss or diminution. Even a small effort made on the path propels us forward to greater gains, and those gains are never ruined.

The drastic changes are far fewer than novel changes and novel changes are far fewer than cosmetic changes. Most of the time, what people call a dramatic change is just a cosmetic change. It does not put us into a new cycle of rise and fall. It moves us forward in the same cycle but demands greater effort, which increases the returns, but not close to the returns on investment in the initial part of the cycle.

Kuhn's Idea of Scientific Change

I will now try to demarcate the differences between cosmetic, novel, and drastic changes using a cyclical pattern articulated by Thomas Kuhn in the book *The Structure Scientific Revolutions.* Prior to Kuhn, scientific progress was thought to be *linearly* progressive. This idea has deep roots in Western thinking where time is believed to move linearly, and bring continuous progress. Kuhn modified this idea to usher in the idea of *revolutions*—i.e., there is a long period of incremental change followed by a phase of disruptive change, which is again followed by a long period of incremental change.

Based on the distinction between incremental and disruptive, Kuhn constructed a cycle of change that involved five phases and rested on the key idea of what he defined to be a scientific *paradigm*.

1. The phase of "normal science" where new phenomena are explained using current assumptions, and the current assumptions prove quite sufficient for explaining the new phenomena.
2. The phase of "model drift" under which the phenomena that cannot be explained by the current axioms are explained by postulating new axioms without breaking the current paradigm.
3. The phase of "model crisis" under which new phenomena cannot be explained by adding or tweaking axioms to the same paradigm without breaking the current paradigm.
4. The phase of "model revolution" under which both old and new phenomena are explained using completely different assumptions. But only the new phenomena justify the revolution.
5. The phase of "paradigm shift" where the new model of explanation becomes the new *paradigm* for all of science. It is applied repeatedly and recursively to revise all previous theories.

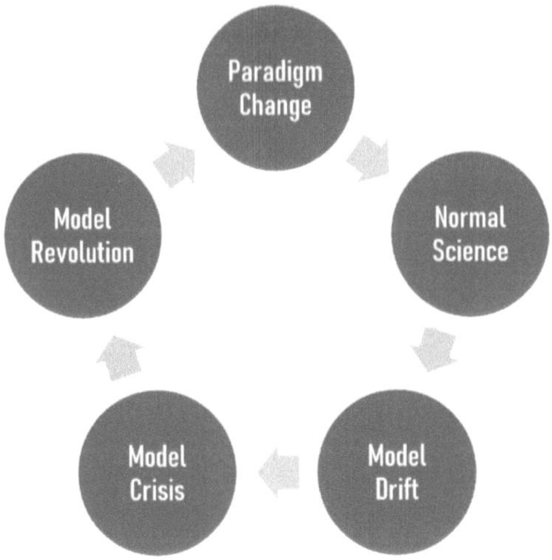

But there are two significant issues in Kuhn's idea of scientific progress, which often go unnoticed.

- Kuhn could not guarantee that the new paradigm would be *final.* It meant that the new paradigm would also lead to a model drift, model crisis, and model revolution. He did not entertain the possibility of science walking a path free of revolutions and paradigm changes.
- Cyclical history entails that history repeats itself or rhymes with itself, and the older ideas return in a new form, preserving the dichotomies of the past although seen in a new way. Cyclical history is not progressive. If this idea is accepted, then science would never progress.

Kuhn's idea of scientific revolutions tries to take the best out of two worlds—cyclical and linear histories—without accepting the conditions that come along with them. Cyclical history is not progressive. And progressive history doesn't have revolutions and paradigm changes.

So, if science was to progress continuously, then it could not have revolutions. However, since Kuhn believed that the current models could not be considered final, therefore, a revolution in paradigm was imminent. When such revolutions occur, they repeat the dichotomies of the past, and there is no long-term progress. Basically, Kuhn's idea of continuous progress through a succession of revolutions is pure fiction.

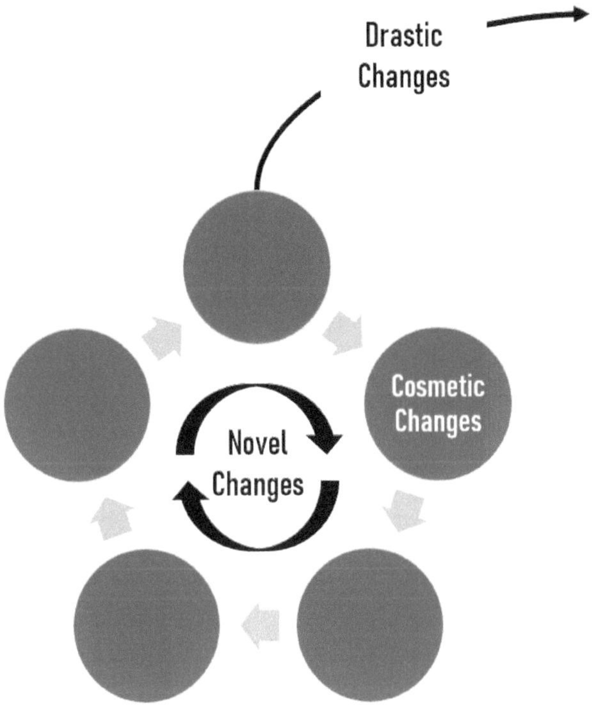

I will term Kuhn's cycles *novel* changes, but not *disruptive*. The paradigm change is significant in the sense that it puts science into a new cycle of rise and fall. However, since this is a cycle too, therefore, another paradigm change must occur in the future. The cycle of paradigm changes is the cycle of non-disruptive novelties that preserve most previous assumptions and changes a few of them. A drastic change would be that which leaves the cycle for a path free of revolutions and paradigm changes.

Long-Term Cyclical Changes

Kuhn's illustration of cycles is deceptive because modern scientific thinking is less than 350 years old. It is hard to derive structural conclusions based on a short period. We can see the longer-term patterns of change by looking at a longer—over 2500 years—history of Western ideologies. Since Greek times, Western ideologies have been caught between the horns of dualisms that take different forms.

- During the Hellenistic period, it was being vs. becoming.
- In Socratic debates, it was ideal vs. real.
- In Platonism, it became form vs. substance.
- In the hands of Aristotle, it became theoretical vs. practical.
- During the Middle Ages, it became faith vs. reason.
- Descartes created the dualism between mind vs. body.
- During Enlightenment, it became religion vs. science.
- For empiricists like Locke, it was primary vs. secondary properties.
- For skeptics like Hume, it was *a priori* vs. *a posteriori*.
- For Existentialists, it became essence vs. existence.
- For Analytic philosophers, it became empiricism vs. rationalism.
- For Structuralists, it was signifier vs. signified.
- For economists, it became individualism vs. collectivism.
- For sociologists, it became individuals vs. institutions.
- For political thinkers, it became freedom vs. regulation.
- For post-modernists, it became universals vs. individuals.

These are *novel* dualisms. But they are not *drastic* changes. All these dualisms are either mutually equivalent or parts of a broader tripartite distinction. History cycles through these distinctions, allowing one idea to dominate over the other, temporarily. If we study history, then the same structural oppositions appear in new ways. Hence, history *rhymes* with itself. Sometimes, it repeats itself.

Shorter-Term Cyclical Changes

We can see the same recurring patterns even in the evolution of modern science. This problem is not restricted to philosophy. Cyclical history—that repeats the oppositions—exists in every domain.

- In physics, history is caught between:
    - Particle vs. wave

    - Determinism vs. probabilities
    - Continuity vs. discreteness
- In biology, history is caught between:
    - Holism vs. reductionism
    - Structure vs. function
    - Heredity vs. environment
- In psychology, history is caught between:
    - Conscious vs. unconscious
    - Cognition vs. emotion
    - Nature vs. nurture

You can pick literally any time in history and you will either find greater importance being assigned to one side of the dichotomy, or you will find equal weight being assigned to the opposing sides. Kuhnian analysis of the history of science sees *progress* even through a *cycle*. It doesn't recognize the persistent dualisms and dichotomies that (a) remain unsolved, (b) repeat over time, (c) are mixed in various ways to create new dichotomies, and (d) even as the debate shifts from one dichotomy to another, *structurally*—i.e., as the debate about which of the two sides of the dualism is correct, and why both sides of the dualism are necessary and yet logically irreconcilable—remains unchanged.

Kuhnian Cycles and Diminishing Returns

We can rephrase Kuhn's cycle in terms of the Law of Diminishing Returns. Under this rephrasing, the phase of "normal science" is the productive phase in which small investments lead to significant returns. Then, the phase of "model drift" is the phase of declining returns where the model has to be constantly tweaked with new assumptions to explain the new observations. Finally, the phase of "model crisis" is the phase of negative returns where any additional assumptions required to explain the observations contradict the existing paradigm. We have to discard that paradigm if we want to progress at all.

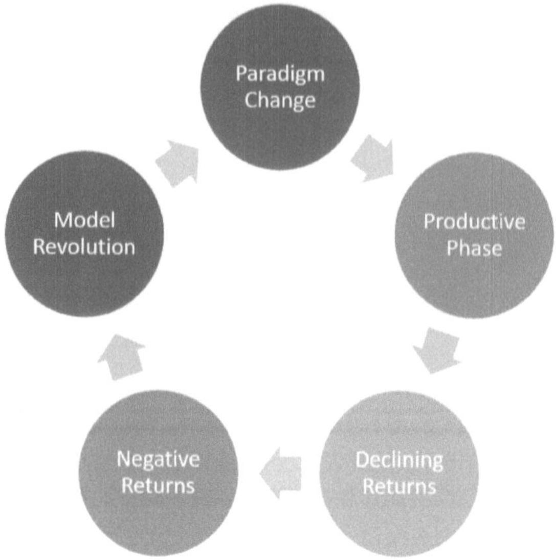

In this rephrasing, whatever Kuhn called a *model revolution*, is nothing but the remixing of old dualisms into new dualisms. For example, classical physics had a dualism between matter vs. light—they were described by gravitational and electromagnetic forces. Quantum theory partially reconciled this duality into a theory that applies to both matter and light (called fermions and bosons). This reconciliation, however, introduced the dualisms of waves vs. particles, determinism vs. probabilities, and discreteness of quanta vs. the continuity of space-time, within quantum theory. We can look at this historical evolution, and say that science *progressed* because quantum theory unified the separate theories of light and matter. But science hasn't progressed because the situation isn't *structurally* better. The problems of resolving the new dualisms aren't easier than the problems of resolving the older dualisms.

There was a productive phase in physics from 1900 till the 1930s after the advent of quantum theory. Then the phase of declining returns began as the Standard Model of particle physics was constructed by trying to fit the model with observations through arbitrary tweaks. This lasted until the 1960s. Then the phase of negative returns began as large particle colliders were built to find supersymmetric particles. Despite thousands of papers and tests, no supersymmetric particles were found. This lasted until the 1980s.

Then a model revolution occurred in physics in the 1980s with the advent of String Theory. By some estimates, there are 10^{500} possible String Theories, none of which can be empirically tested. So, we cannot weed out some theories based on empirical data. String Theory went rapidly from the productive phase to the phase of declining returns and then to the phase of negative returns.

Kuhnian Cycles are Not Perpetual

We can see the problems in Kuhn's concept of cycles—(a) science doesn't always progress with paradigm shifts because the same dualisms recur over time, (b) by mixing and mutation, the number of contradictory models increases over time, and we cannot eliminate any model rationally or empirically. We can no longer decide which of these models should be discarded, and where the effort must be focused. As effort and focus are diluted, the chances of progress reduce. The return on investment is negative—All the time, money, and effort that you throw at the problem only lead to more models, and the problem of deciding on a specific model over others worsens. This is when we can use some wisdom: If you find yourself in a hole, stop digging. But physicists cannot do that due to their benchmark—publish or perish.

Kuhnian cycles are not perpetual because, in the phase of negative returns, money moves away from science into other things. For example, at present, computer programmers with a B.Tech. in technology earn more than Ph.Ds. in science. Financial analysts that mine stock market data earn more than academic professors. People with an M.B.A. from prestigious colleges earn far more than science Post-docs from the same college. This is because science is now less valuable. Most smart kids in the next generation will avoid low-paying endeavors. They will prefer to be computer programmers, financial analysts, or corporate managers because it gives them a much better life.

The Crisis in Modern Science

Modern science is suffering from two problems: (1) a crisis of reproducibility, and (2) predetermined ideological biases. The more complex the phenomena under study, the lesser the reproducibility. If you cannot reproduce the results, then using that theory to make decisions will not lead to the expected results. Since the theory does not predict or explain correctly, it has no value. The crisis of reproducibility is attributed to ideological biases in research—people want to prove their predetermined ideological commitments through data, so they select the data that fits and neglect what doesn't fit. They repeat the experimental process until they find the data that fits their view.

These are actually not new problems. Underdetermination of theory by experiment and experiment by theory is well-known: A single theory can be used to explain some subset of possible phenomena, and a single phenomenon can be explained by some subset of possible theories. The problem is that there are too many theories and too many phenomena to contend with. We have to either fix the phenomenon and iterate over theories, or fix the theory and iterate over the phenomena. But we cannot do either of these due to the fragmentation of the academic process—each department and/or person is entitled to create their own theories and phenomena. All departments and persons are now Towers of Babel. Nobody is inclined to look at everything that everyone is doing. Their goal is not collective progress. Their goal is personal advancement. They cannot focus their efforts, and they cannot stop other efforts because they don't know what to encourage.

As the academic system is paralyzed by too much fragmentation, it starts losing value rapidly. There are too many viewpoints, which can be selectively justified by cherry-picking evidence. All these viewpoints make different predictions, which work for some cases and not for others. All these viewpoints explain the same predictions in different ways, which are applicable for some cases and not for others.

Diminishing Returns of Division of Labor

We can recall the problem of division of labor. As we divide the work and distribute it among many people, initially we see linear growth in productivity. But slowly, the incremental productivity attained by adding more people begins to decline. Ultimately, we find that adding more people to the task reduces productivity. Science suffers from the Law of Diminishing Returns caused by the division of labor. A little division is useful. More division is useless. And even more division is harmful.

The fact is that any amount of division of labor will work if the divisions *cooperate*. If the workers stop cooperating, then the division of labor is counterproductive. Cooperation works well in small groups. This is why some division of labor is useful, more division is useless, and even more division is harmful. The reason is that cooperation, common goal orientation or purpose, and communication between the workers breaks down when the group size increases—especially if the workers are *individualistic*, have been given the freedom to drive their agendas, and are rewarded by competition with others.

When science is dominated by individualism, competition, and the absence of a common purpose, then scientists work against each other, rather than with each other. That leads to diminishing and negative returns. We cannot solve this problem in any way other than by altering the underlying philosophy of life. That philosophy needs an answer to the dualism between individualism and collectivism. The collection has a shared purpose, and individuals have different roles in fulfilling that purpose. If each individual decides their own purpose, then the collection will act cross-purpose with diminishing and negative returns.

Perpetuity is Iterative Progress

The *superstructure* of historical evolution under diminishing returns is continuous decline. Within it, the *substructure* can be governed by Kuhnian cycles. It is like a marble rotating in a bowl—it descends lower with every iteration until it halts at bottom of the bowl. The only question is: How deep is the bowl? How many more paradigm revolutions before it halts? Or, how long can the people who fund science allow the scientific paradigm to keep digging before someone realizes that they are headed in the wrong direction?

Continuous progress requires a general solution to the problem of dualities. We can visualize it as an inverted bowl, or better, an inverted tree—root at the top, trunks below it, branches emanating out of the trunks, and twigs and leaves emanating from them. We have to *rise* on this inverted tree to solve the problem of dualism because each upward step converges the diversity and reduces the duality.

Each upward step on this tree requires us to solve a new kind of dualism, yielding greater model unity. In contrast, the path of diminishing returns mixes the dualisms and subdivides them to produce greater model diversity. Both processes are generally iterative. That is, you iteratively produce more model unity or more model diversity. Thereby, both can have Kuhnian cycles as they rise up or fall down.

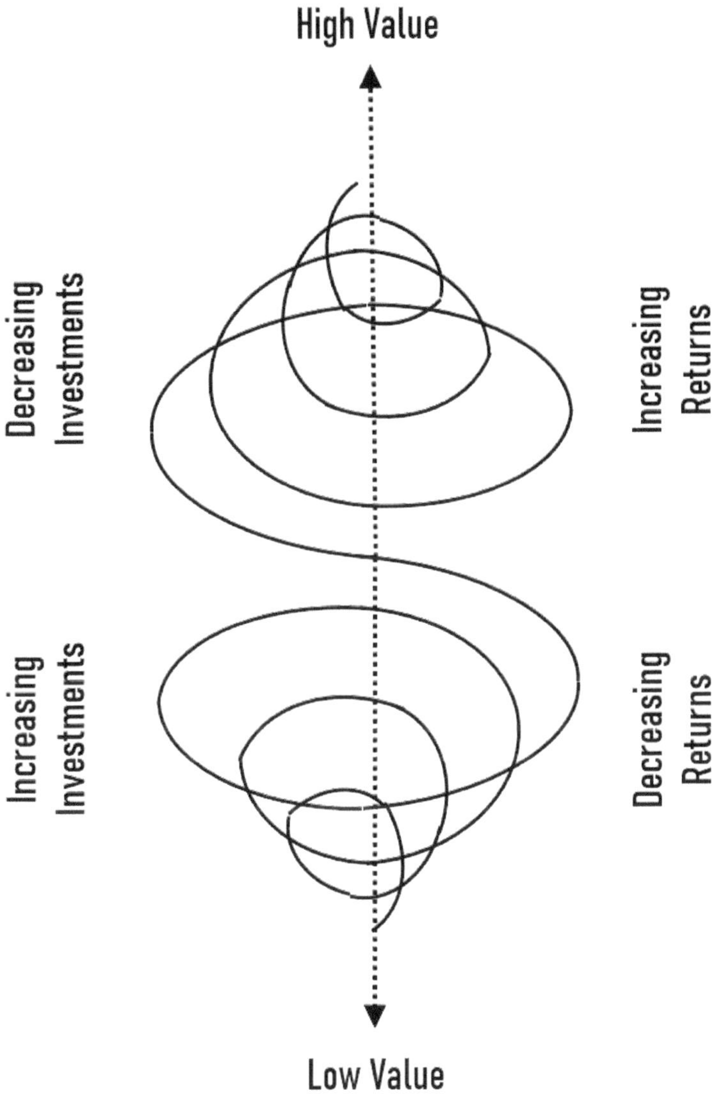

In contrast to the Law of Diminishing Returns, the upward path involves a Law of Increasing Returns, because the solution to one dualism benefits other domains. As all these domains lift almost simultaneously, they begin converging. Now, you can think of one subject in terms of the concepts of another, and cross-fertilization of ideas benefits both. The solution to one problem in one domain becomes the solution to another problem in another domain. The Law of Increasing Returns delivers increasing benefits as it progresses iteratively.

There is hence no conflict between linear and iterative progress—if the path is an upward spiral. Iterative cycles are not always progressive—if they are on a downward spiral. Finally, cycles may be neither progressive nor regressive if they are just cycles, rather than spirals.

Cause of Decreasing and Increasing Returns

Diminishing returns are the result of duality. Each side of the duality is useful in some scenarios, useless in others, and harmful in the rest. Initially, we see the useful applications of one side of the duality. But over time, their continued use is either useless or harmful. We can try to *balance* them—i.e., use different sides for different problems, places, times, etc. But that also produces diminishing and negative returns. The scenarios where they have to be combined are far more numerous, than the scenarios where one of them works perfectly, or they are balanced by alternation. Since we cannot reconcile them, the result is always diminishing returns followed by negative returns.

The time it takes to reach a diminishing or negative return depends on our capacity to (1) use only one side, (2) use both sides for different problems, and (3) try to balance opposites alternately in a problem. By using successive methods we can delay it, but not eliminate it.

Increasing returns are the result of non-duality. Non-duality is the capacity to embed one opposite inside the other, without a contradiction. Opposites in this case are mutually defined, employ non-binary logical conditions, and are not independently separable. As we embed more and more dualisms within each side of dualism, the system of non-dualism gets richer and more applicable to more scenarios.

Duality is *fragmentation* and non-duality is *unity*. Fragmentation appears in an individualistic society. If each person thinks that they are independent of others, they create ideas opposed to the others. Each person chooses their goals, comes up with their own ideas, selects their own data to fit their chosen theories, and competes with other people who have chosen different theories and data points. Under individualism, academics are divided into departments and subareas, subjects and theories, which are encouraged to pursue their own ideas and required to compete with others. All these departments, subareas, and individuals compete with others for funding.

Ideologically, diminishing returns are the result of fragmentation caused by the mixing of dualities. Each duality can be subdivided by another duality to create more diversity. There is no limit to this mixing and fragmentation. As time passes, there are too many ideas, each of which is actually useful for a very small subset of phenomena, but such ideas are never *contextualized* because each individual tries to *universalize* their ideology. The result is that every single theory is partially right and mostly wrong. Since no theory works correctly in all cases, and nobody is inclined to acknowledge that their opponents are right, the system of academics leads to negative returns.

Non-Dualistic Conception of Truth

The modern system of individualism, speculative ideas, and competition is rooted in a universalist idea of truth. Truth is one; it cannot be many. People assume that in a universalist conception of truth and reality, one of the viewpoints about the truth will naturally win over all other viewpoints. But that is not the case because the truth is one, but it has many aspects. Even the seekers of truth are many aspects of the truth. Hence, they prioritize or prefer different aspects over others. Their views may not be *false*, but they are not the *whole truth*. The dichotomy between true and false is incorrect. The correct dichotomy is between *higher* and *lower* truth s. The higher truth is truer than the lower truth. The higher truth is also a bigger truth that has its aspects as smaller truths. This is the inverted tree of truths.

The different aspects of the whole truth can be logically contradictory. Each of the opposing aspects is true—contextually not universally. The non-dualistic solution to this problem requires us to reject binary universalist truth conceptions. Instead, we have to envision an inverted tree of truths in which the parts of the tree can be logically opposed. That opposition is not a self-contradiction, because the self must be on one of the branches to observe that truth. By treating the branches as *perspectives* on the truth, duality becomes non-duality.

The Nature of Dualistic Sciences

Validating one side of the duality is regular science. But as the other side of the duality is discovered, a model crisis is created. When these dualities are mixed to create a new theory, scientists call it a paradigm shift. But it is just a cosmetic change. If instead, we use a new kind of dualism, then we can produce a completely new cycle. That is also a paradigm shift, but it is a novel cycle. After a few such cycles, there aren't enough new dualisms to go around. Then, as we mix them again and again, we produce a path of diminishing returns. Changes are no longer scientific revolutions. They are history rhyming or repeating itself. This cycle comes to a halt after it hits a phase of negative returns.

Based on these considerations, we can provide alternative definitions of cosmetic, novel, and drastic:

- Cosmetic: That which mixes existing dualisms. That mixture produces short-lived cycles within a declining trend. That is, as we mix existing dualisms to produce a new dichotomy, there is a short-term spurt, but when it ends, the new normal is lower than before.
- Novel: That which creates or envisions a new dualism. It produces a longer-term cycle, which eventually starts declining. As it starts declining, the opposing sides of dualism are mixed to produce short-term cosmetic changes with short spurts.
- Drastic: That which takes us out of the dualism to produce unity. That path is also iterative because there are many kinds of dualisms.

Different domains of modern science are in different phases of diminishing and negative returns; some departments of science are much further down the path of diminishing returns than others. They are being sustained by ever-increasing time, effort, and investments to create a semblance of progress. Some departments are in negative returns, such that every passing day worsens the problem. The issue is that they cannot diagnose the problem they are facing because they think— (1) the truth must be one; it cannot be many truths, or (2) there is no truth; the truth is whatever you believe to be. Under these two false assumptions, the path of diminishing and negative returns continues.

If someone believes that there is no objective truth, then they are much less constrained by evidence. They fragment faster because their costs are very low. Social sciences are examples of this today. They progress rapidly to negative returns. Conversely, if someone believes that there is only one truth, then their model crisis leads to many models, in the attempt to solve the crisis. However, instead of resolving the crisis, it worsens and deepens it, because people can no longer decide which model to pursue further. Natural sciences are the prime example of this today. Then if someone believes that there are many truths, constrained by evidence, then their models multiply but they are used for different scenarios. The prime example of such fragmentation is medicine today. They invest in model fragmentation but are careful to use different models for different problems. They can stay in the phase of diminishing returns much longer because they don't face a model crisis: Each department of medicine uses a different type of model to cure different diseases.

Comparing Dualism and Non-Dualism

If we understand the problems of dualism, then we can appreciate non dualism i.e., that it follows the Law of Increasing Returns, instead of diminishing returns. The investment in both cases decreases over time—in the law of decreasing returns because high investments produce low returns and in the law of increasing returns because low investments produce high returns.

Since the non-dualistic scientific system requires progressively lesser investments, therefore, the cost of knowledge declines over time. You don't need to invest money in experiments, testing, speculation, and invention. You just need teachers who can preserve and impart this knowledge over generations. And because the costs of education are so low, therefore, it can be imparted freely to everyone qualified and inclined towards it. The system of knowledge that formerly existed in India was such a non-dualistic system. It required no technological apparatus to know the truth, and imparted that truth freely to anyone interested in it. It was sustained by scholars who had received it through a succession of masters and disciples.

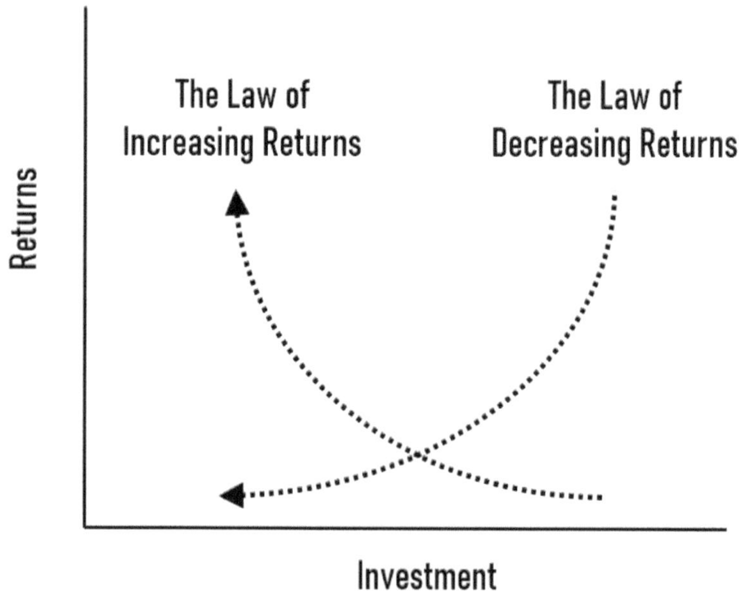

At present, people ask: How could advanced scientific knowledge exist in India without instruments, machines, electricity, etc.? All such claims must be false. This is because they think in terms of dualistic knowledge which requires growing investments to get declining returns. To support this growing investment, knowledge must be converted into technology and business. Students have to pay for this education, researchers and professors have to be paid big salaries, there must be competitive journals that junk and trash each other's ideas to see which ones remain standing through the process of attrition, and a lot of money has to be invested into research laboratories. Without converting knowledge into a business, there can never be scientific progress. Hence, science must be married to industrialization and vice versa.

Technological industrialization is not necessary to sustain progress in non-dualistic knowledge. Even if some experiments have to be performed occasionally, the investments decline over time. You can do more and more scientific work with pencil and paper, if not with your mind, because you are trying to reconcile ideas and models. You only need teachers who have this knowledge and can keep passing it through generations. And the students don't have to pay exorbitant fees to schools, nor is there any monetary investment in scientific research. The industrial business model of dualistic education is quite different from the voluntary teacher-disciple model of non-dualism.

Peg and Hole Knowledge Analogy

Factually, anyone who invests a little time in non-dualistic education will reap far greater benefits than those obtained through a dualistic education. Furthermore, the investments over time decline; if you understand one subject completely, you can understand all subjects completely. Every additional understanding in each subject contributes to additional understanding in all subjects.

And yet, people don't invest even a fraction of the time in non-dualistic education that they invest in dualistic education. They are prepared to work harder and harder to get lesser and lesser benefits through the system of modern science, industrialization, and business economics. But they are not prepared to invest time and energy into something that will yield greater and greater benefits almost for free. This is due to an innate revulsion against traditions, and an innate love for modernity. It is cultivated. But it is not true.

When non-dualistic knowledge is presented, people want to "evaluate" it in a short time using dualistic standards. They don't realize that acquiring knowledge is like fitting a peg into a hole. If the shape of the hole doesn't match the shape of the peg, then we cannot insert the peg in the hole. This means that the time spent learning is changing our way of thinking to allow the peg to fit in. If it takes longer, it is because our thinking is more at variance from the peg. Instead of blaming the knowledge, we have to be a little humble.

If we cannot be humble and patient, then the Law of Diminishing Returns will humble us. It makes the current dualism useless and harmful over time. But there is still a choice: We can pick a new kind of dualism to produce a new cycle or step into a continuously progressive path.

What Is Causal Closure?

The Reason for Writing This Article

In a recent conversation, someone asked me: "Is the universe causally closed?" For a moment I was stumped because I realized that what he is really asking is whether God intervenes in the universe. If God intervenes in the universe, then the universe is not causally closed because God is supposedly outside the universe. If He doesn't intervene in the universe, the universe must be governed solely by what is within the universe, and it would be causally closed.

I was trying to get this clarified by asking the questioner the meaning of "causally closed", but I did not get a pointed answer. Meanwhile, I remembered the invocation from Iśopaniśad: "That is complete and this is complete. The complete produces the complete. After producing the complete from the complete, the balance is complete". Based on this I responded: "Yes, the universe is causally closed". I'm quite certain that the listener would have taken this to mean that "God does not intervene in the universe", so I thought I should clarify this.

The Scope of Causal Closure

Let's begin by expanding the scope of closure—each individual person is causally closed. This means that everything happening to me is caused by me, and me alone. If I'm enjoying in a certain way, both the enjoyment and the specific way in which I'm enjoying are caused by my past actions—the opportunity to enjoy is due to karma, the ability for a specific kind of experience is due to chitta, and the desire to use the ability and opportunity to enjoy is due to guna. Similarly, if I'm suffering in some way, both the suffering and the specific way in which I'm suffering are caused by my past actions—the circumstance of suffering is due to karma, the ability to have a specific type of suffering is due to chitta, and the fact that I consider it suffering is due to guna.

Guna, karma, and chitta divide into the 24 categories of Sāñkhya creating various types of bodies, sense perceptions, senses, minds, intellects, egos, and moral senses. To illustrate this point with an example, we can consider the gross body. Due to guna, my body has certain proclivities—e.g., it likes or dislikes hot, cold, and windy climates. Due to chitta, my body has a certain sensitivity toward the hot, cold, or windy climates. And due to karma, I am put into a hot, cold, or windy climate by which my body suffers or enjoys, subject to my like or dislike (guna), and the sensitivity toward the climate (chitta).

Causal Closure and the Unconscious

The guna, karma, and chitta together constitute the unconscious, but we cannot perceive these three *individually*. Only their *combinations* can be perceived. This is true of the three aspects of the soul—*sat*, *chit*, and *ānanda*—too. The pleasure or pain we experience is associated with some sense by bringing them into a relationship with their objects. That relationship produces a sensation, and that sensation creates the feeling of pain or pleasure. The relationship is established either due to my desires and aversions or the consequences of past actions.

Each person's unconscious determines their experience, leading to *causal closure*. The collective unconscious of all the persons in a society is the society's unconscious which determines all that occurs in society. The collective unconscious of all the societies in a planet constitutes a planet's unconscious, which determines all that happens in the planet. Finally, the collective unconscious of all the planets in a universe determines all that happens in a universe. Everything from a person, to a society, planet, and universe is causally closed. This is not difficult to see if everything from an individual person to a society, planet, and the entire universe is treated as an individual person.

Eternity and Responsibility

The invocation from Iśopaniśad means—"A causally closed person produces many causally closed persons". There is a *Supreme Person* who produced His children out of His choice, and He is responsible for those choices. Those children can also choose and be responsible for their choices. If they make bad choices, then they own the consequences, but the parent also has to live with the consequences of His choices—creating children with the capacity to choose. The parent cannot take away their choices, even if they choose badly. He has to endure the fact that He created them with choice. Hence, the capacity of the children to choose is eternal due to God's responsibility for His choices.

The equivalence between *eternity* and *responsibility* is often missed, so it is worth dwelling on it. There is no way to rationally explain and justify why some people are born poor or rich, beautiful or ugly, intelligent or dumb, capable or incapable, healthy or sick, other than to say that these differences are due to their past actions. Similarly, there is no responsibility for one's choices if one commits immoral acts in this life but evades punishment, and there is no subsequent life where he has to face the consequences of his actions.

We cannot talk about responsibility without eternity and eternity without responsibility. The concept of karma and rebirth is synonymous with the eternity of the soul. If someone doesn't believe in the eternity of the soul, then they will also not believe in responsibility for their choices. This is why when a society embraces materialism, it first rejects the eternity of the soul and then becomes immoral because they think that if they can evade the consequences of their actions in this life then they have evaded them permanently.

Temporality and Immorality

This point is abundantly illustrated in Cārvāka's materialism when he says: "As long as you live, you shall live happily; take out loans and drink ghee; after all, once the body has been burnt, where is the question of coming back?" The implication is that you don't have to repay your liabilities in your next life, which is one of the many examples of immoral behavior. Similarly, some countries accumulate debt to be repaid by future generations because John Maynard Keynes, a famous economist, convinced them that "This long run is a misleading guide to current affairs. In the long run, we are all dead." Keynesian economics is identical to Cārvāka's materialism in this sense.

The idea that life ends with death is the idea that we can escape responsibility for our actions. Hence, when we talk about the soul's eternity, we should call it moral responsibility. Materialists love to say that a materialist foundation for morality is possible but they have never developed such a foundation and their actions have been immoral. So, the rational foundation for morality is absent and the empirical evidence is immoral. This is because there is no responsibility without eternity and no eternity without responsibility.

The connection between eternity and responsibility has been severed in many present religions. Morality based on universal principles of truthfulness, kindness, charity, sacrifice, austerity, renunciation, cleanliness, etc. has been replaced by localized ethical systems that apply to a socio-political-ethnic group alone. For example, "thou shalt not kill" only means that you should not kill others in your socio-political-ethnic group. Killing people from other socio-political-ethnic groups is ethical (even if it seems immoral). And people who follow such ethical (but immoral) systems of religion supposedly attain eternal life in heaven because they do not bear responsibility for their actions.

Everything is Causally Closed

The separation between eternity and responsibility is false; they are identical concepts, which is why "eternal life" can be substituted with "responsible life". Responsibility also creates causal closure. God is causally closed because He is responsible for His choices. Each person produced from God is causally closed because they are responsible for their choices. God is responsible for the system of responsibility for His children because otherwise,

His choices would be irresponsible. God's responsibility for creating children ends with a system of ensuring responsibility because He has made a choice and acted responsibly rather than choosing to create without any responsibility.

Thus, everything from the Supreme Person down to the smallest living entity—i.e., the atom—is causally closed because their experiences are the byproduct of their choices and their responsibilities, as they are co-created. There is no choice without responsibility and no responsibility without choice.

Space and Time of Experience

The unconscious covering the soul and its mixing by time produces the *content* of experience. That content *restrains* choices. The three aspects of the unconscious are the root of a three-dimensional space from which springs the diversity of experiences—like a tree emerges from a root—when these dimensions are mixed by time. All experience is thus a *position* in a space (constructed from chitta, guna, and karma) that changes with time. The universal space is hierarchically subdivided into universes, planetary systems, planets, and places within them, and based on the type of responsibility intended for a specific duration of time, the soul obtains a short-lived life (in a certain body, society, and planet) to reap the responsibilities for what it has sown. As the soul makes new choices while enduring these responsibilities, the unconscious evolves, and in due course of time, the soul is moved to a new short-lived life (in a certain body, society, planet, and universe).

Therefore, the soul is a free individual but covered by an unconscious because choice comes with responsibility. This responsibility is nothing more that the soul's temporally changing position in a space of worldly experiences. We can think of the soul as a particle that moves in space and time. This evolution is not totally deterministic because the soul can choose differently to create a new covering of responsibility. However, it is not totally free either because every choice lawfully entails a different kind of covering of responsibility.

Objections to Causal Closure

Someone can say: Each person is not causally closed because they have to face responsibility, and that would be true. Someone can say: That responsibility is converted into an experience by time, which is not under each person's control, and that would also be true. Since material space and time are partial aspects of God, therefore, someone can say that God intervenes in the soul's life, and that would also be true. Finally, someone can say: Since God intervenes in everyone's lives, therefore, He is intervening in the working universe, and hence, the universe is not causally closed, and that too would be true.

But there is a false assumption embedded in such objections—that a universe governed by mathematical equations is causally closed. This assumption is false because we cannot find a universal computer that receives the current state information of all material particles, computes the mathematical equations governing their next state, and then delivers the results of computations to each particle in the universe.

Even if we postulate such a ginormous computer, its working must be governed by an even bigger computer computing the equations governing the computer. In the logical limit, infinite computers computing the equations for the next computer are required, for a single universe to be governed by mathematical laws. Each of these infinite computers must be powered by increasing amounts of energy. Hence, a universe of finite energy must spend infinite energy in computing its mathematical laws.

To terminate this infinitely cascading hierarchy of computers, there must be a self-started, self-driven, self-governed, perpetually moving computer. No such computer is mathematically conceivable. Hence, those who talk about causal closure—with the assumption that a mathematically governed universe is causally closed—don't have causal closure because their assumption is not causally closed and it is impossible to causally close that assumption since it requires an infinite cascade of computers and infinite energy to run them.

Self-Perpetuating Causal Closure

The system of possibility, choice, and responsibility is such a self-computing system because every choice automatically produces a responsibility, which expands or constrains the possibilities for future choices. M. C. Escher conceived of a self-computing system as two hands that draw each other. We can extend this to three hands—possibility, choice, and responsibility—that circularly draw each other. This is a causally closed system in which the choice of a possibility produces a responsibility, which is then activated by time to change the possibility, leading to new choices and responsibilities.

God is involved in this causally closed system as the guarantor of responsibility for every choice. If someone considers this a problem, they can try to construct an alternative causally closed universe, and based on the above problem of infinite cascading, we can confidently say that such a causally closed universe would never be constructed. The system of possibility, choice, and responsibility is necessary because no other system of causal closure is feasible. It is already sufficient as a causally closed system. Hence, the system of possibility, choice, and responsibility is both necessary and sufficient.

Of course, if someone has a problem with responsibility, then they can live alone self-satisfied where their choices are limited to one alternative—the self (called Brahman). It is a choice that puts an end to all other choices. However, even that choice is not without responsibility, because we can do whatever we want to ourselves, and we would still be responsible for those choices.

Science, Religion, and Causal Closure

Thus, everything in science and religion can be summarized in one sentence: "All laws are the laws of choice and responsibility". The problems in science and religion begin with the desire for choice without responsibility since nobody wants responsibilities without a choice. People envision a society, religion, and science in which they have rights, freedoms, and entitlements without any responsibility. If they get these rights, freedoms, and entitlements, then they call these naturally bequeathed upon them by God. But if they don't get these rights, freedoms, and entitlements due to the responsibilities enforced as effects of previous choices, then they blame God or other people.

Therefore, every conversation on religion, science, or society must be based on the simple principle of possibility, choice, and responsibility. Unfortunately, this is not how most religions, societies, and sciences operate. Everyone wants the freedom to experiment and speculate, with all the rights reserved to change those experiments and speculations over time, without any sense of responsibility. This conception of science, religion, and society is the antithesis of reality. If you make bad choices, then you will be held responsible. People generally call this the "law of karma" but it is much more than that (because, as we have discussed, apart from karma there is also guna and chitta).

Morality and Religion

Many people want to discuss the nature of the soul and God without discussing possibility, choice, and responsibility. They speculate and experiment, and reserve the right to change those speculations and experiments over time. They don't realize that their actions are also subject to responsibilities. If you mislead someone with attractive false ideas, you will be misled by someone else's attractive false ideas. The misleading ideas will match what you find attractive, and the result will be your misdirection. Hence, the principles of possibility, choice, and responsibility are more important than any ideology about soul, God, and salvation.

This emphasis on choice and responsibility is evidenced in that Buddhism and Jainism—which grew in India—did not reject the "law of karma" even when they rejected the soul and God. They have always preferred to treat it as a natural law although they cannot explain how that law is enforced (just like mathematical laws of science). They envision salvation as something that puts an end to the cycle of birth and death, enjoyment and suffering, as entailed by the "law of karma" instead of their ascent into an eternal spiritual world.

Factually, this kind of responsible atheism is better than the theism that recklessly speculates on the nature of matter, soul, and God without responsibility. When people make it a habit to experiment and speculate on the nature of matter, soul, and God, then the number of deceptions multiplies exponentially because every cheater has to be cheated by another cheater in a new way. Ignorance of the principle of possibility, choice, and responsibility thus leads not just to immorality but also to a dramatic increase in falsehoods.

Religion Begins in Responsibility

When the number of cheaters and cheated increases exponentially, then it is impossible to decide what the truth is because everyone is experimenting and speculating on the truth without any idea about the future that awaits them. This irresponsible behavior can only be curtailed by teaching people about the principle of possibility, choice, and responsibility.

Reckless experiments and speculations may hurt others, but they are equally harmful to the person who indulges in them or justifies them because: (a) every liar believes in his lies, and (b) every liar will be deceived in the future, reinforcing his tendency to cheat.

We cannot blame anyone else for this deception because of causal closure. Everything that is happening to anyone—good or bad—is entirely the result of their previous choices. Whatever choices people are making right now will be reciprocated in kind in the future. So, everyone can choose, but we must choose choose wisely knowing that it will be reciprocated.

Causal closure is "what goes around comes around". It is closed-loop causality. There is something external to each person's choice that closes the loop of responsibility. We can study the scientific principles of how that loop is closed, or how choices create a responsibility that changes our experiences. Vedic dharma is nothing more than closed-loop causality or causal closure. It is augmented by the discussion of various kinds of causally closed-loop realities called "complete" and "self-sufficient" worlds. These worlds have sprung from the complete principle of possibility, choice, and responsibility. They hold each person accountable.

Three Aspects of Absolute Truth

Before we get lost in the study of different kinds of complete and self-sufficient worlds, we should know the principle from which they have sprung—i.e., the causally complete principle of possibility, choice, and responsibility. Many complete worlds have sprung from one complete principle. These worlds are just examples, illustrations, or instantiations of the complete principle of possibility, choice, and responsibility. That principle is complete and this world is complete. The complete principle produces a complete world. After producing the complete world, the complete principle remains complete. Completeness is responsibility of choice.

That principle is the Absolute Truth, the Supreme Truth, and the Supreme Person. We may call Him by many names. Since He is the cause of all the words, all the names will correctly describe some aspect of His persona. But we can also discuss His nature just by discussing the principle of possibility, choice, and responsibility that He embodies. In Vedic texts, this principle is called sac-cid-ānanda-vigraha; sat is responsibility, cit is possibility, ānanda is choice, and vigraha is the complete form of these principles. The meaning of complete form is that this principle is realized in many ways in different self-sufficient worlds. They are all parts of the complete form and produced from that form. When infinite worlds can be summarized in three words, then we should use those words to understand everything. Discussing these words is talking about the Absolute Truth, the Supreme Truth, and the Supreme Person.

Four Defects of Human Knowledge

Descriptions of Verbal Testimony

Vedic texts cite four fundamental defects of souls "conditioned" by the material energy—(a) imperfect senses, (b) illusions, (c) committing mistakes, and (d) cheating propensity. All living entities are incapable of acquiring perfect knowledge through their senses, mind, and intellect due to the presence of these four defects. The Vedic texts describe the processes by which one becomes free of these defects. Finally, the same texts reference those individuals that have been freed from such defects by following the above mentioned processes.

The above description is substantiated by histories of conversations between enlightened souls and those seeking enlightenment, and how by following the methods discussed during those conversations, those seeking enlightenment attained what they were searching for.

This simple argument for placing trust in Vedic texts is generally neglected while discussing epistemology or the method of science, how the epistemology or the method of science suffers from the same four defects as humans, and hence it cannot provide the truth.

In this post, I will connect the four human defects to the epistemological and methodological problems of modern science that make the discovery of any scientific truth impossible. We will see how the four human defects appear in science and discuss their examples. These human defects have led science astray despite thousands of people working for centuries and cross-validating each other—because every human has the same defects and science as a human activity of discovering the truth by flawed individuals is always flawed. We will talk about the symptoms of the absence of these defects, and how they are progressively eliminated.

The Description of Four Defects

The concept of "truth" is not easy, due to two empirical problems—(a) the presence of evidence is not evidence of presence, and (b) the absence of evidence is not evidence of absence. If I hallucinate, there is presence of evidence, but it is not evidence of presence, since I'm hallucinating. Similarly, if I'm blind, there is absence of evidence, but that is not evidence of absence, due to my blindness. I have to prove that if I don't see, then I am not blind (i.e., not incapable of perceiving the truth), and if I see then I am not hallucinating (i.e., creating my perceptions) before I can infer presence or absence as truth.

A different set of problems exist with reasoning—(a) a working theory is not necessarily true because I may have an oversimplified or overcomplicated theory that works for some cases, and the data that falsifies it may not be available to me, and (b) despite the availability of contravening data, I might continue upholding a false theory as I don't want to acknowledge the failure.

These four flaws are described in Vedic texts as—(a) illusions such as hallucinations, (b) imperfect senses such as blindness, (c) committing mistakes of misconceiving reality during speculation, and (d) cheating propensity.

- Instruments can self-create detections, which are just like hallucinations. We eliminate these hallucinations by repeating experiments. But rare occurrences are not repeatable. Should we treat a rare occurrence as a hallucination or a fact that occurs rarely? We can treat some hallucinations as rarely occurring facts, and some rarely occurring facts as a hallucination.
- We don't know if we have a complete set of necessary and sufficient properties. If some necessary properties are missing, then we will not notice failures of a theory because

we are not measuring a necessary property. If we have more than necessary properties, then our picture of reality would be erroneous because it is incorporating unnecessary properties in the theory.

- The data that falsifies a theory may not be always available because we consider that data to be outside the domain of the current study. Since the scope of a theory is arbitrary—i.e., the scope can be expanded or contracted—therefore, we don't know whether a theory is true or false because the assumptions we make in the theory are suited for one type of phenomenon and not others.
- When a theory is falsified, it is not easily rejected either due to a lack of alternatives or because incentives are attached to maintaining the status quo. Those who have invested time, money, and effort in creating a theory, try to solve a problem by making minor modifications. They try to magnify the importance of successes and diminish the importance of failures.

All four human defects exist in the scientific method, but they are either ignored or their importance is minimized. Due to these flaws, there is no way to *discover* the complete truth using the processes of reasoning and observation.

The Necessity of Revelation

Truth has to be revealed for us to know it. A revealed truth can be *verified* partially within the scope of my limited perception. Everything in the revealed text cannot be verified unless my perceptual capacity is enhanced. A revealed text is supposed to give us the truth, which we can verify, and while everything may not be currently verifiable, what is verifiable must never be falsified.

Trust is established if we can verify some claims, there is a reasonable path to verify the currently unverified claims, and none of the verifiable claims are falsified. Then, we "trust but verify" the text on the principle of "innocent until proven guilty". Trust is destroyed if we can falsify some verifiable claim and if claims are not verifiable. If enough of these claims have been falsified, then we have to operate on the inverse principle of "guilty until proven innocent".

We can consider a text to be of divine origin if all its claims are verifiable, there is a reasonable possibility of verifying the presently unverified claims, and none of the verifiable claims have been falsified. We must treat a text to be of human origin if its verifiable claims are falsified or the unverified claims are not reasonably verifiable. Trust is not blind faith if it is based on verification, high chances of verification, and the absence of falsification. The faith grows incrementally as we verify more claims and no claim is falsified.

The Principles of Revealed Epistemology

Whatever we call "Vedic epistemology" is rooted in the principles that

- There are four defects commonly found in most humans,
- They make an empirical and rational discovery of truth impossible,
- Therefore, revelation is necessary to know the truth,
- Revelation is trusted if some of it is verified and nothing is falsified,
- Progressively more and more of its claims can be verified.

When we contrast Vedic philosophy against modern science, we demonstrate (a) why existing evidence falsifies current scientific theories, (b) why Vedic philosophy is not falsified by the evidence, (c) how this philosophy can be used to build better scientific theories, and (d) how this application establishes *trust* in the Vedic texts—that some claims are currently verified and no claims are currently falsified. If we don't show that existing evidence falsifies current scientific theories, then there would be no need for an alternative. If we don't show why Vedic philosophy is not falsified by current evidence, there would be no difference between Vedic texts and other scriptures. If we don't show why this philosophy can be used to build better scientific theories, the hopes for future verification will not exist. Without the above three, there will be no trust in the Vedic texts to pursue further verification of unverified claims.

The Critique of Modern Science

The critique of modern science is necessary but not sufficient because the falsification of science isn't the verification of Vedic texts. Similarly, the verification of Vedic texts makes sense only if these texts are not falsified by current evidence and the potential for verifying claims exists in the future. This is how we trust Vedic texts although everything is not immediately verified.

There are many kinds of scientific critiques, some of which are more fundamental than others. A damaging critique is that which questions the fundamental aspects of a theory and a cosmetic critique is that which questions the superficial aspects of a theory. We can critique modern science to the most fundamental principle—binary logic—and its assumption of "one thing is only one thing" because each thing is the potential for many things, some of which are hidden when others are revealed at different times, places, and relations to other things. Binary logic is the foundation for separability—i.e., either one thing is itself or something else and it cannot be both itself and something else. Binary logic is false because reality is entangled and separability is false.

Science has axiomatized separability and reductionism because they are entailed by binary logic and don't have to be proved separately. For instance, under binary logic, the whole and parts must either be separable things or they must be identical things due to the principle of excluded middle. If the whole and its parts are neither separable nor identical to each other, then binary logic is broken. Once binary logic fails, we don't have a system of reasoning. Without separability, we lose the capacity to count things. Without counting, we don't have numbers, space, time, objects, or mathematical laws.

If the most fundamental idea at the foundation of science collapses, then the rest of the edifice collapses. We don't have to critique a structure on its surface if we can critique its foundation. We may feel embarrassed by this failure. After all, this edifice has been created over centuries by many people from all parts of the world. How can all of them go wrong over such a long period of time?

The answer is that there are four fundamental human defects that make any empirical or rational *discovery* impossible. Any humanly constructed knowledge will fail due to these four fundamental defects because (a) we don't have all the data before we make a theory nor the capacity to collect all possible data, (b) much of the data we collect contains errors due to faulty measuring instruments, (c) we create simplifying assumptions to process the data we have, and (d) if we get some success we ignore the outliers, postpone their reconciliation to the future until we can no longer ignore it.

Contextualizing the Four Steps

We can show that Vedic philosophy is not disproven by the available evidence, so it is better than modern science. We can show that the evidence is entailed by an alternative conception of reality. That is not a verification because we can always suspect the possibility of alternative explanations, but it is already better than other religious scriptures and scientific theories that are being falsified by evidence. An unverified claim is not equal to a falsified claim. If something is not falsified by evidence, and it is a plausible explanation of the evidence, then we have (a) rejected the cheating propensity of keeping an ideology despite its falsification and (b) the propensity to commit speculative mistakes because there is no evidence of a mistake if a claim hasn't been falsified.

Overcoming the other two defects—(a) illusions, and (b) imperfect senses—requires the development of the perceptual capacity to stop seeing the illusion and to see what we don't see right now. They pertain to overcoming the two flaws of empiricism noted above. Conversely, by understanding the critique of modern science and how Vedic philosophy is free of these problems, we overcome the two flaws of rationalism—(a) cheating propensity, and (b) committing the mistakes of postulating falsifiable axioms—noted above.

We can trust Vedic texts because they are not falsified by the evidence unlike modern science, they correctly predict and explain the available evidence, but we cannot call them verified truths until we eliminate alternatives through perceptual enhancement that destroys illusory perceptions and creates the capacity to perceive the truth. The truth in the Vedic texts is established rationally, but verification by observation is still pending.

Why Scoffing at Revelation is Pointless

Discussions on Vedic epistemology are misunderstood because when we say that verification requires perceptual development, people scoff. They don't know that existing evidence has already falsified their scientific and religious claims so they don't have any rational reason to place trust in those places. Scoffing at something that is not yet verified is pointless if everything else you have is already falsified. Scoffing at something because we set a higher bar for truth—i.e., verification by observation, not merely the absence of falsification, as is the case in science—is pointless because, by the low bar for truth set by science, the Vedic texts are already true since they are not falsified.

This is not a question of trusting one source vs. another. There is no other source in which you can put trust at present because all their claims have been falsified by evidence within the current limited scope of observation. If you keep trusting them, you are putting your trust in something already disproven. But if you trust us, we can assure you that (a) nothing has been falsified, (b) current evidence is predicted and explained, and (c) we only insist on verification to eliminate any *other* alternative explanation.

Empiricism is rooted in the Lockean *tabula rasa* or "blank slate" consciousness in which what we see is the result of external impressions. This is false because we can dream or hallucinate what we have never seen before. Due to imperfect senses, we may not see all that exists. The philosophy of rationalism is rooted in the Aristotelian idea of logical proof indicating a universal truth, but "proof" is itself based on assuming that one thing is always one thing—patently falsified when one thing is many things that are true not universally but contextually. Rationalism also rests on axiomatizations without proof—the axioms we use in reasoning are definitionally believed to be true without any proof.

The scientific method was constructed by disregarding or underestimating the four human defects. The methods of science inherit all the defects of humans because (a) instruments may not measure correctly, (b) instruments may not measure everything, (c) mathematical reasoning cannot capture a reality that is many things at once and yet it becomes one of those things contextually, and (d) we refuse to accept that human defects also exist in the human scientific method despite its failures. The defects of science are not *new*. They are the defects of humans that creep into anything created by humans. The answer to these defects is knowledge given by those who don't have these defects.

Illustration of False Modeling

A simple example of misperception and misconception is modeling a hammer as a drill. A hammer can work as a suboptimal drill. Since it works, although suboptimally, you can say that my modeling of a hammer as a drill is correct—after all, I am able to drill some holes based on my model. This is the problem with the pragmatic conception of truth—the truth always works and it works perfectly, but what works is not necessarily true, because it is working suboptimally although we don't know that unless we find an optimal drill that drills much better holes. Then, if we additionally discover that this thing is optimally used as a hammer, we can say that this is indeed a hammer and not a drill. Knowing that something is a hammer requires us to know other things that are ideal drills and that this thing is best described as a hammer.

Pragmatic claims are hard to falsify because we can treat a hammer as a drill, not drill all possible holes, the holes we drill consume more effort, but because you can drill some holes even with a hammer, therefore, you never search for the ideal drill and claim that the hammer is the drill because by modeling it as a drill we can get suboptimal pragmatic successes in drilling some holes.

The rational proof of incompleteness in science is the indirect result that indicates the modeling of a hammer as a drill because we cannot drill all the possible types of holes using a hammer. The failure of the hammer to drill all possible holes is *incompleteness*. The holes you can drill with a hammer are also drilled suboptimally.

However, since you can drill some holes with a hammer, although suboptimally, you can also refuse to accept the possibility of an ideal drill. Thereby, science can forever continue to drill holes with hammers.

Falsification Precedes Verification

The critique of science that involves demonstrating its failure in explaining evidence is the proof of (a) incompleteness, and (b) the likelihood that we are modeling the hammer as a drill—it can drill some holes but not all holes. We still don't know if there is an ideal drill and that the thing we are modeling as a drill should be modeled as a hammer, and its use should be restricted to hitting nails, and nothing more. To be a better tool, we have to show that the ideal drill can also hammer nails better. You may still not have seen an ideal drill in your entire life, but you can imagine its *possibility*. You then go in search of the drill. When you find it, the postulate of a drill is completely verified.

The fact is that you will never go in search of a drill unless we show that this hammer that you equate to a drill is incapable of drilling many holes. Incompleteness is indirect falsification—we are showing the hammer is not working as a drill should, so it is not a drill—but those accustomed to calling the hammer a drill like to obfuscate the issue: Maybe we cannot drill all holes, but we will keep calling it a drill. This is what we call "cheating propensity". It is the rationalization of speculative mistakes as not being too bad because we can drill some holes even with a hammer and we cannot drill anything without it.

Four Defects Summarize Epistemology

The template of four faults makes it easy to remember the problems of the epistemology as the method of discovery, why these flaws necessitate revelation, why revelation made by a person free of human flaws is never falsified by the evidence, it explains why the falsifying evidence is merely the evidence that we have misconceived or misperceived reality, what that reality is, and why to verify its existence, we must go in search for something we cannot see at present, at which point can replace our current concepts with much better concepts. Thereafter, the ignorant men may keep using hammers to drill a few holes, but the intelligent men will always use a drill to efficiently hammer nails and drill holes. They will no longer have any use for the hammer.

All that we currently call science and technology is a hammer. It is suboptimally used to drill some holes. It cannot drill all holes, which is its incompleteness. But if we can rise to the level of seeing the failure as a misconception of calling a hammer a drill, replace it with a drill, then the ignorant men can keep using the hammer to drill some holes, but the intelligent men will replace the hammers with drills. The process of realizing the flaws of the current science and technology involves four steps—(a) seeing the incompleteness of what we call the "drill", (b) inferring it as implying that what we call a "drill" is actually not a drill, (c) realizing that what I called a drill is just a hammer, and (d) finding the drill that replaces the hammer. The first two are rational falsification and the last two are empirical verification. You cannot go to verification without falsification. So, falsification is the prior and preliminary step.

Curing the Four Human Defects

This four-step process cures the four defects. When we accept the incompleteness of current science and technology, then we have rejected the cheating propensity. When we accept that this incompleteness implies that we have fundamentally misconstrued reality, then we have rejected the tendency to use speculation as a way to know the truth because it can lead us to mistakes that last for centuries. When we can accept that whatever I called a drill before is just a hammer, then we have gotten out of the illusion of thinking that science is giving us some truth about the nature of reality. And when we see that the thing we use to hammer better is a drill, then we have cured imperfect senses.

Therefore, when we say that the truth is ultimately known by curing the imperfection in our perceptual capacity, we are talking about the fourth step of complete verification. It involves the prior step of falsification of the current idea due to incompleteness, the realization that reality cannot be known speculatively because we oversimplify reality to match (a) hallucinations or (b) blindness, rejecting the axioms that make current science incomplete due to binary logic, separability, and reduction, and overcoming these flaws in a new conception that is at least tentatively the complete conception of reality. We still don't know if this conception is indeed the truth unless we perceive it. But we know that it is better than current science because it hasn't been falsified, it predicts the falsifying evidence and obviates reasons for falsification.

This is how we build trust. After that, we undergo the process of perceptual development to perceive the truth. If you don't perceive the truth, you still don't have a better truth to rely on. Hence, you can either claim the absence of any truth, or you try to develop your perception to see what is rationally indicated to be the truth. The understanding of these four defects gives us a useful template by which we can explain the current problems and how they can be progressively overcome to realize the complete and perfect truth.

PLATONISM VS. UNIVERSALISM

Transformation of Platonism into Univeralism

Plato is credited with the idea of a world of pure forms, of which the present world is an imperfect reflection. For example, there is a pure form of man, after which ordinary men are modeled as imperfect reflections. Thus, according to Plato, we compare ordinary men to the pure form, and due to the similarity between the pure form of manliness and the imperfect men of this world, we call them men. A natural implication of Plato's philosophy is that everyone should try to emulate the perfect form, and even imperfect men should try to become perfect men. This is essentially a morally virtuous idea.

However, this is not how Platonism has been interpreted. It was quickly perverted by saying that a select group of men—initially Greeks and subsequently Romans—were ideal, while others (Africans, Arabs, and Asians) were non-ideal. Thereby, Greeks and Romans did not have to do anything to perfect themselves. They were already perfect by their birth, features, culture, ethnicity, and so on. However, everyone else was imperfect. Therefore, the Platonic idea of emulating the perfect form did not apply to Greeks and Romans. It only applied to the other races. In fact, since the Greeks and Romans were already perfect, emulating these men was the goal for every other society, ethnicity, culture, and so on.

Thus arose, from the Platonic theory of pure forms, multiple oppressive, sectarian, and exclusivist ideologies, including Christianity, which borrowed Plato's ideas and weaponized them for their purposes. In each such ideology, one group of people is supreme. Those who try to emulate this group are better, although not on par with the supreme. Everyone else exists only to serve the supreme group of people. While Plato did not contribute to this development, he is not entirely innocent of it either because he never defined any pure form.

The History and Problems of Defining Universals

Saying that there is a pure form of manliness is not wrong. But what good is that pure form unless we define what that pure form is? Plato left all these questions unanswered, creating a vacuum in which later generations simply filled their traits as the traits of the pure forms.

Platonism is a reformulation of Greek pagan religions in which there were numerous demigods in some heaven. Greek gods and goddesses included the deities of fire, air, water, sun, moon, fertility, war, etc. However, pre-Socratic Greek philosophers decided to abandon Greek religions and pursue what we would today call "secular philosophies". They would talk about non-religious ideas like Being and Becoming, the nature of reason and passion, to arrive at some non-religious view of the world. But they did not succeed. The paradoxes they ran into—such as the paradox between Being vs. Becoming—paralyzed Western thinking for centuries.

The standard problem with everything was providing a *definition.* Let's say we try to define a man as a two-legged animal. Then should we say that a man who lost a leg in a war is no longer a man? How about a man with six fingers? Is he a man? Socrates debated these kinds of issues and showed that nobody had a definition. A secular philosophy was thus impossible.

The Conversion of Truth into Popularity

Plato then revived the Greek pagan religious idea by transforming demigods into pure forms. The pure forms were in heaven and their imperfect reflections were on earth. But to avoid most men becoming imperfect, the perfect form was defined as the most abundant type of man found in one society. Men with two legs and five fingers were more perfect because they were the most *abundant* types of men. Thereby, a Platonic form came to be defined by the most commonly found traits, making almost all men perfect and imperfection an outlier.

We can extend this problem of defining pure forms to everything. What is beauty? It was whatever the Greeks thought was the most common idea of beauty. What is justice? It was whatever the Greeks thought was the most common idea of justice. Purity was decided by the *popularity* of some particular idea among the Greek elites. The opinion of slaves was irrelevant because by the consensus of elites, they were imperfect men, so their opinions were also imperfect. Thus, by the thumb rule that the most common opinion among a select group of people was the pure form, all pure forms were constructed by a consensus among a select group of people. Now, truth equaled popularity. The popular definition was the truth.

It is hard to overestimate the problems when everything is decided by popularity among those who call themselves perfect people. If we take away their sense of superiority, then there is no rational foundation for their claims. Therefore, all such claims are preserved by suppressing and destroying all other alternatives. The destruction of the alternative is called *universalism* because the opinion of some people is elevated to the universal truth. Universalism always comes with a racist, supremacist, or oppressive idea of forcing the truth by fiat, rather than by proving that it is the better idea. Thus, Platonism is transformed into Universalism and pure truth is replaced by the opinion of some individuals whose claim to fame is their sense of superiority. We see this pattern repeat at every key juncture in Western history.

The Use of Popularity to Construct Exclusivism

When Romans accepted Christianity, hundreds of people wrote their stories about Jesus and called them Gospels, which were circulating among their respective bands of followers for about four centuries. Most of these Gospels did not agree with the other Gospels on numerous core principles. Then a select group of people gathered to decide which of these Gospels should be accepted or rejected as the universal truth. While this group called themselves the Catholic Church (catholic means all-embracing), they burned, buried, and banned most of the circulating Gospels to synthetically construct what is today known as the Bible.

Most people don't know that the Bible did not exist for four centuries after the crucifixion of Jesus and was cobbled together from a variety of conflicting religious narratives by a select group of people. The method by which some Gospels were included in the Bible remains opaque to historians. All they can say, after the study of the surviving but excluded Gospels, is that they differ significantly from the Bible. The fact is also that even the Gospels included in the Bible don't concord with each other on numerous questions although the disagreements between the included Gospels are smaller than with the excluded Gospels.

How Persecution Defined Modern Science

The synthetic construction of the Bible, and its elevation to the universal truth, is a common method by which the most important claims have been constructed in Western history. Their purity and truthfulness remain in doubt. Hence, those who questioned them were often killed. Anyone with the greatest power can enforce his opinion as the highest and purest truth.

A similar process was used to construct modern science. A group of people gathered together to form a society that then received royal patronage and came to be known as the Royal Society. All early members of the Royal Society were faithful followers of Francis Bacon, and they had gathered together inspired by his writings. Those writings, which delineated the idea of a "controlled experiment", were inspired by Bacon's profession of witch-hunting.

Those called "witches" were pagans who worshipped nature. Christianity, which depersonalized nature, called nature worshippers Satanic. They were captured and tortured according to prevailing laws until they revealed the names of other witches, after which, they were often hanged and burned. All these jobs were done by witch-hunters, such as Francis Bacon. Bacon's idea of a scientific method was based on the interrogation of witches. An experiment was the courtroom of witch interrogation. The torture of witches through mechanical implements was became the universal paradigm by which nature had to be compelled to reveal her secrets.

Like interrogators put criminals in a box, science creates "controlled experiments" assuming that nature has been put into a box.

The fact is that nature is inside the box, outside the box, and the box. The box is not cutting off nature's access to itself because that box is also nature. The isolation of nature from nature by nature is just a delusion. Even the idea that a criminal's behavior inside the box is exactly his behavior outside the box, is worth only a laugh. And yet, modern science rests on this laughable proposition. It claims to discover some truth through a "controlled experiment" which is extended to everything after removing the controls.

The fact is that "controlled experiments" are the root cause of all problems in modern science because they divide reality into hundreds of imaginary boxes which only exist in the laboratory and not outside of it. Through artificial and imagined fragmentation, every subject becomes incomplete because the boxes don't exist, whatever is outside the imaginary box influences what is inside it, but the scientist ignores what is outside the box and looks for causes inside the box. This is the legacy of the British elites influenced and impressed by the writings of a witch-hunter. Their consensus defines modern science, although even a casual examination would reveal its fallacies. Therefore, the scientific method defends itself by calling everything else "pseudoscience" because it cannot justify itself without name-calling alternatives.

False Consensus at the Roots of Democracy

The same process of collectively agreeing on what is rationally indefensible was used during the drafting of the US Constitution. A select group of "representatives" gathered to frame a constitution for the United States. The main item of compromise was slave ownership under which those states that had abolished slavery would return escaped slaves to their owners in states that continued to legally endorse slave ownership. Slavery and democracy were equally accepted within the US Constitution disregarding the conflict between the two.

The US Constitution stated: "We hold these truths to be self-evident, that all men are created equal, that they are endowed by their Creator with certain unalienable Rights, that among these are Life, Liberty and the pursuit of Happiness." But the equality of all men did not apply to slaves. Life, liberty, and the pursuit of happiness were not for all. Since the constitution stated that these were self-evident truths for all, the conclusion was that slaves weren't human.

How Consensus Truth Deals With Outliers

This is a common method for dealing with outliers and exceptions to whatever worthless dogma is created through consensus. When something doesn't fit the artificially concocted doctrine, it is labeled by the opposite word. The method of shaming by naming has been used repeatedly while defining pure forms, religion, science, and constitutions through a consensus among a select few. Those who don't fit the Greek elite's definition of beauty are ugly. Those who don't follow the Roman elite's religion are Satanic. Those who don't conform to the British elite's definition of science are pseudoscientists. Those who don't fit into the American elite's definition of men are barbarians. Name calling the outlier supports illusory universalism.

After the completion of negotiation among the few who are part of the consensus-building group, the definition produced through compromise amoung the chosen few is raised to the level of Platonic pure truth. The Greek idea of beauty became the pure idea of beauty. The Roman idea of religion became the pure idea of religion. The British idea of the scientific method became the pure idea of science. The American idea of government became the purest form of government. Nobody knows how we go from a negotiated settlement in this world to pure Platonic truth in the transcendent world. But quite habitually, a compromise reached during a closed-room negotiation is elevated to the level of Platonic pure truth.

The Abuse of Platonism for Exclusivism

A constitution has dozens of amendments to suit the needs of the time. Religious texts are modified hundreds of times for political purposes. Scientific theories change frequently to fit the new data. The ideas of beauty change with every fashion fad. But they are all called pure and eternal Platonic forms. There is no imperfection in them as far as the outsiders are concerned. The insiders, however, are free to change whatever suits them whenever they want. The system of universalism is hypocritical to the hilt. Double standards are standard.

There is always a machinery, developed, designed, and deployed to suppress any alternative viewpoint. Even if something escapes the suppression, their proponents are called enemies, heretics, Satanic, witches, and pseudoscientists, and are burned at the stake, often literally and sometimes metaphorically. Universalism thereby always breeds exclusivism.

In general, well-meaning wise guys defining something for a larger group would be welcome if their definitions were improving everyone. For instance, if a pure human was defined as a truthful, selfless, kind, and generous person, then emulating that person would benefit everyone. But if those who lack the above purity call themselves pure, then the result will be disastrous. Hence, the principle of wise guys defining a pure form for everyone should not be equated to a select group of guys calling themselves wise guys while excluding others.

Western universalism is a front for some people to force their opinions on others. The self-appointed wise guys have no clue what a pure form is. Their definition is not open to a rational discussion. The persecution that follows any opposition is not justifiable. The self-appointed wise guys expect to be treated nicely for proposing bad ideas. But they don't extend the same courtesy to others who propose good ideas. The mentality of the self-appointed wise guys is seen in the claim that God sends a heretic to eternal hell while sending the believer to eternal heaven. These are fictions concocted by self-appointed wise guys to justify the elimination of those who disregard their claims while calling that elimination "God's will".

Therefore, Platonism is the most abused philosophy as it allows some people to play God, without the good qualities of God. They are not interested in pure forms. They concoct ideas they find convenient to their interests and elevate them to pure forms. Then they use propaganda to convince everyone. Then they intimidate others to instill fear in everyone. And those who are not convinced and intimidated are made examples to reinforce the message. I doubt

Plato could have imagined the extent to which Platonism would be abused.

Universal Truth vs. Supreme Truth

Platonic pure forms have some similarities to the idea of Param-Satyam in Vedic texts. This term is translated as the highest truth, best truth, and original truth. It does not exclude lower truths, good truths, and subsequent truths. This is just like there is a pure form of human, but there are other humans, who could be impure to varying extents. There is no good vs. evil binary in which Param-Satyam is good and everything else is evil. There is instead a ladder of truths, and something is called evil if it is very low on the ladder. However, even those low on the ladder are encouraged to rise up the ladder. The concept of eternal punishment and eternal hell does not exist. This is not an endorsement of those who are low on the ladder. It is the endorsement of minimal punishments that can raise a person on the ladder.

Platonic pure forms were transformed into Universal Truths during Greek and Roman times, creating the good vs. evil binaries by priests and emperors to anoint themselves as pure humans, bringing everyone under their control. This idea became so entrenched in Western thinking that people today don't know the difference between Platonic pure forms and Universal Truths. The difference is that a Platonic pure form is the Supreme Truth expanding into a ladder of lower truths, while a Universal Truth is the only truth. The purity of the Supreme Truth is established by proving how it is the topmost rung of a ladder but no such proof for the Universal Truth exists. A Universal Truth is always axiomatized by a powerful establishment and then forced upon everyone through intimidation and persecution.

Keeping the distinction between Platonism and Universalism obscured suits some people because if the distinction was known, then we will return to discussing what the pure form of everything is, and realize that it is not that which "wise guys" designated as a pure form.

GUNA, KARMA, AND PERCEPTION

There is a common but false belief that everyone can know everything. It was created at the dawn of modern science to take away the privileged position of Catholic priests and emperors. In Roman times, the emperor was said to be in direct communion with the gods. He was most privileged. The priests were less privileged than the emperor but more privileged than the commoners. At the dawn of Christianity, priests got the privilege of communicating with God and the emperors retained the power over the state. The Pope and the Emperor carved reality into "that world" and "this world", which is noted in the Bible as: "Give unto Caesar what is Caesar's and unto God what is God's".

However, the Protestant Reformation took away the privileges of priests and emperors. Everyone could communicate with God and everyone played a role in deciding the government. Priests did not have special privileges to interpret scripture; everyone was equally empowered to do so. The emperor was not uniquely empowered to make laws. Every adult was empowered to make laws through a democratic franchise. The doctrine of rights was created to formalize these ideas. The right to freedom of religion meant that everyone had the freedom to interpret the Bible in their own way. The right to freedom of government meant that everyone had the freedom to vote democratically for laws.

Modern science was created under the umbrella of this equality. John Locke stated that we were all blank slates at birth, disregarding the fact that some people are born artists, poets, musicians, sportspersons, politicians, or mathematicians. Nobody was born sinful, against the Biblical doctrine of earthly beings being the children of Adam and Eve. There was no life before this one, and hence nobody had any prior impressions. It was the impressions of this life (i.e., education, upbringing, and society) that defined a person. An education system that treated children as blank slates followed. It imparted all subjects to all children. This was the way that everyone was supposed to be equal.

The belief in equality has been a tour de force in Western thinking since then. Just saying that one person is less qualified than another is considered offensive. A musician or artist by birth is not considered educated unless he has learned calculus, mechanics, and evolution. Equality is not just a belief but a dogma of Western thinking. It must be upheld against any evidence of differences. No evidence disproves them. Evidence is tailored to prove the dogma. If this dogma collapses then it will take away the basis of modern Western society.

In Vedic philosophy, we reject the dogmatic equality of Western thinking. We accept that each person is unique consistent with ordinary experience. Nobody has identical proclivities, abilities, or opportunities. Some people are more capable musicians. Some are not capable of music but deeply interested in music. Some people get the opportunity to hone their abilities and demonstrate them, while others do not.

Thus, we construct experience through the combination of ability, proclivity, and opportunity. If you see a musician perform on stage, it is because—(a) he is capable, (b) he got the opportunity, and (c) he was inclined to use it. If you went to watch the musical concert, it is because—(a) you are capable of paying for the ticket, (b) you got the opportunity to buy a ticket, and (c) you were inclined to go to the concert.

Ability and proclivity are collectively called *guna*. Opportunity is called *karma*. Thus, two words—*guna* and *karma*—collectively describe our experiences. Since the abilities, proclivities, and opportunities of each person are different, therefore, equality is a false dogma.

Our eyes cannot smell. Our noses cannot see. Even if light from an object hits our nose, the nose cannot see color. If some molecules of smell hit the eye, the eye cannot smell. Each sense is designed to perceive one kind of property. That design limits the ability to perceive other kinds of properties. Every mind cannot understand every subject. Some minds are suited to mathematics. They can perceive a conceptual mental realm of structures, relationships, and ideas. They are often not well-suited to memorize dates, places, names, faces, and events, as required for a historian. A historian's mind is well-suited for memorization but not for abstract concepts required for mathematics.

Against this experience, science argued the possibility of instruments that can measure all properties *simultaneously*. The limitations of humans were supposedly overcome by instruments. However, quantum mechanics disproved this idea with the Uncertainty Principle. If the position is known precisely then the momentum is infinitely uncertain. If momentum is known precisely then the position is infinitely uncertain. Neils Bohr coined the term *complementarity* to describe necessary properties. Position and momentum were like the front and back of a person. We cannot see both at once. We can see one by one. The human limitations of senses and mind thus returned to science.

There are further problems of quantum collapse which indicate that even if something is knowable it may not be knowable at all times. A particular quantum arrives at one detector, occasionally. Only that detector knows that quantum, not all detectors. Only that detector measures a quantum, occasionally. Other detectors never detect the quantum. No detector measures the quantum consistently.

To understand the quantum problem, we can treat the battery of detectors as our senses. One detector detects heat, another one roughness, another one heaviness, another one form, another one color, and so on. Some detectors never detect anything. This battery is an observer measuring reality with his senses. The detections are not simultaneous. Every observer cannot detect everything. There are probabilities for different percepts. Each observer is inclined toward some detections based on which, at some times, we can focus more on one sense perception than another. The things on which we focus become more common at the moment but less common at a later time.

Let's apply this idea to a simple problem of distance measurement. Suppose one of the many detectors is measuring distance. Suppose also that photons arrive at this detector more frequently, just for a short time. Their quicker arrival doesn't violate probabilities if they arrive slower during subsequent intervals. The temporary burst of photons will be interpreted as the greater *intensity* of light. The Inverse Square Law of light intensity would be invoked to say that what seems *brighter* is *closer*. If after some time, the rate of the arrival of photons reduces, then the same Inverse Square Law of light intensity would be reinvoked to say that what seems *dimmer* is *farther*. Factually, nothing may be moving. And yet, an illusion of movement can be created by altering the rate of arrival of photons at a detector.

Since all measurements depend on the arrival of some photons, but the arrival rates of photons are not fixed, therefore, no measurement is reliable. The arrival rates can vary from one instrument to another. They can vary from one place to another. They can vary from one time to another. There is no current theory that predicts or explains why, when, how, where, how, or which detector receives a photon.

The problem of photon arrival is the problem of ordinary sense perception. All assumptions of instruments objectifying reality by removing subjects, and all subjects being equally capable of knowing everything, are false. The dogma of equality, uniformity, and universality has been falsified empirically. Of course, we did not need science to do that. Any commonsense observation of the world would also tell us that the dogmas of equality, uniformity, and universality are false. But since science insisted on axiomatizing or universalizing such dogmas, hence, they can now see their dogmas falsified. Modern science has used 300 years to confirm what every child knows intuitively from birth.

And yet, dogmas are evidence-free claims. No amount of evidence can falsify them in the believer's mind. Dogmas are not blind faith. They are faith against evidence. The dogmatic believers keep trying to find ways to prove the dogma. The dogma cannot be rejected as long as there is money in the believer's pocket. He will spend money to search for proof of the dogma until he runs out of money. Thereby, falsehoods are not corrected rationally. They die when the dogmatic run out of money. The false dogma is rejected as the option of last resort. Until then, money is spent to find the proof, claim that the proof is just around the corner, or motivate people to search for proof of the falsehood.

The problem of measurement is as complicated as the quantum problem—to explain why, when, how, where, how, and which detector receives a photon. The measurement problem is as complicated as the human perception problem—to explain why, when, how, where, how, or which sense or observer receives a photon. The claims of universality, uniformity, and equality are simply false dogmas.

To solve these problems, we need to understand guna and karma. Everyone cannot digest alcohol. Everyone who can digest alcohol doesn't want to drink alcohol. Everyone who can digest alcohol and wants to drink alcohol doesn't have access to alcohol at all places, times, and situations. Everything is constructed from the combination of ability, proclivity, and opportunity. A capacity to digest alcohol and a proclivity to drink alcohol is guna. The opportunity to drink alcohol is karma. When the ability and proclivity to drink alcohol develop, then many other abilities and proclivities die. That is just like a thermometer cannot measure speed and a speedometer cannot measure temperature.

Everyone is not equally capable or inclined to understand everything. That is because understanding is *digestion*. The samāna prāṇa digests. The digestive capacity is limited by a person's guna. Thereby, everyone cannot digest everything. Some people are allergic to some types of food. There is an assimilative prāṇa called vyāna. Sometimes, even if we can understand something, we cannot assimilate it with our existing ideology. Even after understanding it, we excrete it. The power of excretion is also a prāṇa called apāna. If this excretory power is weakened, then undigested or unassimilated ideas linger around in the mind creating an internal conflict within a person. The process of ingesting, digesting, assimilating, and excreting ideas is as complicated as the process of ingesting, digesting, assimilating, and excreting food.

But what happens if someone says that the mind is a blank slate? That everyone can ingest, digest, assimilate, and excrete everything equally well? Unaware of the working of guna and karma, they will blame others like a person who cannot digest spicy food may blame the cook for having cooked spicy food. He wants spicy food, but he cannot digest spicy food, and hence, he blames the cook who makes spicy food. Everyone cannot digest all types of knowledge, just as they cannot digest all kinds of foods. This is obvious to people who understand how both mind and body are produced from guna and karma. Others trying to quantify the body through instruments don't understand that measurements suffer from the problems of sense perception, differences between individual observers, and their prior actions.

This doesn't mean that the door to knowledge is closed to those who cannot digest it presently. The solution is practice. If we continuously practice, then the ability, proclivity, and opportunity develop, just like a person who cannot digest alcohol can develop that digestive capacity by drinking. He will slowly develop the proclivity to drink. And then he will find the places and times where he can drink. Practice makes a person perfect or imperfect. If we have earlier practiced imperfection then we cannot become perfect overnight. It takes a lot of practice. The process requires enthusiasm, determination, and patience, continuously practicing perfection, abandoning the practice of imperfection, and associating with those who are either perfecting or perfect. The door is open for those who are eager to walk through it.

But that door is closed the moment we blame the cook rather than our digestive system. This blame assignment has become standard practice for those who have eaten only one kind of food. They think that since they have never eaten something they could not digest, therefore, they can digest everything. That is the dogma of equality, blank slates, universality, and absence of privileges. It is all false. Everyone is not equal. Rather, almost everyone is conditioned by a different combination of guna and karma. But by practice, we can change both. Therefore, everyone is not capable of knowing everything. But by practice, we change our guna and karma, and then we become capable of knowing. There is a path for those who are enthusiastic, patient, and determined. There is no path for those who blame the cook.

The preliminary step for everyone under the dogma of equality is to understand the problems of modern science and get rid of their false ideas of equality. They are the results of the political history of Christianity and have nothing to do with the truth. Those who endured these histories reacted to them by creating a new set of false dogmas. They think that the former is the lie of religion and the latter is the truth of science. They don't know that both science and religion are lies, although they won't die as long as the dogmatic have money.

The Inseparability of Epistemology, Ontology, and Logic

The Effect of Western Dualisms

Since Greek times, Western philosophy has separated subjects from each other. These include epistemology (how we know), ontology (what exists), and logic (relations between propositions). The separation relies on two dualisms. First, the dualism of mind and body in which epistemology pertains to the mind and ontology to the body (even if the mind is recognized in the ontology it is only to say that it is separate from the body and hence plays no significant role in the understanding of the body). Second, the dualism of this world and the Platonic world in which ontology pertains to this world and the logic governing this ontology resides in the Platonic world.

Thus, we arrive at three separate subjects, namely, epistemology, ontology, and logic that respectively belong to three worlds—the mental world, the material world, and the Platonic world. As long as these worlds remain separate, the Platonic world rules over the mental world and the material world. The mental world can at most rule over the material world as it tries to create many models of the material world within the confines of logic. The material world cannot rule over the mental or Platonic world. Nor can the mental world rule over the Platonic world. The worlds, therefore, have a strictly hierarchical relationship. At the top is the Platonic world, below it is the mental world, and at the bottom is the material world.

Some people might say that Greeks did not explicitly recognize the mind. They just thought of the material world as substances.

The mind-body dualism is also a later Cartesian addition, and it did not exist during Greek times. All this is true. But it doesn't mean that Greeks did not speak about thought and reasoning and did not separate it from the world. The Greeks called the mind psyche and it existed although not as a mental substance as in Cartesian dualism. The mind as thought and reasoning remained separate from the material world even though it was not explicitly recognized in an ontology. What remains rather obscure is if Greeks ever gave serious attention to knowing the self. The study of the psyche, mind, self, soul, and so on, was never given great emphasis in Western thinking until the 18th century when German Idealism was born. After that, there was a flurry of philosophies talking about the mind, but never applying the principle of Greek logic to such study.

If we follow the Greek notion of logic ruling over the whole world, then logic must govern epistemology too because knowledge in the mind pertains to the ontology of the body and since the ontology is governed by logic, therefore, the concepts being used to describe the body must also be governed by logic.

The Problem in Thinking of Logic

Let's now look at the problems arising from the separation of these three worlds. Let's begin with the application of logic to the mind. Thinking about the mind isn't logical because the same idea can at once exist in many minds although the same body cannot exist simultaneously in many places. The Principle of Identity uses positioning in space to identify one thing. If the same thing can be at many places at once, then it would be many things, leading to the contradiction that "one thing is many things".

Therefore, the logic by which we think of bodies in Greek thinking cannot be extended to the mind. If that body-bound logic happens to be the only logic applied to the entirety of reality, then we can never logically think about ideas or the mind that creates them. Thus, even as we assume that logic must govern all thinking in order to obtain knowledge, the first principle of knowledge (namely, that many people can know the same truth), is patently contradictory to the first principle of logic—i.e., Identity.

Similarly, we cannot think of logic itself using logic because thinking assumes a difference between knower and known—the former is the mind and the latter is the body. If a thinker starts thinking about himself, then calling the self-thought bad would mean that the thinker is itself bad. All his criticisms of thoughts about himself become his personal criticisms of himself and should be disregarded as the thoughts of a bad thinker. Likewise, if logic is used to speak about logic, then any logical criticism of logic that itself employs logic will result in self-contradiction. Logically speaking, we must reject all self-contradictory claims. Thus, we can never logically criticize logic while using logic for criticism.

In this way, even if we can see that the logic used for the body cannot be extended to the mind, we cannot criticize it logically because such criticism of the logic using logic will just produce self-contradiction and cannot be considered a valid argument. This is how bad logic becomes irrefutable if we have accepted that logic for thinking about all future things. We cannot even step out of logic to criticize it.

Separation of Theoretical and Practical

To summarize the separation of worlds, logic in the paradigm of Western thinking resides in the Platonic world and can be applied to the material world *by the mind* but logic cannot be applied *to the mind* itself. The application of logic to the mind denies the possibility of knowledge since one idea could never exist in more than one mind. Thus, if one man knows something, then nobody else can know. We cannot even criticize logic for this flaw using logic because criticism will result in self-contradiction.

To justify this limited role of logic (i.e., that it can be applied by the mind but can't be applied to the mind), Aristotle additionally created a *separation* of theoretical and practical forms within the Platonic world of forms, thus dividing the material world also into two groups. The theoretical forms (such as triangles, circles, squares, etc.) reside in the material world, in the mental world, and in the Platonic world, and can be comprehended through logic, arithmetic, geometry, and so on. The practical forms (such as art, music, poetry, dance, etc.) also reside in the three worlds but logic, arithmetic, and geometry do not apply to them. We can precisely say if something is a circle or not. But we cannot precisely say if something that someone calls music, poetry, dance, or art is definitively a practical form or not.

The separation of theoretical and practical forms becomes necessary because logic doesn't apply to everything in the specific sense that we cannot precisely say what something *is* or *is not*. If we cannot apply that basic Principle of Identity, the Principle of Non-Contradiction and Principle of Excluded Middle also don't apply. Thereby, the Platonic world, the mental world, and the material world are split into two haves—logic doesn't apply to any practical form and its use must be restricted to theoretical forms.

How Western Thinking Is Impersonalist

Matter could never exist in the mind or in the Platonic world. Similarly, the mind could not exist in the Platonic world because there is only one of everything in the Platonic world. If the mind could ascend to the Platonic world, it would become a pure mind, and there can only be one pure mind. All the individual minds would have to be merged into a single mind for those minds to ascend to the Platonic world. There could not be many individual minds thinking pure thoughts because that would mean that each mind had become a separate individual Platonic world, creating infinite such Platonic worlds.

Aristotle's thinking thus breeds impersonalism in the sense that individual minds are separate only as long as they are impure minds. The moment they become pure they must merge into a single mind. The individuality of each mind is therefore an illusion that can be sustained only while it is impure. If the mind dies at the death of the body, then there is no ascendence to the Platonic world in the afterlife. If the mind merges with the other minds into a single Universal Mind, then individuality is ephemeral.

Since the Greek separation of logic, epistemology, and ontology is used universally in the West, hence, all Western thinking is at its root one of two things—(a) materialistic in the sense that there is no life after death, or (b) impersonalist in the sense that going to the Platonic world means merging all minds. As time passes, therefore, the use of the Greek separation of subjects can only result either in materialism or impersonalism. Either the mind dies at death or all minds merge into a single mind after death. The separation of the minds into many individuals can at best be called dividing an ocean into many pots filled with water. Death must destroy the individuality of a person by breaking the potted minds.

Christianity's Double Standard

Isn't it surprising then that for over 2000 years Christianity has used a double standard—(a) each mind is individual, and (b) all minds must think exactly the same because truth cannot be more than one? The reason this double standard exists is that Christianity borrowed Aristotelian ideas to create a rational system, never realizing the eternal separation of three worlds (material, mental, and Platonic) and the eternal division of forms (theoretical and practical), restricting logic's use to the material world. When the universalist ideas of Aristotle—which he had restricted to theoretical forms (triangle, circle, square, etc.)—were extended to the whole of reality, then they were extended to the mind (or the soul) as well. As we have noted, the mind can use logic to think about matter but logic can't be applied to the mind.

Now, owing to universalism, there could not be more than one Platonic truth. Everyone who believed in something else could not be correct. This immediately led to exclusivism in religion, simply by extending the idea that circle, triangle, and square have one definition, hence, religion must have one definition. Any other definition could not be true. Acknowledging any other religion means falsifying one's own.

From an Aristotelian perspective, religion should have been treated as a practical form which means it is not dealing with circles, triangles, squares, arithmetic, and geometry so the principles of logic that were restricted to theoretical forms should not be extended to religion. But Christianity extended the use of Aristotelian theoretical forms to religion, in total contradistinction to what Aristotle had prescribed.

The double standard resulting from this extension is that there are multiple minds thinking the same thing, going to a Platonic world of pure minds, where there cannot be more than one instance of purity. Any variation in any mind thinking slightly different from each other would mean that there are multiple definitions of circle, triangle, and square. Since that is not permissible therefore every mind must think of identical ideas. Why then would we call them separate minds when separation of minds means that there is at least one unique idea in each mind that does not exist in any other mind in the same way?

On one hand, Christianity upheld Greek Universalism to destroy all alternative ideas. On the other, it talked about individual freedoms to think and create, justify and refute, competing in the marketplace of ideas, which led to hundreds if not thousands of theories, claims, and ideologies. Under Universalism, all except one idea must be false. In so far as each person thinks something different, they are unique minds that cannot be fitted into a Universalist worldview. If they die, then all of them cannot go to the Platonic world. At most one person can even go to the Platonic world—if he has the correct idea. Otherwise, all the minds must be merged into a single mind to destroy all kinds of individualism and free choices.

And yet, Christianity has upheld the radical double standard of universalism and individualism. The former allows one to destroy and refute all ideas except one's own. The latter allows one to create their own new ideas. If someone accepts another person's idea, their individuality has been subordinated to a universality. If instead, they assert their individuality, it comes at the cost of universality. Universalism and individualism cannot be true simultaneously. However, Christianity upholds this double standard in a unique way—my claims are the universal truths whereas every other claim is a complete falsehood.

The result of this double standard is that all Western thinking has always been exclusivist and will remain so until the age-old dogmas of three separate worlds, theoretical vs. practical forms, universalism, and individualism, the application of logic to matter but not to the mind, and the contradictory idea of many minds existing in the Platonic world even as they cannot exactly agree with each other in this world, are collectively and summarily discarded. That of course would be the end of Western civilization.

The Use of Extra-Logical Thinking

We have to use some extra-logical thinking to imagine a post-West scenario. That alternative way of thinking is found in the Vedic system. Therein, there are infinite individual minds both in this world and the supposed Platonic world or spiritual world. Both these worlds are idea-like rather than object-like in the sense that the same ideas can exist in many minds—the idea is one and yet it is in many places. Since logic cannot deal with one thing that is at once many things, therefore, we have to call this extra-logical. We can never subsume this thinking under Aristotelian logic rooted in object thinking. We have to begin with mind-thinking in which the same idea can exist in infinite minds so it is one and many at once.

The body must also be just like an idea—namely, that the properties of the body (such as taste, touch, smell, sound, and sight) can also exist in many places so each property would be simultaneously one and many. And yet, each body can be a *unique combination* of ideas, namely, a unique composition of the properties such as taste, touch, smell, sound, and sight. Some of these unique combinations can be called the truth while the other combinations must be called myths. The temporary combinations can be called myths while the eternal combinations must be called truths. The properties are eternal and true. But the combinations of these properties also need to be checked—if they are truths or myths.

To do that, we have to apply the same principle as we apply to test the truth and myth of ideas. Remember, both minds and bodies are just like ideas. They are truths if they are *consistent* with some Absolute Truth and they are myths if they are *inconsistent* with some Absolute Truth. This is how we test for validity of ideas in our minds—if something is inconsistent with an irrefutable truth then it must be false, but if it is consistent with the irrefutable truth, then it must be true. Thereby, we don't reduce all truths to just one truth. There can be infinite truths if they are consistent with an Absolute Truth. There can be infinite myths as well if they are inconsistent with an Absolute Truth. The principles that we apply to truth and myth in our minds can now be applied even to bodies and individuals because they are all ideas. Thereby, we don't have a dualism of mind vs. body or this world vs. the Platonic world. We just have the dualism of truth vs. myth based on whether it is consistent with the Absolute Truth.

Something consistent with the Absolute Truth can be found both in this world and the Platonic world. But something inconsistent with the Absolute Truth can only exist in this world and not the Platonic world. Therefore, the truth can "incarnate" in this world, but the myth cannot "incarnate" in the Platonic world. By seeing the truth incarnate in this world, we can become consistent with it and ascend to the Platonic world. If we reject that truth incarnate in this world, we must remain within this world.

The Necessity of Alternative Logics

To uphold this alternative worldview, we have to think of an alternative logic that is modeled after the nature of the mind and ideas rather than the ideas of the body and objects. The essence of that logic is that one thing can be present in many places. The same idea can exist in many minds. The same properties of taste, touch, smell, sound, and sight can simultaneously exist in many bodies. That is the breakage of all the principles of Aristotelian logic—(a) the Principle of Identity is false because the same thing is in many places, (b) the Principle of Non-Contradiction is false because one thing is many things and many things are one thing, and (c) the Principle of Excluded Middle is false because the same thing is one and many.

These are not strange properties. Everyone knows about these properties every day when they think of minds and ideas. They are falsified only when we elevate the thinking of bodies and objects to universal thinking, eliminate the possibility of ever understanding the mind, and separate reality into the Platonic world, mental world, and material world, such that the minds can either die or merge in the Platonic world, followed by the creation of contradictory double standards of universalism and individualism.

Therefore, the problem of logic comes down to just one thing—namely, Aristotle created a system of three worlds, two types of forms (theoretical and practical), the universalism of theoretical forms and individualism of practical forms, which were then repeatedly mixed to create endless confusion, all rooted in the simple system of logic that was itself derived from thinking about material objects. If we get rid of Aristotelian thinking, then all the problems can be solved. Of course, it will end the Western civilization too. We can anticipate that those attached to Western civilization are the opponents of the Vedic alternative because it is in all fundamental respects opposed to Western civilization.

The Inseparability of Multiple Subjects

The Aristotelian model of subject separation—articulated initially as ontology, epistemology, and logic—has been the foundation for the continuation of such separation in the form of dozens of modern departments of knowledge such as mathematics, physics, chemistry, biology, cosmology, economics, sociology, law, political theory, and so on. When the worlds are not separate—since a truth consistent with the Absolute Truth can exist in this world—then why should the departments be separated?

If we model reality like mind and thoughts, then ontology is mind and thoughts. Epistemology is not about knowing some material object. It is also a property of the mind expressed as thoughts and it is true if it correctly understands the other mind and thought, and it becomes true if it is aligned with the Absolute Truth. Likewise, logic can be used on the mind and thought to check if they are consistent with the Absolute Truth. Thus, epistemology, ontology, and logic become identical subjects when we talk about mind and thought. They are separated when we talk about material objects when pure forms reside in the Platonic world which then governs the material world, and this logic of Platonic forms—embodied as arithmetic and geometry—cannot be applied to the mind because the same idea is in many minds but the same object cannot be in many places. The separation of epistemology, ontology, and logic is itself materialism and their inseparability is itself spiritualism or the nature of mind and thought.

When we take out the foundation of this separation that began with Aristotle, then we start merging many subjects together. There is no such thing as physics because reality is mind and thought. The thing that is physics is also the thing that is psychology. The thing is psychology is also the thing that is biology. The thing that is the biological study of organisms is also the study of the cosmos as a bigger organism with trillions of smaller organisms within it just like organisms within our bodies. Likewise, society, economics, and government are simply the regulation system of mind-like organisms.

The moment we get rid of Aristotelian trialisms, dualisms, and contradictions, knowledge begins to coalesce into one subject of mind and thought. There are infinite types of minds and thoughts, so let us not think that this coalescing makes life trivial. It is indeed very complex. But it is no longer a collection of *contradictory subjects*. Complexity can be addressed. Contradictions cannot be addressed. Factually, epistemology, ontology, and reasoning are one subject. Mind, matter, and rationality are one subject. Religion and science are one subject. But only if we model everything as mind and thought.

The Paradigm of Face and Mask

The Nature of First-Order Logic

What most people call *logic* is technically called *first-order* logic. The nomenclature suggests that there must be second-, third-, fourth-, and infinite other higher-order logics. Most people are unaware of these higher-order logics because they violate the three principles of first-order logic—(a) the law of identity, (b) the law of non-contradiction, and (c) the law of excluded middle. As a result, higher-order logics are generally disregarded in all of modern science, which then relies exclusively on first-order logic.

To understand the necessity of many logics, we can take a simple example. Let's assume that we have to talk about an apple logically. We can look at a specific thing that is an apple and say: "this is an apple". This statement relies on first-order logic because the three principles of identity, non-contradiction, and excluded middle apply. For instance, if this is an apple, then it cannot be an orange. It cannot be both an apple and not an apple. It also could not be neither an apple and not an apple.

First-order logic applies to *objects*. Each object has one nature, by which it is called. The object is an individual and the nature is a universal. First-order logic maps an individual to a universal. It is assumed that such a mapping can be done for all individuals, such that each individual will have a *type*.

The Need for Higher-Order Truths

The situation, however, gets complicated if we ask: How do we determine something's nature? For example, we can try to define the method by which an apple will be identified. We could say that an apple is red, round, and sweet. Redness is a color, roundness is a shape, and sweetness is a taste. We are using three *properties* of an apple to decide if it is an apple. Without these properties, we could not know if the thing in question is an apple or not. Hence, properties are absolutely essential.

Each object has many properties. We can classify them based on sense perceptions and say that each object has five classes of properties measured by each sense. Within these classes there are many subclasses. For example, color, shape, and size are subclasses of sight. Hardness, roughness, and heaviness are subclasses of touch. Therefore, to be certain that we have an apple, we have to apply all the properties required to determine if something is indeed an apple. Without properties, we cannot know.

The properties of an object are *second-order* truths about the object; the first-order truth being the nature of the object. However, the first-order truth depends on the second-order truth, since we have to know the properties in order to know the object. For instance, apple is the first-order truth, and shape, color, and taste are second-order truths. The first-order truth depends on the second-order truth.

Similarly, to know that something has a shape, color, and taste, we have to know its precise shape (such as round), its precise color (such as red), its precise taste (such as sweet). Red, round, and sweet are third-order truths about the apple. The second-order truth depends on the third-order truth, just as the first-order truth earlier depended on the second-order truth. If we cannot know that something is red, round, and sweet, then we cannot know that it has color, shape, and taste, and then we cannot know that it is an apple.

The Distinction of Is and Has

The second-order truths are tied to the first-order truth using the connector *has*. For example, "the apple *has* taste, color, shape". In contrast, the first-order truth uses the connector *is*, such as in "this *is* an apple". However, this transition from first- to second-order truth isn't used consistently with further higher-order truths. For example, even as the apple has taste, we say that the taste is sweet and the apple is sweet. Similarly, even if the apple was dark red, generally nobody says that red has darkness. We just say that red is dark and the apple is dark red. The has connector is unpopular compared to is.

But if we drop the has connector for higher-order logics, and just stick to the is connector, then we would run into a new problem where "this is apple", "this is sweet", and "this is round" would mean that "round is sweet" purely by the use of the identity principle that two things that are equal to one thing are equal to each other. The identity principle doesn't apply to has, and therefore doesn't suffer from this issue. But we don't use has as often and as rigorously as is. Then how are we getting along with the use of is, when clearly that use results in logical absurdities such as equating the taste to the shape?

The answer is that the is connector works in one direction and not in the reverse direction. For example, the apple is red but red is not apple. Or, the red is dark but dark is not red. The is connector is works just like the has connector—in one direction and not in the reverse direction. Therefore, we can continue using the is connector just like we would use the has connector but it is no longer an identity.

The Nature of Mathematical Logic

If we were to replace all the words with numbers, then identity becomes equality (=). This equality holds for the first-order statements but not for second-, third-, fourth-, or higher-order statements. Therefore, mathematical logic can work with first-order statements of numbers, not with higher-order statements. Since "order" in logic means a hierarchy of concepts, properties, and values, therefore, mathematical logic also cannot work with the hierarchical constructions. It can only work with a one-tier reality.

Since reality has many tiers, therefore, limiting it to one tier would clearly limit mathematics to objects and disallow their properties and values. Mathematics solves this problem by redefining an object as a *set* of properties. An object is thereby replaced by two curly braces. For example, using set theory in classical mechanics, a particle is denoted by a pair of properties as {x, p}, where x is position and p is momentum.

Sets use the connector has to say that a particle *has* the property of position and momentum. Or, the property x has the value of 10 while the property p has the value of 15. Now we get a solution where the is connector is used only for equality while the has connector is used for set memberships. By this process, logic is restricted to first-order entities whereas set theory is used for all higher-order entities.

In mathematical logic, I cannot say that "the particle is 10" like I could say "the apple is red" in ordinary language. Instead, I have to say: "The particle has the property of position, the property has a value of 10". A strict hierarchy from the object to property to value is maintained by this construction.

The Problem of Quantum Mechanics

This construction, however, collapses in quantum mechanics when a quantum ensemble "collapses" into one state. That collapse is precisely equivalent to saying "the apple is red" for one time, place, situation, and person while saying "the apple is sweet" for another time, place, situation, and person. This collapse in which the whole (apple) becomes one part (red, round, or sweet) is possible in ordinary language but not in mathematical language. Thus, quantum mechanics cannot describe ordinary experience.

Quantum mechanics now resorts to assigning probabilities to different statements such as P (apple is red) = 0.1, P (apple is round) = 0.3, P (apple is sweet) = 0.2, etc. The whole reduces to one part for a given time, place, situation, and person, but this reduction is not universal truth. It is a spatial-temporal-situational-personal truth. By using probabilities, we make it appear like it is a universal truth.

However, despite this appearance, the set theoretic model of science is broken because all members in the set of apple := {red, round, sweet} are not observable at once. We cannot say that apple *has* some members is an objective truth if it is not true for all times, places, situations, and persons. With the collapse of objectivity and universal truth, everything beginning with logic collapses. But this problem is not understood because objective-universal truth is replaced by probabilities.

Reality as Non-Objective Potentials

To solve this problem, we have to revise the notion of reality as *potentials*. An object, under the potential way of thinking, is a collection of potentials, one of which is first-order object, some of which are second-order properties, many of which are third-order values of properties, and so on. An observation of these potentials requires the selection of some potentials by a choice, to produce *facts*. Sentences can pertain to the reality, the choice, or the facts. We have to know that these three kinds of statements are not identical.

For example, when we say that an apple is red, round, and sweet, we are talking about three potentials which can be observed one after another by some consciousness that uses a choice to experience them. At the point of observation, we can say that the apple is red, because three potentials—apple, color, red—have been activated at once. Strictly speaking, there is a hierarchy between them, so we should say that the apple has color which has redness. But there is no harm in saying that apple is red if we don't invert the proposition to claim that red is apple. Either type of connector works if we are careful.

However, there is another serious problem because there is nothing in logic that necessitates that apple is an object, color is a property, and red is the value of a property. For logic, color could be an object, red could be its property, and dark red could be the value. Similarly, an apple could be a property of the object fruit. Thus, we cannot fix what we mean by first-, second-, or third-order logic unless we say that there is indeed a first object relative to which all other entities are second, third, fourth, and so on. When we cannot fix the first-order entity then we cannot even use first-order logic universally because for someone else the same thing could be a second-, third-, or fourth-order entity.

This problem also requires us to treat reality as potentials. For instance, the apple being an object is just one of the potentials of the apple. The apple being a subset of the properties of fruit is yet another potential. Likewise, redness can potentially be an object, a property, a value, and so on. Everything is potentially infinite things, because it can potentially be treated as first-, second-, third-, or successive order truth for some time, place, situation, and person. It doesn't become a universal truth. Only that which is the original object remains the first-order truth universally.

Three Kinds of Incompatible Claims

We can illustrate the viewpoint of potentials by the idea of a face and a mask. The face is the object and the mask is a property. As successive masks cover a face, each mask can potentially be called a face for the next-level mask. For someone looking at the face covered by numerous masks, the third-order mask is required to know the second-order mask, which is required to know the first-order mask, which is required to know the face.

Thus, all properties, values, and other higher-order attributes described by second-, third-, and higher-order logics are like *masks* while the object described by first-order logic is like a face. When we see the face covered with the mask, we say that the face is the mask but what we really mean is that the face has a mask on. The mask on the face can change. At that point, the face would be known by the new mask, although what we really mean is that the face is now wearing a different mask.

In this face-mask reality paradigm, it is true that when we see the mask, there is a face behind it, so by the mask, we identify a unique face. It is also true that the mask is not truly the face. And it is true that the face can acquire many masks. Thus, we can make three kinds of claims: (a) the face has a mask, (b) the face has many masks, and (c) the face has all the masks but none of the masks exclusively have the face. With the is connectors, we can say: (a) the face is a mask, (b) the face is many masks, and (c) the face is all the masks but none of the masks is exclusively the face. The last claim is the denial of universal truth since the same face is known by many masks but none of the masks is the full truth of the face.

Refuting Some Misconceptions

The face-mask reality is called Brahman and Māyā in Vedic texts. It has been misinterpreted as truth and illusion, although there is indeed a sense in which the mask is an illusion and the face is the reality. The misunderstanding is that the mask is separate from the face, when the mask is actually a part of the face and has been produced or manifested from the face. The mask is one of the many personas of the face so it is reality. Since the masks are seen one by one and appear separate from each other, therefore, the illusion is the separation of the masks. All masks are aspects of the face.

This misunderstanding is clearly understood when we treat the face as a concept. For example, if mammal is the face then dog is one of the masks but there are other masks like cows and horses. The masks called dogs, cows, and horses are parts of mammal and yet faces of the mammal. The dogs, cows, and horses are not illusions although they are masks covering the mammal in the sense that we cannot see the complete mammal by seeing either dogs, cows, or horses. But while seeing a dog, horse, or cow we also cannot say that the mammal is invisible. The masks of dogs, cows, and horses reveal the mammal and yet not fully. Hence, the mask is neither fully an illusion nor fully the reality. The mask is just a later-order truth compared to the face. It cannot be equated to the original truth nor can it be called an illusion.

Seeing the mask means seeing diversity and seeing the face means seeing the unity. When both diversity and unity are seen, then the diversity ceases to be an illusion. The diversity appears as an illusion only if we think that the diversities are separate from each other and the face. But in the face-mask paradigm, each individual observer is a mask of a face and what he sees are also masks of a face. Those who can see the masks as an aspect of the face, are in knowledge. Others are in illusion. This means seeing oneself as simultaneously a part of the face and yet a covering of the complete face.

The three seemingly incompatible claims can therefore also be restated as: (a) there is a face, (b) there are many masks, and (c) the masks are at once a part of the face and the covering of the face. The inside of the mask is congruent with the face and the outside of the mask appears uniquely different. By this understanding Brahman becomes the whole truth and Māyā becomes an aspect of the whole truth.

Revisions to the Logical Paradigm

Aristotelian logic has no distinction between face and mask. What we see is the reality. Since we see many different things, therefore, there is diversity without a unity. In this logic of many separate things, there can be nothing common between two things—i.e., there can be no face behind the mask. Two things are either identical or different. They cannot be simultaneously identical and different. Each different thing must also be an independently existing reality rather than a potential to be seen.

Factually, this conception of reality applies only to the face and not to any of the masks. The face is the universal truth and the masks are the temporal, spatial, situational, and personal truths. The masks are neither false nor the universal truth. Therefore, universalist thinking is false for all the masks.

Since the mask can expand into more masks, hence, there are many tiers of truth. The first-order truth pertains to the face, the second-order truth pertains to the first mask, the third-order truth pertains to the second mask covering the first mask, and so on. The successive masks are objects because they are covered by successive masks. The successive masks are just masks because they have manifest from a face. Only the original face is just a face and not a mask. But the other masks are both faces and masks. Their being faces is responsible for their diversity and their being masks is responsible for their unity. The original face is inside each of the masks and yet the face is also outside of each of the masks.

The face-mask paradigm requires us to see many tiers of truth. The original face is the Absolute Truth and the successive masks are Relative Truths, parts of the Absolute Truth, and yet, Individual Truths. We have to treat the same thing as a Relative Truth, a Partial Truth, and an Individual Truth, and contrast it to the Absolute Truth, a Complete Truth, which is also an Individual Truth. One Individual Truth is Absolute, Complete, and Original. Other Individual Truths are Relative, Partial, and Derived. A Relative,

Partial, and Derived truth cannot be a thing-in-itself, defined by itself, for itself, and by itself. It is defined relative to the Absolute Truth. All thing-in-itself conceptions of truth become fundamentally flawed and false.

Vedic Theology Reduces to Logic

When we start talking about face and mask, the mask being a part of the face, and yet distinct from the face, the distinction between Absolute and Relative truth, the distinction between Whole and Partial truth, then the whole of Vedic philosophy is transformed into an exercise of an alternative logic. By logic, we mean the process by which the Absolute Truth becomes Relative Truths, or how the face produces many masks, enjoys wearing many masks, and reveals or hides different aspects of the face through those masks. This is not the logic of many independent truths. It is the logic of one Absolute Truth expanding into many Relative Truths that are *individual* truths but not *independent* truths.

Infinite individual truths merge into one Absolute truth—if they are just individual truths rather than independent truths. Infinite independent truths just remain infinite independent truths and no universal truth can ever be found except by saying that all independent truths are the same truth. Effectively, universalism operates by destroying diversity to establish a universal truth. However, the Vedic system embraces diversity, and establishes unity within it. Unity in diversity is not universal one truth.

Those who want to understand unity in diversity have to discard the logical thinking rooted in universal one truth. Their logic is a hindrance to understanding the Absolute Truth. Their ideas of reality are contrary to conceptions of face and mask. Their notions of objectivity are alien to the idea of potentiality and choice. Everything in Western thinking is a hindrance to understanding Vedic philosophy. If that thinking is discarded, then the whole of Vedic philosophy is nothing more than an exercise in logic. But it is not Aristotelian logic. Even the universalization of logic is a Western theme, not a Vedic one.

The Principle of Underdetermination

The Bhedābheda Mind-Body Doctrine

Many people equate the mind to the brain, based on the neuroscientific experiments, in which injecting electrical signals into the brain results in novel experiences. This equivalence is in no small measure the result of the mind-body duality created by Descartes and readily embraced by Christianity as the soul-matter duality. Literally everyone, since that time, has held that the negation of *duality* entails *identity*. This article discusses why this belief has no foundation, what the relation between mind and body is, why that relationship differs in the material and spiritual worlds, and how these differences are subsumed under the Bhedābheda doctrine.

According to this doctrine, mind and body are at once different and non-different. In the material world, the mind-body difference is that by observing the body you cannot know a person's thoughts, judgments, goals, values, emotions, and relationships. However, since thoughts, judgments, goals, values, emotions, and relationships have an effect on the body, therefore, mind and body are also non-different. In the spiritual world, by observing the body, we can know a person's mind, which means that mind and body are *equivalent*, and yet, because knowing that mental reality is not thinking, feeling, judging, valuing, intending, or relating in that way, hence mind and body are still different. Thus, mind and body are always different and non-different, although it is never mind-body duality or identity.

Percept-Concept Non-Equivalence

Let's begin with a simple distinction between percepts and concepts. If you don't think that percepts and concepts are two separate realities, don't worry; I'm not insisting that they are right now. I will establish the necessity of this realism as we go along. Right now, we just need an experiential distinction between percepts and concepts to begin discussing the general problem of conscious experience.

Philosophers for the last few centuries have tried to reduce all concepts to percepts, and they have always failed. The most overt of these attempts was Logical Positivism, which set out to prove that all concepts can eventually be reduced to percepts, and whatever cannot be so reduced must be a meaningless concept. They had hoped that ideas like beauty, justice, and morality were such meaningless concepts because we cannot reduce them to percepts. They did not realize that even a simple concept like a chair cannot be reduced to percepts, which is why Logical Positivism failed.

The reason is that chairs can have three, four, or six legs. There can be wooden or steel or plastic chairs. Some chairs can have a backrest and hand rest, while others may not. Some chairs can be fixed while others are revolving. Chairs can be designed for use in a garden, kitchen, offices, or bedrooms. As you can see, you can never reduce the concept of chair to a specific percept, because the concept has many incarnations. That, however, doesn't mean that the concept-percept association is arbitrary. Fire and water are not chairs. Although you can sit on a tiger or an elephant or a tree, these are not chairs.

Likewise, Willard Quine famously argued that percepts cannot be reduced to concepts because the same data or percept observation can be explained using many different concepts. Even if a concept explains the percepts, it doesn't mean the concept is true, because it might not explain other percepts. That problem then led to the thesis of falsification, namely, that theories are never verified, only falsified. The alternative theory that explains the new and old data would be a concept that will explain the same percept although in a different way. Hence, percepts are not reducible to concepts, in general.

But if we arrive at the perfect truth, then we can equate all percepts to concepts. For example, it is alright to equate red, round, and sweet to an apple, since from apple you can derive that it is red, round, and sweet. The knowing of apple is *summarized* knowledge and red, round, and sweet are *elaborated* knowledge. The summarized is still not identical to the elaborated, but since the elaborated can be derived from summarized, and vice versa, therefore, we can say that they are *equivalent*. This equivalence exists only if knowledge is perfect. Otherwise, it doesn't. For most of the remainder of this article, I will assume non-equivalence of percepts and concepts, and return to equivalence toward the end of the article.

Percept-Concept Underdetermination

If you think long and hard about this issue, you will conclude that *percepts and concepts underdetermine each other*. It doesn't mean that percepts and concepts are *independent*. And it doesn't mean that percepts determine concepts or concepts determine percepts. The situation is very nuanced.

Each percept tells us what the concept cannot be, although it doesn't tell us what it will be. For example, if you see something red and round, you cannot be sure whether it is an apple or nectarine. But you can be sure that it is not a banana. Similarly, each concept tells us what the percept cannot be, although it doesn't fix the percept. For example, when talking about a chair, we know for sure that it cannot be fluid, and it should not burn the person sitting on it. But you cannot precisely say what it will be.

This is the meaning of underdetermination—each percept will fix what the concept cannot be, and each concept will fix what the percepts cannot be, but we cannot infer one from the other. Hence, you cannot say that percepts are totally independent of concepts and don't have any role in deciding the concept, or vice versa. And you cannot say that percepts fully determine the concept or vice versa.

Why Underdetermination is Problematic

The problem is that you can never represent the relationship of underdetermination in logic or mathematics, using an equation of the type X = F(Y). If X is percepts and Y is concepts, then if F exists, Y must determine X. But if F doesn't exist, then X and Y are totally independent variables. Logic and mathematics force us into the dichotomy that X and Y are either *determined* or *independent*.

The relationship of underdetermination is neither one of determination nor one of independence. Hence, it can never be captured in conventional logic or mathematics. That makes it *inconceivable*.

Mind-body dualism says that mind and body are independent, and mind-body identity says that the body determines the mind. Both these positions are operating under the same idea of logic and mathematics, under which Mind = F(Body), such that mind-body identity insists that F exists, and mind-body dualism insists that F doesn't. Since logic is conceived in a binary manner, it always follows that F must either exist or not exist, which leads to a mutual exclusion of identity and duality. This binary mutual exclusion implies that if duality is somehow falsified, then identity must be implied.

Thus, mind-body dualism and mind-body identity are simply two opposing poles of the same binary dichotomy in which two things are either identical or independent. Now, if you show any relation between mind and body—e.g., by injecting electrical signals you get some sensations—then it must follow that mind and body are identical because, by mutual exclusion, they are *not* dualistic.

It is unimaginable how Western thinking has been so caught up in these dichotomies for centuries. But that is the fact, and we can see how it makes elementary ideas like underdetermination inexplicable.

Percept-Emotion Underdetermination

This problem is not limited to percepts and concepts. Rather, it can be extended to a wide variety of categories. For example, emotions underdetermine percepts and vice versa. Let's consider mental illnesses such as anxiety, depression, and PTSD. Since they have many common symptoms, therefore, the symptoms underdetermine the specific type of mental illness. For instance, all three can cause headaches, so merely by the percepts of headaches, you cannot determine the type of mental illness. This is one of the key reasons why each type of mental illness is often misdiagnosed as others.

Likewise, a given type of mental illness—e.g., depression—doesn't always create the same percepts. In some people, it can create disorders like overeating. In other cases, one may eat fine, but may not be able to digest the food. Thereby, mental illness doesn't fully determine the bodily symptoms.

Thereby, emotions underdetermine percepts and percepts underdetermine emotions. If you have a headache, you can rule out nail or beard growth as the cause. But you can't fix the cause. Likewise, if you have PTSD, you can rule out nail and beard growth as effects, but you can't fix the effects.

Extension to Other Experienced Categories

We can now generalize this problem of underdetermination to several categories. Within percepts themselves, we can say that observations of the knowledge senses don't fix the observation of the action senses, but the former *restricts* the latter, and vice versa. For example, a knife—with some definite shape, size, hardness, etc. obtained by the knowledge senses—does not fix the actions for which it can be employed: A knife can be used to cut vegetables, tighten screws, or attack a person.

Similarly, the actions of cutting vegetables, tightening screws, or attacking a person do not imply the presence of a knife; even a saw can cut vegetables, a screwdriver can tighten screws, and people can be attacked using guns. Again, you can say that a knife cannot be used for certain things, but you cannot say what it will be used for. Then, the things that it is used for can also be done by other things. Therefore, we can assert that the senses of knowledge and action underdetermine each other.

In the same way, we can extend this underdetermination to values, goals, and beliefs. Values restrict possible goals, but they don't fix the goals. The goals restrict possible values, but they don't fix the values. Goals and values restrict possible concepts and percepts, but they don't fix the concepts and percepts. Concepts and percepts restrict possible goals and values, but they don't fix the goals and values. Your beliefs restrict possible goals and values; however, the beliefs do not fix the goals and values.

Is Neuroscience Really a Science?

Let's say you insert an electrode into the brain and pass some current. That current is some percept, and the mental experience will be a concept. Since percept doesn't determine the concept, and yet, there is always a concept, therefore, every electrical current will produce a mental experience, although you cannot *predict* what it will be. Likewise, since the same current creates different experiences in different people, hence, you cannot explain why the same cause produces different effects in different people. In essence, you can neither make an accurate prediction nor explain the different experiences.

Similarly, electrical current is neither necessary to cause an experience (the experience can be caused in other ways) nor sufficient to cause an experience (because there is a range of experiences that can be created).

Thereby, neuroscience doesn't satisfy the traditional definition of science, because (a) you don't get accurate predictions, and (b) the explanations are neither necessary nor sufficient. Neuroscience is still considered a "science" by loosening its definition to *the prediction of a range of possibilities and impossibilities using a non-necessary and non-sufficient explanation.*

This idea has broad acceptance everywhere because it is true for most everything called "science" today. You will not find academics objecting to the problem, because everyone is in the same situation as a result of the problem of underdetermination. However, since the root cause of the problem is never explicitly stated, therefore, most people are unable to recognize how science is no longer what it was supposed to be at the dawn of Enlightenment. The Enlightenment dream about science has failed, and the new working definition of science is "whatever works to whatever extent". Of course, the public is never told about the failure of civilizational dreams, until the last hurrah is finally done. Hence, science is continuously marketed as something useful and worthy because at least it is something that is better than nothing. Calling it "not a science" will preempt funding, research, publications, conferences, journals, interviews, prestige, promotion, and tenure.

Modern science is like the British empire toward its end, organizing pompous displays of grandeur for the monarchy to make poor people think that it was still powerful when it was actually collapsing. Sweeping claims of science are like the pretentious displays of long-lost grandeur. They project strength to cover up the fact of a collapsing empire. One such claim is the mind-body identity (1) driven by a dualistic "either independent or determined" mutual exclusion, (b) ignoring the serious problem of underdetermination. That mind-is-the-brain assertion is the pretentious display of grandeur while the problem of underdetermination is the collapsing empire.

The Paradigm of Complementarity

The problem of conscious experience is incredibly complicated because it is defined by numerous categories that underdetermine each other. We can never solve that problem using the models of modern science. We can never reduce the explanation of all these categories to one category because each category is underdetermined by every other category. We can never predict the effects because the effects are underdetermined. Hence, sensation, action, concepts, beliefs, goals, and values, are *unique irreducible categories*. They are however not *mutually independent* in the sense that you cannot superimpose arbitrary values, goals, beliefs, concepts, sensations, and actions.

Your actions can tell us what your thoughts, beliefs, goals, and values are not. But we can never identify the precise thought, belief, goal, and value underlying the action. This is why in legal dramas, when the lawyers have circumstantial evidence, they try very hard to establish your mental state—i.e., your beliefs, values, thoughts, and goals—in order to get a conviction because actions alone won't.

It is far too tempting for me not to note that this is a general paradigm of six perspectives employed all over Vedic philosophy. It appears in the problem of Six Causes—why, how, what, when, where, and who. It appears in describing reality from six perspectives in the Six Systems of Philosophy. And it appears in our experience as the six-fold division into action, sensation, thought, belief, goal, and value. The last four are considered the Antaḥkaraṇa or the "internal instrument" and the first two are called the Sthūla-Sarīra or the "gross body". They can be loosely equated to the "mind" and "body" of Western nomenclature. And yet, they are neither mutually separate nor are they mutually identical.

We can rather use the term *complementarity* to describe their nature, which means that each of the six aspects underdetermines the other five; by knowing one of them, we can eliminate many possibilities about the other five, but we cannot fix the other five. However, by defining more and more of the six aspects, we keep *narrowing* the possibilities of what the remaining aspects can be because even more possibilities have been eliminated by the characterization of successive aspects of experience.

Complementarity in Yoga Practice

Therefore, by changing our sensations and actions, we can change our thoughts, beliefs, goals, and values. Conversely, by changing our thoughts, beliefs, goals, and values—or even one of them—we can change our sensations and actions. Any change made to any of the six aspects will have an effect on the remaining aspects. Thereby, spiritual progress can be made through a moral life, by dedicating ourselves to a superior goal, by the study and analysis of philosophy, by always thinking of God, by meditating on a sound using our knowledge senses, or by using our action senses for serving a great person.

Each of these constitutes a certain type of yoga practice, and they are all useful, because they are complementary, which means if we eliminate some activities from our life, then we restrict the possible thoughts, beliefs, goals, and values. Then, as we fix our life on some activities, then we restrict the possible thoughts, beliefs, goals, and values. Different people can focus on one of these more than others. Accordingly, by doing the thing that we can easily do, we make other things easier.

In the final analysis, we must change all six of them, but we can begin with whatever is convenient. As we progress, we can employ a complementary method to make further progress, because, as we have noted, these six aspects of experience are not separate, and yet, they are not also not identical.

For those more familiar with Vedic philosophy, this is the conclusion of Bhedābheda, which stands for "different and non-different". Bodily activity is certainly different from the philosophical study. But because philosophical study changes bodily activity, and vice versa, therefore they are non-different.

Pointless Mind-Body Debates

The fact is that tired and tiresome positions of mind-body duality and identity are both false. Empirical evidence shows how both are false—since bodily changes trigger a mental change, therefore, mind and body are not separate; likewise, since bodily change cannot predict the mental change, therefore, they are not identical. The problem is that we don't have a conceptual framework to understand this empirical evidence. The materialist advances a false agenda about identity although he cannot establish identity. He is successful because people imagine that the only alternative is mind-body dualism. And the dualist advances a separation although he cannot explain the neuroscientific evidence.

In these debates, each side thinks that their position is correct, and whatever doesn't fit into that position, is either irrelevant, can be explained away, or simply doesn't exist. This makes the debate endless because you can either keep arguing forever or just shift from one side to another.

Futility is the essence of mind-body debates based on the false dichotomy of identity vs. duality, as both these positions are false. Both sides operate on the same binary logic, and they never employ the principle of underdetermination, which then leads to complementarity. Without these general principles, we can never progress into the understanding of the numerous types of complementarities.

Facet Contradiction Causes Material Change

Through the study of Vedic philosophy, and its confirmation in our ordinary experience, we can say that the soul has six complementary cognitive aspects, called action, sensation, thought, belief, goal, and value. Similarly, there are six emotional and relational aspects. Each aspect is sometimes *dominant* which means that it is the cause of changes to the remaining aspects. Then sometimes it is *subordinate* which means that it changes as an effect of the changes to one or more of the other aspects.

In the material world, however, the different aspects of the soul are never *consistent,* and the soul's experience evolves to create greater inner harmony. This simply means that we try to align our values, goals, beliefs, and thoughts with each other, and with sensation and action. The entire life is a struggle for this alignment, because sometimes the world forces sensations and actions inconsistent with our values, goals, beliefs, and thoughts, and changes one or more of them, creating an inner conflict. Then to resolve that inner conflict, we act on the world, which produces consequences, which then lead to new contradictions, and the attempt to resolve the inner contradictions.

As we have discussed at the beginning, no aspect of conscious experience is equivalent to the others. This non-equivalence is the evidence of *falsity*. If red, round, and sweet, are correctly identified as an apple, then there would be equivalence although not identity, because the concept of apple is summarized, and percepts of red, round, and sweet are elaborations of that summary. Truth makes aspects equivalent although not identical. Falsity makes the aspects internally contradictory and causes changes. If this falsity pertains to the self, it can also be called the ignorance of the true nature of the self.

Facet Reconciliation Causes Spiritual Eternity

However, if the true nature of the self is known, then the inner contradiction is resolved, and each person is at peace with themselves. In this situation, each aspect is equivalent (although not identical) to other aspects. Vedic texts identify three further subdivisions within this state of equivalence.

In the first subdivision, the end of inner and outer conflict entails the end of experience; only the self is known, and the self is at peace with itself. Thereby, the person is absorbed in the self. In the second subdivision, the end of inner and outer conflict means a world of perfect cooperation, although with freedom. Freedom means the absence of dependence. Everyone is fully capable, self-reliant, and self-satisfied, and yet, they cooperate as equals rather than compete for domination. This is a perfectly egalitarian society. Finally, in the third subdivision, freedom is replaced by mutual dependence based on loving attraction. Nobody thinks that they are capable, self-reliant, or self-satisfied. Rather, they are so strongly attracted to others that they are helplessly bound and inseparable from each other.

Thus, there are four worlds—(a) the material world of inner and outer conflicts, (b) the self-absorbed world called Brahman devoid of conflict, (c) the self-reliant but cooperative world of freedom called Vaikuṇtha, and (d) the loving and dependent world called Goloka. All these worlds are based on the multifaceted nature of the soul. The difference is that the facets can be (a) contradictory and conflicting, (b) reconciled and silenced, (c) reconciled and cooperative, and (d) reconciled and dependent.

We have to remember that opposites need not always conflict. They conflict if they limit and obstruct each other. They cooperate if they allow each other freedom. And they are the basis of mutual attraction. Three out of these four worlds are free of conflict and contradiction; only the material world is conflictual. Hence, the material world is called *duality* while the other three are called *non-duality*.

Mind-Body Equivalence and Non-Equivalence

Contradictions between the aspects make the aspects non equivalent, but reconciliation between them makes them equivalent. This simply means that in the material world, you cannot know a person's mind completely by looking at their body; hence, you can say that there is a difference between mind and body. However, in the spiritual world, you know a person's mind completely by looking at their body, because the body is equivalent (although not identical) to the mind. The mind-body equivalence is that you know what a person is thinking, feeling, valuing, believing, perceiving, and doing by just looking at their body. However, the two are not identical because knowing what they feel is not the same as feeling it.

In the spiritual world, everyone has "bared their soul" and there is no "mental privacy" or ignorance of the other person's nature. And yet, there is "mental privacy" because *knowing* others is not *being* them.

The material world is mind-body complementarity and underdetermination, due to which you see a person's body but you don't exactly know who they are. The spiritual world is mind-body equivalence without a mind-body identity, such that you know exactly who they are without becoming them. In neither case do we get mind-body dualism or mind-body identity, hence these are totally false.

The Ubiquity of the Bhedābheda Principle

Both spiritual and material worlds can be studied scientifically if we grasp the principles of equivalence and non-equivalence. However, this science cannot be captured in binary logic because non-equivalence defies identity vs. duality dichotomy, and equivalence still doesn't imply mind-body identity. Both doctrines are various forms of Bhedābheda. Complementarity with underdetermination is one kind of Bhedābheda, and equivalence without identity is another kind of Bhedābheda. Since both forms of Bhedābheda go beyond binary thinking, therefore, before we can explain this science, we have to understand Bhedābheda via the analysis of experience, philosophy, and the practice of yoga.

Bhedābheda can be known via the analysis of ordinary experience, philosophical reasoning, and mystical practices, and each aspect reinforces the others. Bhedābheda can be explained easily to everyone by exploring the relationship between the facets of experience. It can be arrived at via complex philosophy using concepts like underdetermination, complementarity, dominant-subordinate, cooperation vs. reconciliation, etc. And it can be confirmed by the practice of yoga, as we get more contentment, then voluntary cooperation with the devotees of the Lord, and finally loving dependence on the Lord.

The principle of Bhedābheda through these varied processes tells us about the nature of the soul, how our experience evolves in the material world, and the differences between the various worlds. Finally, if we understand Bhedābheda, then we can easily grasp all problems of modern science and how they are stuck in intractable contradictions and paradoxes, and what the solution to these problems is. This is the power of Bhedābheda that we can succinctly capture everything in a single word—Bhedābheda.

Observer-Dependent Ontology, Epistemology, and Logic

Summary and Overview of the Article

The Vedic conception of reality doesn't comport with the Western ideas of reality widely enshrined in modern science and taken for granted by almost everyone reading the Vedic texts at present. Reality, by definition, in the West is something observer-independent. Anything personal and private is by definition not part of reality. In contrast, reality is observer-dependent in the Vedic texts. Even those parts of reality that seem observer-independent (i.e., observable by our senses) are the body of an observer. Without the observer, the body will not exist. Rather, the body is developed based on the observer's history and is hence observer-dependent. But since the history is not the observer, therefore, identifying an observer through the body is called māyā which means "that which is not". Most people studying Vedic texts skip the understanding of māyā and assume that all reality is observer-independent.

In this article, I will discuss the Western ideas on reality and what is wrong with those ideas, even as everyone takes them for granted. We will discuss how all epistemologies based on these ideas have systematically failed leading to the abandonment of the search for truth in science and its replacement by *pragmatism*, which means claiming victory in the quest for truth through success in technology.

We will then discuss alternative ideas of reality found in Vedic texts and how they lead to a complete epistemology. I will try to contrast the Vedic ideas of reality to their Western scientific counterparts. The article will be useful to those familiar with Western ideas of reality to see their contrast with the Vedic ideas. The article may open the eyes of those who assume that "reality" means the same everywhere.

The Birth and Demise of Western Realism

Realism is defined in Western philosophy in three ways: (a) reality is that which exists outside the observer, (b) reality is that which works without an observer's observation, and (c) reality is objective, which means it is not open to personal interpretation. Realism has many further variations such as Naïve Realism and Scientific Realism. The latter has many divisions that we will briefly discuss below.

Naïve Realism says that the reality that exists outside the observer in just the same way as the observer knows it. For example, if you see a red and round apple, reality is a red and round apple. The redness, roundness, and appleness of the thing seen by the observer aren't a subjective view of the observer. They are also the very nature of reality. In stark contrast, Scientific Realism says that what we call redness, roundness, and appleness is an illusion created by the observer's senses and the mind. The reality is instead mathematical objects (such as particles and waves) and instrument-measurable properties (such as position and momentum). The world is not anything like the way we see it.

Naïve Realism is problematic because everyone doesn't perceive the world in the same way. The shades of colors can seem darker or lighter to different observers. The tastes can seem more or less sweet or bitter to different observers. Two observers might disagree about whether something is a sedan or a wagon. To uphold Naïve Realism, we have to say that one of many observers seeing the world differently is seeing it correctly. Or, we might decide to vote to determine where the majority opinion tilts. Either way, we would have refuted the idea that the world exists outside the observer just the way we see it. At most, we would be able to say that some observers know the reality while others are illusioned. This is not necessarily a false view. It is just hard for anyone who is called "illusioned" to accept it.

Enlightenment thinking chose to move away from Naïve Realism. It tried to replace human sensations with instrument measurements and human concepts with mathematical constructs. This move slightly reduced the problem of Naïve Realism but did not totally eliminate it. For example, who is to say that some instruments are better than other instruments—a counterpart of the question of whose senses are giving the true nature of reality? Who is to say that some mathematical constructs are better than others—a counterpart of the question of whether someone calls the same thing as a sedan or a wagon?

Enlightenment thinkers solved this problem through the *institutionalization* of knowledge. It says that measuring instruments will be selected by a committee of informed people who shall designate some instruments as standards to be used for all measurements. The mathematical constructs will be selected by a committee of informed people who shall designate them as the preferred models of reality. The scientific method of institutionalization of knowledge borrowed heavily from established methods of the Church. Just as Christianity had institutionalized religion through the Church, similarly, Enlightenment thinkers institutionalized science through a reformed and reformulated system of universities.

Institutionalization doesn't guarantee truth. Debate among well-intentioned members of the institution may eliminate obvious mistakes, but every institution has an ideology. Nobody knows if that ideology is true and the ideology is therefore accepted on faith. Scientific Realism chose an ideology of materialism, reductionism, and mechanism. Materialism says that reality comprises objects that exist independent of observers. Reductionism says that complex things must necessarily comprise simpler things. Mechanism says that the objects and simple things conceived by science must follow mathematical laws.

The ideology of science has now comprehensively failed. Mechanism is false because mathematical systems cannot deal with sentences in the same way they deal with objects. A sentence has a meaning, a reference, and a truth value, but an object has none of those. If these are described using numbers, then contradictions are created because a number now has many interpretations. Therefore, a world comprising sentences cannot be modeled by mathematics. Even the most rudimentary cognitive system is outside mathematical reach. Reductionism is false because we cannot always separate complex things into simpler things. A system that cannot be so reduced is called quantum entangled. Materialism is false because the outcome of experiments depends on the observer's state. We cannot call the outcome of an instrument measurement an observer-independent state of reality because other observers performing the same type of measurement using the same instrument come up with different results.

After the comprehensive failure of Scientific Realism, there arose a new breed of philosophies that tried to rescue science from its quagmire—Operationalism, Instrumentalism, and Pragmatism. Operationalism says that words like mass or energy have no meaning outside of the instrument we use to measure them. Instrumentalism says that a theory that aggregates such concepts is just a tool whose worth has to be measured not by whether the theory is true or false but by whether it explains and predicts the data. Pragmatism says that the value of science is that it contributes to socio-economic-political progress.

The main conclusion was that reality and truth are not the focus of science. The focus was building technology, fueling economic growth, reducing social disparity, and bringing political stability. Nobody who knows science at present says that science gives us the nature of reality or the absolute truth. Their argument for the continued funding of science is that it has improved the lives of people. Along with this shift, those parts of science that do not explicitly contribute to such goals started to be defunded.

The Birth and Demise of Western Idealism

The demise of Scientific Realism has led to the revival of interest in Idealism which was considered dead and useless during Enlightenment. Idealism is defined in three ways: (a) whatever we call the world exists inside the observer, (b) the world in the observer works due to its observation by the observer, and (c) the world inside the observer necessarily depends on the observer's personal choices or will.

Idealism arose from the problems of Realism. Factually, (a) we can never know reality as it exists outside our observation because we have no access to a world behind the observation, (b) everything inside our observation is subject to our interpretation and defined by our choices, even if those include the choice of measuring instruments and scientific theories, and (c) nothing works the same for all observers even if the differences across different instruments and measurements seem negligible in most cases.

However, Idealism has a profound flaw: (a) while living our lives, we don't enjoy suffering, (b) we don't voluntarily create our suffering, and (c) we want to get out of suffering. Therefore, in so far as there is suffering caused by the world, the world cannot merely be our choice, interpretation, or creation. The world should instead (a) be forced upon us, (b) exist outside our control since nobody willingly creates their personal suffering, and (c) must, therefore, be accepted as an external reality.

The falsification of Idealism, however, doesn't end its allure. It has given rise to a new breed of hybrid Realism-Idealism theories that can be called Simulated Reality or Virtual Reality philosophies. The rising popularity of such themes can be seen from the fact that popular magazine articles that assert that we must be living in a Simulated or Virtual Reality go completely unchallenged. A thought experiment called Brain in the Vat says that we could be brains submerged in a beaker filled with some preservative fluid with probes connecting different parts of the brain to a computer that injects electrical signals to create the illusion of a rich worldly experience when the only reality outside the brain is a beaker, preservative fluid, probes, wires, and a computer with a programmer writing control software.

Thought experiments like Brain in the Vat cannot be refuted through any kind of argument or evidence because all arguments and evidence assume that there is truth, justice, and goodness in the world. If truth, justice, and goodness are replaced by delusion, injustice, and malevolence, then we have no foundation on which to base our arguments and evidence. Therefore, thought experiments like Brain in the Vat are irrefutable. There is no evidence for them. But there is no counterargument against them either.

Simulated Reality, Virtual Reality, and Brain in the Vat are not Idealism because there is something outside the observer. Since we can never know what is outside the observer, therefore, these theories are consistent with the failure of Scientific Realism. Even though we might reject Idealism because it is contrary to suffering, the fact is that most people trying to escape suffering fail in their endeavors. Failure is not the end of the story. Instead, a theory is created to rationalize the failure—our failure to understand reality and escape suffering is not our fault but the fault of the *system* that put us in it.

The human mind has an exceptional need for rationalization. It rationalizes failures too. People are drawn to Simulated Reality because it rationalizes their failure to find the truth and escape suffering. We cannot find the truth because Simulated Reality makes it impossible to know the truth. We cannot escape suffering because Simulated Reality doesn't allow us to escape its control. The need to rationalize failure makes Simulated Reality inevitable especially because there is no counterargument against it.

Simulated Reality is a form of Nihilism in which life has no purpose other than helpless suffering or pleasure and death is nothing more than whatever puts an end to this suffering and pleasure. Nihilism is not the rejection of reality—after all, the Brain in the Vat is some reality. It is not the rejection of the self—after all, the self may be enjoying and suffering through the Brain in the Vat. Nihilism is a rejection of the *value* in asking questions of truth, justice, and happiness. It is not that answers to such questions exist that we don't know about. It is also not that the questions are unanswerable. It is rather that the questions have been comprehensively answered by denying that they are meaningful questions.

Nihilism creates a sense of helplessness and hopelessness. You cannot find the truth on your own. You cannot put an end to your suffering. You cannot choose to create the reality of your liking. You exist because you haven't died. You have no control over your life. The West has now formally entered the stage of boundless intellectual Nihilism. We see it in the cynical attitude with which every proposal is received as merely a person's opinion. There will be no end to social decline unless we can re-establish the possibility of finding the truth and escaping suffering clearly and unambiguously.

An Overview of Vedic Realism-Idealism

Most of us can accept that we exist, seek happiness, and work to create happiness for ourselves through our actions. We don't need to know anything other than ourselves to accept these claims, provided they are true of us. Of course, they are not universally true for every person. Some people are too lazy to do anything, even for themselves. Some people are too masochistic to seek their own happiness. Some people are too asleep to even perceive their own existence. Outside of these exceptions, for most people, our existence, our quest for happiness, and our readiness to work for our happiness can be taken for granted. Each person can decide if this is true for them. If it is, then it is confirmed for them.

Assuming you are aware of your existence, seek happiness, and are prepared to work for that happiness, you would seek the company of like-minded people. You would not want the company of lazy, asleep, or masochistic people. They deserve to live with their own kind. You may be awake, but not seeking pleasure, and not working towards it. You would seek the company of like-minded people. You would not like to be with people who are asleep, masochistic, or working to hurt themselves. You will also not prefer the company of people who are awake, seeking happiness, and working toward it.

The Vedic system elevates this simple idea of people living with like-minded people to a universal fact. The birds of the same feather are flocked together. The soul with the bird mentality is born as a bird to live with birds. The soul with an elephant mentality is born as an elephant to live with other elephants. The demons and demigods live on different planets. Those with the human mentality are born into a human body to live with other humans. They don't mix with all other humans. Instead, they are separated by societies, cultures, religions, ideologies, professions, and interests for the most part, mainly because they want to live with like-minded people. There are infinite different universes to facilitate different kinds of lives. Those who transcend the material world, live with those of their mentality on planets suited for a different life with that mentality. Segregation of life forms based on their mentality is the big picture of Vedic cosmology. It describes infinite realms, universes, planets, and classes within which life forms with different mentalities live together with others of a compatible mentality.

Within this big picture of reality, there is a minor picture of different kinds of living forms interacting occasionally. Some people keep dogs and cats as pets. Some people tend to domestic animals. Some people ride horses. Some people work in circuses with different animals. Due to globalization, people of different cultures, societies, religions, and ideologies have begun mixing recently. However, even as we see the mixing of different life forms, we find that they generally prefer to live within a species if what they want is available within it. The Vedic texts explain that a desired mixing between different kinds of living forms is the result of their previously diversified mentalities and the result of prior good actions. When mixing is undesirable, it is forced due to the results of one's previous bad actions. Still, the diversity of experience created by such mixing is infinitesimal compared to the diversity across planets, universes, and realms. Segregation of life across the cosmos is infinitely bigger in comparison. The minor picture of life forms mixing with each other is either the fulfillment of the desires in a previously diversified mentality due to good actions in the past, or it is the result of undesirable mixing as a result of previous bad actions.

The big picture of the cosmos and the segregation of life forms indicates that there is no universal reality. Consequently, there is no counterpart of the word "reality" in Vedic texts because everyone has a different personal reality. The word "reality" appears in the Western lexicon under the assumption that there is some universal truth regarding all times, places, circumstances, and persons. That idea is alien to the Vedic system.

We find ourselves in a world because of our previously acquired nature and the results of our actions. If we were radically different, then we would be in another world. The way we perceive, interpret, and understand the world is also the result of our previously acquired nature. If we begin perceiving, interpreting, and understanding the world differently, then we will gradually develop a different nature, and upon death enter a different world. The process of the change of life, change of species, and change of place is just birds of the same feather flocking together. There is a fixed place for each kind of bird. There is a simple process of flocking the birds.

Karma, reincarnation, transmigration across species, and the existence of varied life across the cosmos are features of the Vedic system that even newcomers can see from miles away. We don't need a specific sūtra, verse, or doctrinal name to spell it out. Every Vedic text presents such descriptions. But we have to assimilate this idea better. We have to understand that what we see in this species, life, and planet, is not an observer-independent reality. Rather, what we see, why we see, how we see, where we see, and when we see are the result of who we are. These may not be our eternal unchangeable nature. But it is our current nature. The world simply mirrors who we are. We are in a specific world because of who we are. If we evolve, then we will change our world.

We can call this *Observer-Dependent Realism*. There is a world of living forms with commonalities. Those forms are not confined within my awareness because I don't control what they do. They have to be accepted as distinct realities because they are beyond my control. Idealism in the sense of something that exists solely in my awareness has to be therefore rejected. But that rejection doesn't establish an observer-independent reality. The reality that I see is that which conforms to my nature. If I had a different nature, then I would see a different reality. Therefore, my reality is not universal. My nature filters all that exists cosmically into an infinitesimally small subset that corresponds to my nature.

We are not blank slates passively observing the world from a place that is nowhere and nowhen. We are actively filtering the cosmos during observation to see something compatible with our nature. Our senses, minds, and intellects are filters through which we see limited parts of the cosmos in a limited way. The study of senses, minds, and intellects has to begin with the idea that they filter the complete truth and present a narrow picture, which we arrogantly elevate to the status of universal reality.

Humility is required to understand that there are infinite other types of realities that we don't see presently. Humility is required to accept that our senses, minds, and intellects are acting as filters of the complete truth. Humility is required to acknowledge that we need to change the filters of our senses, minds, and intellects to even see what is being filtered right now. The problem of not seeing things found in other parts of the cosmos cannot be solved if we insist on using the same filters.

This problem is sometimes called *The Frog in the Well*. We are frogs in the small well we see presently. We are in the well because we are frogs. If we were bigger fish, we would be in the river or the ocean. But the frog in the well thinks that even rivers and oceans are just like wells. The frog cannot imagine that the fish in the ocean see millions of different species of life that remain invisible to the frog in the well. Observer-Dependent Realism is a fancy term for the simple idea stated by the frog in the well.

An Overview of Vedic Epistemology

Modern Western epistemology was developed to counteract the problem of sin in Christianity. The problem of sin says that we are all sinners (having inherited the sins of the sinful Adam and Eve) and therefore we cannot know the truth by ourselves. The truth has to be revealed to us by God and His messiahs after which we have to simply accept their conclusions on faith. Meanwhile, the priests were secretly crafting the "revealed truth" calling themselves the ones uniquely blessed by the Spirit of God. Enlightenment thinkers decided to break away from this trap of sinning, being blessed by a spirit, and revelation. They postulated that every human can know the whole truth by reason and observation.

All Vedic epistemologies accept reasoning, observation, and revelation as methods to the truth. In contrast, Western scientific epistemology rejects revelation and Abrahamic religious epistemology rejects reasoning and observation. Despite this stark contrast, nearly all modern students of science and religion have disregarded the methods of reasoning and observation and equated the Vedic texts to revelation (if not something much worse, such as fanciful imagination and speculation). Little to no effort has been made to explain how reasoning, observation, and revelation work together. The Western science-religion methodological dichotomy is always taken for granted.

Therefore, let's spend a moment trying to understand how the Vedic epistemology reconciles reasoning, observation, and revelation. To do that, we need to distinguish the *discovery* of truth from the *verification* of truth. Revelation pertains to the discovery of truth while reasoning and observation pertain to the verification of truth. There is a famous P≠NP problem in computer science. It says that we require non-polynomial (NP) time to discover the truth while we need polynomial (P) time to verify the truth. An example of a computer password can be given. Discovering the correct password through trial and error requires non-polynomial time but verifying the password requires polynomial time. Revelation is like telling a person the password after which they can verify the correctness of the password through reasoning and observation. Revelation, reasoning, and observation all require polynomial time.

Reasoning and observations can be further divided into—(a) what we can think and perceive under the current senses, minds, and intellects, and (b) what we can think and perceive if the filters in the current senses, minds, and intellects were removed or changed. Accordingly, there are grades of verification by reasoning and observation. Some things can be verified using current senses, minds, and intellects. If that establishes trust in the revelation, then one can pursue the path of removing or changing the filters in the senses, mind, and intellect, to confirm that even more revelation can be verified. The process culminates in the conclusion—after the progressive removal of current filters—that every revelation can be confirmed either by unfiltered or appropriately filtered senses, minds, and intellects.

This is *Observer-Dependent Epistemology*. Every revelation cannot be verified by every sense, mind, and intellect. However, every revelation can be verified by every person, because the person is not the sense, mind, or intellect. The former is the person seeing and the latter is the goggles of seeing. We change the goggles to see something different. Since the reality we see depends on the goggles we wear, therefore, epistemology is observer-dependent. However, that confirmation is neither confined to some observer, nor does it have to be accepted on blind faith, nor can it be gotten by everyone without changing goggles. Observer-Dependent Epistemology is simply a fancy name for trying to change oneself to see what one cannot see right now. What we see is not common for all observers. It is limited to those who want to see, will endeavor to change their goggles of filtering, and use them to see in a new way.

Before we see something new, we learn to see whatever we see right now in a new way. Some new ways are better while others are worse. The better way of seeing predicts and explains more data than the worse way of seeing. Therefore, we can also ladder the better and worse ways of seeing by the capacity to predict and explain more or less data. We always introduce a new way of seeing based on the fact that it explains and predicts more data. We establish that this new way of seeing is already better with the currently available data before we ask anyone to pursue this way of seeing to its logical conclusion. The Observer-Dependent Epistemology therefore moves slowly unlike the leaps of faith made in speculative sciences and religions. We are not interested in quick wins. We want to establish that a new way of seeing is a pervasively better way of seeing and the old ways of seeing must therefore be discarded.

Vedic epistemology is a trust-but-verify system of knowledge. It is not the Abrahamic religious system of trust without verification. It is not the modern scientific system of verification without trust. Bundling Vedic epistemology with the epistemologies of modern science or Abrahamic religions is a fundamental category error. Without knowing all the categories, we are likely to make such erroneous judgments.

Effects of Vedic Realist Epistemology

A grounding in the theories of reality and epistemology in the Vedic system is necessary to understand all other descriptions. These include the descriptions of Prakṛti in Sāñkhya that present the nature of sense objects, senses, mind, intellect, and even further personal levels of reality. The basic principle is that we have to understand everything in three ways if we want to understand it completely. These three ways can be called perceiving, generating, and filtering, based on what we have discussed so far.

Let's begin with our senses. The senses generate dreams while we are sleeping, and they can generate hallucinations while we are awake. The senses also perceive the truth. Finally, the senses filter the reality to conform to their nature. Every sense cannot perceive everything even if it exists. We don't have to be shocked by this idea. Thermometers cannot measure speed and speedometers cannot measure temperature. Material instruments are capable of measuring specific properties only. Each instrument is capable of measuring to a different level of accuracy. We cannot use a meter to measure millimeter lengths. All material instruments spuriously generate measurement results even when nothing is being measured. They are just like the hallucinations and dreams in the senses. Therefore, even ordinary instruments measure reality, generate reality, and filter reality. Our senses also perceive, generate, and filter. The difference is only that senses deal in qualities while instruments deal in quantities.

Similarly, the mind generates thoughts, which we call creativity. The mind perceives thoughts in other minds, which we call sixth sense intuition. The mind filters reality to what it is interested in. Everyone is not interested in science, philosophy, sports, music, movies, or literature. Those things may exist in the world but the mind filters them to see what it is interested in. The mind blocks ideas alien to its culture, religion, and society. Due to the filtering of the mind, people may not understand each other. Modern psychology uses the idea of *unconscious bias* to describe how people attend to what they want to attend to, ignore what they are not interested in, and interpret others based on their preconceived notions.

Every element or component in Sāñkhya possesses this tripartite nature of senses and the mind. The intellect generates truths, perceives truths, and filters truths. The ego generates intentions, perceives intentions, and filters intentions. The mahattattva, or the moral sense, generates values, perceives values, and filters values. The tripartite nature of senses and minds pervades the entire psyche.

The same tripartite nature of perceiving, generating, and filtering exists in the elements that constitute the gross body. Sāñkhya describes how in the process of the creation of the world, the Ether generates Air, the Air generates Fire, Fire generates Water, and Water generates Earth. It then describes how in the process of the dissolution of the world, Water absorbs Earth, Fire absorbs Water,

Air absorbs Fire, and Ether absorbs Air. What is not discussed, but can be understood just like the other elements, is that these five elements also filter other elements due to which elementary properties don't get mixed up into one complex property. The complex property can always be partitioned into elementary properties. The taste, touch, smell, sound, and sight don't get mixed into one property. They remain distinct.

In physics, the filtering property of matter is seen in the mutual independence of physical properties such as mass and charge. Applying an electromagnetic field to a mass particle doesn't change the mass and applying a gravitational field to a charge particle doesn't change the charge. A charge particle moves in a gravitational field as if moving in empty space and a mass particle moves in an electromagnetic field as if moving in empty space. The filtering property of matter is therefore taken for granted in modern physics. What doesn't exist in modern physics is the perceiving and generating property of matter.

Sāñkhya emphasizes the perceiving and generating properties of matter and the filtering property is simply taken for granted. It should be noted that these three properties of matter are not mutually independent in Sāñkhya. That is, when properties are mixed, they don't always remain independent. However, that is a deeper issue that we will not get into here as it will distract us from our focus.

The tripartite way of looking at everything appears in three varied descriptions of the chitta, when it is described as (a) the generator of waves just like an ocean, (b) the reflector of images just like a mirror, and (c) a blocker of an observer's vision just like dirty goggles. Chitta perplexes people because we are not accustomed to anything that can be simultaneously called an ocean, a mirror, and goggles. However, this is not so perplexing if we know that everything is a perceiver, a generator, and a filter. The chitta is an ocean because it is a generator. The chitta is a mirror because it is a perceiver. The chitta is goggles because it is a filter. A tripartite approach is necessary to understand the meaning of chitta.

The Three Modes of Sāñkhya Philosophy

The basic thesis of why one thing is three things at once has deep roots in the rest of Vedic philosophy. Prakṛti, for example, is described as comprising three qualities or guna called Sattva, Rajas, and Tamas. Sattva-guna contributes to the perceptual capacity, Rajo-guna contributes to the generative capacity, and Tamo-guna contributes to the filtering capacity. For example, a mind with Tamo-guna prominence filters everything and is therefore said to be asleep. A mind with Rajo-guna prominence is preoccupied with self-generated thoughts and is said to be distracted. A mind with Sattva-guna prominence is awake but silent and is said to be an alert perceiver. The three modes are mutual opposites of each other.

- Sattva is neither asleep nor distracted, hence opposed to both tamas and rajas
- Rajas is neither asleep nor alert, hence opposed to both tamas, and sattva
- Tamas is neither awake nor distracted, hence opposed to both sattva and rajas

By different prominences of sattva, rajas, and tamas, many kinds of sense objects, senses, minds, intellects, egos, and moral senses are produced, with different capacities for perceiving, generating, and filtering. A combination of these capacities then becomes numerous mind-body complexes of a person, which are then aggregated into different realms like birds of the same feather flocking together.

The logic that describes the senses, mind, intellect, ego, moral sense, and then the body compatible with the observer's cognitive apparatus, is *Observer-Dependent Logic*. The logic that describes the body independent of the observer's cognitive apparatus is Observer-Independent Logic. Aristotelian logic is Observer-Independent Logic. The logic involved in Sāñkhya is Observer-Dependent Logic. The former type of logic describes how something is either inside or outside something else. The latter type of logic deals with how the world is both inside and outside the senses. The world inside the senses is at once one with the senses and distinct from them. We can call it non-binary logic.

We cannot conceptualize the three modes of Prakṛti in Aristotelian binary logic because (a) one thing has to be just one thing and not three things, (b) one thing cannot be opposite things at once, and (c) nothing can be neither opposite such as asleep and awake. Two opposite things can be added to each other without canceling each other. The uncancelled sum of opposites can generate those opposites. The non-binary logical properties of the three modes of Prakṛti are inconceivable within binary logical thinking. That doesn't mean they are inconceivable per se. The problem of conceivability is created by Aristotelian logic.

The Three Aspects of Vedic Personhood

The three qualities of Sāñkhya are not the only tripartite ways of thinking in the Vedic system. There is also the tripartite description of a person as sat-chit-ānanda. Everything in the Vedic system is these three properties of personhood, which means that everything is a person. For example, based on this tripartite distinction of personhood, whatever people called "matter" in modern science or ordinary thinking is described in three ways as Śakti, Prakṛti, and Māyā. Śakti is the *sat* aspect of material nature, Prakṛti is the *chit* aspect of material nature, and Māyā is the *ānanda* aspect of material nature.

The Śākta texts emphasize Śakti, the Vaiṣṇava texts emphasize Prakṛti, and the Śaiva texts emphasize Māyā. This emphasis is relative. No text excludes the discussion of the other two. But the subject matter is so complex that they have been separated into different schools quite like the departments of physics, chemistry, and biology are separated in modern academics. Practically nobody at present says that the departments of physics, chemistry, and biology must be giving contradictory theories of reality. But almost everyone at present says that Śāktism, Śaivism, and Vaiṣṇavism must be incompatible schools.

In modern academics, dozens of departments study different secular subjects. One department of religion studies all the religions together. Within the religious study departments, the study of the Vedic system remains almost an afterthought, a box that you have to tick to prevent the appearance of bias. No religious studies department has to date spent any effort in trying to understand the different concepts of personhood. They take the Western definition of personhood—as someone with rights and capable of negotiating contracts—as the only theory of personhood. Since rights and contracts are the subject matter of politics and law, therefore, theories of personhood come out of law and political science departments rather than religious studies departments. Religions simply assume the legal and political definition of personhood, rather than delve into the spiritual meaning of personhood. God, in Abrahamic religions, for example, is defined as a person who enters into a legal contract with the whole of humanity, in contrast to humans who generally have limited contracts with fewer persons.

Given the abject neglect of the study of personhood and capitulation to a political and legal dogma about personhood that originated in Jewish Law, there is little understanding of how a person is defined differently in the Vedic system. Then the idea that everything in the cosmos is a person because it originates in a Supreme, Complete, and Original Person, also escapes notice and discussion.

Rivers, mountains, oceans, lands, and planets are persons in the Vedic system. Since a deity made of stone, wood, or metal can embody a Supreme Person, therefore, seemingly dead things can also be persons. In the Ramayana, Ahilya was cursed to become a stone until she was touched by Lord Ramachandra's feet. The Vāstu Śāstra personifies buildings and other man-made things through the presence of a Vāstu Puruṣa. Nature and Earth have historically been called mothers in all traditional cultures. Every noun in Sanskrit has a gender (masculine or feminine). There are separate word-form tables for these genders and nouns with different genders follow different word-form tables. Essentially, even geology and oceanography are sub-departments of the department of personhood.

Impersonalism of nature is the gift of Abrahamic religions. They removed deities, demigods, karma, and reincarnation from pagan religions and depersonalized nature. The impersonalism of modern science was developed from the impersonalism of Abrahamic religions. It pervaded the world via colonization and became an accepted norm. Abrahamic religions also developed legal and political doctrines of personhood. Since they denied rights and contracts to trees, animals, birds, and fishes, therefore, nature was depersonalized through mathematical laws in modern science.

Without a firm alternative idea of personhood, there is no capacity to understand how traditional cultures personalized nature.

That alternative requires us to reinvoke the principle that one thing is three things. *Sat* is the relational capacity in persons. *Chit* is the cognitive and conative capacity in persons. *Ānanda* is the intentional, emotional, and willing capacity in all persons. A person can be described as a complex of will, intention, emotion, cognition, conation, and relation. If someone has a problem with this terminology, they can use the shorter terms sat-chit-ānanda. There are no rights or contracts. Nobody is born with a Bill of Rights in their hands. They are born with a capacity for will, intention, emotion, cognition, conation, and relation. Therefore, to say that everything is personal is to say that everything has the capacity for will, intention, emotion, cognition, conation, and relation. That capacity may be diminished in things that seem non-living but it is not absent. The stark distinction between living and non-living doesn't exist.

Sāñkhya elaborates personhood into 24 components. Tantra extends these 24 components into 36 components. The grossest of these elements called Earth, Water, Fire, Air, and Ether are embodiments of smell, taste, sight, touch, and sound which means that even the grossest of material things exist for perception, they were generated from the senses, and are filtered to varying extents by different perceivers. The observer is central to this understanding. This was not a strange idea in traditional cultures that personalized nature. It is strange to Aristotelian logic, Abrahamic religions, and modern science since they have depersonalized nature for the last 2,500 years.

A person doesn't produce anything impersonal. But a person can *depersonalize* a person by modeling him as a substance, object, thing, particle, wave, field, equation, idea, force, process, and many such speculative constructs. All such constructs prove inadequate to model a person correctly and completely. Each of these constructs is false, illusory, and deceptive. And yet, in the material world, this is the primary way in which everyone thinks, which hides the true nature of reality—a person. The collection of all such illusory, false, and deceptive constructs is māyā. The material world is māyā because everyone uses one or more of the speculative constructs different from the true ontology of personhood.

Māyā is not an ontological truth. Māyā is an epistemological delusion. That delusion is created in the process of trying to depersonalize a person. The models created by such depersonalization are not true. Hence, they are "that which is not". To the extent that this delusion exists within us, we can say that we are deluded about the nature of reality. The world is not false. Our conception of the world is false. Reality is not impersonal. But our modeling of reality is impersonal. Since the impersonal model can be falsified (as it fails to model a person), Māyā does not eternally delude anyone. Escaping Māyā is knowing the truth and ending the suffering created by delusion. The theory of salvation is not separate from the theory of the world. The two theories are identical.

Depersonalization of reality begins from a deep-seated egotism that makes a person selfish. A selfish person depersonalizes other persons and models them as substances, objects, things, particles, waves, fields, equations, ideas, forces, processes, and so on. A selfless person removes such models and sees the person as he is. Thus, everyone will not personalize reality. The egotistic, selfish, and individualistic persons will depersonalize others while the humble, selfless, and altruistic persons will personalize others. This is also Observer-Dependent Epistemology that allows personal choice of models.

Those who depersonalize others will be flocked with like-minded persons who will depersonalize them in turn. Those who personalize others will be flocked with like-minded persons who will personalize them in turn. Nobody wants to be depersonalized. They just want to depersonalize others. But they must be flocked with like-minded people to correct their flawed ideas. When a person is flocked with those who depersonalize him, he realizes the flaws of his thinking. The Vedic system therefore has no problem with any ideology because it says—you can live with people of your ilk. Of course, it warns—choose your ideology carefully because you will come face-to-face with it.

When the basic model of reality is personhood, then the contradiction between Realism and Idealism disappears. After all, there is something other than me, which is a person. Therefore, realism is just like idealism. This is not equivalence with the Western ideas of Realism or Idealism. In the West, Realism is a multi-observer theory and Idealism is a single-observer theory. Western Realism is reductionistic, materialistic, and mechanistic but Western Idealism is not. The Vedic system violates these categories. It is a multi-observer instead of a single-observer theory. Therefore, it is like Western Realism. But it is not reductionistic, materialistic, or mechanistic because both observer and observed are persons. Therefore, it is like Western Idealism.

Overview of the Problem and Its Solution

Aristotle systematized Western philosophy by dividing it into epistemology, ontology, and logic. Initially, Abrahamic religions and then modern science adopted Aristotle's system of systematized philosophy. Their ontology is observer-independent realism, their epistemology is based either on revelation or reason and observation, and their logic is binary. The Vedic ontology is observer-dependent realism, its epistemology is reason, observation, and revelation, and its logic is non-binary. Since neither logic, nor epistemology, nor ontology match, therefore, it is impossible to understand the Vedic system if anyone carries over the vestiges of Aristotelian philosophy, Abrahamic religions, or modern science.

But since the Aristotelian system of philosophy is deeply ingrained in modern science and Abrahamic religions, and the assumptions of this system have been globalized during colonization, hence, practically nobody is free of this thinking at present. They carry its assumptions consciously or unconsciously, try to judge and fit the Vedic system into their assumptions, and fail to comprehend almost everything.

Since they cannot understand how one thing is many things at once, they see conflicts between different Vedic schools that describe the same thing in many different ways. Since non-binary logic appears self-contradictory in binary logical thinking, therefore, they assume that the Vedic system can only be accepted on faith. Since Vedic Realism is something in between Western Realism and Idealism, they cannot subsume it either under Realism or under Idealism. Since Vedic epistemology integrates reason, observation, and revelation, which are separated by Abrahamic religions and modern science, therefore, they are unable to categorize the Vedic system as either science or religion. Since the Vedic idea of personhood is spiritual rather than legal and political, therefore, followers of legal and political definitions of personhood are unable to understand how everything in the universe is modeled as a person.

The problems are easily identified but they are harder to diagnose and fix. The diagnosis of the problem is that the Vedic system has nothing in common with Aristotelian logic, Abrahamic religions, or modern science. The fix to that problem is that there is an alternative ontology, epistemology, and logic under which the apparent problems disappear. Therefore, the problems are simply the result of trying to fit the Vedic system under the categories created by Aristotelian logic, Abrahamic religions, or modern science, rather than studying it as an independent system with its own epistemology, ontology, and logic.

The virtue of studying Aristotelian logic, Abrahamic religions, or modern science is simply that we can understand their flaws and failures and irrefutably establish the need for an alternative. However, the study of Aristotelian logic, Abrahamic religions, or modern science is not going to make our study of the Vedic system easier because we have to leapfrog the previous systems given their proven failures.

Internal, Marginal, and External Knowledge

Three Categories of Knowing

In Vedic texts, the Supreme Lord is said to have three kinds of energies—internal, marginal, and external. The spiritual world is said to be the expansion of His internal energy, the soul is said to be the expansion of His marginal energy, and the material world is said to be the expansion of His external energy. Many people use these words but I have doubts whether they are clear about what they mean. Therefore, in this article, I will try to explain the meaning of internal, marginal, and external energies as three kinds of knowledge of the same thing. We will discuss the many applications of this tripartite distinction.

Let's begin with an ordinary example. Suppose that person A is eating ginger. Person B comes along and they start discussing the taste of ginger. Assume that B has previously tasted ginger. Suppose A says: This ginger is more astringent than bitter but the ginger that I ate last week was more bitter than astringent. Through A's words, B will get a rough idea about what A is talking about since B has previously tasted ginger, and possibly other bitter and astringent foods. Nevertheless, there are many kinds of gingers, which don't taste alike. Therefore, despite getting a rough idea of what it tastes like, B will still not know precisely how the specific ginger that A is eating tastes. That precise taste can be known only if B also tastes the same ginger. Words to him can communicate the taste approximately but not precisely.

Now suppose a third person C comes along and begins participating in the discussion. Assume that C has never tasted a ginger before. Assume also that he hasn't tasted anything astringent either. A tells C that the ginger is more astringent than bitter. C has no clue about what A is saying. To help him understand the taste of ginger, A might try to explain the meaning of astringent. He could say that the astringent taste is not sweet, not sour, not bitter, not pungent, and not salty. Assuming that C has previously tasted sweet, sour, bitter, pungent, and salty foods, he will know that ginger is not those things. But mostly, he will remain clueless because knowing what something is *not* is not knowing what something *is*.

Naming the Three Categories

Let's give names to these three types of knowing. The meanings of these names are limited to this discussion. Outside of this discussion, the same name may have other meanings. I don't expect to use these names outside this discussion, so their meanings should not be extended to other situations.

A's tasting ginger is first-person knowledge. It is precise and accurate. It can be called the perfect truth because A is tasting the ginger unlike B and C who are just watching A taste ginger. B's knowledge is second-person knowledge. He has not tasted the specific ginger that A is tasting. But he has tasted other gingers in the past. He can think of the class called ginger rather than the specific ginger that A is tasting. Since gingers can have varying flavors, therefore, he could be off the mark in guessing its taste, even though he would not be totally wrong. B's knowledge is neither perfect nor false. C's knowledge is third-person knowledge. He has no clue what ginger tastes like. He hasn't ever tasted astringent foods. But he has tasted sweet, sour, salty, pungent, and bitter foods. Therefore, when he is told that ginger is neither of these things, his knowledge is also neither precise nor false. But it is worse than B's knowledge.

A, B, and C can all be said to know the truth. But they are not the same kinds of truths. A has perfect knowledge, B has approximate knowledge, and C has negative knowledge. By perfect knowledge, we mean knowing something precisely and flawlessly. By approximate knowledge, we mean knowing something in the ballpark but not precisely. By negative knowledge, we mean what something is not.

Alternative Kinds of Three Names

While all these are more-or-less good descriptions, personally I prefer to use the terms *ideal, possible,* and *impossible* knowledge. A's tasting of ginger is ideal knowledge. When he says that ginger is bitter and astringent, it becomes imprecise knowledge. Many foods can be included in those categories. For B, the taste of all those foods, including varying types of ginger, are possible. When B hears that A is tasting a ginger that is more astringent than bitter, he carves out a subset of all those tastes. That subset has many possible tastes. Since B cannot pick one out of the many members of the subset, therefore, his knowledge is a possibility. Finally, C knows what ginger could not taste like. He knows what is impossible.

The knowledge of impossibility is the least perfect. We know something, but negatively. The knowledge of possibility is better. We are closer to the truth but cannot pinpoint the truth. Finally, the knowledge of ideality is best. We know the precise, perfect, and accurate truth, without any ambiguity. If this system of tripartite division of knowledge still appears confusing, then we can take a different example.

Suppose you have a pen in your hand. Ideally, you are supposed to write with it. But if you are bored, you could play with the pen, instead of writing with it, and then it becomes a toy. However, that pen will never become (at least under normal circumstances) a car for you. Hence, ideally, we know something to be a pen. Possibly it is also a toy. And impossibly it is a car (i.e., the thing in question will never be a car). If you call something a toy (which is ideally a pen), you are not wrong. But it is not the ideal truth. If you call something not-car (which is ideally a pen), you are not wrong. But it is not the possible truths.

The Tripartite Conception of Reality

The possibility and impossibility are non-binary categories of truth. They are not false, and yet, they are not ideal truths. We cannot fit them into the binary true-false categories of either true or false. The world around us is many possibilities, many impossibilities, and one ideal truth. To know the world, we can begin with what it is not. That is not precise, but it is knowledge. To know the world better, we can proceed to all that is possible. That is also not precise, but it is knowledge. Finally, to know the world perfectly, we must proceed to what it is ideally. That is not just precise. It is also the perfect truth.

The knowledge of possibility and impossibility expands from the knowledge of ideality. For example, we aim to produce a pen. There is purpose and meaning in our action. Based on that meaning and purpose, we produce something that may be non-ideally used as a toy but cannot be used as a car. Since there are infinite possible truths (e.g., a toy), therefore, we can never completely enumerate all of them. We try to overcome this problem by defining the impossibilities. Since they too are infinite, hence, we can never completely enumerate them. Therefore, the knowledge of possibility and impossibility always remains incomplete. Even knowing the ideal truth (e.g., a pen) is not complete because we don't know what it possibly could be and what it will never be. Only the combination of ideal, possible, and impossible constitutes the complete truth. Even ideal truth is incomplete without possibility and impossibility.

This tripartite conception of reality can now be applied to the discussion of internal, marginal, and external energy. An energy is a description of reality. The description pertains to the reality; therefore, the energy is never independent of reality. If the description were separated from reality, then it would become a falsehood. Therefore, reality and its description have to always be paired. Nevertheless, the description of reality can pertain to what the reality is ideally, possibly, or impossibly. The internal energy is the description of what reality is ideally, the marginal energy is the description of what reality is possibly, and the external energy is the description of what the reality is impossibly. They are just like pen, toy, and car. The external energy is the negative knowledge of the truth. It is a non-binary category of truth. It means that it is not false, and yet, it is not the ideal truth. By knowing the external energy, we don't know the possibility and the ideality. Hence, this knowledge is also equated to ignorance although it is not complete ignorance because knowing the impossibility is also knowledge of the same reality.

The Physical Conception of Reality

In stark contrast to the above description of energy stands the physical conception of reality in which everything is described as precisely what it is, rather than what it could or could not be. For example, when someone looks at a pen, they will say that it is just a pen. They might call a toy an interpretation of the pen, which is not objectively true, because in their conception reality must objectively be one thing. Similarly, the statement that a pen is not a car would not be considered objective physical truth because the car's absence cannot be measured in a pen. We can only measure presence and not absence.

Thus, possibility and impossibility are excluded from a physical conception of reality. The pen is just a pen. Toys are personal interpretations of the pen, not an objective fact about the pen. Negation of cars is a logical statement about the pen, not a physical truth, because physical truth is what something is, not what it is not. Thus, the physical conception of reality is *incomplete* because it eliminates the possible and impossible truths, and restricts the truth to just one thing—presumably the ideal truth of that thing. All that can be said through a description about the pen is not part of the physical conception of reality.

The physical conception of reality creates a stark divide between reality and its description because the description includes possibility and impossibility whereas the physical reality just pertains to ideality. This is not an accident. It is derived from Greek philosophy where everything is assigned one word, is said to represent just one form (even if imperfectly), and therefore has just one truth. The idea-form represented (or incarnated) in something was considered its ideal truth during Greek times. Under binary logic, all that was not ideally true, was designated false. Under binary logic, calling something a toy (when it is ideally a pen) is false. Calling something not a car (when it is ideally a pen) is trivially implied by binary logic because if one claim is asserted, all other claims are automatically rejected.

Thus, binary logic easily accepts the ideal and the impossible categories, but has serious problems with possibility. Factually, a pen can be a toy, doorstop, paperweight, weapon, and so forth.

There are infinite possible descriptions of the pen which are all true and yet not the ideal truth. Binary logic rejects all such non-binary truths. It relegates them to personal interpretations of the mind, not the truth or reality.

The Semantic Conception of Reality

Therefore, if we were to describe the above notion of energy accurately, we will have to revise our notion of reality and align it with all descriptions of reality. The toy, doorstop, paperweight, weapon, and so forth, must be as much part of reality as the pen. The negations of car, house, tree, cow, and so forth, must be as much part of reality as the pen. The reality cannot just be one thing. It has to be one ideal thing, many possible things, and many impossible things. They should all be part of one thing so that all true descriptions of reality can be applied back to reality and be considered true statements.

I call the conception of energy (as given above) *semantic reality* and contrast it against the physical conception of reality because possibility and impossibility are part of semantic reality whereas they are rejected from a physical reality. A physical conception of reality insists that reality is just one thing. A semantic conception of reality insists that reality is one ideal, and many possible and impossible claims. All the things that can be said about reality through sentences are inherent in reality. All such things are not part of a physical reality. Therefore, reality is sentence-like rather than object-like. Everything around us is a collection of sentences—those very sentences that can be said to be true about something.

Sentences can make negative claims—e.g., "this is not a car". Their presence indicates an absence. The sentence is not absent. The sentence is present and true. However, the truth of the sentence implies an absence. The presence of negative sentences can be measured. But it cannot be understood correctly, or differentiated from positive sentences, unless we treat them as sentences with meaning and truth. The absence of the sentence is not the same as the presence of a sentence that indicates absence.

The Negative Conception of Matter

When the material world is called the external energy of the Supreme Lord, and often described as māyā (which means that which is not true), many people interpret it to mean that the world doesn't exist, when it actually means that it exists, it is true, and yet, it is the collection of negative sentences. The material world is a true description of the Supreme Lord, as sentences that indicate what He is not, quite like "this is not a car" is a true and present description of something that is ideally described as a pen.

However, the material world is not eternally experienced quite like most of us seldom think about how something that is ideally a pen is a not car. We are generally preoccupied with ideality, occasionally interested in the possibility, and rarely aware of the impossibility. It doesn't mean that the impossibility is a temporary truth. The impossibility is also eternal truth. And yet, we are seldom interested in it. Accordingly, the external energy is also eternal. And yet, it is rarely experienced. The eternally true negative statements appear and disappear with the passing of time due to which the world appears to be temporary. It is still eternal truth. But because it is negative truth, therefore, it is temporary.

Take for example our present bodies. Their essence is birth, death, old age, and disease, which is not the nature of the Supreme Lord. He is neither born, nor does he die. He never becomes old and is never diseased. Therefore, if our body is treated as a negative sentence describing the Supreme Lord, then it is eternally true, and yet, in a negative sense. Or, take for example our temporary pleasures such as eating, sleeping, mating, and defending. The Supreme Lord never becomes hungry, tired, lusty, or fearful, which are the causes of eating, sleeping, mating, and defending for us. If He eats, it is not because He is hungry. He can go on eating forever without indigestion. If He wants, He can isolate Himself and become self-absorbed without losing self-awareness. If He loves someone, it is free of the desire to dominate or control others, which are the essence of lust. If He avoids something it is not because He is afraid. Thus, both material suffering and pleasure are the negations of the Supreme Lord's suffering and pleasure.

Science Inverts Material Negation

However, when science studies the material world disregarding the existence of the Supreme Lord, then all the negative statements are treated as facts. They are indeed facts. Birth, death, old age, and disease are all facts. Eating, sleeping, mating, and defending are also facts. But they are not *positive truths*. They state what the Supreme Lord is not. As descriptions about Him, they are eternal truths, provided we understand that they are negations of His nature. With such an understanding, we would also be able to explain why the material world is temporary despite being an eternal truth. Without the negative conception, we will suffer from the impersonalist paradox—what is temporary cannot be true, what is not true but appears to exist must be a hallucination, and hence the world is a hallucination.

Everyone can accept the simple idea that truth is eternal. They can also accept the fact that the world is temporary. By combining these two claims, we must conclude that the world is not true. This conclusion then makes the study of the world futile. After all, what could be the value in studying hallucinations? What would be the value in working in this world or doing our duties if what we are doing is just a hallucination? The impersonalist position—perfectly logical and well-argued—results in a complete collapse of life, unless we know that the material world exists as eternally true negative sentences. The negative truth is not the ideal truth. It is also not false. It is a non-binary category of truths.

The non-binary truth cannot be modeled by binary logic. Since the whole world is non-binary truth, therefore, the application of binary logic begins by accepting the world as facts, and *elevating* those facts to truths. Thereby, birth, death, old age, disease, eating, sleeping, mating, and defending become truths. Theories are constructed to explain the changing world and those explanations are also called truths.

Since truth is supposed to be eternal, while the world is temporary, eternal truth is defined as the unchanging laws of nature governing the changing world. Mathematics is used for such laws because it is considered eternally true. Consciousness is removed from the explanation of the temporary world because mathematical truths don't need our awareness to be true. Science is expected to make the world a perfect place, disregarding the fact that the world is all that perfection is not. Each of these problems arises because we elevated negative truths to positive truths by elevating facts to truths.

To undo this problem, we can bring back the idea that the world is negative statements. For that, we must accept a semantic conception of reality in which the world is sentences, not objects. Then we have to explain why the world is temporary—consciousness is not interested in negative truths. It moves from one negative truth to another, and the experience of change results from movement of consciousness. Change is like a person walking in the garden whose constituents are negative sentences. That makes the world eternal truth, a changing fact, and a fact explained by the movement of consciousness.

Three Types of Experience Revisited

Within the realm of negative statements, we can further demarcate the distinction between first-person, second-person, and third-person knowledge. For example, if I am sick with fever, then only I know exactly how that fever feels. Nobody else experiences the fever when I am down with fever. Others who have earlier been down with fever can approximately guess what I am experiencing based on their past experiences. Since everyone doesn't have the same type of fever, or the same experience with fever, hence, their guesses may be neither completely precise nor completely false. Then, someone who has never had fever cannot even theoretically understand what I'm experiencing. He can only conjure negative ideas about my condition, namely, that I'm not healthy, energetic, vigorous, or awake.

Thomas Nagel wrote a paper talking about the first-person feeling of being a bat. He argued that this first-person feeling is what we primarily mean by conscious experience. We can extend Nagel's argument to second-person experiences had by other bats. They can know—based on their first-person knowledge of being a bat—what the other bat feels approximately. They cannot know precisely what it means to be a specific bat. A bat's understanding of other bats is an approximation based on their first-person experience. Then there is third-person knowledge of a bat had by humans. We cannot even know what it means to be a bat. Of course, we can say that a bat is not a horse, donkey, bird, fish, tree, and so on.

In a first-person experience, we have direct encounter with the cause, such as fever. In a second-person experience, we don't have a direct encounter with the cause. Rather, we have a first-person experience of an effect from which we infer a cause—e.g., fever—based on our prior first-person experiences. In a third-person experience, we directly encounter an effect from which we cannot infer the cause—e.g., fever. We can only say that the symptoms indicate what the cause cannot be, not what it is.

Vedic philosophy calls the first-person experience Pratyakṣa, or direct experience, e.g., the experience of fever. A second-person experience is not Pratyakṣa. It is Anumāna, which means guessing what the cause could be based on prior similar experiences. A person who has earlier experienced fever can make a reasonable Anumāna that my fever is just like someone else's fever. However, a third-person experience is neither Pratyakṣa nor Anumāna. It is the detection of an effect. Thereafter, a person can say that that cause cannot be one of the known ones, because the effect departs from those of the known causes.

Three Kinds of Material Realities

This understanding can be applied to understand three ways of looking at matter, each of which is true, and yet not the complete truth. We can call them—pursuant to the previous nomenclature—perfect, approximate, and negative knowledge. Perfect knowledge is being a bat. Approximate knowledge is a bat seeing some other bat, and guessing what it feels like. Negative knowledge is a human seeing a bat, not being able to guess what it feels like, but asserting that it feels different than being a cow or a horse.

Thus, within the negative statements we can make three further distinctions based on understanding—(a) the ideal understanding of the negative statement, (b) all possible interpretations of the statement that are not always ideal, and (c) not understanding the statement but correctly asserting that whatever it means, it must mean something different from other statements. We have to remember that each of these three types of understandings is incomplete. However, they are complete put together.

Even if a bat knows itself perfectly, it doesn't know that it is a part of a species—that feels similar but not identical to it. Similarly, the bat doesn't know that it doesn't feel like a cow or a horse. Perfect knowledge of oneself is not complete knowledge unless it includes the knowing of all other beings. Thereby, we must distinguish between perfect or first-person knowledge and complete knowledge. Knowing the truth of what it means to be a specific bat is not knowing the complete truth. The tripartite structure of knowledge makes it impossible to get each of three types of knowing simultaneously. Of course, we can get them one after another. They are distinct, compatible, but complementary modes of knowing.

Three Divisions of God's Energies

The internal energy is like first-person experience. Under it, the world knows exactly how the Supreme Lord feels, quite like the bat knows how it feels. The marginal energy is like second-person experience. Under it, the world knows the Supreme Lord approximately, like a bat knows other bats. The external energy is like third-person experience. Under it, the world knows the Supreme Lord negatively, quite like a human knows what a bat is not. Together, the three energies constitute the complete knowledge of the Supreme Lord. Therefore, even the material energy is accepted as a part of the complete truth, although it is a negative idea of the Lord, different from the approximate and precise knowledge of the Lord.

Those who are in the material world are encouraged to know the material world perfectly to get an idea of what the Lord is not. We can call it material science. But it is not modern science in which negative truths are elevated to positive truths. Material science means knowing that the world is māyā. When the world is studied as negative truths, then the approximate and ideal truths become a necessity. Then nobody can be an atheist denying the existence of a world beyond the material world. It is only when the negative truths are elevated to positive truths that such a denial appears. In short, if matter is studied as māyā, then the students of the material world would never be atheists. They are atheists because they are studying the world as positive truths. They think that because this world is positive truth, therefore, there cannot be another positive truth. If they knew that this world is negative truths, then they would be compelled to accept that there are approximate and ideal positive truths beyond this world.

Impersonalism has polluted the understanding of māyā by calling it a delusion. Calling birth, death, old age, and disease a delusion doesn't work. Nobody can accept that suffering is just a delusion. Suffering is real. The world is not a delusion. It is negative truths. But elevating that negative truth to a positive truth is indeed a delusion. The Vedic system never elevated the negative truth to positive truth. Modern science did that. Therefore, modern science is a delusion. Most people cannot accept that. They claim that science has given us so much comforting technology, so it must be the truth. They cannot see that their technology is just like cola, burgers, and fries—very pleasing to the tongue and very harmful to the body. Then there are personalists who ignore māyā. They elevate the material world to positive truths, just like modern science. They cannot understand or explain why the material world is called external energy.

The problem is created because knowledge isn't properly analyzed. The word is taken to mean positive truth. Then the knowledge of the material world is elevated to positive truth. The impersonalist negates this claim and makes the world a delusion. Everyone else rejects impersonalism and makes the world a positive truth. Both positions are wrong. A negative truth is neither a positive truth nor a falsehood.

The Eyes of Knowledge

I recently changed the byline for Shabda Blog to "Through the Eyes of Knowledge". This is called jñāna-cakṣu in the Vedic texts. Kṛṣṇa uses this term in Bhagavad-Gita 15.10: "The foolish cannot understand how a living entity can quit his body, nor can they understand what sort of body he enjoys under the spell of the modes of nature. But one whose eyes are trained in knowledge can see all this." I thought I should explain this term, especially because the idea of perception in Vedic texts is quite different from its counterparts in modern thinking. This article is devoted to the meaning of "eyes of knowledge".

The Failure of Scientific Empiricism

Let's begin by talking about the idea of perception in modern science which states that light enters our eyes and creates an image on our retina to make us see. In scientific empiricism, all eyes are blank slates. So, when light enters our eyes, we see the world just as the world is. Thus, perception gives us the truth.

Now a little consideration will easily falsify the scientific idea. First, we see things during dreams even when the eyes are closed and no light enters the eyes. Second, we can see patterns of light if we press our eyes; again, light doesn't enter our eyes but the pressure of the fingers does. Third, even while seeing the world with our eyes open, we might misperceive reality, e.g., see a snake where there is a rope. Fourth, if we don't pay attention, we don't see even if we are looking in the direction and light should have entered our eyes to create a retinal image. Fifth, everyone doesn't see the world in the same way, so there is no foundation for saying that perception gives us the true nature of reality.

Given these problems, modern science replaces eyes with instruments. It is assumed that instruments do not dream, that if they indicate a value it must be correct, and all properly calibrated instruments must consistently produce the same results. Even this claim is false. Instruments register values even when there is nothing to measure; we call those "faulty instruments", but there is no way to know that the instrument is faulty other than by comparing it with other instruments, which still begs the question: Which of the many instruments (detecting or not detecting) is correct? The same instrument registers different values on repeat measurements making it an unreliable source of results. Different instruments register different values too, shattering the idea that instrument calibration makes results reliable.

This problem now has an official name and is called "the crisis of reproducibility in science". Some of the crisis pertains to people publishing tampered data to derive a conclusion that will be quickly accepted by a journal whose editors are already committed to proving the conclusion. Another part of the crisis pertains to instrument or human errors or both. Yet another part of the crisis pertains to the fact that the same thing doesn't behave in the same way at all times, places, and situations. The crisis could also pertain to unknown variables in a complex system where it is extremely hard to account for all variables.

Some years ago, the prestigious journal Nature published a paper with the opening statement: "More than 70% of researchers have tried and failed to reproduce another scientist's experiments." At the start of science, it was assumed that this value would be negligible if not zero. That was a false belief.

This compels us to rethink our ideas of perception *and* measurement because (a) measurements do not fix the problem of misperception, (b) the problem of measurement seems much worse than the problem of misperception, and (c) the problem of misperception was bad enough for perception to not be a basis of knowledge. That a serious problem of measurement and perception undercuts the scientific method so viciously is little known and even less understood. This should be a cause for alarm but it is not.

The Vedic Description of Perception

I will now turn to the Vedic idea of perception and illustrate it with an example. Think of your eyes as a drum, the world as a stick that beats the drum, and your perception as the sound that results from beating the drum. The drum is not a blank slate because there are endless types of drums that do not produce the same sound. Even if the two drums looked identical, they might produce different sounds based on differences in their materials, the tautness of the skin on the drum, the age of the drum, and the environmental conditions (such as weather). Accordingly, the same stick would produce different sounds and two different sticks can produce the same sound. Drums that appear quite different can produce the same sound and drums that appear identical can produce different sounds. The sound you hear is the result of the drum, stick, and the act of hitting the drum with the stick. They correspond to the observer, the observed, and the act of observing. There are three logically distinct variables, not just one, unlike the blank slate idea in which the observed is the only variable because the observer and the method of observation have been "fixed". That fixing of two out of three variables is presumptuous and false.

This idea of perception has a formal name and is called Satkāryavāda, which means that the effect (the sound) is present in the cause (the drum) and could be produced from the cause either due to an agent (the stick) or spontaneously. We don't expect drums to vibrate spontaneously but this is easily true in the case of our senses. The senses are the cause from which perceptions are produced either due to an external agent (the world, during the waking stage) or spontaneously (during the dreaming stage).

There is no hard-and-fast line dividing waking and dreaming. We could be daydreaming, imagining, or hallucinating during wakefulness. We could be misperceiving—i.e., mixing components from waking and dreaming—during wakefulness. We could be half dreaming and half wakeful—e.g., we could imagine that someone talking to us outside our dream is actually talking to us within our dream. We can only talk about waking and dreaming *theoretically* as (a) a perception created due to something outside our mind, and (b) a perception produced spontaneously from our mind unrelated to anything outside the mind.

Satkāryavāda compels us to rethink perception as something produced from the senses and the mind and therefore "conditioned" by their nature. Everyone's senses and the mind are not the same. Instead, they are conditioned—in Vedic philosophy—by previous lifetimes of experience. They might also be modified by our current emotional, intellectual, or situational state. Thus, a fearful person might see a snake where there is only a rope. A person conditioned to thinking in terms of particles and waves might try to always reduce every phenomenon to particles or waves disregarding what doesn't fit within this reduction as an aberration. Contextually, a person might use a concept differently, such as interpreting the word "field" differently in the context of physics and farming. Or, a person might shift their conceptual repertoire completely, such as using different set of words at home and at work.

The Origin of the Concept Jñāna-Cakṣu

These problems then lead Vedic philosophy into a radically different epistemology in which the senses and the mind have to be "purified" of their "conditioning" to be reliable sources of knowledge. The purification doesn't make the senses and the mind blank slates. It rather gives them a pure, ideal, or perfect set of percepts and concepts in terms of which the world is interpreted correctly. The hallmark of correct interpretation is that contradictions between theories disappear, we can reconcile all theories into one comprehensive theory, confirm that the theory always works, and thus prove its truth.

The purified senses and mind are the jñāna-cakṣu or the "eyes of knowledge". They are not blank slates to simply picture an objective reality. In fact, the eye becomes more and more sophisticated over time as it acquires newer types of percepts and concepts closer and closer to the perfect truth. When we see the world through the eyes of knowledge, we see it differently than other eyes. We may see what others could not see, although it was present. We might emphasize or prioritize things that others might have considered less important or irrelevant. We might use different concepts to aggregate seemingly different things as quite similar while separating seemingly similar things as quite different. We might judge the world differently, describing different things as truth, justice, and beauty. We might value, desire, and cherish different things than those who might not have the eyes of knowledge.

Finally, as Kṛṣṇa states in Bhagavad-Gita 15.10: "The foolish cannot understand how a living entity can quit his body, nor can they understand what sort of body he enjoys under the spell of the modes of nature. But one whose eyes are trained in knowledge can see all this." In more esoteric Vedic texts, this is called the reflection of the soul in the mirror of the mind, by which a self-image is seen. That self-image, called ahaṅkāra, is false in a contaminated mind and true in a pure mind. The symptom of that purification is that one can see oneself separate from the identities enforced on the soul due to the body—race, religion, nationality, gender, age, culture, status, profession, ancestry, and so on.

Thus, there are both external and internal symptoms of this vision. Externally, the eyes of knowledge lead a person to formulate a consistent and complete theory of the world. Internally, the same eyes of knowledge lead a person to formulate a consistent and complete theory of the self. The hallmark of a consistent and complete theory is that it doesn't change. Externally, this means that the theory of the world remains unchanged because it is always verified and never falsified. Internally, this means that the self-image doesn't change because it is always verified and never falsified. The theory and the self-image are called truth because they don't change and are eternal. Thereby, truth equals eternity.

The Senses as the Limbs of a Tortoise

There are further nuances to the eyes of knowledge in which the eyes go out into the world quite like a tortoise stretches out its limbs. Kṛṣṇa states in Bhagavad-Gita 2.58: "One who is able to withdraw his senses from sense objects, as the tortoise draws its limbs within the shell, is firmly fixed in perfect consciousness." In many cartoons, we see a protagonist being stunned by what they are seeing, their amazement symbolized by their eyes popping out of their eye sockets. Many people indicate a similar experience in the presence of advanced personalities—i.e., they can "see through them".

The scientific idea of perception is that light enters our eyes, which means that (a) I have no choice in seeing what I see because I will be forced to see that which enters my eyes, and (b) I cannot see that which others cannot see because the light is not entering my eyes. In short, perception cannot be controlled by will. Both these ideas are falsified when perception advances through sense control and purification. Now, if the eyes are withdrawn, we need not see what others are seeing. If the eyes are extended outward, we can see what others might not see. The conditioned eyes are not under the control of will but the purified eyes are. They can choose to see what they want to see, avoid things they don't want to see, and see things that might not be visible to others. This is perceptual advancement.

The eyes of an advanced personality can go out like the limbs of a tortoise, and enter another person's body and mind, to understand their state. Now, we cannot even say that light must enter our eyes for us to see; instead, we must say that the eyes can also go out to see what might be unseen by others. The things that others cannot see are not absent. They are just unmanifest. The unmanifest is manifest if the eyes interact with the unmanifest and make it manifest by going out to see what others can't see.

Sun and Moon as the Eyes of God

This brings us to the final point in which the Sun and the Moon are called Kṛṣṇa's eyes in Bhagavad-Gita 11.19: "You are without origin, middle or end. Your glory is unlimited. You have numberless arms, and the sun and moon are Your eyes. I see You with blazing fire coming forth from Your mouth, burning this entire universe by Your own radiance." According to modern science, the Sun shines because of nuclear reactions and the nuclear fuel will run out in 5 billion years. Of course, none of us may be around to confirm that. But from Vedic texts we understand that the universe goes on for 311 trillion years, defined by the shining Sun. Additionally, darkness is the unmanifest state of reality and when the

Sun shines, it is not emitting light (as in modern science) but *seeing* the world—quite like an advanced person's eyes probe and reveal the hidden—to make the unmanifest manifest and thereby visible to everyone.

In quantum mechanics, each particle exists in a potential state. It changes state when it absorbs or emits energy but the precise moment of this emission or absorption cannot be predicted. Some philosophers of science have proposed a role of consciousness in this emission, calling the change of state a "collapse" from many potential states into one definite state. The idea in the Vedic description is different. There is a person—the Sun in this case—who probes reality and transforms it from unmanifest to manifest. That state change is called the emission of light, which triggers an action in our senses, and we see. In short, we see because the Sun sees. If the Sun stopped seeing, the world would be dark and we would not see.

The Sun is called the eyes of Kṛṣṇa in the above verse. It means that we see because Kṛṣṇa sees. If He stopped seeing, then the world would be dark. The world is lighted because Kṛṣṇa is seeing it. While the proposed nuclear fuel in the Sun may run out in 5 billion years, Kṛṣṇa's eyes will not run out of the power of seeing in that time. He will continue seeing for as long as required, which in the Vedic texts, is about 311 trillion years. The world is lighted not by the emission of photons but by the power of Kṛṣṇa's eyes.

True and False Ideas of Knowledge

This brings us to a comprehensive picture of seeing and we can note the following: (a) the eyes are not blank slates as everyone doesn't see everything, (b) what they see may not be seen consistently, (c) this problem is not unique to perception and exists even in measurement, (d) a person's vision could be the result of their past conditioning, (e) when this conditioning is removed, a person acquires the eyes of knowledge by which the true nature of reality is seen, (f) such eyes of knowledge can see what many others cannot see, (g) that is because the eyes of knowledge can reveal the hidden by moving out and converting the unmanifest into the manifest, (h) the process of the senses moving out and revealing the previously hidden is responsible for the Sun lighting up the world for us to see whatever we see, and (i) the world is not lighted by a random emission of photons unpredictable under the laws of quantum mechanics but by the movement of senses, ultimately under the control of the Supreme Will.

While the last conclusion might seem drastic to modern science, it would be naturally obtained if we began with the problem of perception, and tried to obtain a certifiable epistemology, without assuming that the senses are fundamentally different from the instruments under a presumed mind-body divide. The irreproducibility of scientific experiments is the result of the movement of senses, which reveal and hide different things, and no two results can be precisely equal unless all senses move identically.

The crisis of reproducibility in science is not uniform across all subjects. The crisis is less in physics, some more in chemistry, even more in biology, even higher in psychology, and the highest in sociology. That is because the crisis results from the movement of the observer's senses. The more we can remove the observer from the observation, as in the case of physics, the less of a crisis there is. The greater the role of the observer in an observation, as in the case of sociology, the greater the crisis there is. All assumptions of objective reality, its measurement by instruments leading to objective truth, are false. The failures of scientific empiricism are established empirically by the irreproducibility of scientific experiments. They are being published in the most prestigious journals. But will science take those failures seriously to revise its assumptions about observation, measurement, and the scientific method? Unlikely.

There are two ideas of perception—(a) knowledge comes outside-in, and (b) knowledge goes inside-out. They can be called waking and dreaming. Dreaming is a more advanced state of consciousness than waking in the Vedic texts because it represents creativity and a power of seeing that reveals that which might be hidden from others. But modern science is based on waking and disregards dreaming. In fact, dreams are only part of Freudian or Jungian psychology, not even parts of mainstream psychiatry.

The eyes of knowledge are difficult to understand because a carefully crafted set of false assumptions has been mainstreamed in science, popularized in society, and widely accepted as true. We can peel those assumptions, see their problems, and reject them to get back to the eyes of knowledge.

What Is Māyā?

The Meaning of Truth and Delusion

In classical Indian epistemology, illusion was defined by the example of seeing a rope and thinking it was a snake. Truth was defined as distinguishing a rope from a snake. The method by which we could reject the idea that there is a snake and conclude that there is a rope was epistemology. The essence of illusion was seeing the similarity between two things—rope and snake—and thinking they are the same.

This essence of illusion constitutes Māyā. We see two things, we find some similarities, and we conclude they are the same because we ignore the differences. For instance, when God appears in this world, He eats, drinks, sleeps, marries, travels, and fights. We could compare this to an ordinary person and say that all those who eat, drink, sleep, marry, travel, and fight are God. This is a delusion because we have taken some similarities between God and ordinary people and concluded that they are the same.

Why the Material World is a Delusion

This delusion is all-pervasive. The gopis dance with Kṛṣṇa in Goloka Vrindavan. And so, women and men think that if they danced, they would be in heaven. Everyone in the spiritual world is well-fed. And so, we believe that if we feed everyone, it will be heaven. Nobody in the spiritual world is homeless. And so, we believe that if everyone had a home, it would be heaven. Everyone in the spiritual world is playing. And so, we think that if everyone started playing it would be heaven. Nobody in the spiritual world has to work for their survival. And so, we believe that if nobody had to work for their survival, it would be heaven.

Under these delusions, we want to stop working, start playing and dancing, and expect food and home. When we don't get that, we ask: If it could happen in the spiritual world, then why not here? The answer is simple: The spiritual world is a snake and the material world is a rope. You saw a rope and thought it was a snake. Your delusion is your problem, not of the rope or the snake. Both exist, but one thing is not the other thing. That you can't see the difference has to be blamed on you, not on the rope or the snake.

The Cause of the Material Delusion

The soul comes to the material world from the spiritual world. Since it has been in the spiritual world, it knows that people in the spiritual world have homes and adequate food, they dance and play, and they need no job to survive. All these things are provided by Kṛṣṇa. He can supply everything and He supplies them for free to His devotees. But the envious living entity thinks: I can get these on my own and I don't need Kṛṣṇa. And so, the living entity comes to the material world to become an independent enjoyer. After he arrives, he realizes that I cannot supply everything for myself just by willing it. I have to work in a job, to earn food and home, before I can dance and play. And yet, the innate memory of the spiritual world is still there due to which everyone wants everything in the spiritual world for free without Kṛṣṇa.

The delusion is that a world without Kṛṣṇa can also be the spiritual world. That we don't have to work for survival, that we will have a home and food, and that we will play and dance, without Kṛṣṇa. In this delusion, we see a rope and think of a snake, justify it based on the similarity between rope and snake, and ignore the differences. The difference to most people isn't obvious since the difference is that Kṛṣṇa is absent. The delusion exists when Kṛṣṇa is forgotten. The delusion disappears when Kṛṣṇa is remembered.

The Inversion of Truth and Delusion

Advaita inverted the concept of truth and illusion. Now, both rope and snake became illusions and not distinguishing between the two became the truth. All methods of epistemology that could be used to distinguish between rope and snake became irrelevant. You could equate anything to anything else, and claim that they were essentially the same thing. Epistemology—the attempt to distinguish between rope and snake—itself became an illusion. Thus, in classical Indian epistemology, the illusion was confusing a rope for a snake, while the truth was distinguishing between the two. Advaita inverted this epistemology such that distinguishing between rope and snake is the illusion and equating them is the truth.

At present, the Advaita definition of Māyā is the common idea about Māyā. When we talk about Māyā, people think we are saying that the world is a delusion (which is true) but it is *interpreted* to mean that the world doesn't exist (that what we see is a simulated hallucination) when the original description of Māyā was that there is a rope which we see as a snake. The world, in the original Indian epistemology, was real; the illusion was the misunderstanding about the world in the observer. Advaita made the world and all its understanding an illusion removing the need to distinguish between rope and snake.

Elevating Ignorance to Knowledge

Knowledge in the Vedic tradition has always meant the capacity to discriminate, which involves three steps. The senses help us distinguish, the mind helps us identify, and the intellect helps us prioritize. The combined result of these three is that we organize things in a hierarchy, prioritizing the truth over falsehoods, the just over the unjust, and the good over the bad. However, under Advaita, discrimination is itself the main problem. Instead, not discriminating, not organizing in a hierarchy, forcibly equalizing, and dissolving the obvious differences as illusion is called knowledge. If you see higher and lower, Advaita calls it ignorance. Dissolving their difference is knowledge.

Essentially, Advaita elevated ignorance to the status of knowledge. Those with the capacity for discrimination were called ignorant while those without such capacity were called enlightened. The capacity to discriminate is described in Sāñkhya. Advaita called it a byproduct of Māyā. Advaita justified these things as the teachings of Śaṅkarācārya, who is an incarnation of Shiva, without noting that Shiva is also the personification of tamo-guna, the quality and condition of ignorance.

The purpose of renunciation in the Vedic tradition was to stand apart from reality to see it clearly and not be biased due to attachment to some part of reality, such as family, nation, culture, language, color, gender, class, and so on. Detachment separates us from the world to help us see it correctly so we can discriminate and organize hierarchically. But if there is no difference between the self and the other, what is the need for detachment? Why separate yourself and magnify the illusion of separation when you can dissolve it by staying attached? Why do penances, in which one tortures one's body and mind, only to magnify the appearance of the self-other difference?

When we organize things in a hierarchy, the higher level is superior and the lower level is inferior. The lower level serves the higher level and through this service, the lower level ascends to the higher level. And yet, there is no limit to this ascent. There is always someone higher, due to which progress and service are eternal. Advaita reduced eternal progress to static eternity supposedly attained by flattening the hierarchy and dissolving all differences. The elimination of eternal progress, and its replacement by a static emptiness, became the supreme Vedic conclusion.

Why Advaita is a Tamasic Ideology

Advaita is actually the elevation of tamo-guna to the state of intellectual supremacy. Indian history bears out the effects of the tamo-guna ideology. People became lazy, ignorant, selfish, complacent, and greedy. Their identification with their local region, language, culture, food, empire, and customs grew with time and their identification with the wider Vedic civilization declined. Their attachments to their narrow world grew while their detachment from this world, which Advaita called an illusion, declined. Instead of accepting that all material things are an illusion, as Advaita claimed, they became even more attached to all things that Advaita called an illusion. They abandoned their dharma, which is based on their higher and lower status determined by their qualities and activities, and started doing whatever they wanted on the presupposition that they were all equal. Everyone wanted the right to do everything without the duty to do a specific thing. Advaita destroyed dharma in India.

Therefore, I say this with great responsibility: Advaita is a tamasic ideology. It is not the highest, but one of the lowest. It is not violent, so it is not as bad as violent ideologies. But it destroys duty, austerity, detachment, discrimination, and broad-mindedness and makes people lazy, ignorant, selfish, complacent, greedy, and narrow-minded. Their attachment and identification to local region, language, culture, food, empire, and customs grow instead of decreasing with time. Contrary to Advaita, diversity increases and unity declines. People get deeper into material attachment instead of coming out of it. Advaita claims that we will come out of material illusion if we follow its ideology. The facts of history show that we descend deeper into materialism.

The Confusion of Māyā and Māyāvāda

At present, when we talk about the original definition of Māyā, most people think we are talking about the Advaita interpretation of Māyā. Originally, getting out of Māyā meant distinguishing the rope from the snake. In the modified Advaita interpretation, it means dissolving the distinction between the two.

The Advaita view of Māyā is actually called Māyāvāda, different from the original view of Māyā. Māyā is not Māyāvāda. The resolution of Māyā is distinguishing rope from snake. The resolution of Māyāvāda is discarding the distinction between the two. And yet, because everyone equates Māyā to Māyāvāda, hence, discussing the nature and problem of Māyā is taken to mean the discussion of Māyāvāda.

The Confusion of Unity and Oneness

Māyā is the principle of separateness, which is called duality. All reality comprises opposites such as hot and cold, bitter and sweet, heavy and light. Each of these opposites is contextually useful and nothing is universally harmful or useful. If these opposites are used correctly, i.e., in the right context, they all aid progress. The pen and sword can both be used for the same purpose. They are opposites but not enemies, if there is a common purpose. They become enemies only if a common purpose is replaced by an individual purpose. A common purpose contextualizes the opposites; an individual purpose universalizes them. Hence, conflict is not due to opposites but the replacement of a common purpose with an individual purpose.

The actual Vedic doctrine out of this conflict of dualities is a shared or common purpose. It creates *unity in diversity*. Advaita replaced it with *oneness*. God is the unity in diversity, the shared common purpose of everything. If everyone serves God, according to their capacity and ability, then there is unity in diversity. If God disappears from society, then the unity is destroyed and replaced by individualism. Now the individualists can talk about oneness but it will never happen. Their misdiagnosis of Māyā as opposites rather than individualism will neither destroy opposites nor create oneness. It will simply fragment a society due to the loss of shared purpose. The dogma of oneness is intellectually appealing and practically harmful as the rejection of the basis of unity, i.e., God, fragments society into selfish individuals.

God is the soul of the social body that unites the people in a society quite like parts of our body are united as long as there is a soul. When the soul leaves the body, the body starts fragmenting. Similarly, when God leaves society, the unity within the society disappears, and the society starts fragmenting. A godless society is just like a dead body, that continuously disintegrates. The initial sign of disintegration is that people don't do their duties or dharma anymore. They begin lying and cheating while not performing their duties. Merit is not respected and good people born in that society start immigrating out of that society. Mostly, the unfortunate, the helpless, and the immoral are left behind. Over time, society is infested with immorality and people stop taking religion seriously and become immersed in materialism. Advaita is a godless religion that converts a living and strong social body into a dead and decaying social body.

Advaita Destruction of Vedic Traditions

According to Advaita, temple deities are man-made illusions, and Brahman is the only truth. There is no such thing as God or Supreme Being because all beings are ultimately one. The concept of the Supreme Being requires distinguishing between various beings and is false. But if you want to retain the idea of God, then God is a self-realized man, and self-realized men are God. If you want to worship God, then worship self-realized men as God. Thus, men claiming to be self-realized came to be known as Godmen in India because there is no difference between God and self-realized men in Advaita. These men were worshipped as God because they had become God. Some men even prefixed their names with Bhagavan. There was no philosophical challenge to men being called Bhagavan because men and Bhagavan were the same.

The worship of Godmen was a substitute for the worship of the deities in temples. The images in the temples are just statues of self-realized men, just like the statues of kings and queens in public places. They can serve as reminders of their deeds, virtues, and ideas but nothing comes from worshipping these statues. Instead of giving special status to priests who worship these statues, we must treat everyone equally Brahman. The priests in temples are not worshipping God. They are, at best, worshipping statues of self-realized men. The less intelligent people worship statues while the more intelligent people focus on the deeds, virtues, and ideas of self-realized men.

The Vedic tradition deifies the cosmos. Water, Fire, and Air are all deified. This deification is a problem in Advaita. Instead, of deifying the cosmos, as elements governed by higher beings, we must take a scientific approach to reality in which these deities are replaced by laws of nature. Since the traditional Vedic education system deified the cosmos, it must be replaced by a modern education system.

Secularism and Favoring Monotheism

According to Advaita, even followers of other religions are Brahman, and conflict between them is based on an illusion. It doesn't matter whether you believe in Hinduism, Islam, Christianity, Buddhism, Sikhism, Jainism, and so on, because they are all illusions. Only the oneness of Brahman is the truth. Advaita took a moral high ground above all religions, calling all of them illusions on the one hand and arguing for their harmony on the other. All other religions were the children fighting with each other. Advaita was the adult among these children calling for peace.

Indian secularism was merely an extension of Advaita. Since all religions are illusions, it doesn't matter what religion you choose. Even atheists can align with Advaita, and they do so in the West because Advaita considers all religions false and delusory.

Advaita accepted and encouraged the iconoclasm of Abrahamic faiths because deities and temples were illusions. Praying in a Mosque or Church without an image of God was closer to the truth than worshipping an image of God in a temple. Hindus fighting against Muslims or Christians was farther from the truth because Muslims or Christians worshipped God without images while Hindus worshipped images.

Advaita argued against the exclusivism of Abrahamic religions too, based on the oneness of Brahman. But it argued against Hinduism more, based on the principle of rejecting deities and temples. When push came to shove, Abrahamic iconoclasm (opposition to images) was closer to the truth than people worshipping hundreds of different images in temples. The monotheistic religions were closer to the oneness of Brahman than polytheistic Hinduism. While playing the adult in the room filled with children, criticizing both sides based on its ideas of oneness, Advaita ultimately tilted in favor of monotheism, Buddhism, and its own impersonalism.

Advaita Destruction of the Economy

Wealth must be equally distributed among people because they are equally Brahman. The rich man must give his wealth to the poor and should be taxed to dissolve rich-poor differences. The underclasses must be especially empowered to bring everyone to the same status. Governmental controls must be applied to ensure that economic disparities are not created because they lead to social discrimination, undermining the concept of oneness. Entrepreneurs and businessmen are evil while poor farmers, small shopkeepers, and working classes are good. Laws must push the entrepreneurs and businessmen down while lifting the farmers, shopkeepers, and workers.

Advaita ideologues coined the term Daridra Nārāyaṇa, or that the poor are Nārāyaṇa, thereby linking Indian economics to religion. Nārāyaṇa, the husband of Lakṣmī, the deity of wealth, became poor. Wealth was supposed to come to India by deifying the poor. When India became independent, there was a famous slogan that we rarely hear today: Service to man is service to God. If the government was serving the people, then it was serving God. If the government created jobs and reservations for the poor, it had a spiritual legitimacy. Meanwhile, those who encouraged entrepreneurship, created economic disparity, were not serving God, and hence, had no spiritual legitimacy.

Most people at present don't know that Indians did not take socialism from the West. It was already in India as Advaita. Small groups of Indians took Marxism, Communism, and Maoism from other places, but Indian socialists rejected it because their vision of India was not violent like the imported ideologies. Indian socialism was a benevolent idea of uniformity and it rejected violence. Wherever Marxists, Communists, and Maoists came to power, socialists bitterly fought against them. That is because Indian socialism was not materialism. In fact, matter is an illusion and spirit is reality in Advaita. Indian socialism was the political extension of Advaita philosophy.

The Kingdom of God Without God

Indians today can't see the elephant in the room—Advaita—responsible for the destruction of the Vedic traditions, insertion of secularism, preferential treatment of Abrahamic religions, the socialization of the economy, and how all this delights India's former colonizers. Colonizers elevate Advaita above the Vedic traditions, giving it more respect and importance, because it keeps India backward. But if you are angry about something, you can blame individual politicians, political parties, religious groups, and conversion schemes without looking at the real culprit giving intellectual, moral, and emotional support to all of them, i.e., Advaita. One blamed party can be replaced with another, as long as the underlying ideology continues.

Srila Prabhupāda called this the kingdom of God without God. But I like to call it sleeping with the enemy because (a) people are sleeping, (b) the enemy is ruling them, and (c) they believe that their enemy is their protector. This destruction is rooted in the one idea that diversity is an illusion and oneness is the truth.

Someone put this to me as gold is real but the gold earrings are illusions. Hinduism, Christianity, Islam, Judaism, Buddhism, Jainism, Sikhism, and all others, are gold earrings. They are all tolerated because they are equally illusory. They are all rejected because none of them is the truth. The pragmatism of Advaita lets it outwardly accept everyone while inwardly rejecting everyone. That is a wolf hiding in sheep's clothing. It is nobody's friend but pretends to be everyone's friend.

Flawed Attempts to Create Unity

People influenced by Advaita believe they are the adults in a room filled with fighting children. There is insurmountable hubris in these people, which makes them think that they will bring brotherhood and peace to the world based on their ideas of oneness. Every few months I meet some such people.

- Some try to reconcile the Vedic tradition with Abrahamic religions by attempting to align their histories, reducing the Vedic history to a few thousand years, and overlooking the immense differences in the ages of the universe as given in these traditions.
- Some try to unite the West with the Vedic tradition based on the study of the mind, disregarding the enormously complex descriptions of the mind in the Vedic tradition, hoping that these could be equated to the overly simplistic ideas in the West.
- Some cite Western philosophers, find similarities to their claims in the Vedic tradition, and try to equate the two, neglecting the fact that philosophy in the Vedic tradition is a system of infinite diversity while that in the West is a system of universal uniformity.
- Some cite verses of love and devotion from the Vedic texts

and equate them to similar verses from Abrahamic texts, disregarding the multifaceted conception of God and the soul in the Vedic texts, and mono-faceted conception in the Abrahamic texts.

- Some try to digest Vedic science descriptions of qualitative nature within Western science axioms of quantification trying to make the Vedic tradition appealing to the Western world, disregarding the logical contradictions between these ideologies.

This is not an exhaustive list of baseless attempts; these are just the most prominent ones that I have seen personally. All these attempts are an illusion because the similarities are emphasized while the differences are ignored. People want to see a rope as a snake. There is obviously some similarity between the two. The differences are even greater. Due to these differences, none of their attempts succeed. But they don't stop trying. They are gripped by Māyā, which in classical Indian philosophy meant seeing a rope as a snake. But they don't see it as Māyā either because Advaita redefined it as the illusion of diversity hovering over the oneness or because they consider the Western worldview the standard against which everything else must be understood.

There is a great similarity between Western Universalism and Advaita Impersonalism: In both cases, the diversity of ideas is false and universality is true. Both subscribe to a binary conception of truth, i.e., there is only one truth and everything else is false. The actual Vedic conception is a ladder of truths in which there is some truth even in the lowest rung of the ladder but the truth grows to become complete truth at the top. Attempts to reduce a ladder of truths to a binary truth are like reducing infinite colors to black and white. Unable to discard Western ideas, the supremacist West tries to merge Vedic ideas into itself while the mentally colonized Indians try to coalesce themselves into Western universalism. The net result is that neither moves even an inch on the ladder but they believe they found the only truth.

Blatant Violation of Vedic Injunctions

All over Vedic texts, we find stories of Asuras attacking Devas, Devas taking shelter of Viṣṇu, who then supports Devas in their war against Asuras for the protection of dharma, despite both being His children. Before the Mahābhārata war, Arjuna argues with Kṛṣṇa against fighting a war with his cousins, the Kauravas, who were equally related to Kṛṣṇa. And yet, Kṛṣṇa urges Arjuna to fight for the protection of dharma, despite Pandavas and Kauravas being cousins and equally related to Him. In different Vedic texts, Viṣṇu appears in different forms to kill his servants—Jaya and Vijaya—who had become demons due to the curse of the Four Kumaras, protecting His devotees, for the protection of dharma.

There is simply no equivalence between Devas and Asuras, Pandavas and Kauravas, devotees and demons anywhere in the Vedic texts. But Advaita created that equivalence by calling both sides equally illusory. To do that, Advaita undermined the Purāṇa and Itihāsa where these pastimes are discussed in detail, upholding an impersonalist philosophy of Advaita based on the Upaniṣads and Vedānta Sūtra although the Advaita conclusions have to be twisted out of these texts through misinterpretations.

The fact is that Advaita has never been a Vedic tradition. It was a tradition outside the Vedic system but railroaded it when Śaṅkarācārya wrote commentaries on the Vedic texts, marginalizing large portions of the Vedic system, twisting limited portions to extract an interpretation that was refuted over and over by successive generations. At the heart of the Advaita misinterpretation lies a redefinition of Māyā or illusion, not as seeing a rope as a snake, but as the illusion of both rope and snake, creating an equivalence between Devas and Asuras, Pandavas and Kauravas, devotees and demons, contrary to all Vedic texts.

The Western Rejection of Realism

Advaita currently finds great resonance in the West because of the failure of modern science to account for mind and consciousness. This has to do with the fact that science separated the mind and the body as secondary properties (qualities) and primary properties (quantities), implying that quantities are primary and qualities are secondary and that we must reduce the qualities to quantities. Factually, no such reduction is possible because quantities use binary logic and qualities use non-binary logic. In the Vedic tradition, there are ternary opposites but in Western thinking, there are binary opposites. The Vedic ternary opposites are codependent while the Western binary opposites are mutually exclusive. The difference is so profound that there is simply no way to reduce qualities to quantities. All quantity sciences are also fundamentally flawed because reality is ternary and codependent opposites.

Western Realism is also divided into two main positions. One, in Naïve Realism, the world is just as we see it and knowing the world is no problem because everyone already knows it from birth. Two, in Scientific Realism, there is some difficulty in knowing the world but it requires no changes to ourselves. As Francis Bacon, who formulated the scientific method, put it: Nature is a witch who must be tortured to reveal her secrets. Torturing the witch is slightly more difficult, but it requires no changes to us.

Scientific Realism is a response to Christianity in which each person is evil, having descended from the evil Adam and Eve, and they cannot know the truth due to the evil in them; truth has to be revealed to them by a savior-messiah. The Scientific Realism response to Christianity is: We are not evil; we are fully capable of knowing nature. This is sometimes described as *mind is a blank slate.* As the slate is blank, there cannot be evil. Rather, upon observation, the world is clearly imprinted on the slate. However, nature is an evil witch for having hidden all her secrets from us. The method of knowing nature is torturing her to make her reveal her secrets. Scientific Realism transfers the evil from us to nature. In Christianity, man is evil and cannot know. In Scientific Realism, nature is evil but can be tortured.

The Western Adoption of Advaita

But the failure of Scientific Realism both in mainstream science and in the study of consciousness and mind has now compelled the West to reject Realism and look at Idealism. Idealism doesn't require the distinction between primary and secondary properties because there is no reality. What we see is the qualitative appearances and we have no way of knowing what, if anything, causes it. The best way to get out of the problem created by the inability to know reality is to say that it doesn't exist. Thereby, the world we see is an illusion or delusion created by consciousness. Of course, if that consciousness was us, then we should know that we are creating that delusion. In fact, we should be able to precisely forecast what next delusion we will see. Since that is not possible, therefore, you have to look at a delusion creation mechanism in which we are not creating the delusion, and yet, we are experiencing it. The West hopes or believes that Advaita has an answer to this problem, although Advaita itself doesn't know it.

Advaita is nearly identical to Western Idealism because in both cases, there is no reality, what we see is just our experience, and due to the absence of reality, this experience is a delusion. Since the delusion is painful in Advaita (we are suffering in the world), therefore, dissolving it is preferred over keeping it. Thus, Advaita goes a step further than Idealism to say that an illusion exists and we must get out of it. Idealism doesn't take this step or says that it cannot be taken. Thus, in Idealism, the illusion continues, we have no way of getting out of it, and even if that illusion is suffering, it can never be resolved.

The West has coopted Advaita in the name of studying and prioritizing mind and consciousness over the realist stances. Advaita is already non-religious, so you can't be blamed for siding with one religion. You can also say that the study of mind and consciousness is scientific, so you cannot be called opposed to science. Thus, the West walks the tightrope between not being anti-scientific and not being pro-religion. It is factually anti-scientific because science means mathematical realism which has already failed, but if you don't say that openly, then it's okay. It is also factually pro-religion because the ideas of consciousness and mind are being drawn out of the Vedic tradition but reformulated in a secular language, but if you don't say that part out loud, then it's okay. The tightrope of Western Idealism is just hypocrisy.

The Creation of Escapist Ideologies

Māyā is neither Western Realism nor Idealism. A real world exists but we misperceive it. So, in a sense, the evil is in us, rather than nature. We cannot torture nature to know her secrets. We have to purify ourselves to know the truth. But this evil is not inherited due to our ancestry—i.e., Adam and Eve—so revelation is not necessary to know the truth. At most, revelation can tell us about the nature of the truth which we have to confirm via reason and observation. Thus, the focus of Western Scientific Realism is on torturing nature to make her reveal her secrets while the focus of the Vedic doctrine of Māyā is on torturing ourselves to purify ourselves after which we know the truth automatically.

Most people don't like torturing themselves. Some people prefer that the truth be revealed to them so that they can have blind faith in that revelation without having to torture themselves. Other people would like to torture nature to get to the truth, instead of torturing themselves. Yet other people want to avoid torturing nature, or having blind faith in a revelation, or torturing themselves, and they prefer to dissolve the world by calling it an illusion. All these are escapes from self-torture. Christianity escapes self-torture by having blind faith in a revelation. Scientific Realism escapes self-torture by torturing nature. Advaita escapes self-torture by calling the entirety of the conscious experience an illusion.

The Creation of Veda Through Austerity

In contrast to these escapist ideologies, the doctrine of Māyā insists that the reason we see a rope and think it is a snake is due to problems within ourselves. Factually, the rope is not a snake; we cannot call it a snake because it doesn't bite us. Factually, there is a rope; we can confirm that there is a rope by using it as such. Factually, the misunderstanding of a rope as a snake is due to a problem within us; the rope can be confirmed and the snake can be denied, so our seeing a snake in a rope is our problem. Factually, this misunderstanding can be removed; we have to distinguish between a rope and a snake, confirm a rope, and disconfirm a snake, and through this process, we have to change our understanding.

Factually, this process involves self-torture, although we find the truth in this way and there is no other way.

Vedic texts describe how Veda (i.e., knowledge of truth) was created—Brahma was born on a lotus, he didn't have a clue about who he was or what he was supposed to do, then he heard the word *tapa* (austerity), proceeded to perform austerity, and after a long time having removed the delusion within himself, the truth automatically appeared in his mind. Then Brahma gave this truth to his sons, which could be called a revelation, but they went on to perform austerity, to realize the revelation. These sons then expanded the revelation to more revelation, and yet, everyone was still expected to perform austerity to realize it. Thus, austerity is embedded in the Vedic tradition from the beginning.

Why Kali-Yuga Creates Escapist Ideas

But in Kali-Yuga, people become hedonistic and cannot do austerity. The body and mind are so weak that they cannot stand hardship. They invent varieties of schemes to avoid austerity—such as blind faith in a revelation (Abrahamic religions), torturing nature (Scientific Realism), claiming that what I see without austerity is the truth (Naïve Realism), or claiming that the world is an illusion (Māyāvāda). The varieties of religions, ideologies, philosophies, and theories are just schemes to avoid austerity. They are all delusions because they try to shut the door on the only way of knowing the truth—i.e., austerity. They cannot succeed because they never address the problem of Māyā, i.e., purifying oneself. And yet, every such scheme seems extremely alluring because it promises the result without a lot of effort.

Vedic texts describe how greatness is achieved through austerity. Sages performed austerities for thousands of years to attain greatness. Very few people could perform such austerities even in the former times, hence greatness was limited, and those who had done such austerities were respected. The Bhagavad Gita states that out of thousands in this world, hardly one endeavors for perfection; out of thousands endeavoring for perfection, hardly one attains perfection; of the thousands who have attained perfection, hardly one knows God. While no one is forbidden from pursuing perfection, in practice, it is known that perfection is rare. Nobody equalized the opinions of everyone.

But in Kali-Yuga, people cannot do austerity. They also cannot accept that they lack greatness. So they equalize everyone's opinion as free speech. Every lazy man incapable of austerity comes up with a new scheme of staying lazy and attaining greatness. In Abrahamic religions, you go to the kingdom of God without the purification of consciousness. In modern science and Western philosophy, you create an Earthly kingdom of God by trial and error. In Advaita, you become God by calling everything an illusion. There are unlimited options to elevate mediocrity to supremacy. Each person's option is based on their level of mediocrity. Choose the one you like. Of course, the fact is that none of these elevations are factually true. They are simply different kinds of self-delusion to stop the austerity but make the mediocre think they are on the path to greatness and supremacy. This self-delusion is temporary; it doesn't end suffering; in fact, it exacerbates it. And yet, most people cannot stop believing the delusion. They shoot the messenger who tells them about the futility of their endeavors.

All Forms of Dharma Involve Austerity

Each of the four principles of dharma—truthfulness, kindness, cleanliness, and austerity—is nothing but austerity in Kali-Yuga. If we tell the truth that the delusion is in each person, everyone is offended and they shoot the messenger. If we show kindness in any form, people think that we have something to gain and attack us trying to undermine out of envy. If we ask them to follow a systematic approach, they remain unsystematic, fail to achieve anything, and accuse the person who gave them the systematic approach of having given them a bad approach. If we take the austerity of guiding anyone, they dump their austerity onto the person who is showing them the path of austerity and end up torturing the person who shows that path. Simply doing dharma is very hard in Kali-Yuga.

This is why Kali-Yuga is almost completely hopeless, except for those who are ready for austerity. There are literally infinite imaginary schemes for avoiding austerity, which delude people into futile pursuits. Everyone who tries to take them out of this futility is shot, attacked, accused, and tortured.

We can summarize it succinctly: If it is simple, it is probably not true; if it is cheap, it is probably not a diamond; if it is easy, it is probably not great. That doesn't mean we make the truth unnecessarily complicated, make diamonds unnecessarily expensive, or make greatness unnecessarily difficult. We simply focus on the truth, diamonds, and greatness, and accept the minimum necessary and sufficient complexity, cost, and hardship required for it. Māyā is the delusion that the simpler is truer, the cheaper is more valuable, and the easier is greater.

Rapid Expansion of Escapist Ideas

The original form of Māyā is a delusion in the self as an independent enjoyer. It develops into numerous schemes of independent enjoyment. As that independent enjoyment is not fulfilled, but the tendency to enjoy independently is solidified, it becomes the inability for austerity to end the original delusion. To justify the inability for austerity, Māyā expands into infinite schemes for avoiding austerity, which are also delusions because they won't remove the original delusion, and instead further reinforce it.

At each successive step, Māyā increases and keeps the soul trapped in its control. The original delusion is very simple, but as it progresses, it becomes more and more complex and becomes harder to escape. Most people are enamored by the simplicity of the original delusion; they think that they can easily remove it. They don't realize that the original delusion has expanded and solidified immensely.

Most people think that there is some truth in modern science, Western philosophy, Abrahamic religions, Māyāvāda, and dozens of such things prevalent today. They don't understand that these are expansions of Māyā—i.e., to perpetuate the delusion of the self being an independent enjoyer, firming the tendency for hedonism, reducing the capacity for austerity, justifying the hedonism, and trying to avoid austerity. Since there are infinite schemes to avoid austerity, which keep appearing, disappearing, and evolving, everyone trying to avoid austerity keeps jumping from one scheme to another thinking that even if the previous scheme failed, the new one will succeed. Thus, new theories, religions, philosophies, and ideologies keep popping up. They are quite popular because they promise the impossible goal of independent enjoyment. Deluded by these escapist ideologies, the soul remains trapped in Māyā.

Why Escape from Māyā is Very Hard

This is the infinite and inescapable trap of Māyā. The root cause is the inability to take the austerity of purifying oneself, coupled with the renunciation of the idea of independent enjoyment. Everyone wants a heaven in which they don't have to work for survival, that they will have food and a home, and they will simply play and dance. But they don't want God in that heaven. While God would have given all these things for free, we want the kingdom of God without God. This is the real meaning of Māyā.

But to avoid the austerity of purifying oneself, and accepting God, Advaita created a misunderstanding of Māyā in which the distinction between rope and snake is an illusion. After that, you don't have to talk about the difference between the two. You can abrogate differences and focus on similarities. Of course, the differences don't disappear just because we don't want to look at them. They come back to bite us when we least expect it. The redefinition of Māyā is therefore nothing but a delusion. While Advaita likes to call the world a delusion, the fact is that its imaginary notion of oneness is the actual delusion.

This delusion is not harmless. As India's history shows, it is extremely harmful because when you state that you are not separate from your enemy, then you have to part with your wealth, property, and life for the enemy. Your enemy will now exploit you, take everything that you have, while you are standing silently hoping to attain oneness with him. Therefore, if someone doesn't agree with the problems of Advaita based on the Vedic texts, then there is a secular and empirical confirmation of that problem. Of course, precisely due to Māyā, even when you see your self-destruction, you will blame individual politicians, political parties, religious groups, and conversion schemes, rather than yourself.

Sexuality in the Vedic Tradition

The Essential Nature of Sexuality

The Importance of Sex in Vedic Texts

In Tantra philosophy, the entire material creation is described as the sexual intercourse of Śiva and Śakti. But because sex has become such a taboo subject these days, discussing it openly, in any detail, seems vulgar. The shame associated with sex within religion has pushed the discussion of sex outside religion. But calling sex shameful, taboo, or despicable doesn't reduce its prevalence. In fact, what is forcefully suppressed as shame goes deeper in the mind and then comes out bigger in the body. I have also refrained from talking about this subject openly because of this perceived taboo and vulgarity.

The result of not talking openly about sex are manyfold—(a) we don't understand how the entire material realm is sex, (b) we don't understand how the spiritual realm is love and not sex, (c) we don't understand the difference between love and sex, (d) we don't understand what masculine and feminine means in terms of their roles and powers, (e) we apply the roles and powers of men and women to each other and try to create equality between them, (f) don't understand how a sexual marriage in this world has to be lived, and (g) we don't understand how to get out of the sex desire by moderating it.

Therefore, after a lot of consideration, and going back and forth in my mind, I decided to write an elaborate article on sex. To put this article in context, there is no sex in the spiritual world.

The spiritual world is based on love rather than sex. But at present, people equate love to sex. Therefore, I will use this article to explain the difference between the two and why sex is such an important subject in the material world, completely absent in the spiritual world, and yet going from matter to spirit requires us to understand sex deeply to enable its removal. Simply suppressing the topic does not work.

A General Meaning of Phallus and Vulva

Sex involves a phallus (lingam) and a vulva (yoni). For most people, these are just the genitalia. But in the Vedic texts, they are not limited to genitalia. Rather, every part of the body is genitalia because lust exists in every part of the body. The Brahma Vaivarta Purāṇa describes that when Indra seduced Ahalya (the wife of Sage Gautama), Brahma cursed him to bear a thousand vulvae on his body. Brahma could have cursed Indra to have a thousand phalluses since Indra is a male. Then why a thousand vulva? To understand this, we have to go deeper into the meaning of phallus and vulva, beyond the genitalia. It is best to begin with the deepest meaning of genitalia, and then we can understand everything else.

There is a vulva in our hearts, which is the hole of emptiness, loneliness, and unfulfillment. We try to fill this hole with the phallus of gadgets, money, and prestige. The attempt to fill the vulva with the phallus is sex. As the hole in our hearts becomes bigger, we need a bigger phallus to fill it. That means as we feel more empty, lonely, and unfulfilled, we need more gadgets, money, and prestige. Likewise, as the hole in our hearts gets smaller, we need a smaller phallus to fill it. That means as we feel less empty, lonely, and unfulfilled, we need less gadgets, money, and prestige. When people pursue more gadgets, money, and prestige, we must know that they have a bigger vulva in their heart, i.e., emptiness, loneliness, and unfulfillment. When the lust for material things reduces, the vulva in the heart also shrinks.

Differences of Providers and Consumers

The lingam is the provider and the yoni is the consumer.

The pleasure of the yoni is the pleasure of consumption and the pleasure of the lingam is the pleasure of production. These are not always mutually exclusive because in this world everyone is required to provide in order to consume. However, when the capacity and proclivity to consume increases, and the capacity and proclivity to provide decreases, the person becomes more yoni than lingam. Conversely, when the capacity and proclivity to provide increases, and the capacity and proclivity to consume decreases, the person becomes more lingam than yoni. A society that consumes more than it provides is a bigger yoni and a smaller lingam. A society that provides more than it consumes is a bigger lingam and smaller yoni. Masculinity is the capacity and desire to provide and femininity is the capacity and desire to consume. When a society becomes a net consumer, it becomes feminine because it demands more than it supplies. When a society becomes a net provider, it becomes masculine because it supplies more than it demands.

Whenever there is hardship in society, the role of the masculine provider grows. Whenever there is comfort in a society, the role of the feminine consumer grows. The feminine demands more rights while the masculine performs more duties. However, if men start demanding rights rather than performing duties, they too become effeminate. Similarly, if women start performing duties rather than demanding rights, they too are masculinized. The bodily gender can be different than the mental nature.

The person who performs more duties and demands fewer rights must always have the upper hand in a society because duties are necessary and sufficient to fulfill rights whereas rights are neither necessary nor sufficient to perform duties. Production is necessary and sufficient for consumption but consumption is neither necessary nor sufficient for production. The provider has an upper hand over the consumer. Hence, men who supply more and demand less have an upper hand over women who demand more and supply less. Sex for a man is being accepted as the provider in the dominant position over the woman. Sex for a woman is being accepted as the consumer in a subordinate position to the man.

Sexuality as a Model of Cosmic Reality

The Mechanistic Scientific Model of Reality

Every scientific description of the world takes after a *model*. The model for nature in modern science is a machine; it takes in energy and outputs work. It is a failed model of reality because sometimes there is more energy input but less work output and sometimes there is more work output with less energy input. We can never make a mechanistic model of nature if nature can't be treated as a machine. Science assumes that nature is a machine under the process of depersonalizing and objectifying nature.

Mechanistic models of reality are unidirectional—the producer gives something to the consumer but the consumer gives nothing back to the producer. This mechanistic model is drawn from a depersonalized picture of nature—nature gives something to man but man gives nothing to nature. These models began with religions in which God gave man a lot while man gave a lot less to God; as time elapsed, the giving continuously reduced while taking continuously increased. The same ideas were then formalized into ideas of society in which each person minimizes the giving and maximizes the taking. Colonial atrocities were perpetrated on the same unidirectional principle of taking a lot and giving a little. All mechanistic models of reality operate on the unidirectional concept of force. It creates an oppressive, exploitative, coercive, and non-reciprocal understanding of everything.

Mechanistic models of nature construe an amoral conception of reality under which one simply takes and gives nothing, or takes a lot and gives a little. However, if we were to add morality and fairness back to nature, then each party would give and take fairly, but they must also give and take different things. This reciprocal idea of causality cannot be understood simply by reversing the giving into taking. For instance, if one person gives something to another person which the other person returns, then there will be no change, and no need to explain it with a cause. The reversal of unidirectional models of causality doesn't mean giving back the same thing that one has received—as Newton conceived his 3rd law of action and reaction, where the action and reaction are equal and opposite. Giving and taking must involve different things, based on what each party needs or wants. Newton's model of reciprocity says that when I push something, it pushes me back. But a producer and consumer don't push each other. Even if one person's purpose is to advance, the other person's purpose must be to retract. Through such compatibility between purposes, the interaction becomes mutually relishable.

The Reciprocal Scientific Model of Reality

A reciprocal model of causality requires two opposite kinds of desires and pleasures—there is a desire to provide and a desire to consume, a pleasure in giving and a pleasure in taking, a desire to control and a desire to be controlled. If both parties want to consume (and no party wants to provide), or both parties want the pleasure of taking (and no party wants the pleasure of giving), or if both parties want to control (and no party wants to be controlled), then causality is pushing and being pushed back. Sure, this is a part of reality, but an exceptional case where things *don't* work the way we want them to work. It is not the normal case where things *do* work. If producers and consumers push each other away, there will be neither production nor consumption. They have to attract each other, and form mutually beneficial bonds, for either to exist.

Mechanistic models of reality are inevitable in a culture dominated by Aristotelian universalist thinking in which opposites simply cannot coexist. If X is true, then not-X must be false, and what is false cannot exist. They are also inevitable in a culture dominated by Abrahamic universalist thinking in which the opposites are God and Satan, forever locked in a battle that ends in God destroying Satan. A reciprocal model of causality requires opposites giving and taking. But if these opposites are eliminated due to Aristotelian logic or Abrahamic universalism, then we get the idea that the world must be moving due to force. Now, each side minimizes the giving and maximizes the taking, and whoever can apply greater force takes more while giving less. This amoral (or immoral) conception of reality is the result of Aristotelian and Abrahamic thinking.

In the Vedic non-mechanistic model of reality, the opposites are masculine and feminine. The existence of one doesn't eliminate the existence of the other. The masculine and the feminine are not at war with each other like God and Satan, which must culminate in God destroying Satan. The masculine and the feminine are rather two opposite natures involved in sexual intercourse. They are both persons, but their desires are opposite—one enjoys providing and the other enjoys consuming, but in return, the consumer gives pleasure and the provider takes pleasure. There is no mathematical equation governing sex.

Of course, in some limited sense, the repeated entry and exit of the phallus into and out of the vulva can be approximated as a machine. However, in so far as this machine doesn't work the same for every time, place, situation, and person, it is not a machine. Something that looks like a machine but doesn't work the same everywhere and everywhen is not a machine. However, both working like a machine and not working like a machine can be explained as sex. The non-mechanistic model of reality is sex.

Mechanistic and Non-Mechanistic Models

The reasons that sex doesn't work like a machine are numerous and diverse. I will list them here. The aim is not to provide an exhaustive list of possibilities that explain why the behavior is both mechanistic and non-mechanistic. The aim is only to provide suggestive examples of how this often happens.

- After every desire is fulfilled, the desire disappears temporarily, but returns after some time; the disappearance and reappearance are not exactly periodic, to create a machine.
- After every desire is fulfilled, a new desire is created, which follows the same cycle of association and dissociation, and yet, it is a different kind of machine than the previous one.
- As one kind of emptiness reduces, another type of pre-existing emptiness magnifies, pushing the mechanistic behavior out of one type of machine into another type of machine.
- If the desire doesn't perfectly match the thing trying to

fulfill it, there is displeasure even during association, which means the mechanistic behavior is not precisely periodic.

- Mismatches in desires can stop and start the intercourse, decelerate or accelerate the intercourse, and due to these inconsistencies, the behavior is not periodic.
- Mismatches in desires create coercion in which each party tries to change the other, which may or may not succeed, and the result of change or no change isn't deterministic.
- Mismatches in desires can temporarily pause the intercourse but restart it as pausing the pleasure brings back the desire for pleasure which restores the previous state.

Sex is repeated association and dissociation between the producer and the consumer. It is not limited to genitalia, although everything we see in the world can be modeled as the intercourse of genitalia, so talking about sex in detail becomes an easy way to understand the world, as the model of reality.

Sexuality and Conscious Experience

Spiritual and Material States of the Soul

Before entering the material world, the soul is fulfilled, loved, peaceful, and happy. Vedic texts describe how Māyā—"that which is not"—transforms the original state into its opposite: feeling empty, unloved, anxious, and unhappy. This feeling triggers the desire to acquire gadgets, money, and prestige, and for the time that this desire is fulfilled, and the soul feels worthy, valuable, loved, and pleased. Māyā is hence described in two ways—throwing and covering. The feeling of emptiness, loneliness, anxiety, and unhappiness is the state of *throwing,* and the reversal of feeling wanted, worthy, valuable, loved, and pleased is the state of *covering*. The second state of Māyā looks to the original state of being fulfilled, loved, peaceful, and happy, although it is not. There are three kinds of states—(a) the original state of happiness, (b) its reversal as anxiety, and (c) its reversal as pleasure. Pleasure is not the same as happiness, although they seem similar.

Happiness is internal and pleasure is external. Happiness is the state of internal satisfaction and fulfillment due to which a happy person doesn't need external validation. In contrast, unhappiness is the state of internal dissatisfaction and unfulfilment due to which an unhappy person always seeks external validation. Therefore, the double-reversal from happiness to anxiety to pleasure doesn't take the soul back to its original state, although it temporarily reduces the misery, suffering, and unhappiness. Over time, people accustomed to pleasure completely forget about happiness. They cannot imagine a state of inner contentment, satisfaction, and fulfillment. They accept that every person is by default empty and the only way to fill that emptiness is through the acquisition of gadgets, money, and prestige. Thus, in many modern cultures, pleasure has replaced happiness. Due to its dependence on external things, pleasure is not just fleeting, but also binding a person to the world as he depends on the world for pleasure. In contrast, happiness is not just permanent but also liberating, as it frees the person from external dependence.

Sex as Union of Senses and Sense Objects

The things that give us pleasure are contrasted to Māyā as Puruṣa. Māyā creates desires and Puruṣa fulfills them. Māyā is the desire and Puruṣa is the object of desire; if that object of desire is acquired, the desire is fulfilled. Our senses are expansions of Māyā—they are ways in which we are empty, lonely, and unfulfilled. The objects of the senses are expansions of the Puruṣa—they are the ways in which we try to overcome the feelings produced from Māyā.

Therefore, every union of the senses with their objects is sex. Sex is not just with genitals. We are engaged in sex even while hearing, touching, seeing, tasting, and smelling because each of these involves a union of senses and the sense objects. As our fingers touch one thing after another, there is a union of senses with the sense objects and hence that is sex. As our feet move one step at a time, there is a union of the senses with the sense objects and hence that is sex. As our tongue moves up and down and unites with the outgoing and incoming breath, there is a union of the senses with the sense objects and hence that is sex. As the urine passes via the urethra, there is contact between the senses and the sense objects and hence that is sex. Then of course there is genital sex, which everyone calls sex.

Sex is a general concept in Vedic texts and it means desire (kāma) in the senses and fulfillment of that desire by the sense objects (bhūta). Genital sex is a special case of the general concept of the union between senses and the sense objects. This is why sex is discussed so brazenly in the Vedic texts in contrast to so much shame being associated with sex in all other religions. While every other religion is thinking about genital sex, the Vedic texts are talking about the union of senses with their sense objects. If perception is also sex, there is no shame in talking about it. When the entire material world is based on desires for material things, which lead to the union with those things, then the whole world is just sex.

The Material World as Observer Experience

The cosmic sex is described as the intercourse between Śiva and Śakti—Śakti is desire and Śiva is the object of that desire. Śiva is Puruṣa (the object of desire) and Śakti is Māyā (the desire for the object). The senses are Śakti and Śiva is the object of the senses. When Śiva and Śakti unite, their children are produced. These children are *experiences* produced through the union of senses and their objects.

Our body is not a substance, object, or matter. It is an experience that materialistic people who don't know about Śiva and Śakti have objectified and are studying the world as objects due to their own Materialism—i.e., ignorance of Śiva and Śakti. If they develop the bare minimum understanding of the world, then they will realize that the world is simply experiences—cognitions, conations, intentions, emotions, and relations—to which the soul is attached due to its own will to experience. That will stops temporarily when we go to sleep so the experience ends although that is not the end of the world because even as we are sleeping, Śiva and Śakti are engaged in their pleasurable intercourse. That intercourse lasts for 311 trillion years, after which both of them rest in each other's embrace.

Ignorant people call the material world evil, malicious, and wicked, but even that is described so beautifully in the Vedic texts that it will put to shame anyone who calls the world evil, malicious, and wicked. The beauty of the spiritual world is even greater, which we will discuss toward the end.

Technical Treatment of Sexuality Topics

Sāñkhya: Indriya, Bhūta, and Tanmātra

All our experiences are produced from our senses; during dreaming, they are produced without contact with any objects, and during waking, they are produced due to contact with objects. In Sāñkhya, the senses are called *indriya*, the sense objects are called *bhūta*, and the experiences generated from the senses due to the interaction with the sense objects are called *tanmātra*. Factually, we never see the *bhūta* because they are "behind" the experience of *tanmātra*. For us, the *tanmātra* are the appearances and the *bhūta* are the reality behind the appearances, but that reality is just a hypothesis. In principle, we could say that even waking is just like dreaming—i.e., I have created my experiences and there is no world causing it. However, this begs the question of why self-created experiences are painful. If I were fully in control of my experience creation, then I would only create happy experiences. The problem of suffering creates a necessity for something other than the self, although we don't know what it is.

In Plato's allegory of the cave, the cavemen simply see the shadows (*tanmātra*) but never see what is causing those shadows (*bhūta*). They also don't accept that the shadows are self-created. Thereby, the person is not dreaming. He is awake, he sees the appearances, but not their cause. As a result of not seeing the reality behind the appearance, there is speculation about it in Western philosophy, science, and religion, and they conclude that there must be some "objects"—e.g., particles, waves, electrons, protons, neutrons, quarks, leptons, baryons, hadrons—that must be causing our experiences.

Differences of Seer, Seen, and Seeing

In the Vedic texts, what we don't see behind the appearances is Śiva; what we see is Śakti. What we see is produced from our senses as an appearance due to interaction with a world that we never see. Hence, we can experience our desires, and then experience the images of the world, but never the world. In short, Śakti is all that we are experiencing while Śiva is the real unseen cause of appearances.

Śaṅkarācārya, an incarnation of Śiva, called this invisible reality behind the appearance Brahman. He was talking about Himself—"I am Brahman" by saying Aham Brahmāsmi. But everyone assumed that Śaṅkarācārya was talking about them; his statements about himself were misunderstood as statements about everyone, and thus, everyone began claiming to be Brahman. Traditional Advaita followers worship Śiva, and that is good. But many equated themselves to Śiva and then said that even Śiva is an imagination while the self is the only reality.

The main question is: What is reality? Is it *behind* the appearances—i.e., the thing we are not seeing? Or is it *before* the appearances—i.e., the seer who is seeing appearances? The answer is that the reality behind the appearances is Śiva, and the reality before the appearances is the soul. The appearances lying in between reality and the self are caused by Śakti. Hence, there are three causes of experience—Śiva, Śakti, and the soul. We are the seer, we develop a desire to see and then see an appearance due to the effect of Śakti, whereas Śiva is the actual seen but He remains unseen. We develop a desire for Śiva because we are under the control of Śakti who is desiring Śiva. The thing that is *behind* is not that is *before*. The seer, the appearance, and the reality are three distinct categories responsible for experience.

In the Tantra Āgama, Śiva is worshipped in five forms called Sadyojāta, Vāmadeva, Aghora, Tatpuruṣa, and Īśāna, which correspond to the five *bhūta* or Earth, Water, Fire, Air, and Ether, respectively. These elements are not substances, objects, or matter. They are the five aspects of Śiva, the reality behind the appearances, the *bhūta* behind the *tanmātra*. Anyone who depersonalizes these elements is ignorant of Vedic texts (there are many people who want to construct mathematical models of the *bhūta*). Even these *bhūta* are only the body of Śiva, behind which are His mind, intellect, ego, and the self. Hence, the thing we are not seeing—and calling it reality—is not impersonal. It is rather a person—Śiva.

Differences of Subjective and Objective

At this juncture, I will draw a distinction between the *subjective* and the *objective*, quite different from how these words are used at present (and in the Western world) to illustrate why appearance is distinct from reality, why appearance can depict reality accurately, but also why it can mislead us.

Let's take the example of a pen to illustrate what we mean by subjective and objective. Ideally, it is a pen. But non-ideally, it could be a weapon, ornament, or paperweight. Whether I call it a pen, weapon, ornament, or paperweight is my subjective choice. However, this choice is not limitless since I can never say that the pen is a car, ship, or an airplane. While different people can call the pen a weapon, ornament, or paperweight, nobody can call it a car, ship, or airplane. Therefore, pen, weapon, ornament, or paperweight are true for some people (subjective truth) while not being a car, ship, or airplane is true for everyone (objective truth). The objective truth is not an object; it is a limitation on the possible subjective claims. We can also say that the pen is the ideal truth, weapon, ornament, and paperweight are possible truths, and not being a car, ship, or airplane are the impossible truths. The ideal and the possible truths can be subjectively chosen, but the objectively impossible truths can't be chosen. And thus, subjective and objective exist side-by-side as they pertain to the possible and the impossible. We don't see the impossible truths because we either see the possible or the ideal. The positive is seen and the negative is not seen. The subjective truth is not private because others can see the world in the same way. The objective truth is not public because nobody is able to see the impossible truths. Thus, two kinds of dominant claims are false—objectivity is not public, and subjectivity is not privacy. Both can be established through the example of a pen.

This objective, but non-object reality, is a person, i.e., Śiva, who we don't see because we never see the whole appearance. He can be described in five different forms if we want to personify each element. In simple words, subjective truth means pertaining to each soul, while objective truth means pertaining to Śiva, the Lord of the material realm. Since Śiva is one, hence the objective truth is one. Of course, the subjective truths are many, corresponding to each soul seeing a part of Śiva. Thereby, subjective and objective truths are both personal, although different as the soul and God. The depersonalization of the objective truth at the hands of Western thinking is a false dogma because even when a simple thing like a pen can be described as a weapon, ornament, or paperweight and established to be true by reason and observation, then the pen cannot be called an object. Thus, nothing in the world is an object. And yet, there is an objective truth—true for everyone—which is all the impossible truths for something. It is objective also in the sense that it transcends every soul's experience and it hides behind the phenomena.

Now we can understand why there is an objective reality and yet we don't see it—our experiences are the results of our desires, and since these desires are limited (i.e., our senses are limited), we can never see the whole reality. We see parts, but we don't understand that these are parts of the body of Śiva and we objectify them. Our experience is a vision created by our desire, which is a subjective truth, different from the objective truth. The objective truth limits the subjective experience but doesn't fix it.

In simple words, we see parts of Śakti but not Śiva. And yet, we can *infer* from the subjective experiences that the objective reality must exist. Hence, the Vedic worldview is Realist and not Solipsist, which means that there is an objective reality and my experience is not self-created. But Realism is not Materialism. It is also Theistic in which reality is Śiva. The world is working because of Śiva's will, not mathematical laws. Since the objective truth is what we don't see, therefore, all that we see is a byproduct of our desire. Since that desire is for pleasure rather than happiness, it is both temporary and illusory. The vision produced due to that pursuit is an illusion, or Māyā. Thus, Realism in the Vedic texts is fully compatible with our experience being an illusion, unlike in Western philosophy where the existence of a real universe entails that we must see it just as it is.

Varied Descriptions of the Same Reality

The Objective Reality is Also Cosmic Time

The situation of the material world can be summarized as seeing a movie projected by a movie projector. We don't see the projector, the actual cause of the movie. And yet, both the movie and the projector exist. The movie we see isn't a substance, object, or reality. But behind that movie is a projector, the reality. That projector can project any number of movies. To see a movie without seeing the projector is an illusion. And yet, without the projector, there will be no movie. And thus, the world we see is at once an illusion and an indicator of reality.

Since this merger of Realism and illusion confuses everyone, therefore, we can add a nuance to it from the Vedic texts—the reality or Śiva is also Cosmic Time. We can see space or Śakti, but we cannot see Śiva or time. And yet, time is the reality and what we are seeing is an illusion. Our vision is illusion or Māyā and reality is Puruṣa. These two are not enemies, like God and Satan of Abrahamic religions at war with each other, even as they are opposites. They are husband and wife romancing each other.

In the movie *The Matrix*, there is a gigantic computer that simulates the experiences of people trapped in its control. Those experiences are illusions created by the computer or the Matrix, which is never seen by the people in its control. That computer or the Matrix that we never see is Cosmic Time, but it controls us. As experiences appear one after another, we see an *effect of time*, but never time itself. This is why in modern science it has been very easy to measure time but very hard to say what time actually is. We have seen moving things in space, but we have never seen time. We simply *infer* that time exists.

Time is cyclical in the Vedic texts because it is sexual intercourse. Normally, we don't like to talk about sex, so we just say that time is cyclical. But if we want to understand this cycle, then it is that of sexual intercourse. As the masculine enters the feminine, the world expands. As the masculine withdraws from the feminine, the world contracts. These two are creation and destruction. In between, there are periods during which the masculine stays within or outside the feminine, and that is called maintenance.

Nyāya, Buddhism, and Advaita Ideologies

Thus, there are many descriptions of reality—the five *bhūta*, the reality behind the appearances, the projector projecting a movie, the objective truth different from the subjective truth, the truth different from the illusion, the Cosmic Time that moves everything but remains invisible although it can be inferred, and even the Matrix under whose control were are all seeing a world, and while we cannot see the Matrix itself, we can infer its presence, and ultimately, Śiva who is seen, desired, and loved by Śakti, but Her children cannot see their father. Of course, the children can ask who their father is, and the mother will tell them about Him.

In Nyāya philosophy, there are two basic categories of reality called Bhāva and Abhāva, or presence and absence. That absence in its primordial form is desire while the presence in its primordial form is the person being desired. We can also say that the absence is our senses and the presence is their objects. When presence and absence interact, a presence (experience) is created from absence (desire). The soul is inside Māyā or absence, and the presence (experiences) it sees is created from that absence. Hence, in one sense, it is correct to say that everything is created from "nothing" because it is indeed created from absence. However, it is not factually nothing. It is the desire for presence, which is not "nothing".

Buddhists elevated the principle of creation from absence to the only truth, disregarding the presence. Śaṅkarācārya then appeared to say that there is indeed a presence, although what we see is created from absence. Thus, a conflict between Buddhism and Advaita was created. Factually, both are partially true—the Buddhist absence is Śakti and the Advaita presence is Śiva. A world is created from desire, so discarding the desire also ends the world experience. Likewise, that desire is for something real that we don't experience so there is a reality behind the phenomenal appearances. Buddhism and Advaita depersonalized Śiva and Śakti as *being* and *nothingness* when they are the object of desire and the desire for it. Meanwhile, many Buddhists accepted Shakta Tantras and many Advaitins accepted Shaiva Tantras. If we understand Tantra, then their godlessness is a false dogma forced upon Śiva and Śakti, respectively.

The central problem of this age is depersonalization. In Buddhism desire becomes emptiness. In Advaita, the object of desire becomes an impersonal being. In modern science, reality becomes a mathematical entity. In monotheistic religions, God is depersonalized as a formless entity, and giving it any form means limiting it, due to which exclusivism, universalism, and iconoclasm are married into such religions. The world is suffering from various kinds of ideologies created by varied types of depersonalizations. There is only one alternative—the Vedic tradition—which explains how everything has to be personalized.

Many people at present say—we have seen material reality but we have never seen God. The response to this argument is that you have never seen material reality and hence you have never seen God. What you are seeing is a phenomenon, and you infer there must be a reality working under the influence of time. We infer the same, except that reality and time are identical. You postulate that reality is physical properties, to be modeled using mathematical equations, and time is a linear arrow. With these postulates, all you got is probabilities and contradictions. Hence, your inferences are false. There is a different way to infer, in which there is an eternal divine couple—Śiva and Śakti—engaged in their mutual enjoyment.

How Cosmic Sexuality is Simply Self-Love

Māyā is often described as the power of the Puruṣa. The power is the capacity to know, desire, and relate to the Puruṣa. Just like we see, desire, and relate to something through our eyes, similarly, Māyā is the power of the Puruṣa to see Himself, desire Himself, and relate to Himself. Māyā is the inner eye of the Puruṣa, by which He knows Himself, loves Himself, relates to Himself, and enjoys with Himself. So, there is no conflict in saying that Māyā is senses and the Puruṣa is the object of the senses and then saying that Māyā is power and Puruṣa is the powerful, or that Māyā is desire and Puruṣa is the object of desire. The description in terms of power and powerful is preferred if we don't want to talk about sex. The description in terms of senses and their objects, or desire and its object, is better if talking of sex.

The sexual intercourse in divinity is self-love. Some ancient cultures—such as Mesopotamians and Egyptians—did not have a good way to describe self-love, so they described it as masturbation, which caused an ejaculation, and the world was said to have been produced from this ejaculation. That type of description was sometimes complemented by saying that there is a personality that is both male and female, and the creation was partly sexual. Then there were descriptions that stated that there is a couple, and the creation was the progeny of this couple. Abrahamic religions removed the feminine and could also not accept masturbation. Hence, the world was created from nothing, i.e., *ex nihilo*.

The Vedic texts explain how the divine couple is one and two—the power of seeing is seeing the object of seeing, but that power is the inner eye of the object of seeing as it wants to see itself. The desire in the eyes to see is just the desire for self-seeing. If the eyes are not separated from the person who wants to see, then he cannot see himself. Hence, one becomes two. Their sexual intercourse is self-love. Sex is not taboo in the Vedic tradition because it is between the seer and his power of seeing. The power of seeing is originally in the seer but separates from him, the seer then enters the power of seeing as the seen. Sexual intercourse is simply the seer entering the power of seeing to become seen. This seen is technically distinct from the seer, but in the act of self-seeing, the seer, seen, and seeing are one.

Advaita impersonalists described self-love as self-seeing, and it appeared that there is just one thing—Brahman—when factually there are two. They also pretended that self-seeing is asexual when self-love is sexual. Thus, a gender-neutral ideology was created from a gendered ideology. The former rejects the deities and their genders, making divinity impotent. Well, if someone wants to be eternally impotent, that's fine. Nobody is asking them to be potent. But they should not demand that everyone be impotent. Advaita is accepted by the Personalist schools as a state of impotence. It is not the supreme truth, let alone the universal truth, but it can be one's choice. We have the choice to reject the better truth.

Entrapment, Renunciation, and Delusion

The Vagabond and the Domesticator

Men are often described as uncivilized vagabonds who don't want to be tied down to a woman and women are often described as civilized domesticators who want to tie down a man. Śiva is the archetype of the uncivilized vagabond and Śakti is the archetype of the civilized domesticator. Śakti domesticates the vagabond and He becomes a responsible father and husband. Thereafter, He is tied to Her because in some corner of His heart, He wanted to be domesticated by a civilized wife, and She is tied to Him because, in some corner of Her heart, She wanted to domesticate a vagabond as Her husband.

The feminine is powerful if she can attract the masculine and keep him entrapped by her power of giving pleasure. Holding onto the masculine—by employing the power of pleasure—is real feminine power. The masculine is powerful if he is detached. If he can withdraw, the feminine can't control him. Śakti is the power who entraps Śiva by Her desire for Him and Her proclivity to keep Him entrapped by Her capacity for pleasure. And yet, despite being married to Śakti, Śiva remains sovereign and renounced. Their residence is a mountain, they live in the company of wild creatures, and their pleasures are simple. Due to the combination of Śiva and Śakti, the world is both barbaric and civilized, demonic and divine.

The Śiva-Śakti relation tells us about the nature of masculine and feminine powers. The feminine power is being able to entice, entrap, and please the masculine. The masculine power is being able to renounce this enticement, entrapment, and pleasure from the feminine. Sex for the feminine is an affirmation of her power to give pleasure, appreciation for her capacity to please the masculine, and proof that she can keep a masculine domesticated. Sex for the masculine is an affirmation of his power to take pleasure, recognition of his attractiveness for the feminine, confirmed through the receipt of pleasure. These two powers dominate alternatively, such that the feminine power entraps and the masculine power renounces. The alternating recurrence of entrapment and renunciation is sexual intercourse.

In the Vedic tradition, men were taught about celibacy from childhood, and women were taught how to keep the men pleased. The power of a woman was her capacity to give pleasure and the power of the man was his capacity to renounce pleasure. The woman entrapped the man by giving pleasure and the man liberated the woman by renouncing pleasure. The vagabond asserts his independence through renunciation, establishing that he is still a vagabond, while the domesticator asserts her control over the vagabond through pleasure, establishing that she is still a domesticator. The domesticator must prove that she wants the vagabond domesticated and is ready to keep him happy in domestication. The vagabond must prove that he is ready to renounce the domestication as he prefers independence. The price of domestication for a vagabond is receiving pleasure from the domesticator. The reward of that pleasure for the domesticator is that the vagabond stays domesticated. Thus, there is sexual tension between the vagabond and the domesticator due to their respective proclivities for renunciation and pleasure.

The essence of this tension is that the masculine is independent, vagrant, and renounced while the feminine is entrapment, civilization, and pleasure. This is eternal life for Śiva and Śakti, hence, in their creation, there is a fine balance between independence and entrapment, vagrancy and civilization, renunciation and pleasure. Those who want to live in this material world happily must also create that balance. This is a materialistic life of sexual enjoyment, but it is very sophisticated and scientific.

Why Sex Enjoyment is a Material Delusion

The material world is called a delusion in the Vedic texts because—(a) when we gain something, we lose something else, (b) we become dissatisfied with what we have and crave for what we don't, (c) as we try to fulfill more desires, the desires increase even more, (d) there is no final fulfillment, and (e) it appears at each moment that if we got one more thing, we will have final fulfillment. Thus, the delusion of the material world is that we can be fulfilled. The reality is that its pursuit makes us more unfulfilled. There is only one way to live in this world, which is to control our desires, remain satisfied with what we have, and not crave for what we don't. When desires are controlled, they reduce and create satisfaction. The answer to the problem of dissatisfaction is not fulfillment but rather the containment of desire.

The simple truth of life is that as we chase and obtain material things, we become more unhappy. But nobody is able to explain why that is the case. The Vedic texts explain this fact based on the description of Māyā and Puruṣa—the thing that we think we need or want is not we needing or wanting it, but an external imposition upon us by Māyā, to then force us to start chasing those things. Material life is temptations insinuated upon us from the inside and enticements given to us from the outside.

For example, even if we are currently satisfied, the Puruṣa will dangle a carrot in front of us, after which Māyā will say—"I want that"—and we will immediately become dissatisfied. If we see others eating the carrot, Māyā will say—"I want that"—and we will be dissatisfied. Even without seeing anyone eating a carrot, Māyā will say—"I want that"—and we will be dissatisfied. If we resist these temptations, Māyā will say—"I just want that and nothing else"—and we will start chasing it. However, once we get that, Māyā will say—"If only I could get the other thing, which I had not realized I needed so badly, I could be happy"—and we will start chasing it. There is no end to these pursuits. If one surrenders to them, he is trapped in the material world, always instigated from the inside and provoked from the outside.

These days, almost everyone knows that people in high and mighty positions are involved in perverse sexuality. The more they have, the more they want. The more of the permitted things they can get, the more taboo, forbidden, and prohibited things they want. Factually, they did not want these things when their status was low and powerless. Most of them were happy with the simple permitted things of life. But as they rose to high and mighty positions, new desires sprung within them to chase the forbidden, taboo, and prohibited. Elevation to a high position in life increases one's sexual perversity. Well-known examples of this perversity these days are voyeurism, pedophilia, and polyamory. As perversity rises, sexual fulfillment is attained through raping, sadomasochism, and killing painfully. When the pleasure of life for us is a painful death for someone else, then life has been transformed into its antithesis.

The things we desire right now aren't the only things we will desire if we don't control our desires. As we chase desires, the desires will increase and will reach a point where we desire the forbidden. As the soul pursues the forbidden, or seeks the permitted in forbidden ways, it is entangled in sinful activities and suffers a lot. The desires go unfulfilled, which gradually reduces the desires, and a person sees some peace in a simple life. However, that state is temporary because Māyā and Puruṣa will trap it again.

Therefore, the material realm is sexuality and delusion. The delusion is that if we keep chasing things, then we will return to a peaceful, satisfied, contended, and happy state. The reality is that as we get one thing, we want something even bigger. Our desires grow, get perverted, and cause immense suffering. In chasing pleasure, we end up suffering. Happiness can never be attained through pleasure. And yet, the fact that everyone believes that happiness will be attained through pleasure is a delusion.

Why Escaping Sex Enjoyment is Very Hard

The soul originally came to the world of its own wish. But once in the material world, it is very difficult to get out. The fall into the material realm takes a moment and liberation can take millions of lifetimes. That is just like an ant can easily fall into a well but it takes a lot of effort to come out of that well. Even though the ant may seem progressing right now, even a small mistake can make it fall to the bottom.

Śakti is irresistible desire and entices Śiva into intercourse. Once begun, the intercourse lasts for 311 trillion years, with smaller periods of resting in between, after which the intercourse regains vigor. It means that even in the material world, there are times when sexuality reduces or stops. That is not the end of sexuality. It is just a pause in intercourse before it restarts again. We can't assume that just because it has stopped for now, that it has ended. It can come back again and often does.

The 3-part movie Godfather tells the story of a soldier who is ready to marry his fiancé. His father is a gang leader, who runs into conflicts with other gangs. As the other gangs try to kill his father, the soldier becomes a killer in trying to protect his father. He had vowed to his fiancée that he would never be part of his father's gang activities, but after killing his father's enemies, he is pulled into his father's gang-related activities and becomes even more ruthless than his father. As time passes, he does more and more atrocious things, until one day he decides to salvage himself from this mess by aligning with the Catholic Church, doing charitable activities, making his business legitimate, and gaining respect in society as a model citizen rather than a vile criminal. But circumstances suck him back into the mess that he was trying to escape. In part III of the movie, the don says: *Just when I thought I was out, they pull me back in.* This is the essence of the material world—entrapment, escape, and recapture.

Many people in this world prematurely accept Sannyasa (the renunciate order of life in which one gives up family and home to become a mendicant teaching others). They think they have escaped the material entrapment but what they have actually done is sublimate their sex desire into a different avenue. As we have discussed, sex is not confined to the genitals; rather, every aspect of experience is a sexual intercourse if it is driven by the emptiness within. Those who prematurely accept Sannyasa are driven by the desire for adoration, prestige, and worship. Even if they renounce genital sex, other forms of sex increase as a result of that renunciation, which is sublimation of sex. They start playing fast and loose with the regulations and requirements of Sannyasa and then the inevitable happens: Just when they thought they were out, they are pulled back in.

Practical-Worldly Aspects of Sexuality

Understanding Genders and Powers

Real masculine power is taking pain and real feminine power is giving pleasure. A man cannot give so much pleasure as a woman. A woman cannot take so much pain as a man. Of course, Śiva and Śakti are different from us because they can take the same level of pain and give the same level of pleasure if the need so arises. Śakti performs great austerities like Śiva, and Śiva enjoys the same kinds of pleasures as Śakti. But Śiva's natural proclivity is taking pain and Śakti's natural proclivity is giving pleasure. Based on these distinctions, we can define the masculine-feminine gender difference. Masculinity is a higher proclivity and capacity for pain and femininity is a higher proclivity and capacity for pleasure.

Spiritual progress can be made by taking pain or giving pleasure, provided they are directed properly. In the Vedic tradition, men took pain for the good of society and returned to a home of pleasure created by the women. Men were leaders outside the home and women were managers at home. Men served society and women served men. Nobody thought they were masters, or made inferior by service. Similarly, men performed austerities of traveling and teaching to spread the message of godhead while women offered pleasures of food and home for such teachers.

Thus, both men and women made spiritual progress, as they were engaging their proclivity and capacity for the right purpose. Of course, nobody stopped women from taking pain for the good of society but most women would not because taking pain is unnatural for women. Likewise, nobody stopped men from offering pleasure for the good of society but most men would not because giving pleasure is unnatural for men. Those who can take pain and renounce pleasure (i.e., men) take pain and renounce pleasure. Those who can give pleasure and relieve pain (i.e., women) give pleasure and relieve pain. These are the ideal gender roles. Their adoption was natural and not coerced, and exceptions were always possible.

The Vedic Prescription for Marriage

Factually, women as the embodiment of feminine power have far more desires than men. A man can lead a renounced life, but when he gets married, his wife needs so many things because her desires are many times greater than the man's. An austere man understands how this pursuit of material things is never-ending because desire fulfillment expands the desires. A good woman understands that her desires can destroy her life and that of her children and husband, which will plunge everyone into unhappiness. She accepts the guidance of an enlightened and renounced man. She knows that if she cannot control her desires, a man should. This control is not domination. It is factually the path to liberation. A spiritually progressive society teaches men to be renounced and women to listen to a man if he tries to control their desires. Through this training, both men and women advance in spiritual life.

The ideal marriage is in which a man is enlightened and renounced, and teaches a woman how to be so, while the woman is desire and pleasure, and teaches a man how to live a comfortable life of enjoyment. In the Vedic tradition, before marriage men led an austere life and women lived a comfortable life. When they were paired, the man who had led an austere life took some pleasures from a woman while the woman who led a comfortable life took some austerities from the man. The woman was taking a little austerity and the man was taking a little pleasure. For a man who had led an austere life, a little pleasure was a lot. For a woman who had led a comfortable life, a little austerity was a lot. Thus, men felt they had enjoyed a lot and in old age left home for austerities, and women felt they had done a lot of austerities and retired in their old age to a life of comfort. Their life ended just as it had begun. But from the viewpoint of a neutral observer, men took far more austerities and women gave far more pleasures.

As men took a little pleasure, they did not feel deprived and did not mind austerity. As women took a little austerity, they learned to control their desires and progressed toward renunciation. Thus, both genders were progressing toward transcendence simply by following the basic rules of marriage. If the man became a transcendentalist and the woman was strongly attached to him, both transcended the world at once because a person always goes to the destination that they are most attached to. If a man goes to God, and the woman goes with the man, then both go to God. Married life was therefore not mundane. It could also become eternal if there was a deep bond between the married couple.

Real vs. False Types of Sex Education

Sex education means an understanding of all these principles—namely, how to live in a world created by sexuality, how to conquer sexuality, and transcend it. The goal is not to increase sex, or how to avoid its consequences, such as childbirth, and then enable unlimited indulgence in sex. The path to reduction of sex goes neither through hyperindulgence nor through abject denial. If there is hyperindulgence, the desire for sex increases, rather than decreases. If there is abject denial, the sex desire is vented through other kinds of indulgences such as overeating, intoxication, violence, and sex outside marriage.

We have to remember that sex is a contact between senses and their sense objects. If genital sex is denied, the desire for contact between sense and sense objects is fulfilled through other means. If there is hyperindulgence then the desire for sex increases which is vented through other means. Thus, unless one becomes free of sex, it must be moderated. That moderate level depends on each person. If sex is moderated, then the sex desire gradually reduces. Therefore, moderation has been the path to control sexuality. Suppression and shame are not the path to control sexuality; they increase sexuality. Hyperindulgence and shamelessness are also not the path to control sexuality; they increase sexuality.

Education about the nature of reality is paramount. At least, an option to educate must exist, but if the people don't take it then they have made their bed in hell. The laws of nature are very harsh. There is no sentimental forgiveness since forgiving just makes things worse. We can see that through the history of religions that forgave sins; instead of reducing sin, they increase it; instead of taking people toward a better life, they degrade their lives. Therefore, nature doesn't forgive. This is because the effect of forgiving sins is well-known. Ignorance is not an excuse against suffering. The fire will burn our hand whether we put it into fire knowingly or unknowingly. It is better to learn that a fire will burn the hand and not to put our hand inside it. This applies to education about sexuality as well.

Modern Perversion of Sexual Tendencies

False Ideas of Masculine and Feminine

At present, many women want to acquire masculine power,

which is the power of enduring pain. Austerity makes the body strong and a strong body handles austerity. Even an austere woman can become strong. However, as the capacity to endure pain rises, the capacity to give pleasure declines. Thus, as women try to get strong, they lose their capacity to give pleasure and become unattractive to men. Conversely, hedonism makes the body weak, which is the incapacity for austerity. As men become hedonistic, they become weak and unattractive to women. The modern social trends are toward inverting the ideas of masculine and feminine—men losing power through hedonism and women gaining power through austerity. The net result of this inversion is that neither gender finds the other gender sexually attractive. Women find men too effeminate and men find women too masculinized.

In general, there are native capacities and proclivities in both genders. Right at birth, men are born with a greater capacity and proclivity for austerity and women are born with a greater capacity and proclivity for pleasure. That means stronger men, with strength being the capacity to endure pain and renounce pleasure. A woman's power is giving pleasure, not enduring pain. Women are born with the proclivity and capacity to give pleasure and relieve pain. Ideal gender roles in society were based on these natural capacities and proclivities, without denying exceptions. Men did jobs that involved taking more pain and women did jobs that involved giving more pleasure. Men focused on jobs that involved renouncing pleasures and women focused on jobs that involved relieving pain. Gender roles were based on their respective capacity and proclivity.

However, at present, the pursuit of gender equality creates more and more perverse ideas about power. For instance, by greater power, many women don't mean enduring greater pain. They mean being employed in a cushy job, working within an air-conditioned office, sitting on a nicely cushioned chair, typing emails to subordinates, and barking orders in meetings on what others need to do while taking home a big pay packet by which they will have more pleasure and less pain. These perverse ideas of power are the results of men having previously inverted the idea of power from the capacity for greater pain to that of greater pleasure. The modern masculine definition of power is more and more pleasure and less and less pain. These are not strong men. They are weak effeminate men. They can't handle austerity and give their austerity to others while taking their pleasure. Many women are simply following the perverse masculine idea of power—i.e., demanding more pleasure and less pain.

Rise of Gays, Lesbians, Transgenders

In the traditional gender roles, where men accepted pain and women relieved pain, and where men rejected pleasure and women gave pleasure, both were compatible. In modern gender roles, as men reduce the pain they take for women and women demand that men take more pain for them, while men demand more pleasure from women and women reduce the pleasure they give men, the genders have become incompatible. Due to the inversion of these gender roles, all relationships are unhappy.

In a traditional marriage, men would work to provide for the family, while women would take care of the home and children. When a man was in difficulty, the women nourished and soothed the men. The home for a man was a place of rejuvenation, after which he could take hardship again. But in a modern marriage, women expect men to work harder to take the woman to vacations and restaurants while renouncing their role of nourishing and soothing a man. As a man finds that he is not nourished and soothed in his home, he pursues other women to find that rejuvenation. That in turn reduces his attention toward the woman at home who wanted more than normal but gets less than normal. Now she looks for another man who will take her to vacations and restaurants and as her attention is diverted away from the family, the man who wanted more than normal gets less than normal. This is a self-reinforcing cycle in which one gender increasing the demand and reducing the supply leads to the other gender reducing their supply and increasing the demand. As each side demands more and supplies less, they both become unhappy and seek a different partner, which ultimately leads to separation.

	Traditional Roles		Modern Roles	
Men	Taking Pain	Rejecting Pleasure	Rejecting Pain	Demanding Pleasure
Women	Relieving Pain	Giving Pleasure	Rejecting Pain	Demanding Pleasure

Also, precisely as a result of this role inversion, there is a rapid rise in gays, lesbians, and transgenders. Non-binary genders are created due to rebirth, as a result of renouncing ideal gender roles in the previous life. As men become more effiminate, in their next life they will become a non-binary gender. As both men and women renounce gender roles, the number of non-binary gender births will rise. The desire to create gender equality always produces gender conflict. Neither gender will be happy through this equality. Rather, their sexuality will be more confused, they will keep rejecting their own gender traits and taking on the opposite gender traits, and ultimately, they will keep changing sex partners.

Modern ignorant societies have created the false dogma that gender is a human creation—i.e., humans defined what gender meant—because they have no idea of divine genders, i.e., Śiva and Śakti. They are deeply influenced by false Hegelian-Marxist ideologies in which a thesis and antithesis merge to become a synthesis and that merger is progress. In the context of genders, it means man and woman merging into a genderless person who is neither masculine nor feminine. Gays, lesbians, and transgenders are simply stepping stones toward an isolated individual who is so confused about their gender that they cannot be attracted to anyone and cannot live with anyone in any stable relationship. But this is precisely what happens in an atheistic society that has no understanding of divine genders.

At present time, men have lost their capacity for austerity and have become hedonistic. Meanwhile, women have lost their capacity to give pleasure and relieve pain. This means that men have been effeminized as women incapable of taking pain, while women have become masculinized as men incapable of giving pleasure. There is nobody to teach men about austerity and nobody to tell women to control their desires. The primary difference between genders is their childbearing capacities.

False Ideas of Patriarchy and Matriarchy

In the Śiva and Śakti relation, Śakti is desire and Śiva is the object of desire. Śakti gives pleasure and Śiva renounces pleasure. The object of desire and the renouncer of pleasure has the upper hand in this relation. When this is emulated in a marriage, men have an upper hand in the marriage over women. The basic principle is that independence is greater than entrapment, vagrancy is greater than civilization, and renunciation is greater than pleasure. The masculine tendencies gain prominence over the feminine tendencies in the case of human society because that is also the situation in the case of Śiva and Śakti.

Ignorant of what divine genders stand for, the inversion of gender roles, and the rise of gays, lesbians, and transgenders, people have started calling the dominance of men in human society patriarchy, driven by Western assumptions where men accepted pleasure from women (and often forced it out of them) while not being domesticated (i.e., being responsible fathers, teachers, and husbands) per the wishes of the women. As women got an unfair deal in these relationships, they have now decided to punish men and tilt the equation of power in their favor. They have no idea about what is about to happen.

Weak men who can't control their desires, or the desires of a woman, start doing immoral activities to fulfill them. When a woman realizes that a man is ready to do immoral things to fulfill her desires, she demands more things from the man, and uses sex as a weapon—i.e., gives sex if she gets what she wants, and denies it if she doesn't get what she wants. Toxic women deny sex even if they get what they want just to prove their power. As a man is deprived of sex, he turns to other women, and the wife loses power over him. Enraged by her loss of power over the man, the woman sets out to destroy the man via separation.

The ultimate result is that the entire family—man, woman, and children—is ruined.

As marital discord becomes unavoidable, marriages are gradually being replaced by the company of pets. The person who lives with a cat or dog becomes a cat or dog in their next life. Meanwhile, he or she cannot elevate a cat or dog to human life because he or she is already non-human. Over time, there will be too many cats and dogs and very few humans, and as these cats and dogs become a nuisance to humans, they will either be put to death by the government or used as guinea pigs for testing cosmetics and drugs. The degradation of humans to the animal state makes the lives of animals even worse.

To avoid this, we must learn about the Śiva-Śakti relation, different from the patriarchy rooted in the exploitation of women. Its essence is that women give pleasure and men renounce pleasure, women are desires and men are objects of desire. A man is attractive if he is independent and a woman is attractive if she is dependent. If men become dependent, and women become independent, then women have to take the pain and austerity of men whereas men will become the ones pleasing the women.

Those women protesting against patriarchy will find themselves carrying the burdens of men, and men supporting this matriarchy will find themselves being treated as pleasure toys by women. If a man becomes desire and a woman becomes the object of desire, women will live a hard life and men will be pleasing women. Factually, neither men nor women can do this, if they are men and women. Hence, those who complain about patriarchy are headed toward marital discord, which ends up living with cats and dogs, which leads to becoming cats and dogs, and then being killed or tortured as guinea pigs.

Transcending Sex and Entering Love

Alternative Meaning of Inside vs. Outside

To discuss the difference between sex and love, we have to define the words "inside" and "outside" in a new way. In the physical worldview, we think that one thing being inside another thing means that the thing is contained within the space of the container. If we observe an apple, the apple is within our mind, and yet, outside it. However, if we hold the apple in our hand, it is in our hand, not in another person's hand. Quantum mechanics establishes why two people cannot observe the same thing simultaneously because photons are emitted one by one, each photon goes to a different destination, so two observers cannot see the same thing simultaneously; of course, they can see it one after another. Likewise, two hands cannot hold the same apple simultaneously; of course, they can hold them one after another.

Thus, the word "inside" means exclusive control, and "outside" means no control. This idea of inside and outside is compatible both with holding an apple in our hand and observing the apple with our eyes. When we observe the apple, the apple is inside us, but the very next moment, it is outside us. It is as if the apple poked us in the eye to make us see and then went on to poke other eyes to make them see. The apple cannot poke many eyes simultaneously. That poking—i.e., photon emission—is one by one. That exclusivity of observation is just like the apple moving from one hand to another, one by one. At each stage, the apple is in control of one hand, but the next moment, it is in control of another hand. This exclusivity of control—i.e., only one person can enjoy one thing at one time—is the essence of the material world. To see the back of a person, we have to stop seeing their front. To focus on taste, we have to defocus from smell. To listen to one person, we must stop listening to another person.

This exclusivity of enjoyment is sex. But if enjoyment were inclusive, then it is not sex. Only one person can enjoy a slice of bread at one time, but everyone can simultaneously enjoy God. Even as everyone is simultaneously enjoying God, He is not in anyone's exclusive control. He appears to be "inside" everyone and yet He is "outside" everyone. A photon enters a detector and is absorbed within the detector, such that the source that emitted the photon loses the photon. However, the vision of God—created as a result of spiritual light emitting from Him—enters a person without being lost in the source. If God lost His light because we saw Him, He would be material. But if we can see Him, without Him losing His light, then He is spiritual. Thus, everyone can see God at once through His light without reducing Him.

Yoga-Māyā and Mahā-Māyā Difference

The freedom from a sexual universe is the freedom from Māyā. It is not the ultimate state of happiness because there are two kinds of Māyā—called Yoga-Māyā and Mahā-Māyā—and the Brahman realization is in between them. The Brahman realization is asexual, while Yoga-Māyā and Mahā-Māyā are sexual. However, the sexuality of Yoga-Māyā is quite different from that of Mahā-Māyā, to the point that Yoga-Māyā is described as the absence of sex. We will now turn to understanding why that is the case.

Under Mahā-Māyā, the limited things of the material world are the masculine. Even if they are desired, they don't precisely match our desire; the mismatch of desire and its object creates discomfort. Since each thing is limited, it also leaves a lot to be desired. As one desire is partially fulfilled, the other desire magnifies, but it can't be fulfilled by the same object. Thus, the sexual intercourse of experiencing the world under Mahā-Māyā creates discomfort (if there is partial fulfillment) and dissatisfaction (because nothing fulfills all our desires) forcing an iterative process of union and separation. The discomfort and dissatisfaction result from the intercourse with limited things rather than the unlimited Puruṣa.

Under Yoga-Māyā, the Supreme Puruṣa is the masculine. He is infinite forms at once, and yet, He takes a form suited to the soul's desire. As He fills the hole in the heart, He perfectly matches the desire of the soul, and that match between the desire and the object of desire creates pleasure. Even if the desire changes form subsequently, the Supreme Puruṣa adapts to that desire, such that there is no pain. The pain is limited to separation from the Supreme Puruṣa. That pain is an unfulfilled desire, rather than discomfort. As the desire for the Supreme Puruṣa grows, it brings Him again in contact with the soul.

When both Yoga-Māyā and Mahā-Māyā involve sexuality, then why do we say that there is no sex under Yoga-Māyā? The answer is that sexuality under Mahā-Māyā is exclusive and under Yoga-Māyā it is inclusive. A material masculine can only unite with one material feminine at one time, but the spiritual masculine can unite with many spiritual feminine at once. Due to the exclusivity of the material union—i.e., only one person can be fulfilled by one thing in one time, place, and situation—the material union is sex because the material thing comes under the control of the person trying to enjoy it. The inclusivity of the spiritual union—i.e., infinite persons can be fulfilled by the Supreme Puruṣa in infinite times, places, and situations at once—the spiritual union is the absence of sex as the Supreme Puruṣa fulfills everyone simultaneously, and yet, He doesn't come under the control of the person trying to enjoy Him.

The Difference Between Sex and Love

The relationship of Śiva and Śakti is a sexually bold marriage, that of Viṣṇu and Lakṣmī is a lovingly shy marriage, while that of Kṛṣṇa and Rādha is a lovingly shy extramarital affair. Along with Brahman, which is asexual, these four are called Chatuśpāda, or four realms of existence in the Vedic texts. The realms of Brahman, Viṣṇu, and Kṛṣṇa are beyond the material world, i.e., the realm of Śiva. Discussing all of them will elongate the discussion enormously, hence I have focused this article on the realm of Śiva while giving some understanding of why it is bondage and what lies beyond the material realm of sex.

The realm beyond the material world is sexuality without sex. As we have seen, sexuality is the senses uniting with their objects. But if senses cannot exclusively control their objects, then it is love. Thus, in the realm of love, seeing the Puruṣa is love, hearing Him is love, touching Him is love, and working for Him is love. Moreover, shyness accompanies love, which is why the clothes are never shed, the body doesn't become naked, the emotions are hidden and suppressed, and come out as laughter and tears, trembling and dancing, touching and embracing, without any genital intercourse. The absence of genital intercourse is also called the absence of sex, although, in every other respect, it can be amorous.

While each of the four realms is expected to emulate the archetypes of Puruṣa and Māyā of that realm, this expectation is fulfilled in the realms of love and often not emulated in the realm of sex. In former times, girls worshipped Śiva to get an enlightened husband

and Śakti to get a husband who would be under her control. Boys worshipped Śakti to get a wife who would value an enlightened husband and Śiva to get a wife who would be attracted to him. But these days, mostly women worship Śakti to get a husband they can control and mostly men worship Śiva to get a wife who will be attracted to them. Neither men nor women are interested in enlightenment. They just want control over their partner.

Women want a rich but foolish man, who will keep giving them material things. In fact, a man who seeks enlightenment rather than richness is abhorrent to women. Likewise, men want beautiful but foolish women. In fact, a woman who desires an enlightened man is abhorrent to men; they want a wife who desires material possessions because that is all that they are capable of offering to the woman.

Thus, both men and women want sex with foolish counterparts. They have no idea that a great man is enlightened and a great woman is one attracted to an enlightened man. An enlightened woman wants her sons to be enlightened like their father and daughters to seek enlightened men; an enlightened man relies on an enlightened woman to produce children who seek enlightenment. But as both men and women seek foolish partners, the nature of Śiva and Śakti are rejected. Men gather possessions to attract women for sex while rejecting enlightenment, to become the opposite of Śiva. Women desire a man's possessions, not the man with enlightenment, to become the opposite of Śakti. The net result is suffering as the result of rejecting the role models of Śiva and Śakti. Highly ignorant people have presently created the false propaganda that everyone is free to do whatever they want. They have no idea that there are preset standard role models to be emulated even in the material world.

There is no suffering in the realms of Viṣṇu and Kṛṣṇa because no living entity violates the behaviors and traits of the role models. This difference shows that there are great dangers in sex but no danger in love. It means that if one pursues the goal of spiritual love, he will eventually become enlightened. But if he pursues the goal of material sex, he will most likely forget about enlightenment and be degraded. In the material realm, the enlightened man is a vagabond and the enlightened woman is a domesticator, due to which the material realm is a duality of uncivilized and civilized, chaos and order, austerity and pleasure, detachment and attachment, destruction and creation. In the spiritual realm, there is no sex and no vagabond; there is simply domestication, civilization, order, attachment, pleasure, and creation.

The Vedic tradition describes myriad practices—rituals, mantras, meditations, austerities, and duties—whose ultimate aim could be sex or love. The difference between them is that when the goal is sex, after a certain level of perfection in a practice, one pauses the practice and starts enjoying the results gained thus far as sex, but when the goal is love, one never pauses the practice and attains the ultimate state of love. The more one can delay the gratification, the higher the state one attains. However, most people cannot delay the gratification. They rise a little, start enjoying the results, and fall. Hence, genuine transcendentalists never discuss sex; they only describe the material world as suffering and the spiritual realm as happiness. It looks like sectarianism to most, but they are not rejecting the other possibilities; they are simply aware of the fact that talking about sex will easily distract most people quickly.

The discussion of sex is a double-edged sword. If we discuss it, there is a chance of getting distracted. But if we don't, then we don't know how to live in this world while seeking transcendence. This double-edged sword is the reason for the ambivalence on sex, although there is no technical ambiguity.

The Vedic Concept of Duality and Non-Duality

The origin of the material world is described in various ways in Vedic texts: (a) the envy in the soul toward God, (b) appearance of duality from of non-duality, (c) the darkness of ignorance and egotism, (d) the separation of what was previously unseparated, (e) the cycle of creation, maintenance, and destruction from eternity, (f) the cycle of relaxation and aggression, and so on. These varied descriptions pertain to different aspects and effects of the same underlying cause and reality, which I will discuss in this article. That discussion will demonstrate how all these descriptions depend on each other.

Origin of Duality in the Soul's Envy

Let's begin with envy in the soul because it makes the rest of descriptions easier to understand. Envy is the alternating love and hate for the same thing. A person wants something that another person owns but hates that person for having it. We can illustrate using wealth. An envious poor person wants the wealth of a rich person, but hates the rich person for being wealthy. Under the influence of envy, the person tries to separate the wealth from the wealthy and attach it to oneself. Wealth is a property and the person-property attachment makes the person valuable. Envy wants to devalue the person by taking their property. To become valuable, the envious want the wealth to be transferred to themselves.

Under envy, the same person is desired (because they have something valuable) and hated (because the envious don't have the same value). The desire for value attracts an envious person toward the person who has the value, but as soon as he comes in contact with the valuable person, he feels shame for not having what they value. That shame in the self transforms into hatred for the attractive person.

At the root of envy is a desire for sovereignty. Each person wants to be self-sufficient, independent, complete, and sovereign. To be sovereign, we must not need anything from others. If a person can give up all desires, he can be sovereign without owning anything. If he did not want to be sovereign, he could be happy depending on others, and if did not feel threatened by good things in others, there would be love without hate. Hatred results from the desire for sovereignty by having everything. Since this desire cannot be fulfilled (we cannot have everything), the desire is futile. Believing that the futility is possible is delusion. And yet, the material world is the place in which nearly everyone suffers from this delusion.

The pursuit of things one doesn't have creates a feeling of inadequacy. As we hope for adequacy by trying to replace others, we fear that others might be trying to replace us. Thus, fear is a transformation of envy. If we want to displace others, we fear that they want to displace us. If we are threats to others, we fear that they are threats to us. We believe that those with more things are more sovereign although even such people try to replace those who have even more. They all suffer from simultaneous love and hate of the same person. They love the person who has more, feel inadequate by comparison, desire to replace them, feel insecure that other are trying to replace them before they can replace others, hate perceived competitors and enemies, and in this way, love transforms into hatred.

Envy would not exist if we did not feel inadequate, even as we do not have everything. Then, we would not want to be sovereign and we would be happy with needing others and being needed by them. We would feel secure in loving relationships, would not perceive competitive threat from enemies, and we would not want to be a competitive threat to others. Attraction toward others will remain love.

The Soul Directs Its Envy Toward God

Envy of others is envy of God: We want to be just like He is, complete, sovereign, and supreme. God is most valuable as He owns six desirable things in fullness—knowledge, beauty, wealth, power, fame, and independence. God is most attractive due to His properties. Since everyone else has these six properties to a lesser degree, they are naturally attracted toward God. If they serve God, they can also receive the same six properties from Him. But everyone doesn't want to do so. They want the six properties without God. An envious person may praise God's glory but once he gets some glory, he forgets God since his praise of God's glory is like the attraction of a poor man toward a rich man, in that it comes with envy due to which the poor man wants to detach wealth from the rich man and attach it to himself.

Thus, many people who initially come to God for His qualities, forget God after they get something from Him. Even if they outwardly praise God's glory, their competition with others is envy of God. A hallmark of envy is pursuit of God's qualities for one's glory, rather than using those qualities to glorify God. Their devotion is conditional upon them getting God's qualities. Their focus on God's qualities, their desire to be sovereign, and competition with others, are all indicators of the presence of envy in them.

The soul free of envy lives in the spiritual world. He is attracted to God due to His attractive qualities. But even as the soul comes into contact with God, he doesn't feel shame for being less than God. Instead, he rejoices at God's greatness, and his smallness, and lives in God's shelter rather than in competition with God. As God shares His great qualities with a pure soul, the soul uses them to increase God's glory, which means enhancing His greatness. This process is never-ending and very pleasing, provided one doesn't feel shame and envy. The soul who feels shame and envy in relation to God enters the material world, and is caught in the cycle of love and hate, attraction and aversion, toward other living entities.

Duality Is Tug-of-War Relationships

Under the love-hate duality, all relationships are a tug-of-war. An employee and an employer enter a relationship because each has something that the other doesn't. An employer has wealth but he wants labor, the employee can give labor but he wants wealth.

They enter into an employer-employee relationship. But since this relationship is envious, hence the employer tries to extract more labor from an employee and the employee tries to extract more wealth from an employer. The employee loves the wealth of the employer but hates the employer for being wealthy. The employer loves the employee's labor but hates the employee for reducing his wealth. They are locked in a love-hate relationship.

The employer dreams of replacing employees with capable, hardworking, and low-cost machines that the employer will control. The employee dreams of replacing an employer with a money-printing and luxury-giving machine, which the employee will control. This is called equal opportunity employment. It means neither employee nor employer are loyal to each other. If the employee can get more money for less work, he will quit the current employer and join a new one. If the employer can get more work for less money, he will replace the current employee with a cheaper and hardworking machine.

The same situation is called a contract relationship. The employer and employee are in a contract with each other, which either side can renegotiate, reducing what they give and increasing what they take. Since both sides are trying to decrease their giving and increase their taking, a contract relationship is a tug-of-war between two sides. There is no loyalty in a contract. The relationship is based on mutual convenience. As soon as something more convenient is found, the relationship breaks down. While the relationship continues, it constitutes a tug-of-war between parties pulling and pushing each other.

Duality Means a Zero-Sum Game

There is no win-win scenario in a tug-of-war. The employer wants to pay the employee just enough to keep him alive, working, and dependent on the employer, unable to leave him. If the employee is paid more, he will go on vacation and work less, decreasing productivity for the employer. If the employee has enough savings, he can go on a strike and demand more compensation. Thus, the employer tries to ensure that the employee lives paycheck-to-paycheck, so that he cannot go on a vacation or strike.

The employee also plays the same game with the employer. He works in a way as to solve one problem while creating more problems, so that he would be needed in the future to solve them. If the employee only solved problems, but did not create new ones, then the employer would need fewer employees. The employee creates the impression of working without solving any problem. For instance, employees organize meetings, then write meeting notes, then organize meetings to discuss the meeting notes, then write meeting notes for the meeting organized to discuss the previous meeting notes, and so on, in a never-ending cycle that solves no problem but creates the illusion of work cheating the employer.

Duality creates the win-lose scenario, rather than a win-win scenario. Each party wants to win. But due to envy, for them to win, the other party must lose. In theory, the winner wants to take it all. But if that happened, the game itself would end. For instance, if the employees bankrupted the employer, they would have to find another job. But if the employee died due to overworking, the employer would have to find a new employee. Therefore, both employer and employee try to keep the other barely alive and functioning, to keep the game going, while trying to ensure that they win and the other loses.

Three Kinds of Value Change Games

Duality disappears if we give up desire for sovereignty, stay happy in our incompleteness, and aspire for interdependence. Then we aren't envious of the other, we depend on them because of their qualities, and we admire that they have qualities we don't. If this interdependence rather than independence is cherished and practiced, then the situation is called non-duality. It is also a game just like duality, but it is a win-win rather than win-lose or lose-lose game. Each person takes something valuable from the other person and uses it to enhance the value of the person they had previously taken the value from.

Value in a win-win game continuously increases because whatever value is taken is used to increase value for the person from whom it was taken. In contrast, in a win-lose game, value remains constant because the winner takes value from the loser. Since both parties are trying to win in a game, quite often value is spent in mutual struggle without creating any new value, and the net value is destroyed, the game becomes lose-lose, and comes to an end. To continue the game, some value must be created even while trying to take more value. Thus, the realm of duality is described as creating, maintaining, and destroying value. Creation is a win-win, maintaining is a win-lose, and destruction is a lose-lose game.

A Misleading Theory of Value Creation

Matter or energy in modern science is never created or destroyed. All physical sciences operate under the assumption that matter or energy is conserved. They believe that matter or energy is transferred from one place to another, transformed from one form to another, but never created or destroyed. This is because they don't think in terms of value. Their idea of reality is material stuff rather than the six kinds of value—knowledge, beauty, independence, wealth, power, and fame. These six kinds of values can be created, maintained, and destroyed, but material stuff is supposedly never created or destroyed in a physical science. This makes physical science incompatible with all value-based sciences.

For instance, economics believes that wealth must grow. But how can wealth grow if matter and energy are conserved? The original answer in economics was that matter must be given a *form* to increase its value. For instance, if we transform wheat into bread, we have given it a form, and increased its value. But the form of the bread is temporary; if we eat the bread, the form will be destroyed. The economist will say that after eating bread, we can do some work, which will again create value. But whatever we create after eating will also be destroyed. It naturally follows that there can never be economic growth.

This is when economics shifts the definition of value to *perception*. If we *think* that what we are creating is more valuable, then it is economic growth. For instance, if we think that jeans are greater value than dhoti, then by replacing dhoti by jeans we have created economic growth. Now, economic growth depends on changing our perception—i.e., making us believe that the present is better than the past. To continue this process forever, we must continuously change our value assignments, e.g., after saying that jeans is more valuable than dhoti, we must say that torn jeans is more valuable than intact jeans.

At this juncture, advertising is married to the possibility of economic growth to change our perception to make us think that the latest thing is the best thing. Creating new things is called innovation, changing our perception that it is better is called advertising, and people are made to work harder and harder just to keep chasing the latest thing because the old thing is becoming less valuable in our perception. In reality, the new thing is often the less valuable thing and we spend our life trying to reduce value.

A Correct Theory of Value Creation

To create any theory of value creation, we have to first identify that thing which can continuously grow, and not be subject to inevitable destruction or constrained by the law of matter or energy conservation. There is only one such thing in this world—knowledge. It can be created, preserved by passing it from one generation to another, never destroyed if it is preserved, and can continuously grow. Based on the one non-reducing thing, we can talk about other values. Wealth is that which makes it easier to grow and preserve knowledge. Power is that which makes it more likely to preserve and grow knowledge. Fame is that which makes it easier to preserve and grow knowledge for more people. If knowledge is what society pursues, everything else that supports, enhances, or strengthens this pursuit is valuable.

Knowledge can continuously grow because when I give you knowledge, I don't become ignorant. The act of transmitting knowledge is net increase in knowledge. Then, if you expand and enhance what I gave to you earlier, and give that expanded and enhanced knowledge to me, both of us benefit. This is a win-win game. By giving you knowledge, I don't become ignorant, but you gain knowledge. This is net increase in value. But it is interesting only if you can take the knowledge and grow it further. If you are not keen on knowledge, and you cannot grow it further, then transferring knowledge is not interesting. Over time, knowledge will die, and every other attempt to increase value will be futile because everything other than knowledge is temporary. It is only knowledge increase that makes everything else valuable.

How Everything Becomes Valuable

This brings us back to the question of duality, which is a cycle of creation, maintenance, and destruction. We can connect this cycle of change to the above theory of value creation. The connection is that if we focus on knowledge, the cycle of change is replaced by continuous growth. The cycle of change exists only because we focus on things other than knowledge. If we focused on knowledge, it will only be creation and maintenance, without any destruction. Everything that assists the protection, preservation, and transmission of knowledge will be valuable due to its association with knowledge. If we disregard the value that can actually be preserved and grown, and focus on other things, the situation is duality. But if we focus on the real value that makes everything else valuable, the situation is non-duality.

If computers and the internet are used to spread knowledge, they are valuable. In and of themselves, they have no value. In fact, they may be destroying value, if they take us away from knowledge. Likewise, if trains, cars, and airplanes are working in support of spreading knowledge, then they are valuable. In and of themselves, they have no value. In fact, they may even be destroying value if they are taking us away from knowledge. If peace protects, preserves, and grows knowledge, then peace is valuable. If war protects, preserves, and grows knowledge, then war is valuable. There is no measure of value besides knowledge because only knowledge can grow while everything else is created and destroyed.

Material and Spiritual Worlds

Broadly speaking, the material world is duality because most people deprioritize knowledge and prioritize wealth, power, beauty, fame, and independence. The pursuit of the latter, devoid of the former, makes the latter temporary—i.e., subject to creation and destruction. As the latter becomes temporary, everything seems *finite* and people create the laws of conservation. Thereafter, the pursuit of the latter leads to win-lose and lose-lose games because everyone wants to grab the most of the finite. That creates the alternating cycle of love and hate resulting in insecurity, competition, and conflict.

However, if knowledge is prioritized, the pursuit of wealth, power, beauty, fame, and independence makes all of these non-reducing. Now, we don't need laws of conservation because everything is growing and the future is factually better than the past due to this growth. Then games are win-win instead of win-lose and lose-lose. Now, there is cooperation, security, and harmony. Non-duality can exist even in the material world if knowledge is prioritized over wealth, power, beauty, fame, and independence.

Subordination does not mean rejection. Prioritizing knowledge doesn't mean becoming poor, weak, ugly, obscure, and bounded. It is the only way to grow everything and make it non-reducing, eliminate the win-lose and lose-lose games, and create security, cooperation, and harmony. Hence, non-duality can also exist in the material world, if we prioritize knowledge. Non-duality is not a feature of the spiritual world alone, as impersonalists like to claim. The material world is not fully duality if we prioritize knowledge. The material world becomes duality because we prioritize things other than knowledge.

Pessimistic and Optimistic Outlooks

The Vedic tradition shows both great pessimism and optimism about the material world. It is optimistic if knowledge is prioritized; it is pessimistic if things other than knowledge are prioritized. The pessimism overrides optimism because most people prioritize things other than knowledge. Pessimism is the result of destroying Brahmanas who preserve, transmit, and enhance knowledge while giving greater value to other classes that prioritize wealth, power, fame, beauty, and independence. When politics, economics, and culture are given greater importance than knowledge, everything declines, the society is plunged into simultaneous love and hate relationships and destroyed by conflict, insecurity, and disharmony.

All these things can also be reversed if society creates, protects, and encourages Brahmanas, and elevates them to the highest status, not as a matter of caste discrimination but because if knowledge is given the highest priority in a society, then wealth, beauty, power, fame, and independence increase.

The impersonalist depiction of the whole material world as duality is false. Its pessimistic attitudes about the material world are false. Its depiction of knowledge as something shorn of wealth, beauty, power, fame, and independence is false. In fact, when impersonalism rises, pessimism about the material world makes people inactive and incompetent, which in turn destroys all the six values, people are plunged into the struggle for survival, and the defeated by those who have an optimistic view of the world.

Non-duality is not the end of individuality but the end of individualism. Individuality is the idea that I am distinct from others but interdependent with them. I take from others but give back something even greater to them. My taking and giving is a win-win game. In contrast, individualism is the idea that I am sovereign. I take something from others but either give back nothing or try to reduce what I am giving back. My taking and giving is win-lose or a lose-lose game. The impersonalist claim that the entire material world is a win-lose or a lose-lose game is false. Its equating of eternity to something static is false. While static eternity is possible, an even better eternity is ever-growing. Freedom from the cycle of birth and death isn't limited to a static eternity; it also includes ever-growing eternity. In the latter case, eternity simply means that nothing dies; instead, everything is preserved and increased.

The Dominant-Subordinate Cycle

In the material world, there is simultaneous love and hate among the 24 elements of Sāñkhya, which results in inner and outer conflicts. The material elements also play win-lose, lose-lose, and win-win games. Under the win-lose game, when one material quality appears, some other material quality disappears. Under the lose-lose game, the material qualities mutually annihilate each other. But since that ends the game, under the win-win game, material qualities reappear as cooperating opposites. However, that cooperation is temporary as each quality becomes dominant or subordinate relative to other qualities, producing a cycle of alternating prominence among these qualities. As this struggle for domination intensifies, the opposites go to war with each other, and annihilate each other.

The creation of mutually supporting opposites is called *manifest* or *vyakta*. The cycle of each quality going dominant and subordinate is called maintenance or persistence. The destruction of the opposites, resulting from the intensification of their conflict, is called *unmanifest* or *avyakta*. Due to the cycling of different qualities into dominant and subordinate states, there is an objective reality without it being an object. Objectively speaking, there are qualities. But since these qualities go dominant and subordinate, nothing is in a fixed state. We cannot measure anything and elevate the outcome of that measurement to the only truth because upon the next measurement the outcome will most likely be different.

All conservation laws of science are false because things go *vyakta* and *avyakta*. Modern science calls the *avyakta* state "potential energy" although we can never measure this potential until it becomes actual. If we cannot transform the potentiality into actuality, then we cannot know that it exists. Since opposites can be created from a potential state, we cannot know that what we measure as energy right now won't substantially increase in the future. This is related to the problem of Big Bang in which infinite energy must be concentrated in an infinitesimal space-time. No such problem arises if energy becomes manifest from unmanifest—the former is separated opposites and the latter is merged opposites.

Simple Examples of Dualistic Struggle

Once we understand the problem of duality, we can give many ordinary illustrations of this problem to make the description intuitive. In all cases, there is love and hate between two entities that results in the desire for domination, which creates the desire (in the entity being dominated) to be free, which creates the struggle for existence. As this struggle for existence intensifies, the opposites annihilate each other.

This dynamic is seen in all human relationships. Children need their parents to support them, but children dislike their parents for controlling them. Parents need their children to relive their childhood but parents dislike their children being irresponsible. A man needs a woman to take care of young children, but a man dislikes a woman if she becomes the center of children's attention. A woman needs a man to earn, but she dislikes a man if he holds the power of wealth in his hands. A Sannyasi needs a Grihastha to support him, but a Sannyasi dislikes a Grihastha for being disinterested in spiritual life. A Grihastha needs a Sannyasi to guide him, but dislikes the renunciation of the Sannyasi lifestyle.

An employer wants the talent and work of an employee, but hates the fact that he has to recompense the employee. The employee wants the wealth of the employer, but hates the fact that he has to give talent and work in return. A wealthy country loves a poor country if it is a source of natural resources, but hates the fact that the poor country wants to use those resources for its own development. A poor country loves a rich country as the source of good technology and wealth, but hates that country as a dominant, exploitative, and bullying power. A small company loves a bigger company due to its ability to execute big projects but hates the big company for its dominant market position. A big company loves a smaller company for its greater efficiency but hates the fact that it innovates much faster.

When every relationship is based on simultaneous love and hate, then relationships are formed due to love and broken due to hate. People, organizations, and countries come close because they need each other, one side tries to dominate the other, and the relationship is broken. Then one party uses force to control the other, resulting in the other trying to become free. Eventually, they are locked into a mutual battle of domination and are mutually destroyed. Since life must go on, a new relationship of love and hate is created. Again people, organizations, and countries come together and are separated. Again, they struggle to dominate and are mutually destroyed. This is the cycle of the material world. It springs from envy. It defocuses from knowledge—i.e., the dualistic understanding of the world—and encourages domination, competition, and control. Even if it is destroyed, due to envy, it does not reform.

Inconceivable and Conceivable

Every worldly train of events can be narrated as two kinds of opposite stories—love and hate—neither of which is false nor is either of them the exclusive truth. We can describe wars as just or unjust. We can describe marriages as successes and failures. We can laugh at life as a comedy of errors or cry over the utter meaninglessness of life entailed by the errors. We can talk about the same thing as progress over the past or regress to the past. Since neither of these opposites is the exclusive truth, therefore, it is said that reality is *Acintya* or inconceivable because we are conditioned to think in terms of binary truths in which laughing and crying, success and failure, love and hate, just and unjust are mutually exclusive.

The nihilism resulting from the ability to describe the same train of events in opposite ways is called postmodernism, as modernity refers to the idea that there is only one true description of reality, and opposites cannot be true at once. Both modernism and postmodernism are false because of duality. Love and hate coexist under duality. Our stories told under the assumption that only one of the opposites could be true are incomplete. And yet, if we try to complete the story, it becomes inconsistent because it involves opposites of love and hate, laughing and crying, success and failure, just and unjust, etc.

The solution to this problem is a non-binary logic in which opposites are simultaneously true, like two sides of a coin, with the coin (different from its two sides) representing envy. We cannot understand the coin simply by looking at one of its faces—head or tail. We have to look at both faces to understand the coin. Like that, everything has many faces. We cannot understand it fully without seeing all its faces. And yet, these faces are mutually opposed. If we look at fewer faces, we get incompleteness. If we look at all the faces, we get inconsistency. Their resolution is that there is something deeper than the faces that is all inconsistent faces at once. The faces are aspects of that thing, like love and hate are aspects of envy.

Every word has many meanings—the aspects of the word. Every person has many personalities—the aspects of the person.

Every situation has many descriptions—the aspects of the situation. Many of these meanings, personalities, and descriptions are mutually opposed—like the two faces of a coin. If we describe one of those, the description is incomplete. If we describe both, the description is inconsistent. That doesn't mean the word, person, or situation is unknowable or inconceivable. It means that there is a deeper reality—the coin, different from its faces—that reconciles the contradicting aspects.

Three Kinds of Material Dualities

This duality is further divided into types, which are called sattva, rajas, and tamas. Sattva is least dualistic, rajas is more dualistic, and tamas is most dualistic. In this sense, we could say that duality quantitatively increases from sattva, to rajas, to tamas. But they are also three different kinds of dualities. We can illustrate this difference by the description of three qualitatively different societies.

In a sattvic society, many kinds of partial truths exist and have debates with each other. Each partial truth is missing something than the other partial truths, so each partial truth needs the other. And yet, because it cannot be sovereign and complete without the other, it competes with the other. In this scenario, there is ideological conflict but it is limited to debate, to learn from the opponent, while trying to defeat the opponent. We can cite the example of the conflict between Advaita and Buddhism.

In a rajasic society, there are many kinds of wealth, power, and influence, incomplete without the others. Each type of wealth, power, and influence needs the other, but also tries to be more dominant than the other. But the conflict is limited to fair competition and accepting others when they are better. We can cite the example of markets in which companies agree to cooperate with each other in building common standards but also limit the standardization to create areas of differentiation and competition.

In a tamasic society, competition become subversive. We can cite the example of pharma companies and patients. A pharma company doesn't want a healthy society because that would make the company irrelevant. But it cannot kill their patients because that will make the pharma company unnecessary. Thus, the pharma company creates drugs to control and manage the disease, to keep the patients dependent on the drugs, neither curing the patient nor killing them. The patients cannot kill the pharma companies as it would make their illness unmanageable. They cannot give a pharma company monopoly as it would make their drugs unaffordable. Hence, the patients keep jumping from drug to drug, neither killing the pharma company not giving them a monopoly. Their relationship is subversive codependence.

Duality vs. Non-Duality Difference

Thus, there are subtle but important difference between sattvic, rajasic, and tamasic conflicts. In a sattvic conflict, there is more agreement, less conflict, and people cooperate more, although competition is not absent. In a rajasic conflict, there is less agreement, more conflict, and cooperation and competition are balanced. In a tamasic conflict, the enemies are locked in a mutually parasitical codependence.

The sattvic conflict is lesser compared to the rajasic conflict, which is lesser compared to the tamasic conflict. Thereby, sattva minimizes conflict, rajas increases conflict, and tamas maximizes conflict. They are all material because there is some conflict. But sattva is better than rajas and rajas is better than tamas because the extent and type of conflict reduce. This is why in some places in Vedic texts the material world is condemned as a place of strife. In other places, the different modes are distinguished. All modes are not equally condemned. The praise for something is selective, contextual, and limited.

As society becomes more tamasic, all relationships become mutually subversive codependence in which the death of one side means the death of both. So, they remain together, trying to undermine each other. To some people, this subversive codependence can look like loving interdependence. And hence, people keep talking about love in the age of war, try to create heaven on earth, but they never achieve that. At present, the material world is almost completely subversive codependence. The spiritual world is always loving interdependence. The difference between the best and the worst is so subtle that most people think that the worst is the best. The best and the worst look like each other but they are not.

The Impersonalist Misunderstanding

Impersonalism or Advaita has misrepresented non-duality as a reality without faces, aspects, and descriptions. This is called the *formless* description of the world because a form has a top and a bottom, a front and a back, a left and a right, which are mutually opposed. If we remove the form, the remaining thing cannot be described because all words—top, bottom, front, back, left, right—are rejected. Calling this knowledge, when it cannot be described, is a misdirection. The impersonalist non-duality doesn't exist. At the bare minimum, there is a self-awareness, denoted by the word "I", which itself divides into three aspects called the knower, knowing, and known. The self is the knower of itself; the way it knows itself constitutes the known; the connection between the knower and the known is knowing.

The formless description is also inconsistent with the *sat-chit-ānanda* description of the self because three words are used, each word entails a form, so the self cannot be formless. The conception that all forms are dualistic is also false. If that were the case, then all Vedic texts would be duality, not the source of non-dualistic truth, and hence not worth reading. The impersonalist pessimism about the world is also false as it makes living totally meaningless and purposeless. Any society that takes to impersonalism will self-destruct because it will slowly become lazy and incompetent and will be destroyed by any optimistic society (whether or not their optimism is grounded in the true source of optimism in knowledge).

Advaita talks about how words are rungs on a ladder and we kick the ladder when we reach the highest rung of the formless. The guru is rungs on a ladder and we kick the guru when we reach the highest rung of self-realization. The forms of God are rungs on a ladder and we kick these forms when we reach the highest rung of becoming God. Advaita doesn't respect anything or anyone—not Veda, not the guru, and not God. Everything is a means to an end, the end being the self, and Veda, guru, and God being the means. When this tendency takes hold, the study of the Veda, the respect for the guru, and the worship of God are destroyed. Advaita is an anti-Vedic system, as it inculcates silent individualism in a person. When it takes hold in a society—such as India—its pessimism makes people lazy and incompetent.

Advaita is: (a) self-contradictory, (b) inconsistent with Vedic texts, (c) disrespectful toward Veda, guru, and God, and (d) harmful to each person. And yet, its ideas of non-duality have been mainstreamed by the fact that the actual understanding of non-duality (as opposite aspects of one thing) is comparatively harder. That truth is harder and falsehood is easier should be solved by accepting the hardship.

THE DIFFERENCE BETWEEN MĀYĀ, ŚAKTI, AND PRAKṚTI

Illustration Through an Example

The Vedic texts employ three terms—Māyā, Prakṛti, and Śakti—to describe material nature. They are often used interchangeably although they are not identical. They are also not completely separable. In this article, I will discuss the differences between these three terms and their respective functions. I will begin with an example, and identify different features of our experience. I will call these features Māyā, Prakṛti, and Śakti, without an explanation. However, as we progress, I will explain each of them.

Let's begin with an example. Suppose that I am hit by another person. I feel pain in my body. But this is not all. Additionally, my ego is also hurt. I feel angry and upset. However, if the situation is inappropriate or not conducive to a response, I might control my anger with my willpower and not react to the attack.

In this situation, the pain in the body is Prakṛti, my feeling of anger and hurt is Māyā, and my willpower to control my anger is Śakti. The three are not identical because (a) I might feel pain and yet it is possible that my ego may not be hurt, and (b) I might feel pain and my ego may be hurt but I might still try to control the anger. In the first case, there is a difference between Prakṛti and Māyā; in the second case, there is a difference between Māyā and Śakti. However, this distinction is not always seen. Typically, the moment I am hit, I get angry and respond aggressively. Then, Prakṛti controls Māyā which controls Śakti.

This mutual triggering of Māyā, Prakṛti, and Śakti can also be seen in the person who attacks me. He may be upset or angry, which is Māyā. He may not be able to control his anger with his willpower, which is Śakti. The absence of control may result in him hitting me with his hands, which is Prakṛti. In this case, Māyā controls Śakti, which controls Prakṛti. Each of the three can be controllers and controlled. In each case, there is a specific sequence to the cause-effect relationship. Hence, we cannot say that there is always one cause and one effect. We also cannot mutually separate Māyā, Prakṛti, and Śakti.

Illustration Through a Buddha Story

There is a famous Buddha story about two arrows. A man approaches Buddha and asks Him about the cause of pain and suffering. Buddha tells him: The pain is inescapable but the suffering is avoidable. Buddha gives the example of being hit by an arrow, which results in pain. But as a result, the person hit by the arrow is again hit by a second arrow—the piercing of his ego. The second arrow, according to Buddha, is optional. The first arrow is probably inescapable. Buddha teaches the person to distinguish between pain and suffering and understand that the suffering is completely within his control.

When someone hits me, the pain is unavoidable as it is created in Prakṛti. However, if my ego is not hurt, then I will not feel angry, humiliated, or disrespected. I won't have to think about how to react. The pain of being hit will subside in a moment. The whole thing will be over in a few seconds. Conversely, if my ego is hurt due to being hit, then I will carry the anger, humiliation, and hurt for a long time. If I respond, I might dramatically escalate the situation, which may then lead to more problems. All this will probably elongate not just my pain but also my suffering. However, this elongated suffering was avoidable.

Layering of Māyā, Śakti, and Prakṛti

This distinction depends on Māyā, Prakṛti, and Śakti. Māyā is the deepest layer of covering on the ātmā. It makes the ātmā feel inadequate, incomplete, insufficient, and inferior. The net effect of Māyā on the self is the feeling that "I am not". The feeling is caused by the absence of wealth, power, influence, beauty, knowledge, or freedom, which is Prakṛti. However, the feeling of inadequacy, incompleteness, insufficiency, and inferiority is Māyā. One can be poor, weak, ignorant, ugly, unknown, and bound and yet not feel inferior. One may have wealth, power, influence, beauty, knowledge, and freedom and yet feel inferior. The presence or absence of inferiority is neither fully determined by nor fully independent of the attributes of superiority. Then, even if a person feels inferior, he may not have the endurance, willpower, and resilience to pursue the attributes that will restore his inferiority to superiority.

The typical situation for everyone is that the sense of inferiority creates anger in a person. He cannot stand the absence of self-worth. He wants to restore his pride. He gathers willpower, resilience, and courage to acquire the attributes that will restore his sense of pride and self-worth. However, if he is unable to muster that courage, willpower, and resilience to acquire the attributes that will restore his sense of self-worth, then he falls into even deeper self-loathing and sense of personal inferiority. A person who has tried to restore his self-worth and failed, becomes nihilistic or suicidal. He is a nihilist if he thinks that nobody can do anything. He is suicidal if he thinks that only he cannot do anything.

Based on the distinction between Māyā, Prakṛti, and Śakti, there are different paths of upliftment in the Vedic texts. Those who want to go enjoy a better material life, try to change their Prakṛti; they get better bodies, go to a better place in the universe, and enjoy heavenly pleasures. Better than them are yogis who try to develop willpower, resilience, and endurance through austerities; they pursue Śakti. But even better than them are devotees who try to overcome their sense of inferiority by devotion to Bhagavān; they conquer Māyā because they are happy serving Bhagavān even in a weak and helpless condition.

The Origin of Māyā in Spiritual Reality

By definition, Bhagavān is the completeness of knowledge, beauty, independence, fame, wealth, and power. In contrast, the ātmā has properties of Bhagavān in miniscule. When the ātmā feels jealous of Bhagavān, it is trapped in Māyā, which is the sense of inferiority, incompleteness, inadequacy, and insufficiency. The material existence begins if an ātmā feels inferior compared to Bhagavān. This feeling gives birth to the desire to become equal to Bhagavān. The ātmā enters an imaginary competition with Bhagavān, trying to prove to himself, that he is no less than Bhagavān. Since this competition is imaginary, therefore, Māyā is also called delusion. The desire can never be fulfilled permanently.

Māyā is described in many ways. One, it is the sense of inferiority. Two, it is jealousy. Three, it is the lust for greatness. Four, it is the anger at one's perceived smallness. Five, it is the delusion that one can become equal to Bhagavān. Six, it is the goal to become Bhagavān. Seven, it is the false belief that the goal is about to be achieved. Eight, it is the false belief that one has already become Bhagavān.

To simplify these descriptions, we can summarize Māyā as the inner conflict between inferiority and superiority. The perceived inferiority of the self gives rise to the desire to attain superiority. This desire is occasionally, temporarily, and partially fulfilled giving rise to the hope that it will be fulfilled completely. Then the hopes are dashed and the person returns to the feeling of inferiority, angry at the perceived smallness, lusting for greatness, imagining that greatness is within reach, and endeavoring to get it again, only to be frustrated repeatedly. Under the influence of Māyā, a person is caught in the inner battle between contradictory pictures of the self—Am I great or am I worthless? He cannot accept that he is worthless and he cannot get the greatness of Bhagavān. He lives continuously in inner conflict.

There is only one solution to the problem of Māyā—become devoted to Bhagavān, just like a part of a body serves the whole. The part cannot become whole. But the part need not feel inferior to the whole, and enter into a competition with the whole. Only devotees of Bhagavān conquer Māyā. Everyone else keeps imagining that they are going to become great or that they have already become great.

Distinction of Two Kinds of Māyā

Bhagavān is greatness. Those who think that greatness doesn't exist are either nihilists or suicidal. However, those who want to become that greatness are also hopeless fools. The devotees of Bhagavān are neither of these. They partake in Bhagavān's greatness by expanding it, for His glory, and His happiness. Bhagavān gives them His greatness and expands that greatness by which they do greater and greater things. But there is no competition between Bhagavān and His devotees. The devotee's qualities of greatness and the resulting actions are simply to expand the glory and happiness of Bhagavān. If a devotee cannot expand Bhagavān's glories for His happiness, he feels unhappy, but not for himself. He does not get the feeling of inferiority, the desire to acquire superiority, or the desire for competition with Bhagavān. The devotee just feels inadequate that he has not succeeded in expanding the glories of Bhagavān for His happiness.

Hence, Māyā is also divided into two parts—Mahā-Māyā and Yoga-Māyā. The devotees of Bhagavān always feel inadequate that they haven't adequately expanded the glory of Bhagavān for His pleasure. Since this expansion is potentially infinite, therefore, every finite expansion of Bhagavān's glories seems inadequate. The competitors of Bhagavān feel inadequate that they are not yet on par with Bhagavān. In both cases, there is a sense of inadequacy, incompleteness, insufficiency, and inferiority. But Mahā-Māyā is nihilistic, suicidal, and depressing. However, Yoga-Māyā is enlivening, hopeful, and exciting. A devotee feels that even as he has not done enough to expand the glories of Bhagavān for His pleasure, even as his life has been totally wasted, there is no loss of hope or enthusiasm because Bhagavān is already great.

Hence, Mahā-Māyā can also be characterized as false ego and its refutation—I am not great, I try to become great, I fail, and I get depressed. However, Yoga-Māyā is the true ego, and its affirmation—Bhagavān is great, I try to expand His greatness, I don't feel I have done nearly enough, but I remain grateful for the opportunity and excited about the future prospects.

Once Māyā is understood, then Prakṛti and Śakti are easy to understand. Prakṛti is just Bhagavān's greatness. Śakti is the willpower to increase this greatness. When a person comes under the influence of inferiority, he tries to acquire Bhagavān's greatness for himself, fails in the endeavor, becomes depressed, and loses the willpower to try again. Of course, Mahā-Māyā doesn't allow a person to rest in peace; a person is repeatedly triggered into feelings of inferiority, anger to conquer that inferiority, and struggle to establish superiority, which fails and takes a person back to depression, and then again anger.

Impersonalist Misrepresentations

Impersonalists don't know the difference between the two kinds of Māyā. They think that any feeling of inadequacy, incompleteness, insufficiency, and inferiority is bad. They try to convince themselves that they are eternally and perpetually great. This conviction is not long-lasting because it is the continuation of the same mindset of trying to prove one's greatness under the influence of Mahā-Māyā. Generally, people suffering from a deep-seated sense of inferiority take to impersonalism to quickly and cheaply elevate themselves to the highest status of greatness. However, it is a short-lived delusion. It temporarily ends the cyclical attempts to prove one's superiority and failure in those attempts. But it doesn't make one Bhagavān. Eventually, the impersonalist falls from his self-appointed delusional state of greatness into the grip of Mahā-Māyā.

We cannot be eternal happy trying to prove our greatness or giving up the attempt to establish greatness by assuming that we are already great. Eternal happiness is expanding Bhagavān's greatness. The eternal truth is not cyclical change or static finality. The eternal truth is continuous and endless expansion.

Impersonalists also confuse Māyā and Prakṛti to say that the world is an illusion. The fact is the opposite. The world is real but we are illusioned into thinking that this world is meant for proving our greatness when the world is Bhagavān's greatness meant for expanding His greatness. Thereby, the impersonalist tries to renounce the world but the devotees don't. The devotees talk about renouncing the illusion that the world is meant to establish our greatness. But that is not renouncing the world. It is engaging the world in expanding Bhagavān's greatness. Hence, the devotees don't make a stark distinction between the material and spiritual worlds because both worlds can be used to expand Bhagavān's greatness. The impersonalist desires liberation from the world. The devotee is happy even in the material world if he gets the opportunity to expand Bhagavān's greatness and therefore doesn't aspire for liberation.

The distinction between matter and spirit is stark for the impersonalist because he contrasts them as illusion and truth. However, if this world was completely an illusion, then even talking about liberation from this world would be an illusion. However, if the world is meant for expanding Bhagavān's greatness, then the world is not an illusion although the attempt to establish one's greatness is an illusion.

Distinction Between Puruṣa and Śakti

Each person is capable of infinite Śakti, which means willpower, although, under the control of Mahā-Māyā, this Śakti is missing. We might ask: What is willpower and how does it differ from free will? Willpower is the ability to fix our awareness on something; free will is the ability to choose what to fix our awareness on. The capacity for free will is called Puruṣa and the willpower of that person is called their Śakti. Every Puruṣa doesn't have Śakti, which means that even if they want something, they don't have the power to focus. They try a little, are troubled by the difficulty, and succumb to their weakness for convenience. Therefore, Śakti is acquired by austerity, which means tolerating difficulties against convenience.

Under the influence of Mahā-Māyā, Śakti is occasionally activated (when we are angry or lusty) and then deactivated (when we are discouraged and depressed). Thus, Śakti is controlled by Māyā. Willpower is not always constant. It comes and goes, rises and falls, depending on our current emotional state.

However, a devotee's Śakti is never deactivated because he never becomes hopeless, provided he has become free of Māyā. Even if he doesn't get success—i.e., Prakṛti (knowledge, beauty, independence, fame, power, and wealth)—he remains willful due to his inner excitement arising from devotion to Bhagavān. Bhagavān gives the devotee Prakṛti to fulfill his desire to expand Bhagavān's greatness and glory. Bhagavān gives the devotee the Śakti to persist on a difficult path. If a devotee is eager to expand

Bhagavān's glories, then Bhagavān is eager to expand a devotee's glories. If a devotee is eager to serve Bhagavān, then Bhagavān is eager to serve the devotee.

Three Components of Experience

The tripartite distinction between Māyā, Prakṛti, and Śakti helps us understand, explain, and predict experiences. Hence, this distinction is experientially confirmed. Māyā is the innermost reality, Śakti is the intermediate reality, and Prakṛti is the outermost reality. Therefore, by and large, Māyā controls Śakti, which controls Prakṛti. However, in some extraordinary cases, each of the three can cause the other two. By a good emotional state, we can get willpower and then results. By willpower, we can get a good emotional state and then results. By results, we can get a good emotional state and then willpower.

Each of the three can be cause or effect, although typically there is a hierarchy from Māyā to Śakti to Prakṛti. All three must be combined to produce experience. There is no experience if these three are separated. These three are also three aspects of a person. Hence, they are three, and yet, they are one.

Different Vedic texts place greater emphasis on one of the three because (a) each of the three is immensely complex, and (b) each of the three can be the cause or effect. Generally, Vaiṣṇava texts emphasize Prakṛti, Shakta texts emphasize Śakti, and Shaiva texts emphasize Māyā. However, no text neglects any of the three completely. In former times, Brahmanas studied the Veda as a whole. If they were not experts in everything, they consulted those who were experts in other subject matters. Different schools of Veda were neither exclusive nor contradictory. Exclusivism and contradictions have been created in the last few centuries because all the schools declined, each school wants to prove its supremacy over others, and they neither have the capacity nor inclination to understand others.

Through such neglect, however, we lose the capacity to reconcile different portions of Veda and fail to understand, explain, and predict our own conscious experience. The simplification of philosophy doesn't simplify reality. Simplification only makes reality incomprehensible. Conflicting schools with conflicting claims confuse a sincere student of Veda. Ultimately, under that confusion, the person gives up trying to understand reality. Therefore, the combined understanding is not just in the interest of Veda but also of each student of Veda. If the combination is neglected, then the whole is rejected. That is because the three aspects of reality are inseparable. They are not just three things; they are also one thing.

The Worldview of Contracts

Contracts in Religion

Modern society is constructed on the idea of contracts. This idea can be traced back to Judaism which instituted a "covenant" with God in which God will do certain things for Abraham if Abraham did some things for God. The first covenant of Judaism for instance says: "You shall be circumcised in the flesh of your foreskins, and it shall be a sign of the covenant between me and you". God promised to make Abraham the ruler of the Jews and give him the land of Israel if he obeyed His commandments.

This idea of covenants or contracts between God and man then carried forward in many successive religions, including Christianity and Islam. In Judaism, the people of Israel have a collective contract with God. In Catholicism, the people of this whole world (not just Israel) have a collective contract with God. In Protestantism, each individual person either has or must make a unique covenant with God.

The relationship to God in all these religious systems is not based on love; it is rather based on a contract. This means that *if a* man does certain things as ordered by God, then God will do certain things for man. This agreement of reciprocal exchange defines the contractual relationship to God.

The Western preoccupation with writing things down, history, and records are due to the obsession with contracts. It is also said that this way of thinking originated in the Babylonian civilization and Judaism borrowed it from them. Contracts were used for trade agreements, and that's how people learned reading and writing—they had to negotiate contracts and write them down. The covenants that people drew with each other as trade agreements were then extended to a covenant with God.

Contrast this idea with the Vedic civilization in which things were never written down, and knowledge was transmitted orally. There was no trust deficit in people for things to be written. In fact, they were never negotiating contracts. They were discussing the principles of dharma or duty. They had language, and people were learned, but not out of the necessity to negotiate or write down contracts. When Western scholars look at Indian traditions, they wonder: How can a society exist without writing things down? It must not have existed. This is because their cultural upbringing accustoms them to view society using the lens of contractual documentation.

Contracts in Social Organization

The idea of contracts then leads to the Social Contract Theory in which morality is replaced by contracts. The government is now a legal entity that enters into a contract with the people. Since it is a contract, therefore, it can be revised. The people can replace the government because the ruler is contracted on some terms. Citizenship of a country is a contract that requires the citizens to obey the government's laws. These contracts are drawn based on some principles—which is called a nation's Constitution. Even the Constitution can be amended, so the contractual terms are not true for all times. Thus, the replacement of monarchy with democracy is the extension of contracts from religion to society.

The idea of contracts creates room for fictional legal entities called corporations, which can enter into contracts. When someone is employed by a company, he or she has entered into a contract. Either side of the contracting party—i.e., the corporation or the employee—can terminate their contract if they choose to do so. This is called "Equal Opportunity Employment"— employment is only a contract. A corporation is now not obligated to worry about the people's welfare. It is only interested in its own welfare, and it is obligated only to follow the terms of employment offered at the time of hiring.

Contractual Human Relationships

Then, human relationships are also contracts. The relationship between husband and wife—which is the cornerstone of a family—is a contract, and it can be terminated if either party so decides. Even children can get legally divorced from their parents because the parent-child relationship is a contract. When all relationships are reduced to contracts, then humans are not obligated to care for each other unless documented by a reciprocal contract. Contractual marriages lead to an increase in divorces, single-parent children, and families are destroyed. Now, the government steps in to provide "social security"—i.e., care for the abandoned and old parents, divorced mothers, and parentless children. Why? Because people don't have a binding contract with each other; only the citizenship contract is binding.

Due to the increase in divorces, most people don't want to get married, or even if they get married, they don't want to have children. This means that the tax-paying population declines, and the number of people dependent on the government for social security continues to be the same (or increases). Now, the governments are forced to open their borders to people who are very likely to produce many children, because these children will grow into tax-paying citizens to take care of the government's social security obligations.

People may complain about interracial and interreligious conflicts resulting from the immigration of foreign people, but they have nobody else to blame. This immigration is an inevitable outcome of society advocating a sexual revolution, contractual marriages, leading to increased divorces, increased abortions, and reduction in birth rates; to continue to pay for social security, people who produce more children and are socially not inclined toward sexual liberation, divorce, or abandoning parents, are necessary as tax-paying citizens. Only such citizens will pay enough taxes with reduced social security liabilities to compensate for the social security needs of the others.

Interracial and interreligious mingling in society is now an inevitable consequence of the declining rate of childbirth. And the inevitability of this mingling forced by economic necessities then semi-ensures the conflicts between races and religions, semi-guaranteeing chaos.

Contracts of Scientific Theories

Even modern science evolved out of the extension of moral, social, and religious contracts into the idea of producing contractual laws about nature. Such contracts are drawn up between the theoretician and the experimenter. Curiously, nature itself doesn't enter into the contract about natural laws.

Einstein explained this idea by the example of a person going to a ball dance. As you enter the ballroom, you give your coat to the gatekeeper, and he gives you a token in return. The token can be plastic, metal, paper, cardboard, etc. It can have any number printed on it. The only virtue in the token is that when you give it back, you get your coat back. A token is a contract between the dancer and the gatekeeper. This is how Einstein claimed science works. The theoretician is the gatekeeper and the experimentalist is the dancer. The theoretician can give you any token, and as long as you get your coat (i.e., the observation is predicted), that token is the mutually agreed upon "truth". There is no such thing as reality or truth; it is merely a token agreement of exchange and reciprocity between the theoretician and experimenter.

As a result, different departments of academia can create their own token systems, and as long as the token works for them, it is called the truth, although tokens of one academic department cannot be exchanged in another department. Each department is permitted to create their own collectively negotiated tokens—i.e., they arrive at a contract about how they think of the world. This idea is then formalized as the "philosophies" of Instrumentalism, Operationalism, Pragmatism, Etc. In these philosophies, science is not about the truth; it is about how we like to think about nature with the only condition being that we get our coats back (we can predict and explain observations) by using whatever theory-tokens we happen to invent.

In all these laws, there is no moral *consequence* for actions because moral clauses don't enter the contract. Why? Because such a moral clause is not needed between a theoretician and an experimenter.

These two individuals have a contract about how a gun will work, but no contract about when and whether to use the gun. The use of the gun is a separate contract drawn up with others in a society, or with the government, but not within science and never with nature. Since nature never enters into the contracts about natural laws, therefore, nature cannot punish us for misusing the gun. Only society can punish people for gun misuse because the contract is only negotiated with society.

Postmodernist Contractual Thinking

A common thread about contracts unifies Western thinking from religion to social organization to human relationships to science. That thread makes several stipulations that remain obscure to most people (although they are well-known to the experts in a given field). For example, there is no love between soul and God; it is a contract. There is no love between humans; it is a contract. There is no morality in society; it is a contract. And there is no truth; our conceptions or theories about reality are contracts between scientists.

Postmodernism now takes this up a notch. In postmodernism, there is no such thing as truth; it is whatever people think the truth is. There is no such thing as morality; it is only a socially constructed set of agreements. There is no such thing as beauty; it is whatever people want to think beauty is. There is even no such thing as gender; you can create your own gender pronouns, and the pronoun (he, she, etc.) you call a person by is based on a contract between the caller and the callee.

On one hand, this leads to radical individualism—each person can decide what truth, right, and good means. On the other hand, this radical individualism now leads to problems even in further negotiating the contracts. With radical individualism, people lose the capacity even to sign contracts, because they cannot agree on what is truth, right, and good, and they cannot give up their own ideas of the same.

Religious people in the West may rally against the relativizing trend of postmodernism, but they have to look deeper. This relativization is a direct result of contractual agreements. And they begin in the contractual relation to God. How can there be love between people if the most personal and intimate relationship to God is a contract? How can there be morality in society if morality is reduced to a mutually beneficial contract? How can there be happiness in the people if their only connection to society is through a contract of material exchanges?

Anyone who has grown up in a traditional society where truth, morals, virtues, ideals, and goodness are upheld as non-negotiable principles, will find himself or herself as a fish out of water in a world where everything is based on a contract. And those who have grown up in a society where everything is governed by contracts can never understand a philosophy where truth, morality, virtues, ideals, and goodness are not socially constructed, not determined by contracts, or not accepted as absolute principles. This difference leads to many conflicts.

Vedic Philosophy is Non-Contractual

This is the sense in which Vedic philosophy completely overturns everything the West has thought and practiced over millennia. In Vedic philosophy, God doesn't enter into contracts. We cannot give anything to God that He doesn't already have. So, how can we have a contract with God? A contract is signed between two parties each of whom needs something from the other. When one of the signatories on the contract is God, there is nothing that we have to offer. But we can still love Him. That love is the only thing to offer, and it cannot be a contract. It has to be understood as an act of giving without the expectation of a return. Vedic texts state that God reciprocates that kind of love. All other ideas about contractual relationships with God based on an exchange of mutual benefits are false.

Similarly, moral principles of truthfulness, kindness, austerity, and cleanliness are non-negotiable. We cannot whimsically invent our moralities or ideas of right and wrong and produce temporary laws. These laws don't mean anything, because natural laws of cause, effect, and consequence are based on unchanging moral principles. Indeed, all the socially constructed laws don't save a person from immorality, even though we might say that they are legal. Legality doesn't necessarily imply morality.

Likewise, you cannot create arbitrary token exchange theories about nature and call them "science". And you cannot have different token systems across many disciplines. There is only one theory of nature that explains every single type of experience. Every other theory is false, delusional, and ignorant. The test of a theory is that you must be able to exchange the tokens of physics theories in the psychology department, the tokens of psychology in the economics department, and the tokens of economics in the religion department. And everything has to be exchangeable in the happiness department. If your tokens cannot be exchanged in this way, then they are not the truth.

Non-Contractual Societies

Social relationships are not contracts based on rights; they are social roles governed by duties. We have the right to perform our duty, and no other rights. When we enter the world, we don't negotiate a contract about "I will do this if you do this". This idea of human existence is a pure concoction. Even if we want to think in terms of a contract, the contract is: "Either you perform your duty, or you will suffer". This so-called contract of duty performance without the expectation of a result is meant to give us the training to love each other and ultimately love God. If we can perform our duties without expectation of results, then we come to the point of understanding the nature of love. And the so-called lawfulness of nature is to bring us that understanding. Therefore, if we don't get what we think is our right based upon a social contract with other people or the government, there is no need to be angry, because we never had any rights. We only had our duties.

The idea that we have "rights" is so central to Western thinking that everyone talks in terms of a right to education, right to employment, right to justice, right to equality, and so on. Who gave us all those rights? And the answer is that the social contract is negotiated on the premise of such rights. A contract has to be equitable; everyone must have the right to negotiate a contract and revoke a contract. All so-called rights in the modern world are based on the idea that we are free to negotiate contracts.

That this entire way of thinking about society, human

relationships, and science began in a contractual relationship with God seems too distant now, but that connection lies hidden in plain sight.

How would our societies, human relationships, and sciences be different if we gave up our ideas about contracts? How will we reimagine the world, if our relationship with God was based on love?

Non-Contractual Religion

That alternative way of thinking about the world is Vedic philosophy. It is grounded in a loving relationship to God, and based on that love, social organization, professional employment, human relationships, and science, are defined non-contractually. This non-contractual way of thinking leads us to truth, morality, and goodness. If instead someone is lost in a world of negotiated contracts, arm twisting to get better terms, changing the contract when it suits a person, and giving up on the contract when it seems inconvenient, then they have completely misconstrued the nature of reality. Every theory, idea, principle, or system that follows from the contractual way of relating to God, is a false conclusion.

The contractual worldview is so radically different from the worldview about truth, love, and morality, that it is hard to overstate the incompatibility between the two, and the impossibility to bridge them. The contractual view is also self-destructive because it begins in the attempt to define everything as a contract, and it ends with the inability to negotiate any contract or innumerable conveniently betrayed contracts. The worldview based on truth, love, and morality is the only answer to this self-destruction.

Indian Origins of German Idealism

Background of German Idealism

German Idealism is a collection of ideas developed in Germany during the colonial period in India, after Germans got access to Indian texts, and specifically, an interpretation of these texts, called Advaita, which until that time had been rejected for centuries in India. Christian missionaries during colonial times used to revile all things Indian, including the so-called Polytheism, the so-called caste system, and the so-called lack of scientific thinking. Demoralized by centuries of Islamic and Christian colonization, Indians accepted these insults as their karma and fate. Factually, Indians had lost the sophistication of science and philosophy that had earlier prevailed in India because all the major universities, libraries, and teachers had been destroyed by Islamic rule. Additionally, Indians had no access to the history of Islam and Christianity, so they had to accept the version of Islam and Christianity that was given to them by the preachers of these religions. The destruction of the Indian universities, libraries, and teachers, coupled with the lack of information about the origins of Islam and Christianity, made Indians helpless.

In this situation, some Indians, led by the English-educated and somewhat Westernized Bengali elite, revived Advaita in a land that had earlier been swept by the Bhakti Movement under the leadership of the greatest of all devotees, Śri Caitanya, in the 16th century. Śri Caitanya had defeated Advaita in its erstwhile fortress—Vārāṇasi—and all former Advaita proponents had become Śri Caitanya's disciples. Therefore, the revival of Advaita within

Bengal was an unconscionable betrayal of Śri Caitanya, and it had literally no resonance across the rest of India. But Bengal at that time was the seat of the British Empire in India (the British later moved the capital from Calcutta to New Delhi), and so, the word of the English-educated and Westernized Bengalis became the final word on the Vedic tradition for Europeans.

In this article, I will discuss how Germans took ideas from Advaita, and its predecessor Shaiva and Shakta Tantras, and reformulated them as German Idealism. To do that, we have to understand the Tantra philosophy that preceded Advaita. After that, we can understand how Advaita distorted the Tantra tradition, and how Advaita was then disaggregated into multiple philosophers as German Idealism. Finally, we will talk about how German Idealism was a colonialist project that collapsed after the end of WWII and was replaced by ideologies that have since undermined European supremacist thinking.

Advaita as Reformation of Hinduism

But before we get into these details, we have to understand how Advaita came to be seen as a tool for the ideological subversion of India, and was resurrected and endorsed, after it had already died during the Bhakti Movement in India. How did Advaita come to be seen as a reformation of Hinduism, taking the primitive Hindus engrossed in ritual, worship, and ceremony of many gods, divided into many classes based on ancestry, out of their blind faith into the glorious new age of reason by the Europeans?

To understand this shift, we have to understand the Protestant Reformation in Europe, which had rejected the authority of the Pope and the Catholic Church and articulated a form of Christianity devoid of class, ritual, and ceremony in Catholicism. Protestants believed that Catholicism was contaminated by pagan ideas and practices, and it wasn't Monotheism in its purest spirit. Protestants who wanted to purge classes, rituals, and ceremonies from Catholicism called themselves Puritans because they saw these things as pagan contaminations. During the Reformation, Protestants had rejected the special rights of the kings and the priests, and Protestantism eschewed Catholic rituals and ceremonies.

The British and the Germans, called Anglo-Saxons, applied Protestant Reformation ideas to the Vedic tradition: They saw Acharyas of the Bhakti Movement as the Pope, their teaching institutions were equated to the Catholic Church, and their advocacy of class, ritual, and ceremony was synonymized with Catholicism. Meanwhile, the freewheeling English-educated and Westernized Bengalis were not tied to the Acharyas, classes, institutions, rituals, and ceremonies. They would read and interpret the Vedic texts on their own, not under an established tradition. They were not particularly attached to rituals and ceremonies, or these only had a socio-cultural significance, rather than a spiritual meaning for them. The Protestants resonated with freewheeling Bengalis due to their own theological biases, although the Bhakti Movement had come after Advaita, unlike Catholicism, which had preceded Protestantism.

For the Bengalis, Advaita rejected the diversity of the world as an illusion, and thereby the so-called Polytheism and the so-called caste system. The Bengalis saw the resurrection of Advaita as a path out of the criticism and humiliation by the Christian missionaries to restore Hindu pride. The road to hell is sometimes paved with good intentions. The rejection of diversity and its replacement by uniformity was the clarion call for Protestants as well, so they resonated with the Bengalis. Since all Monotheisms are iconoclastic and reject the worship of deities in temples, Advaita received additional support from Christians due to its own iconoclasm. And thus, Advaita came to be seen as the Reformation for the Vedic tradition, along similar lines as the Protestant Reformation of Catholicism, i.e., purging religion of classes, rituals, and ceremonies, and therefore, in the minds of the Protestants, the superior type of worldview and religion.

The Creation of a Collaborative Project

Advaita proponents now became coconspirators with Christians in the destruction of the Vedic tradition, although operating from within the tradition, rather than outside of it like the Christian missionaries. Christians presented these coconspirators as the true representatives of the Vedic tradition, and they were given inordinate attention in the West, while the true representatives were ignored. Advaita and Christianity walked like brothers-in-arms, talking about the need for the Reformation of Hinduism. Hindus who joined in this project, such as Raja Rama Mohan Roy, who tried to end the so-called evil of Sati, and Swāmi Dayānanda Saraswati, who rejected the Purāṇas as corrupted texts, were called *reformers*.

Many Christians were also tired of the colonial crimes and saw in Advaita a peaceful substitute for their good vs. evil wars. The similarity between European and Indian languages had already led to the coining of the phrase Indo-European languages. Anglo-Saxons in Northern Europe considered themselves separate from the Greco-Roman cultures in Southern Europe, so they needed a separate identity for themselves. That identity, especially for Germans, became Aryan, as Germans believed that giving themselves a different identity from the rest of Europeans would help them conquer and rule the rest of Europe as a race superior to those who had Greco-Roman culture and genes within them (which eventually came true).

For the British, the replacement of deities, rituals, ceremonies, and diversity of India with the uniformity and iconoclasm of Advaita would serve colonial purposes—(a) Indians would stop seeing themselves as different from the Europeans and stop opposing the colonial rule in India, and (b) their adoption of one cosmic spirit rather than many deities would eventually facilitate their conversion into Christianity.

All these diverging interests in the Bengalis, British, and Germans came together into a collaboration we presently call German Idealism. It involved a give-and-take deal—(a) Germans would subvert Christianity and replace the Monotheistic God that kicked out Adam and Eve from heaven with a Cosmic Spirit, (b) Bengalis would subvert the Vedic deities, rituals, ceremonies, and classes and replace them with the same Cosmic Spirit, called Brahman, and (c) the British would rule over India permanently as the ideological differences between the East and West would have been diminished or dissolved. The model could also be replicated in other parts of the world, by giving them German Idealism as a substitute for Polytheism, citing the Indian example. Thereby, all over the world, Monotheism and Polytheism would merge into Monism. The cultural and civilizational disparity between cultures would collapse, and the whole world would then become uniform. In this uniformity, the West would provide the science of matter while the East would provide the science of mind, and that would then pave the way for global harmony.

Subversion Hidden in the Collaboration

Of course, while talking about this bonhomie in the world, there were insidious designs of racial and cultural supremacy in the works. The Germans were going to reformulate Advaita as German Idealism and give it to the world, including Indians, as something uniquely Western. It would be taught in universities as philosophy of the self coming from the West, alongside science, and the university will become the place that teaches theories of the body and mind, removing the need for any other source of information. Even Indians will be taught German Idealism, while Advaita and Tantra texts will not be part of the university curriculum. All those who might have earlier talked about Advaita and Tantra would be discarded as useful idiots who had lived past their date of usefulness. The West will now own both the science of the mind and the body, and the institutional power in Western universities will be used to undermine, revile, and destroy all other classical traditions. While extending one hand in friendship and collaboration, the Anglo-Saxons had the other hand stealthily hidden behind their backs, ready to stab the Indians.

This subversion was seen throughout the collaborative project in the fact that even as Germans were reading, coopting, and transforming ideas from the Vedic texts into their own philosophy, they almost never mentioned the sources of their inspiration. They saw Advaita as a pantheistic philosophy in which the individual annihilated itself into an indeterminate spirit, incompatible with Western individualism. They believed that ideas of karma and destiny made Hindus fatalistic and defeatist. They claimed that the cycles of time in Vedic cosmology lacked the idea of progress and demoralized people into inaction.

None of these is factually true, and their falsehood would be known if their advocates had learned under an Acharya. But Protestants had already elevated everyone to the level of a priest, fully capable of interpreting scripture on their own as one deemed fit. By applying Protestant ideologies to the Vedic tradition and rejecting whatever did not match that ideology as inferior, they filtered the Vedic tradition through the Christian sieve. Thereafter, they cherry-picked what they liked, disaggregated it from the Vedic tradition, made it their own creation, and derided the Vedic tradition from which they took, most of the time.

Hegel, in particular, espoused a hierarchical view of cultures and placed Indian thought on a lower level than Western thought. His false interpretations, premature generalizations, and ignorant criticisms clearly established his motive to establish the supremacy of the Western perspective, relegating Indian ideas to a pre-philosophical or unphilosophical status. He followed the Orientalist practice of relying on a limited understanding of non-Western cultures to reinforce the imagined superiority of the Europeans.

For those who don't know, this is an established process in all Monotheisms—they took preexisting deities, teachings, and practices from pagan religions, reformulated them as Monotheism, presented that reformulation as a divine revelation of a messiah, and used it to conquer territories and convert the pagan followers to Monotheism. The Anglo-Saxons were doing nothing different with Indians than what Christianity had already done in Europe during Roman times. Of course, Indians did not know the history and tactics of Monotheisms, so they thought that the friendship and collaboration were genuine. Subsequently, as history unfolded, German Idealism died while the Vedic tradition strengthened.

Shaiva and Shakta Tantra Philosophy

Since German Idealism is a philosophical movement spanning many philosophers, on the surface, it looks diverse. But all that diversity is superficial if we understand the Tantra philosophy from which these philosophers borrowed different ideas and transformed them in different ways. Once the Tantra system is understood, the differences between the philosophers of German

Idealism are understood as picking different aspects of Tantra philosophy, not truly separate philosophies in themselves.

Within Tantra philosophy, there is a Cosmic Spirit, called Param Śiva, from whom the world originates. He is the embodiment of will that controls the cosmos and is called Causal Time. Within Param Śiva, there is Śakti, His power. This power is, in preliminary descriptions, divided into three parts, called the power of knowing, the power of doing, and the power of enjoying. At present, when people think of power, they think of energy in modern science. In fact, in Sanskrit-English dictionaries, Śakti is translated as energy. It's a bad translation because it inherits European ideas of energy and power (as used in modern science), where it means something inert, dead, material, meaningless, and purposeless. Śakti, instead, is neither inert, nor dead, nor material, nor meaningless, and not purposeless. She is the wife, consort, and eternal partner of Śiva. There is no connotation of Śakti common with energy, except maybe that energy can be equated to a causal force, and Śakti is indeed the causal force in the universe. Of course, when the Sanskrit-English dictionaries were created, false equivalences were the norm rather than the exception.

Śiva and Śakti are one person but two personalities. This concept is rather difficult to understand for the modern mind, so I give the following example. I can cook for myself, but I prefer that someone cooks for me. When I cook for myself, I make a simple meal—one or two items. But when I cook for others, I like to make a feast. While cooking a feast, the cook and the eater are separated. However, that doesn't mean the cook doesn't eat; rather, the cook prepares sumptuous dishes for the eater, according to the wishes of the eater, and after feeding them, the cook eats the same dishes. But the key pleasure for the cook is seeing the eater enjoy the sumptuous dishes, rather than their own eating. Likewise, Śiva and Śakti are one person, but for enjoyment, they separate into two personalities. Śiva becomes the eater, and Śakti becomes the cook. Śakti cooks for Śiva and then eats the same meal Herself. And yet, the key pleasure for Śakti is not Her own eating what She has cooked, but instead seeing Śiva enjoy the sumptuous meal She has cooked.

In traditional Indian culture, women cooked for men, fed them, and then ate their meal afterward. Men and women were considered one person and two personalities. Those who remember traditional Indian culture know that men and women were called "one soul and two bodies". This idea has become alien at present due to the spread of hyper-individualism; under individualistic thinking, each body is one soul, so two bodies must be two souls. This is why it is nearly impossible to understand how men and women were considered one soul and two bodies. But this is crucial to understanding Śiva and Śakti as one person but two personalities. It was the common thing in India earlier, and nobody even bothered to complicate it philosophically. But at present, this concept requires a philosophical explanation.

Tantra Philosophy Through Examples

The explanation is that the self wants to know itself, and for that, the self divides into a knower, a known, and a knowing. Śiva is the knower, Śakti is the power of knowing, and the world is the known. Śiva is the eater, Śakti is the cook, and the world is the food. The world is the portrait of a hero painted by a painter, the biography of a leader written by an author, the song about a star sung by a singer. Śiva is the star, leader, and hero, Śakti is the painter, biographer, and singer, the world is the portrait, biography, and song. The world is created when the hero wishes to see a portrait, the leader wants to read a biography, and the star wants to listen to a song. This is when the knower, knowing, and known are separated. However, these three merge into one when the will for eating, seeing, reading, and listening disappears.

The painter, biographer, and singer have to know the hero, leader, and star before creating a portrait, biography, and song. At the point of knowing, the hero, leader, and star enter the mind of the painter, biographer, and singer. The entry of Śiva into Śakti is called their sexual intercourse. Most people at present think that sexual intercourse is only about the genitals because they don't understand the meeting of the minds. They also think that the body is a substance and the mind is an idea because they have never resolved the mind-body dualism. In the Vedic tradition, the body is an expansion out of the mind, which is why a soul gets successive bodies based on their previously developed mind. And yet, genital intercourse exists because the world is constantly recreated as the children of Śiva and Śakti.

The painter, singer, and biographer create portraits of the hero, leader, and star from their perspective, so each portrait, biography, and song is not the complete representation of the subject they are depicting. If the same painter, biographer, and singer creates new portraits, biographies, and songs about the same subject, from different perspectives, one after another, in each case, the portrait, biography, and song come out different. Thus, the subject enters and exits the mind of the painter, biographer, and singer in successively different ways. This is also called the sexual intercourse of Śiva and Śakti. Śiva enters Śakti multiple times, but each time, the entry and exit are different, and the result is a different world. It is just like a painter, biographer, and singer creating new portraits, biographies, and songs about the same subject, after understanding the subject in a different way, from a novel and unique perspective.

Polytheism vs. Perspective Thinking

Since the creative process is sexual, Śiva is the father, Śakti is the mother, and the world is the children of the mother and father. Sex simply means birth and death; in the spiritual world, where there is no birth and death, there is no sex. In the Shaiva and Shakta Tantras, the changing world is the successive children of Śiva and Śakti. They come one after another, just like the children of ordinary parents. The siblings produced by the same parents are not the same. In fact, as time elapses, different kinds of children are produced successively, and that is the flow of Cosmic Time. But the birth and death of the children don't entail the birth and death of the parents. Factually, in the case of the cosmic creation, the parents are eternal while their children live for a very short time. These children were originally in Śiva, the father; from Śiva, they are injected into Śakti, the mother; after that, they become the parts of a cosmic portrait, biography, and song, the children.

To understand this portrait, biography, and song as a reflection of the creative process occurring between a father and a mother, we have to adopt *semanticism* and *personalism*. The world is not stuff or substance devoid of meaning and purpose. The meaning is that it is a picture, biography, and song about Śiva, and the purpose is that Śiva wants to see Himself from the perspective of the Śakti. Everything is a combination of a subject and a perspective—the masculine and the feminine causes of the world. The soul is a small and insignificant part of this perspective-laden vision, as it sees a fraction of what Śakti sees.

Those who worship Śakti and receive Her grace can see the whole cosmos just as She sees it, at that time. Likewise, those who worship Śiva and receive His grace can see Śiva as He sees Himself, separate from and transcending the temporal perspective of Śakti. Those who worship lower deities, called Devas, and receive their grace, see larger portions of Śiva than ordinary humans but smaller portions of Śiva compared to Śakti. Due to smaller and bigger, longer and shorter, better and worse, perspectives, there is a hierarchy of visions, and there are many kinds of worship in the Vedic texts. They exist to see Śiva from different perspectives, some bigger and others smaller, some longer and others shorter, some better and others worse.

Universalism is Ignorance and Arrogance

Ignorant people consider multiple visions of reality a fiction or Polytheism. It arises due to arrogance—what I see must be all that there is, the only truth, and if someone sees something else, it must be false. This ignorance-arrogance is called universalism in Western philosophy. Under its influence, each limited perspective—like a frog in a well—equates its vision to that of the ocean. Western thinking, since the time of Greek philosophy, tries to see reality as some "objective truth" devoid of perspectives. In science, this is called the view of reality from nowhere and nowhen—transcending the limits of space and time, and pretending to see the world from outside, not inside. In Monotheistic religions, this is called the existence of only one deity. The whole of Western thinking, called universalism, is a frog equating its limited vision of the well to an ocean. It doesn't recognize the role an individual plays in forming a perspective on reality, and the vision that comes from that perspective is neither completely false nor the universal truth.

Western thinking is essentially anti-Idealism because of its universalism. Individuals don't have a choice in how they know the truth. Truth from a perspective is not truth; it is simply personal and irrational opinion. That lack of choice in knowing through different perspectives is the continuation of Monotheistic authoritarianism, where nobody has a choice to know the truth differently or a different truth.

To truly embrace Idealism, we have to discard universalism, i.e., the entire trajectory of Western thinking since Greek philosophy, and go back to pagan religions in which multiple deities see limited portions of reality, organized in a hierarchy, and the higher deity has a bigger and longer perspective, while the lower deity has a smaller and shorter perspective. We have to discard the idea of the same objective truth being known by everyone as the only truth, because the truth is infinite, and we are finite. We can progress from seeing a smaller, shorter, and worse truth to seeing a bigger, longer, and better truth, but that requires vision development through a process. Of course, those who never undergo vision development think they will know the whole truth based on whatever they see right now, exactly like a frog that tries to take bigger leaps within its well, and claims to have fathomed the length and breadth of the infinite ocean.

Coexistence of Truth and Illusion

Simplistically, the changing world is an ordered succession of changing perspectives in Śakti in order to know the same subject, Śiva. New portraits, biographies, and songs are created to depict the same subject from a previously unseen perspective. The changing nature of the world is not an evil, curse, or illusion because the same eternal and unchanging subject is depicted from novel changing perspectives. The illusion is simply that the children think that there is no mother or father, that the world is inert, dead, material, meaningless, and purposeless substance, and each child wants to see the world as a portrait, biography, and song about itself, not the father. The illusion is simply a false interpretation of reality, exactly like someone might see a snake and think it is a rope; the illusion is not in Śiva or Śakti, but only in their children.

Accordingly, there is a difference between Prakṛti and Jagat. Prakṛti is the reality produced from Śakti and Śiva, whereas Jagat is our *interpretation* of that reality. This interpretation is tainted by the soul's desire to be the hero, leader, and star being depicted in the world, which results in the denial of the real hero, leader, and star, i.e., Śiva. Insofar as most children are tainted by this desire, they misinterpret reality, and the Jagat is mostly false. But insofar as we can know reality just as it is, some Jagat can be true. The choice of a correct or incorrect interpretation of reality is in each child. Hence, each child can individually interpret reality correctly or incorrectly. Everyone's interpretation cannot be called illusory. Since correct and incorrect interpretations are possible, therefore, science can coexist with illusion. Knowledge is still a rare, exceptional, and extraordinary thing; illusion is the normal thing, but both are possible.

The Distortion of Tantra Into Advaita

Of course, if we close our eyes, then we see neither truth nor illusion. A blind man also sees no truth or illusion. So, closing our eyes, or becoming blind, can be called freedom from illusion, but it is factually the renunciation of truth as well. And yet, since closing our eyes or being blind is freedom from illusion, someone under illusion can say that closing the eyes or becoming blind frees us from illusion. When we close our eyes or become blind, we see nothing except the self. When the awareness of the external world is cut off, the awareness of the self grows. If we keep our eyes permanently closed or remain permanently blind, we can only remain conscious of the self, which is definitely not an illusion.

This is the Advaita solution—close your eyes, or become blind, stop seeing the world and only see the self. It is certainly one way of getting out of illusion; it is certainly one way of knowing the self as the truth, but it is a marginal, small, and limited truth, not the complete truth which would be possible if we kept our eyes open, and we were not blind, and we learned how to interpret reality correctly.

In Advaita, the world disappears because our awareness is turned inward, so someone can even say that if we turn the awareness inward, then we don't see the diversity of the world. Rather, we only see the self, and that self is the truth, so there is simply one truth—the self, not the diversity of the world. All these statements are true, and yet, they are very marginal, small, and limited truths. Those who want to realize this kind of truth are welcome to pursue it, provided they don't deny a far bigger truth. Advaita became an illusion when it elevated itself to the whole and sole truth, and denied the far bigger truth. The self was equated to Brahman, the Jagat was called illusion, the withdrawal of awareness from the world became the only process for transcendence, and the reality of Śiva and Śakti was denied.

Advaita doesn't recognize a spiritual world; therefore, its asexual portrayal of reality as Brahman pertains only to the annihilated state of the universe in which the knower, known, and knowing are merged, not when they are separated. This is why Advaita proponents have never contributed anything to the scientific understanding of the world. They see religion as essentially separate from science, exactly like the Monotheistic religions that separate the two. Within Advaita, science is about the separation of the knower, known, and knowing, while religion is about their merger into self-awareness.

Use of Advaita in German Idealism

The illusions created by Advaita then spread to the West through what came to be known as German Idealism, because one by one, different German philosophers coopted different aspects of Advaita as their own philosophy.

- Immanuel Kant stated that the world is a phenomenon, and the reality behind that phenomenon was simply unknowable. Whatever science called reality was what the observer added to the phenomena. For instance, space, time, matter, motion, and law were not real things existing outside the human mind; these were simply mental constructs to organize the phenomenon. However, insofar as all humans thought the same, a universal science was possible.
- Carl Jung stated that the divinities that people have

historically worshipped across civilizations were not real entities. They were simply mental Archetypes, the religious equivalent of Kantian mental constructs called space, time, matter, motion, and law. He attributed the fact that the same divinities were worshipped across diverse cultures (Roman, Greek, Egyptian, Babylonian, and Vedic) to the presence of universal mental Archetypes across all human minds.

- Frederick Neitzche read about Śiva and Śakti as will and power, their sexual intercourse as the union of will and power, and created a theory of the world in which Übermensch (men who desire greatness) have a will to power. He called this union of will and power the path to self-determination, which in India was called self-realization. He equated the concept of each person realizing himself as the cosmic Brahman to each person attempting to be Übermensch.
- Arthur Schopenhauer read about how the will in Śiva transforms into His portrait, biography, and song called the world, and created a theory in which the world is a representation of the will of the self. The inner essence of everything in the world, the thing-in-itself, was will, and the outer world we saw was the representation or expression of that will. He even called the world the objectification of will, a clear reference to the idea of Brahman objectifying into a world.
- Georg Hegel coopted the Advaita idea of duality as thesis and antithesis, and that of Brahman free from duality as synthesis. He stated that thesis and antithesis disappear with passing time, and are replaced by synthesis, a typical Advaita idea dissociated from the Vedic tradition, where nothing disappears as dualities are codependent, like the head and foot of a person. Hegel coopted the Advaita idea that diversity is an illusion resolved by conversion to uniformity.
- Johann Fichte took from Advaita the idea of the self as infinite and the world as finitude imposed on the infinite. He called the former freedom and the latter necessity, the

former subjectivity and the latter objectivity. He stated that the self imposes limitations on itself to create its finite experience whose purpose is self-knowledge, because the infinite self is unknowable even to itself, but by imposing a limitation on the self, the self becomes a determinate individual.

- Friedrich Schelling took more Tantra than Advaita and posited that the self and nature are simply two aspects of one absolute and dynamic reality, not the mind and body of Cartesian dualism. He saw nature as a dialectic, constituting expansion and contraction, but still a linear progress. Nature wasn't a mechanism but a living organism. He took the Advaita idea of the world as a positive determinant of the self, and the self was known by negating all that the world was.

Characteristics of German Idealism

There are many critical commonalities between the different philosophers of German Idealism: (a) there is no transcendental world beyond this world, (b) there is no overt reliance on masculine and feminine in the creative process, (c) there are no divine and demonic entities called Devas and Asura in the Vedic texts, (d) there is no reality behind the phenomena or even if it exists, it can never be known, (e) there is no cosmic affirmation or retaliation of good or evil in a person, called karma and rebirth in the Vedic tradition, (f) there is no life other than humanity, and (g) there is no concept of cyclical evolution, simply one of continuous progress, even when dialectical concepts of reality are adopted and advanced.

There are also many crucial differences between German Idealism and the rest of Western thinking up until that time: (a) there is no role for Socrates, Plato, and Aristotle, (b) there is no room for messiah, revelation, covenant, apocalypse, faith, or belief, (c) there is an active attempt to dissolve dualisms, such as that between mind and body, freedom and necessity, substance and form, finite and infinite, while treating consciousness as the bedrock of reality, rather than matter, as was the case previously.

Ideas of German Idealism never made it into science, logic, reasoning, linguistics, and epistemology. They came to be known as Continental Philosophy, separate from Analytic Philosophy. While Analytic Philosophy was used for matter, Continental Philosophy became a tool for the mind; while Analytic Philosophy was used in natural and logical sciences, Continental Philosophy was used in social and mind sciences. In Analytic Philosophy, the body is real and the mind is an epiphenomenon of the body, but in Continental Philosophy, the mind is real and the body is an epiphenomenon of the mind. Analytic Philosophy begins by assuming Realism, while Continental Philosophy begins by assuming Idealism. Since these two have never been reconciled or proven over millennia, there is no hope of doing so in the future either.

Due to commonalities between the different German Idealist philosophers, we can call them part of a single movement. Due to differences between German Idealism and the rest of Western thinking until that time, we can call it a radical departure from the Western tradition. Due to differences with the Vedic tradition, we cannot truly equate the two. And that makes us think that German Idealism is a standalone Western movement, disconnected from both Western and Eastern philosophical ideas. However, if we study Tantra philosophy and its modification as Advaita, we cannot help but notice the cooption.

Religion Justifies Theft of Property

The question is: Why didn't German Idealists take Tantra and Advaita texts and write commentaries on them, as was the case in the Vedic tradition? Why pretend to create a new philosophical movement when every key idea was borrowed? Why not acknowledge the source of inspiration and add to it your own insights or modifications so that others can go back to the source of inspiration if they need it? Why do Western intellectuals demand that others quote their ideas and works, while they themselves don't reciprocate the same standard? Why do they happily cite philosophers that they consider a part of their culture, such as ancient Greeks, but don't cite philosophers they think are outside their culture?

The answer is cultural superiority. As the saying goes, my

money is my money, and your money is also my money. This idea was formally enshrined in the West through the Doctrine of Discovery by the Church: All the lands that Christians discovered became theirs, while their land was already theirs. Germans used the Doctrine of Discovery on ideas. But this wasn't just due to the Doctrine of Discovery. As noted earlier, all Monotheistic religions coopted preexisting deities, teachings, and practices from the pagan religions, reformulated them as Monotheism, and presented that reformulation as the revelation of a messiah, when the fact is that to those who know history also know that there is nothing original in them.

Why the West Couldn't Create Idealism

Factually, the West, after Greek philosophy, has never had any noteworthy understanding of the mind, psyche, or soul. To develop such an understanding requires us to uncover the preconscious, subconscious, and unconscious realities underlying the conscious reality through meditative practices. In these practices, the consciousness is withdrawn from the world into the deeper recesses of the enormous internal reality, and it digs out that hidden realm into the conscious realm. These meditative practices are the precondition to practicing Idealism because without them, nobody can understand what lies beneath the conscious experience, even if they read someone's philosophy. But there has never been a noteworthy meditative tradition in the West; therefore, in principle, the West could never make a systematic theory of the mind, psyche, or soul. At most, philosophers can talk of a hidden reality which accidentally and inadvertently comes to the surface, such as during dreams, which is what Western psychology is about. But what one sees during dreams is so insignificant compared to the actual hidden realm that generalizing it as the whole and sole truth—under the Western tendency toward universalism—is bound to deceive.

There has never been in Western history a tradition that said that the world springs out of the soul. Even when Abrahamic Monotheisms accepted a soul, it was equated to the breath breathed into dust by God. Obviously, the dust existed before the breath was breathed into it; the dust did not emerge from the breath. Modern science also did not provide any insights into the mind because it began by assuming a separation of the body and mind. Science focused on the body, leaving the mind to religion. The study of the mind wasn't even a rational project until then. It was a realm of faith, belief, and opinion, not reason. There was nothing in Western philosophy, religion, or science to talk about the mind, psyche, or soul.

Inferiority Transforms Into Superiority

This was a major cultural disadvantage for the West during the colonial rule in India. While the West claimed to have created modern science, the Indians would simply call the West materialistic. This hurt a lot. The West could not project cultural superiority over India if Indians rejected the West as materialistic. And so, German Idealism coopted what they thought was the pinnacle of Indian thinking—i.e., Advaita—to create their theories of psyche, mind, or soul to wash off the taint of materialism. Now, they could say that they were also spiritual, but additionally, they were also scientific. The trouble was that what they thought was the pinnacle of Indian thinking (Advaita) was an outdated and rejected ideology in India that had been debunked for centuries, and proven to be incompatible with the Vedic tradition.

Indians also called the West barbaric because of the violence they had wrought all over the world during colonial times. This stung very hard. The West was trying to portray itself as a superior civilization, so the colonized people, calling the colonizers barbaric, demolished their claims of superior civilization. The West also wanted to call itself Aryan, and the idea of Indo-European languages was being created at this time. The question was: If Indians and Europeans were the same race, why did India have deep insights about the self while the West lacked it completely? Why was it that religion in India meant yoga and meditation, while religion in the West meant an eternal battle between good and evil? Seeing similarity between the languages is one thing, and seeing the disparity between the ideas is something completely different. Assuming that Indians and Europeans were the same race based on similarities of languages, while disregarding the dissimilarities between their worldviews, could not be more than an idle joke.

Indians rejected Monotheistic theology and the Western materialistic worldview so thoroughly that the West needed to create a new theology that looked spiritual to continue their colonization. German Idealism was that theology, reformulating Indian ideas as Continental Philosophy and teaching them as the theories of the mind in universities all over the world, to overcome the accusations of materialism and barbarity. Thereafter, they could say that Europeans also had the same ideas, while rejecting the rest of the Vedic tradition as barbaric, and then using European advancement in science and technology to construct an overall cultural superiority narrative. But there was no meditative practice backing Continental Philosophy. How could the West know anything about the mind in a few decades when it had not known anything for millennia, and never considered it worth knowing? The answer is that the whole thing was stolen, exactly like Monotheisms stole from the pagan religions and called the theft a divine revelation.

Decline and Death of German Idealism

The Vedic tradition describes two kinds of gurus—external and internal. The teacher is the external guru, a representative of an age-old tradition, originating in God. The Paramātma, or the Supreme Soul in the heart, is the internal guru. These two gurus work hand in hand. When someone has a sincere desire to know the truth, Paramātma in the heart guides a person to the teacher. If the person is sincere, he learns from the teacher, always remains deferent to him, and teaches the tradition to his students as the representative of his teacher, never an independent philosopher, messiah, or thinker. The Paramātma helps a sincere soul from within by constantly inspiring and guiding him toward a greater understanding of what was taught by the teacher. But even with such inner inspiration, the sincere student knows that whatever he is receiving from within is not his creation, but the inspiration from Paramātma due to his sincerity and devotion to his teacher, and ultimately the age-old tradition, originating in God. This is how the Vedic tradition lives forever through a disciplic succession and is therefore called sanātana or eternal.

The reverse happens if someone disobeys, disregards, or disrespects the teacher or the tradition. He may read books, copy and reformulate ideas, but if he disconnects himself from the guru or the tradition, or pretends to be an independent thinker, teacher, or messiah, he loses all spiritual power. Outwardly, he may pretend to be a great philosopher, but inwardly, the Paramātma knows better. The hallmark of the Paramātma withdrawing inspiration and guidance from within is that the philosophy he creates becomes a flash in the pan, a short-lived ideology that cannot answer contemporary questions, and eventually dies. Since the arrogant student has proven to be disrespectful in the past, the Paramātma doesn't guide him to the right teacher or path for a long time to come, and the student simply gets lost in time.

This is indeed what happened to German Idealism. Once the ideas easily accessible through Tantra and Advaita texts had been exhausted, German Idealism died, and Continental Philosophy moved into a dark territory called Existentialism, Post-Structuralism, Post-Modernism, and Deconstructivism, which claimed that there was no such thing as truth, right, and good, and everyone made up their own idea of it. This would have never happened if German Idealism had truly accepted that the self was Brahman, called sat-chit-ānanda in the Vedic texts, and therefore itself the nature of truth, right, and good. Deviations from the true nature of Brahman emerge due to envy of the teacher, tradition, and God, marked by the desire to become independent. The moment one wants to be independent, Paramātma lets a person endeavor on their own. They don't find the right teachers, don't receive the guidance they truly need, invent their philosophies, can't find the answers they want, and eventually get lost. This happened to German Idealism as well. It lasted as long as colonialism. Once colonialism died, German Idealism died too.

There is a powerful and poignant lesson in the birth and death of German Idealism—don't pretend to be independent. Never disobey, disregard, or disrespect the teacher or the tradition, because if you do so, the Paramātma will withdraw the inspiration and guidance from within, and you will be lost. Never think you are superior to the teacher or the tradition, if you want to learn. If someone cannot answer your questions, seek sincerely, and the Paramātma will find a better teacher to answer your questions. But if you start ridiculing the teacher or the tradition, or pretend to be a self-made independent thinker, philosopher, inventor, and teacher, the ideas you have received through grace become impotent. If you have disrespected, disregarded, or disobeyed your teachers, then why will your students care for you?

How to Distinguish Truth and Illusion

There is a general principle regarding how to know the true nature of something; it requires us to know (a) what something is, (b) what it is not, (c) what came before it, and (d) what came after it. Moreover, even to know what something is, we need two considerations: (a) how it appears to us, and (b) what its effects are due to its actions. For instance, something that looks like a snake, but doesn't bite us, is probably a rope. If it has no capacity to move, although it looks like a snake to us, it is probably a rope. If it were a pipe earlier, and/or if it became a rope later, it couldn't possibly be a snake in between.

We can never know anything in isolation, as a thing-in-itself. For example, Advaita rose in response to the problems created by Buddhism, which arose in response to the schism within the Vedic tradition between pravṛtti (enjoyment) and nivṛtti (renunciation), which arose due to the fact that the Vedic texts include those that teach how to live in this world and those that teach how to transcend this world. Successive interpretations of Vedānta, called Viśiṣṭādvaita, Śuddhādvaita, Dvaita, Bhedābheda, and Acintya Bhedābheda, successively solved the logical problems with the previous interpretation.

We can never understand any philosophy without knowing what came before and after it, because that philosophy is a response to the problems of previous philosophy and may have some problems solved by the next philosophy. Likewise, we can measure whether someone truly believes in that philosophy by the effects of that philosophy on those claiming to follow it. Finally, we can know what it is not by seeing how the followers of one philosophy behave differently from the followers of other philosophies.

The Hypocrisy of German Idealism

If we apply all these criteria to German Idealism, we will find that German Idealism had no precursor or successor. There was a pipe before it, and there was a rope afterward, so it could not have been a snake in between. The creation of a new theology didn't change anything for the Germans; they did in Europe what Christians had been doing for centuries in other places, during the colonial invasions and destruction. By the fact that the new theology had the same effects as Christianity, we know that it wasn't anything different. It was simply a new type of exclusivism, confined to the Germans.

The fact is that the philosophers of German Idealism made universalist claims, but they were never extended to other cultures. The Kantian idea of universal categories in all minds, the Jungian idea of common moral virtues in everyone, the Nietzschean idea of everyone becoming Übermensch, the Schopenhauerian idea of everyone's will becoming their representation, the Hegelian idea that we were all in the presence of a cosmic spirit, the Fichtean idea that the self imposes constraints on itself to become determinate, or the Schellingian idea that the cosmos is a singe organism, should have meant that people who believed in such ideas should have treated others with love and respect.

After all, they were equally capable of science, equally endowed with moral virtues, equally desiring to become great men, equally endowed with will, the whole world existed within the presence of the same cosmic spirit, everyone had the will to impose different constraints on themselves to become different, and all these different individuals were parts of a single cosmic organism. Then how could Germans be meant to violently dominate and rule the world? If indeed Germans believed in Idealism, what would be the basis of racial superiority rooted in nothing more than trivial bodily features, which don't determine the mind? How could Germans be superior to Indians, to judge them from their Eurocentric lens, after receiving their ideas from the Vedic texts? The answer is that German Idealism was simply hypocrisy.

Why German Idealism Led to Relativism

The real purpose of German Idealism was to project cultural and intellectual superiority to conquer the world. That was the original intent behind Christianity as well: To create a new theology and scripture to strengthen and expand the Roman Empire. The Aryan identity was meant to indicate that Germans were different from other Europeans and superior to them. A new system of religion-philosophy, separate from the Greco-Roman philosophy and religion, was meant to portray Germans as intellectually and spiritually superior to the other Europeans. The scientific and technological developments were all used to project German superiority. It is this undercurrent of racial superiority that led to two World Wars.

To prevent future wars, Germans had to give up their erstwhile beliefs in racial superiority, for which they were indoctrinated in Existentialism, Post-Structuralism, Post-Modernism, and Deconstructivism, all hyper-relativistic philosophies that reject any possibility of ever knowing truth, right, and good. If Germans had taken Idealism seriously, they would have accepted the meditative traditions to realize the inner reality before writing about it. They would have entered the tutelage of teachers who taught meditation to realize their philosophy. After that, they would have never taken a superiority mindset, not fought World Wars, and they would not be forcibly indoctrinated into hyper-relativism today. But they are, because they used German exclusivism against European exclusivism. This trajectory proves that German Idealism was never about the self or the innate truth, right, and good, but simply about projecting cultural superiority.

The easiest way to disprove something is to show its inner contradictions. The inner contradiction in German Idealism is that between theory and practice. The theory says we are equally good spirits, and the practice says that those who make such claims are culturally superior and entitled to rule the world. After that superiority projection, one gets a reformulation—we are equally good spirits, such that whatever you believe doesn't matter, because someone else believes something else, which is also equally good.

Ignorance of History Perpetuates Illusions

A generation ago, many Indians used to like the Nazis, not because of their ideology, but because they destroyed Europe and ended colonialism with it. The seeds of that destruction came out of India in the form of German Idealism. The Bengalis who tried to reform Hinduism considered themselves culturally, intellectually, and spiritually superior to the rest of India. After that, Bengal was partitioned, and it is today the most economically, politically, and socially backward state in India. The truth is eternal, and lies progressively farther from the truth are progressively shorter-lived. Therefore, if someone cannot analyze truth and lies philosophically, there is an easier way through knowing the temporal longevity.

However, even this easier way of knowing the truth is lost when people don't study history. The true history is never taught in any university at present because it shows the West in a terrible light, and people prefer delusion over truth. Most people are also conditioned to think in terms of linear time: The past is gone, the present is new, and we don't need to worry about what happened in the past. They have no idea that people are reborn, that we are byproducts of our history, and the same tendencies are transmitted over generations through the rebirth of the soul. The parents pass their mentality to their children at the time of conception, and reinforce it throughout their lives. History has enormous importance for a society in which the soul is reborn, and it has little importance in a society in which people live just once. By studying the problems of history, we know that the same problems likely exist in us. The longer the historical trends, the deeper and more resilient the inner tendencies. More conscious effort is needed to uproot these tendencies.

Everyone should study their history and its problems, because these most likely exist within you today. You are born in a society, not by accident; your birth indicates that your mind conforms to the collective ideology of that society, your past still exists in you, and you have to uproot the bad things in that past if you want a better future for yourself and your place of birth. Of course, if you undergo modern science education, you will think that all places are the same and no place carries imprints of the past because the past has ceased to exist. History loses value because of this materialistic outlook. People tell fake stories because they think that by rewriting history in a book, the history inside them would be rewritten. Or, they just don't learn and teach history. After that, nobody learns the lessons of history; the history within remains intact and recreates the past over and over, while historians rewrite or cover up history for self-delusion.

Even as the Bhakti Movement swept across India, it did not totally wipe out Advaita; there were remnants of Advaita leftover in people from the past centuries, due to which Advaita rose like a phoenix from the ashes. German Idealism did not abandon Greek universalism, which is why there was no perspective philosophy in Idealism. The supremacist tendencies in Europeans did not die even when they were reading Indian texts. The tendency in Monotheisms to steal from pagan religions and call it a divine revelation continued with German Idealism, as German philosophers reformulated others' ideas as their own intellectual greatness. This is because history doesn't die unless we kill it with the utmost sincere and conscious effort.

The Meaning of Ṛta

Ancient vs. Modern Ideas of Order

Ṛta is a Rig Vedic concept that means cosmic order. However, that order differs from the order imagined in modern times as religious, scientific, economic, social, and political laws. The modern idea of order is universalist, reductionist, and impersonal—(a) the same laws apply at all times, places, and situations, (b) each individual person or thing is governed by the same laws, and (c) the laws are contracts of give and take between rational self-interested parties, but every party is intrinsically the same. Ṛta instead is based on a contextual, collectivist, and personal idea of order—(a) the behavior differs based on time, place, and situation, (b) order is created by rational collective interest, and (c) each individual person or thing is intrinsically unique and their behavior depends on that unique nature. Due to these fundamental differences between the Vedic and modern notions of cosmic order, Ṛta is hard to understand for those attuned to modern ideas of order. So, I will use this article to describe and explain the differences.

But before we go there, let's first understand how each of the three assumptions behind the modern idea of order is false, and impossible to uphold. If the same laws applied to all times, there would be no laws for emergencies or exceptional situations, but there are. If the same laws applied to all places, there would be no difference between private and public space, but there is. If the same laws applied to all situations, the same person could not behave differently in their family and workplace, but they do. If each individual and thing were governed by the same laws, a policeman would not be governed by different laws than a thief, but they are. If everyone negotiated contracts in self-interest, parents would never sacrifice for their children, but they do. If each person were the same as others, there would never be a disagreement between two people, but there is. If each thing were the same, we would have one universal law of nature, not dozens of partially true and mutually contradictory laws, but we do.

Now, the total number of required laws is the total number of times multiplied by the total number of places multiplied by the total number of situations multiplied by the total number of persons and things multiplied by the total number of collectives of such persons and things. Each one of these multiplicative factors is infinite, so the total number of laws required to create order is also infinite. Thus, it is impossible to know cosmic order or create social order under the modern idea of order. In fact, the application of this idea of cosmic order would result in cosmic chaos because the differences of time, place, situation, person, thing, and collective would be ignored, but nothing would work as expected by such neglect; therefore, all predictions, explanations, and expectations of order would end up in failure.

Infantile and Adult Ideas of Order

With that failure in mind, we can recognize the necessity of an alternative idea of cosmic order. At the outset, we can recognize that order must accommodate infinite unique times, places, situations, things, persons, and collectives, so the assumptions behind Ṛta are necessary. We just have to prove that these assumptions are also sufficient for cosmic order, which is what the rest of the article is all about.

To do that, I will begin by describing dharma, which is related to Ṛta, but not identical to it. I will discuss the differences between those who accept or reject Ṛta, and how they should live separately. I will talk about the source of depersonalizing, reductionist, and universalist attitudes behind the modern idea of order in the idea of an unprincipled, irresponsible, unaccountable, and omnipotent God, who never aimed to create a world of life, but only a playhouse of toys to play with. He wanted His toys to be predictable and obedient, to be used or discarded as He pleased, with no concern for what the toys think or feel, because to Him, they are just lifeless toys. Laws, too, begin as toy models of reality, expected to be predictable and obedient, modified if they are no longer interesting, discarded if they stop working, with no concern for things or persons modeled or governed by laws. The lawmakers reflect the personality of a juvenile God. They make laws just like an irresponsible, unaccountable, and unprincipled child playing with toys.

The adult supervision system for the children is Ṛta, and it comprises responsible, accountable, and principled adults who train, supervise, and control children. This idea also has to be traced back to a responsible, accountable, and principled God. The adults give children toys to play with, but restrict them to the playhouse. Ṛta is the order created by adults. Infants running the world entails cosmic chaos, and adults running the world is the only way to get cosmic order. To understand Ṛta, we have to understand how adults become responsible, accountable, and principled, which is called dharma. Dharma means a world run by responsible adults, not by children playing in a playhouse of toys.

Definition and Nuances of Dharma

Dharma is a Vedic concept that means a person's ability, proclivity, and duty. If we have no ability for duty, we will not do it even if we have the proclivity for it; similarly, if we have no proclivity for duty, we will not do it even if we have the ability for it. For example, someone with a weak body cannot become a warrior even if he wants to, and someone with no inclination to fight will not fight even with a strong body. But one who has the ability and the proclivity for fighting shouldn't fight with everyone, at all times, places, and situations. His abilities and proclivities must be used only in scenarios required by duty. Thus, ability, proclivity, and duty are individually necessary for moral action, but not individually sufficient for it. Sufficiency of action is given by the combination of ability, proclivity, and duty.

Ideally, we aim for the maximum overlap of ability, proclivity, and duty to ensure that we are capable of doing our duty, and have the proclivity for duty, to ensure that duty is done perfectly and consistently. And yet, duty is the main meaning of dharma, such that even if we don't have a great proclivity for some duty, and even if we are not fully capable of doing our duty, we push ourselves to do our duty even with less proclivity and ability. As we perform our duty reluctantly and imperfectly, we develop the missing proclivity and ability, after which our duties are done perfectly and enjoyably, such that the maximum overlap between ability, proclivity, and duty is achieved eventually, even if it was missing initially.

There are two kinds of constraints on duty—(a) not overdoing it, and (b) not underdoing it. For instance, if we are impelled by our ability and proclivity to fight, we would be fighting with everyone, at all times, places, and situations, which is against duty. But if we are demotivated by lack of ability and proclivity, we would not fight even when the duty of the time, place, situation, and person requires it, and that would also be against duty. If we are motivated by profit, we would fight when we find it profitable, and we would not fight when we find it lossy, both of which are against duty. Therefore, duty is the most important meaning of dharma, but others like ability and proclivity are necessary to fulfill duty.

The Vedic Principles of Cosmic Order

The person who performs their duty with desires for rewards receives rewards; the person who neglects their duty with desires for rewards receives punishment; the person who performs their duty without desire for rewards receives liberation from rewards and punishments. These three types of activities are called *rajasic*, *tamasic*, and *sattvic*, and their good, bad, and neutral effects are called *sukarma*, *vikarma*, and *akarma*, respectively. Thus, from an individual standpoint, we talk about *dharma* and *karma*.

Sukarma leads a person to a life where he has more important duties, with more ability and proclivity for doing them. Vikarma leads a person to a life where he has less important duties, with less ability and proclivity for them. Akarma leads a person to a life where he has the most important duties, with the greatest abilities and proclivities for it. Thus, both sukarma and akarma are welcomed in the Vedic tradition. The former elevates a person to higher positions in the material world, and the latter liberates the person from the material world. Only vikarma is condemned in the Vedic tradition because it pushes a person into a life where he has the least important roles, with the least ability and proclivity to do it. Sukarma and akarma are thus virtuous cycles (good deeds elevate a person, which gives them the ability, proclivity, and opportunity to do better deeds, in the protection of better persons, after which they transcend the material realm), and vikarma is a vicious cycle (bad deeds degrade a person, which gives them the ability, proclivity, and opportunity to do worse deeds, in the protection of worse persons, after which they fall into hellish suffering). Obviously, the virtuous cycle is preferred over the vicious cycle.

The question is: Who decides what is appropriate dharma for each time, place, situation, and person? Who gives rewards, punishments, or liberation based on a person's actions? Clearly, there must be some cosmic *system* that teaches us about dharma and then judges us based on our adherence to it; or else, everyone would just do whatever they want, there would be no meaning to individual dharma and karma, and the cosmos would be plunged into chaos. The Rig Veda calls this cosmic system of teaching, judging, and enforcing dharma and karma, *Ṛta*. Loosely speaking, we could also call it *cosmic governance.*

I say loosely speaking, because there are so many types of governments at present that don't accept dharma and karma. In the past few centuries, theocratic, autocratic, and democratic systems that reject dharma and karma have cropped up. They invent their systems of governance, but they don't last. During their existence, they keep evolving and eventually collapse, because they are *local governments* subject to the principles of dharma and karma. While they proclaim their freedom to choose their system of rule (democracy), force a system opposed to dharma and karma calling it a divine rule (theocracy), or replace dharma and karma by violence (autocracy), for the cosmic government operating on a cosmic timescale, they last less than a moment—just long enough for the cosmic government to catch and punish them. The results of their actions, in the form of sukarma, vikarma, and akarma, apply to them as well.

The System of Cosmic Governance

The hallmark of Ṛta is that the principles of cosmic governance never change. Those who do their duties with desires are elevated to powerful positions in the cosmic government, running various departments of cosmic governance, and are called Devas and Devis. They are not above dharma and karma; they, too, are subject to dharma, which they in turn enforce. They are just in higher positions of authority, like ministers or bureaucrats in a government, administering different government departments. The Vedic tradition rejects any system of governance in which different principles apply to the rulers and the ruled.

Ṛta is a stable system of governance because its principles never change. The heads of the government enacting this system are never corrupted, compromised, bargained, dethroned, or replaced. There are three heads of the cosmic government called Brahma, Viṣṇu, and Rudra. Brahma creates a world for a certain duration and defines dharma for varying times, places, and situations within that duration. Viṣṇu maintains dharma by delivering the results of sukarma, vikarma, and akarma according to the previously defined dharma, and when that duration has elapsed, Rudra destroys the previously created world to let Brahma create anew. These new creations become necessary due to the cyclical evolution of time, which we will discuss shortly. Thus, the big picture of Ṛta is creation, maintenance, and destruction.

Among the three heads of government, Viṣṇu is the original; He creates Brahma, who creates Rudra. They are identified as representations of *sattva, rajas, and tamas*, respectively, and due to the hierarchy between *sattva, rajas, and tamas*, there is a hierarchy between Viṣṇu, Brahma, and Rudra as well.

These three heads of the cosmic government, in turn, have subordinates of various cosmic departments. The subordinates of Brahma are called Vasus; they define and teach dharma. The subordinates of Viṣṇu are called Aditya; they maintain dharma by delivering the results of sukarma, vikarma, and akarma. The subordinates of Rudra are called Rudras; they destroy the world created by Brahma to pave the way for a new creation. They are known as the 33 principal heads of departments of the cosmic government.

Deva and Asura Governance Systems

The Vedic tradition also accepts, within the cosmos, the existence of those who are opposed to Ṛta: They are called Asuras, and they create alternative systems of governance opposed to dharma and karma. The Vedic cosmos is divided into two parts—upper and lower; the upper part follows Ṛta, and the lower part is opposed to Ṛta. Even opponents of Ṛta live with like-minded persons. They often worship Rudras to get their favor to destroy the Ṛta, so they can establish their rule even in the upper parts of the universe.

The hallmark of Asuric systems of rule is double standards—different principles apply to the rulers and the ruled. Democracy, autocracy, and theocracy are such Asuric systems. For instance, theocrats keep sinning while they expect people to be pious; autocrats give themselves freedoms and deny freedom to the people; democrats make different rules for themselves and for the people they rule. All Asuric systems of rule are unstable and chaotic, marked by constant fear of corruption, overthrow, and replacement.

Living under the fear of self-destruction, the Asuras demonize the followers of Ṛta and call them a threat to their existence. They tell belittling stories about the followers of Ṛta, to ensure that their own followers would not ask for a similar system, to allow the Asuras to preserve their power. They propagandize their followers into believing that their system is the best that humanity has ever discovered. The Asuras are predators, and they need prey to feed on. They use their followers as predators to prey upon the followers of Ṛta. But if that stops working, they begin preying on their followers themselves and reveal their predatory nature. At all other times, propaganda hides and/or justifies its predatory nature as cosmic perfection.

When one Asuric system begins to collapse, the powerful Asuras give the same system a new name—to appear to have brought real reform and to recreate trust in their system of rule—while continuing the same policies. Deceit and hypocrisy come naturally to the Asuras. They are always cheating their own followers by glorifying themselves and belittling others. Anyone who believes their lies comes under their control, after which they are initially used as a subordinate predator and eventually as prey.

Mutual Exclusion of Devas and Asuras

There are many hallmarks of Asuric life—(a) endless, needless, and lawless violence on those who have done no harm to them, (b) blind faith ideologies that can never be proven by reason and experience and are often contradicted by such evidence, (c) inability to reconcile their own ideas leading to contradicting and conflicting sects, (d) continuous evolution through the passing of edicts, laws, and amendments, (e) double standards between words and actions, between rulers and ruled, indicating the absence of any principled stance, (f) supremacist and exclusivist ideologies that preempt reconciliation, and (g) highly materialistic inclinations of their leaders, teachers, and proponents that result in immorality.

Factually, nobody can be happy in an Asuric system of rule because it oscillates between extremes of fear and greed—greed that we can own the world, and fear that we may be killed in the conflicts arising from trying to own the world. The Asuric mind is not governed by morality, nor does it work rationally, such as being able to comprehend that there is no stable system other than that which leads to cosmic harmony. The Asuric mind is governed by negative emotions, such as fear, inadequacy, jealousy, and anger, which are the antithesis of positive emotions, such as happiness, satisfaction, peace, and contentment.

Accordingly, there are two opposite systems of governance—driven by positive and negative emotions. A mind filled with negative emotions always remains restless and agitated. Pleasure calms a disturbed mind and leads to sleep. Thus, the Asuras are always either in violence, hedonism, or slumber, never in serenity, calmness, or fulfilment. The purpose of dharma is to take a person toward positive emotions and remove negative emotions. Under positive emotions, the mind becomes rational and realizes that an immoral life will never bring happiness. Under negative emotions, such a realization is impossible.

Despite the guaranteed demise of an Asuric system, the followers of Ṛta don't force their thinking on others; they accept that free will is an inalienable feature of every living entity, and nature already has a moral system in place to reward and punish individual actions. The followers of Ṛta ask the Asuras to not force their system on others, live separately from the followers of Ṛta, and separate themselves from the Asuric system. But the Asuras can't tolerate any alternative—(a) they fear that their lies, deceits, double standards, hypocrisies, and blind faith cannot stand against the rationally provable methods used by the followers of Ṛta, (b) they fear that if an alternative exists, their own followers will abandon them after seeing their problems and thus any alternative becomes a threat to their viability, and (c) they project their supremacist mindset on others and believe that alternatives will attack and destroy them.

This insecurity in the Asuras creates wars between Devas and Asuras, and between their followers. To win that war, the followers of Asuras take shelter of the Asuras, and the followers of Devas take shelter of the Devas. That war can always be won on earth, because it is the dominion of the Devas. And yet, if followers of Asuras take shelter of Asuras, but the followers of Devas don't, then the latter are defeated by the former. A lazy, pessimistic, and hopeless mindset then takes over the defeated, which allows the Asuras to rule the world. To restore Ṛta, we have to discard that lazy, pessimistic, and hopeless mindset and fight against the Asuras with the conviction that dharma protects those who protect dharma.

The Contextualization of Dharma

Dharma is unique to each time, place, situation, and person. Each person can play many roles in life—parent, child, citizen, ruler, employee, employer, etc. These roles need to do different things at different times and places. Each person is capable or incapable of different things that must be done in different roles at different times and places. Therefore, dharma is always contextualized and individualized.

The simplest example of changing dharma over time is the Chatur-Yuga system of four ages. There are four principles of dharma—*satya* (truthfulness), *daya* (kindness), *śaucha* (purity), and *tapa* (austerity) within this universe—which are given different emphases at each time, place, and situation, but overall, there is greater emphasis on one such principle during the four ages of the Chatur-Yuga. For instance, during Satya-Yuga, austerity has the highest emphasis; during Treta-Yuga, kindness; during Dvapara-Yuga, purity; and during Kali-Yuga, truthfulness. The contextualization and prioritization of the principles of dharma become necessary because all four principles can't be upheld at once.

For example, normally, we should be kind to everyone, but we can't be kind to a criminal and forgive his crimes; those who have shown unkindness have to be corrected through unkindness. Normally, we are expected to be truthful, but we can't give our bank account details to a thief even if he asks us; we may sometimes lie to the liars because those who cheat have to be corrected through cheating. Normally, we should always be pure, but if someone exploits our purity, we may exploit their impurity, because there is no other way to deal with such persons. Normally, we should be austere, but we can't sacrifice our lives for a thief; in fact, we may have to steal back from the thief what he has previously stolen from us.

If everyone is truthful, kind, pure, and austere, we prioritize austerity—even if someone steals our food, we assume that he must be very hungry and needed food more than us. But as thieves rise, we have to prioritize kindness—ensure that we proactively give away food in charity so that nobody has to steal and they can lead an honest life. As thieves rise more and start abusing kindness by becoming freeloaders, we have to prioritize purity—i.e., engage them in honest work so they can live a life of honest work. Finally, as thieves rise even more, we have to call a thief a thief and punish them by taking away their freedom to steal, because the alternatives of austerity, kindness, and purity increase thievery.

The Presumed Universalism of Laws

The harshest punishments of thieves—such as cutting off their hands or banishing them from a land—become essential if the entire society is corrupt. At this juncture, we get *universal rules*, which remove the options of tolerance, charity, or employment of thieves, because the reality is that hardened thieves can't be corrected. And so, universal rules are the bottommost rung of dharma—when the entire society is irrevocably criminal, and one set of rules is applied to everyone at all times, places, and situations.

Modern legal systems begin with presumed innocence and try to establish criminality before they punish someone. But presumed innocence is incompatible with laws—someone may have stolen food because he was hungry, someone could have stopped stealing if they received some charity, someone could have stopped stealing if they got a job, and so on. Proving that someone stole food isn't enough to decide how to stop theft. If we always incarcerate a thief without knowing the conditions that led to theft, we will make that thief a hardened criminal, and then, instead of stopping thieves, they will increase more and more.

At present, Western societies pride themselves on the rule of law. And yet, some of these societies also have the highest per-capita crimes because people stopped dharma—e.g., letting a hungry person steal food, giving food in charity, or giving them honest jobs, which forced them into crimes, and the harsh punishments made them hardened criminals. The West calls these things *capitalism,* which works only when people have access to food, a home, education, healthcare, and jobs; if some people are deprived of these, and capitalism only benefits those privileged with food, a home, education, healthcare, and jobs, crime continuously grows. The Western societies that initially escaped high crime rates applied high taxes on the privileged and used that money to provide food, housing, education, healthcare, and jobs to the underprivileged. These things are called *socialism,* and they were attempts to follow dharma. But as these became rules, they encouraged the greedy, the freeloaders, and the criminals to exploit the system, when they shouldn't have been forgiven, received the least, were required to work, and punished for crimes. Even when dharma was enacted as rules, the results were adverse, as society drifted towards crime.

And thus, whether we stop dharma by making rules, or whether we make rules to follow dharma, the results are always adverse. The most law-enforcing societies die when they replace dharma with laws because either they subject everyone to the harshest rules and convert the innocent into criminals, or they subject everyone to the mildest rules and allow criminals to escape after exploiting the innocent. In both cases, the result is that the society gradually drifts toward crime simply by following laws.

Deep Causes Behind Lawful Thinking

Asuras don't see unique individuals with unique abilities, proclivities, and opportunities. They replace unique individuals with uniform objects, after which universal laws replace contextual and individual dharma. Asuras also make different laws for the rulers and the ruled, passing the adverse effects of laws to the ruled, and passing the beneficial effects of laws to the rulers, after which the entire society comprises criminals—the rulers are the biggest criminals, and the ruled are the smaller criminals. To ascend to the position of a ruler, the ruled have to demonstrate their capacity for greater crimes.

There are many deep causes behind the replacement of dharma with laws—(a) the depersonalization of individuals into one-size-fits-all objects which allows the application of universal laws, (b) the attempt to justify criminality by legalizing it, so that the criminals can enjoy immorality without punishment, and (c) ultimately to convince oneself of their omnipotence by using the power to make laws for others, while never being subject to those laws, exactly like God is believed to be above the laws that He makes.

The problem begins with a conception of God who doesn't follow the laws that He expects others to follow, and culminates in criminals acting as God by making laws for others while being above those laws. This never happens under Ṛta because God follows the principles that He expects others to follow. Therefore, followers of Ṛta don't expect to make a government whose principles they will themselves neglect. Double standards come from a God who isn't bound by his own teachings. If God is whimsical, His followers will also be whimsical. However, that whimsicality is not true for the deities of Ṛta.

Infantile Conception of the Supreme

This whimsical idea of God owes its origin to irresponsible, unprincipled, and unaccountable rulers who projected their personality onto God. Whom they call God is actually an Asura—oppressive, wrathful, demanding, vindictive, intolerant, whimsical, and jealous. There is actually no such God. This is, at best, the personality of a tantrum-throwing child living in the body of an adult, which is called narcissism. The child demands all kinds of playthings and considers the parent who gives them to be benevolent. If the parent refuses to oblige the child, then the child steals the playthings from other children. He also hates other siblings in case they have received more playthings from the parent, and fights with them.

A child playing with toys hates responsibility, accountability, or duty. And yet, it wants all powers, toys, and freedoms in the world. He expects the toys to be devoid of agency, to be used or discarded as he pleases. If this infantile personality is projected onto God, we get God making a playhouse of toys, not a world of life. These toys are expected to be obedient and predictable, with no concern for the toys themselves because they are just lifeless things. The depersonalizing, reductionist, and universalist attitudes stem from this childlike mindset—everything is a toy that can be taken apart at whim, working according to some gear-and-spring mechanism that remains hidden until we look under the cover.

Infantile rulers who projected their personality onto God were never mature enough to comprehend the complexity of the real world. Their simplistic worldview came from a childish mindset that wanted to continue playing with toys even in adulthood. These were not educated or knowledgeable people. They did not care about the people they ruled over. They modeled the world as toys, not people.

An Infantile Supreme Creates Chaos

We don't expect an infant's playhouse to be organized; we expect it to be chaotic. Some responsible, principled, and accountable adult is required to bring order to a child's chaos. We cannot allow a child to play with other children as if they were toys; otherwise, the child will have no playmates. The child's playhouse is an insignificant part of reality, and the whole world isn't a child's playhouse. A child who treats the world as its playhouse will not live long; it will be dead unless a parent restricts it. Likewise, laws are useful only for an insignificant portion of reality and can't be used for the whole world.

The worldview of a religion that universalizes laws is that of an infant thinking that the whole world is toys. Infantile thinking is seen in other aspects of such religions too—demanding new toys from their father, scheming how to steal others' toys, treating their playmates as toys, and hating other children whom they think have more toys to play with. A child can play with its own toys, break them, kick them, or cry for new toys, but the adults must decide which child's behaviors are acceptable to what extent, when, where, how, and why. If the child doesn't give up its toy mentality, it is never elevated to a responsible position in the cosmos, regardless of what the child might believe about ascending to eternal life in heaven to eternally play with toys. However, if the child has been deprived in the past, the adults give that child some toys to play with temporarily, to check if the child will behave responsibly as an adult.

Once we understand the deep causes behind lawful thinking, it is easy to see that the problem is not democracy, autocracy, or theocracy, but a flawed conception of God Whose omnipotence empowers Him to break all the rules that He creates, change all the rules that He may have made in the past, and never be bound by the rules that He expects others to follow. If we discard this idea of God, then (a) rulers can come from among the common people, so the society can be democratic, (b) rulers can be descendants of previous rulers, so the society can be autocratic, and (c) saints, called Rajarṣi in the Vedic tradition and philosopher kings in other cultures, can rule the society, so the society can be theocratic. At the root of all problems lies a bad idea of omnipotence—irresponsible, unprincipled, and unaccountable.

Contradictory Ideas of the Supreme

Factually, nobody can live eternally with an irresponsible, unprincipled, and unaccountable supreme, whereas everyone can live eternally with a responsible, principled, and accountable supreme. This has nothing to do with what the supreme might be, and everything to do with who we ourselves are.

The Vedic tradition resolves the ambiguity regarding the supreme by saying that He has infinite forms, each matching our nature. If we are irresponsible, unprincipled, and unaccountable, then the supreme ruling over us is the same. But if we are responsible, principled, and accountable, the supreme ruling over us is the same. Since we cannot eternally live with the former type of supreme, by showing us a face that matches our nature, the supreme reforms us into something we can live with eternally. There are still eternal forms of the supreme we can live with eternally, but an irresponsible, unprincipled, and unaccountable form of the supreme is not one of them; that form is temporary, meant to reform us.

Law-making religions contrast God against Satan, but in the Vedic tradition, God and Satan are simply two faces of the same supreme. The supreme shows us a face matching our nature. If our nature is good, we see a good supreme, but if our nature is evil, then we see an evil supreme. If we begin with an evil supreme, it becomes a self-fulfilling prophecy—the supreme shows us an evil face. Conversely, if we begin with a good supreme, it becomes a self-fulfilling prophecy—the supreme shows us a good face. Therefore, there can be no universal definition of the supreme; the supreme matches our nature.

The Universality of the Greatest Good

The recognition of the many faces of the supreme allows us to define dharma as the greatest good. When good deeds are reciprocated, the good is reinforced; when evil deeds are reciprocated, the evil is cancelled. Both are factually good; therefore, the supreme is all-good in an ultimate sense, even if, in a shallow and narrow sense, the supreme might sometimes appear evil to those who did evil deeds.

The principle of the greatest good also helps us understand how dharma is contextual. We don't want to punish a hungry person for stealing food, because once he is fed, he may start working to earn a meal. We don't want to punish the disabled for begging because they don't have a better way to live; we might instead support them through charity, so they will do the best within their disabilities. We don't want to imprison petty criminals because they may be improved by giving them opportunities to use their skills, and imprisoning them will ensure that they won't use their skills and become hardened criminals. We only want to punish those who have opportunities, support, and skills, but choose the path of crime.

Dharma begins by giving the benefit of the doubt to the criminal, assuming that he is a moral person and wants to lead a moral life, but has been forced into crime due to lack of opportunities, support, and skills. Dharma tries to bring that person back to morality by removing the hindrances to it. If all those efforts fail, then harsh punishment becomes necessary. All these contextualized and individualized decisions fall under the universal principle of delivering the greatest good to the greatest number of persons, times, places, and situations. Those who have the intelligence to make such contextualized and individualized decisions are empowered to educate, judge, and correct others. Ṛta comprises intelligent rulers. Even in a human society, those with such intelligence and understanding are given the highest status.

Slow Perversion of the Concept of Ṛta

All governments rely on taxation on the people they govern. Ṛta is no different. Cosmic taxation in the Vedic tradition is implemented as rituals, sacrifices, and duties. The priests perform rituals offering the grains collected from society to the deities governing them; through these rituals, the cosmic governors are strengthened. The warriors sacrifice their lives for protecting Ṛta, as subordinates of the cosmic governors; through such sacrifices, the warriors ascend to positions of cosmic governors because they have shown their commitment to the protection of Ṛta. The farmers grow food to ensure that the rest of society can lead a healthy life. And the workers manufacture all the things that nature doesn't give us, to ensure that everyone has all the necessities of life. Thus, everyone performs their duties according to their capacity to ensure that a society adheres to Ṛta and doesn't atomize itself by selfishness.

All these rituals were misunderstood over time and came to be seen as "pleasing the gods", rather than "paying your taxes". Over time, people couldn't understand how the cosmic government has numerous departments, and began arguing with each other—"my god is better than your god". Then came rulers who rejected the cosmic government, and made their own laws, while calling them divine laws—"God gave me these laws by which I shall rule over you, and if you break my laws, you shall go to hell". Then came philosophers and scientists who said, "The world is run by impersonal laws, with no lawmaker, and we shall discover those laws through observation and speculation". Then comes the realization that we need infinite laws to govern all the times, places, situations, things, persons, and collectives, and because nobody can make infinite laws, the result is the misapplication of laws leading to chaos.

Since infinite laws are required to create perfect order, when these are implemented, everyone would be paralyzed because nobody can even know these laws, and if they don't follow all the laws, they are by definition criminals. Thus, in the scenario where there is perfect order due to infinite laws, everyone is a criminal. And in the scenario where there is perfect chaos due to zero laws, everyone is innocent. Every scenario in between these extremes makes some innocents criminals and some criminals innocents. 3,000 years have passed in this flawed trajectory that lost the understanding of Ṛta. At every step, the situation has worsened, with continuously increasing laws, which constitute increasing bondage.

Legal experts today know that the government can actually catch, indict, and imprison anyone if it truly wants to do so, because everyone violates endless laws out of ignorance. The issue is simply that the government doesn't have the law enforcement machinery to catch, indict, and imprison everyone, so it only targets those whom it really wants to punish. That is not the rule of law, but it can be one of whim, at which point it will be factually no different than any autocratic system in which an emperor could chop off anyone's head if he so wished. At present, those whom the government targets can spend their lifetime in prison waiting for justice, while the government can throw at them endless laws to delay and/or deny justice. The true horrors of laws are known by those who have been unfairly targeted, while the criminals know how to escape the government's legal system. Again, laws often criminalize innocents and often deem the criminals innocent.

There is only one solution to this problem—revive the understanding of Ṛta, learn to practice dharma, reform the idea of cosmic order from impersonal laws to personal government, and give up the infantile idea of the world as toys in a playhouse. Those who can't accept this will destroy their societies.

Why Dharma Can Never Be Religion

Dharma cannot be equated to religion because dharma is unique per time, place, situation, and person, but religion is the same for all times, places, situations, and persons. Religion becomes outdated with the passing of time, differences of places, changes in situations, and variations in persons, but dharma always remains current. Religion becomes rigid as the same beliefs and practices are forced on everyone, at all times, places, and situations, while dharma always adapts to the changing times, places, situations, and persons. This is why religion has a short shelf-life, whereas dharma lives eternally. Anyone who tries to sustain a religion across times, places, situations, and persons has to make innumerable adjustments and compromises discordant with the original idea of religion, while dharma naturally adapts to them.

Dharma would never work without karma—there must be different consequences for sukarma, vikarma, and akarma, for otherwise, nobody will do dharma. Therefore, dharma can also never exist without a cosmic system of governance, i.e., Ṛta. The principles of cosmic order cannot be changed at whim; that is not cosmic order, but cosmic whims. The cosmic order cannot be a recent revelation, because the cosmos has existed for billions of years, and happy and prosperous civilizations existed in the past, which would be impossible if the cosmic order were revealed late. The cosmic order cannot be impersonal laws because when machines govern persons, they replace persons with machines, and since the cosmos has existed for billions of years, impersonal laws should have already replaced persons with machines.

Modernity has inverted truth and myth—everything it calls religion, science, and philosophy is actually a myth, and everything it calls myth is actually religion, science, and philosophy. This is not a surprising thing in the Vedic tradition, because most of the people, in most of the times, places, and situations, are already said to be living in partial or complete myths, delusions, and misconceptions. The perfect truth is extremely rare, while myths are most common. In this age of Kali-Yuga, both complete and partial truths are easily lost, and most people elevate the myth to the truth and degrade the truth to the myth.

But all these myths can be debunked through observation and reason, simply by scaling ordinary ideas of a good government comprising responsible, accountable, and principled rulers to the entire cosmos. Just as a good earthly government has many departments, the cosmic governance does so too. Just as a good earthly government has moral rulers who follow the principles of morality that they enforce on others, similarly, the cosmic government is headed by moral rulers who practice what they preach. Therefore, it is not difficult to understand cosmic governance, i.e., Ṛta, if we are truly interested in doing so.

www.ingramcontent.com/pod-product-compliance
Ingram Content Group UK Ltd.
Pitfield, Milton Keynes, MK11 3LW, UK
UKHW041312190726
13845UKWH00025B/220

9 789385 384585